Caliban's Reason

Books in the Africana Thought series:

Existentia Africana: Understanding Africana Existential Thought
by Lewis R. Gordon

Series Editors: Lewis R. Gordon and Paget Henry

Caliban's Reason

INTRODUCING
AFRO-CARIBBEAN PHILOSOPHY

Paget Henry

New York • ROUTLEDGE • *London*

Published in 2000 by
Routledge
29 West 35th Street
New York, NY 10001

Published in Great Britain by
Routledge
11 New Fetter Lane
London EC4P 4EE

Copyright © 2000 by Routledge

Printed in the United States of America on acid-free paper.

All rights reserved. No part of this book may be reprinted or reproduced or utilized in
any form or by any electronic, mechanical, or other means, now known or hereafter
invented, including photocopying and recording or in any information storage or
retrieval system, without permission in writing from the publishers.

Library of Congress Cataloging-in-Publication Data
Henry, Paget.
Caliban's reason : introducing Afro-Caribbean philosophy / Paget Henry.
p. cm — (Africana thought)
Includes bibliographical references and index.
ISBN 0-415-92645-9 (hb) — ISBN 0-415-92646-7 (pbk.)
1. Philosophy, Black—West Indies. I. Title. II. Series.

B1028. P34 2000
199'.729'08996—dc21   99-047426

Book design by Cynthia Dunne

Contents

For the Anchors

C. L. R. James

Frantz Fanon

Wilson Harris

Sylvia Wynter

and for

Tim Hector,

who has never

stopped asking:

"where is our philosophy?"

Acknowledgments

Writing is indeed a time-consuming activity. Consequently, even small books make large demands on the time and energies of the author and many other people. This has been particularly true of this work, which crosses disciplinary boundaries. Consequently, I am particularly indebted to many people who have given their time and effort to this work. First on this list is Lewis Gordon. I must thank him for insisting that I take the plunge into philosophy, for including some of my early philosophical essays in works he edited, and for reading a draft of the text. Without these acts of generosity, it is hard to imagine this work in its present form.

I would also like to thank other friends and colleagues whose suggestions and criticisms have helped to make this book what it is. Wilson Harris, Sylvia Wynter, Anthony Bogues, Tsenay Serequeberhan, Madhu Dubey, Lucius Outlaw, Charles Mills, Dick Howard, Selwyn Cudjoe, Paul Buhle, Ato Sekyi-Ou, Paula Davis, John Ladd, Patrick Gooding, Rowan Phillips, Roberto Marquez, Neil Roberts, Cleavis Headley, Mali Olatunji, Sophie McCall, Kofi Benefo, Alex Dupuy, Hilbourne Watson, and Robyn Campbell for her special insights into African-American spirituality.

Thanks are also due to successive member of my graduate seminar on culture and social structure with whom I discussed many of the ideas in this book. I also had the opportunity to expose some of these ideas at the Postdoctoral Seminar of the Pembroke Center for the Study of Women here at Brown University. So thanks must go also to the coordinators, Elizabeth Weed and Ellen Rooney, and to successive members of this seminar.

To Ms. Sheila Grant, I owe a great deal of thanks for her diligent work on the manuscript. Without her efforts it certainly would not be in this highly readable form.

Finally, two chapters of this book are revised versions of previously published works. An earlier version of chapter 2 appeared in *The CLR James Journal* 4, no. 1 (1993), and an earlier version of chapter 3 in *Fanon: A Critical Reader*, edited by Lewis Gordon, T. Deanean Sharpley-Whiting, and Renee White. I thank the CLR James Society and Blackwell Publishers for permission to reprint these two pieces.

Preface

One of the peculiar features of Caribbean intellectual life is the near absence of an explicitly cultivated philosophical tradition. Yet the region has produced authors such as C. L. R. James, Frantz Fanon, and Wilson Harris, whose works are brimming with original philosophical insights and arguments. *Caliban's Reason* is an attempt to resolve this apparent paradox. Consequently, it is a work that introduces Caribbean philosophy to the academic community, describes some of its distinctive features, and examines some of its major problems, in particular, problems of internal unity, creolization, and praxis.

By problems of internal unity, I am referring to the cleavages and lack of dialogue that persist between many of its major schools, such as the gaps between historicists and poeticists, or between historicists and traditional African philosophy. Creolization raises explicitly the issue of power relations in determining the ways in which African, Indian, and European philosophies come together to constitute a regional philosophy. Lastly, in many of the formulations of Caribbean philosophy, relations to society have been mediated by the transformative praxis of a number of postcolonial projects. Many of these projects have been thrown into crisis by changes in the global political economy and, hence, are in need of reformulation. These are some of the key issues around which my examination of Caribbean philosophy will be organized.

This comparatively late introduction raises the question: Where has Caribbean philosophy been all this time? This is a question many have been asking. None more persistently than the Antiguan journalist and activist Tim Hector. In his well-known "Fan the Flame" column in *Outlet*, Hector has often asked, "Where is our philosophy?" The persistence of his asking has been a major motivating force for the writing of this book. The short answer to this pointed question is that Caribbean philosophy has been carefully embedded in the practices of nonphilosophical discourses almost to the point of concealment.

Caliban's Reason is the long answer to this question. Consequently, it describes in detail an implicit style of philosophizing that has been embedded

in other Caribbean discourses such as ideological, literary, and religious production. These interdiscursive locations gave Caribbean philosophy only limited visibility. This limited recognition was reduced to naught in the cases of
Afro- and Indo-Caribbean philosophies by clouds of racist invisibility that
descended over them during the colonial period. Consequently, the work of
recovery has taken the form of a double excavation: first, that of the tradition
as a whole; and, second, that of Afro-Caribbean philosophy. Once excavated, I
focus intensely though not exclusively on the school of Afro-Caribbean
historicism.

In many ways, *Caliban's Reason* is a book that has written itself. Four years
ago, it was certainly not among the conscious plans I had for myself. So if it
seems a little unusual that, although trained as a sociologist, I have undertaken
to write a book addressed primarily to philosophers, I share your sentiments.
To my colleagues in sociology, let me assure you that I am not abandoning the
discipline and that there is much here that will be of interest to you. This is
particularly true for sociologists of knowledge, development, and culture. We
don't really have a sociology of philosophy subfield that is comparable to the
sociology literature or religion. Maybe this will change with Randall Collins's
new book, *The Sociology of Philosophies*, which unfortunately was published
after this text was written.

To the philosophers that I hope to reach, I think I should let you know that
my interest in your discipline is not a sudden or passing one. Rather, it has
been a lifelong interest that has played an important role in my work as a sociologist. In fact, the approach I take to philosophy in this book draws directly on
these encounters with philosophy in the course of doing sociological work. As I
reflect on it now, the interests and concerns that came together to produce this
work have been forming for quite some time. Three events in particular stand
out in this process of philosophical development.

First, my interest in philosophy emerged around age fourteen when I was
still in high school in Antigua. Although I did well in school, I was bored with
the books I had to read, except for science texts. Thus on Saturday mornings
when my parents insisted that I go to the library, very often I did not. Instead,
I would jump on my bike and go swimming at Fort James with my friends. One
Saturday, after one of my friends got caught and received a thorough whipping,
I decided that it was time for me to get to the library. So, off I went on foot to
avoid the temptation of riding off if I got bored. As I had done many times
before, I went by the stacks of fiction that my sister had been devouring and
experienced no interest whatsoever. The science collection was extremely
small, and I had already gone through those that interested me. In the midst of
thinking that I should have gone to the beach instead, I spotted among the science collection a book that aroused my curiosity. It was E. C. Ewing's *Ethics*.

Reading the chapter on Kant, all thoughts of going to the beach disappeared. As I decided to take it out, I can remember saying to myself, "So this is why people read." I've been reading philosophy ever since. As an undergraduate at City College in New York, I won the 1970 Frederick Sperling Award for the best student in philosophy even though I was a sociology major.

The second important philosophical concern in my intellectual formation that has made this book possible was the strong interest I took in the methodological debates around the cognitive practices of the social sciences. I was fascinated by these debates and by the contributions of philosophers of science. These contributions shaped my work as a sociologist in two important ways. First, they were extremely helpful as I wrestled with the differences in the nature of the knowledge produced by the empirical and interpretive approaches to sociology. The second was in making my choice of a dialectical approach that integrated history, social structure, and biography. In both of these crucial decisions, I encountered philosophy as a practice that was embedded in sociological work. For me, the encounter confirmed Merleau Ponty's claim that "the sociologist philosophizes every time he is required to not only record but to comprehend facts."[1] Consequently, it is from this experience that I derived the intertextual approach to philosophy employed in this book.

Third and finally, there were the shifting positions of the self that I observed in my own sociological practice and that of others. Far from being a constant in cognitive situations, the self is a dynamic factor, changing and playing different roles as individuals develop. As its horizons widen with new self-definitions, dualities it could not resolve, and positions it had to exclude can now be synthesized in new totalities. This relationship between progressive self-transformations and the resolving of binaries, antinomies, and partial perspectives that often limit thought became a philosophical problem that my sociological development kept ever before me. As a result, this concern with dualities and their inclusion in larger totalizations has become one of the important lenses through which I have examined the texts of Caribbean philosophy. Because of this affirmation of totalizing strategies, it has also meant writing against the postmodern grain, even though my work has been influenced by the linguistic turn.

It is my hope that these prefatory remarks will ease whatever feelings of strangeness the reader may have about a sociologist undertaking this philosophical project.

P. H.
Crosbies, Antigua
Summer 1998

Introduction:
The General Character
of Afro-Caribbean Philosophy

The power of philosophy floats through my head
Light like a feather, heavy as lead

—Bob Marley

There are idealist views of philosophy that see it as an affirmation of the autonomy of a thinking subject. As the primary instrument of this absolute subject, philosophy shares in its autonomy and therefore is a discipline that rises above the determinations of history and everyday life. The distinguishing characteristics of Afro-Caribbean philosophy do not support this view. Here we find a tradition of philosophy so indelibly marked by the forces of an imperial history, and by its intertextual relations with neighboring discourses, that it is necessary to begin with a general characterization of philosophy that is more appropriate to its pattern of development.

1

From the Afro-Caribbean perspective, philosophy is an intertextually embedded discursive practice, and not an isolated or absolutely autonomous one. It is often implicitly referenced or engaged in the production of answers to everyday questions and problems that are being framed in nonphilosophical discourses. However, it is a distinct intellectual practice that raises certain kinds of questions and attempts to answer them by a variety of styles of argument that draw on formal logic, paradox, coherence, the meaningful logic of lived experiences, and the synthetic powers of totalizing systems.

From this intertextual perspective, philosophy appears as an open but diverse discursive field in which ontological, epistemological, logical, ethical, transcendental, historical, and other formations flow into one another. This rather fluid field is responsive to various strategies of organization either from within or without. In cases like the Caribbean, where philosophy functions as a minor or auxiliary discourse, organization usually comes from outside and is often less centralized than in cases in which philosophy is a major or more autonomous discourse. In the minor mode, philosophy's organization usually reflects the pushes and pulls of its interdiscursive connections. In the major mode, organization tends to be from within and reflects the importance currently attributed to particular subfields by philosophers.

The kinds of questions raised by philosophy tend to be those regarding the origins, ends, and truth value of our everyday activities. Consequently, philosophy's primary concerns tend to be foundational, teleological, and discursive in nature. Foundational concerns include the bases of all discursive practices we employ in grasping self and world, as well as questions such as the origin of life and creation. Teleological concerns include the ends of many of our social activities, the fate of the individual, and the ends of creation. Consequently, whenever we write or attempt to answer a significant problem we necessarily raise philosophical issues, which may or may not be addressed explicitly.

The analysis of these kinds of questions may be done by philosophers or nonphilosophers using one or more of the styles of philosophical production indicated above. Indeed, there is a strong tendency to draw lines in the sand around the use of particular styles or around particular subfields such as ontology, formal logic, or ethics. Thus the attempts to reduce philosophy to the making of arguments or to processes of world constitution are cases of unnecessary polarization between these different tendencies. Even the most cursory look at Afro-Caribbean philosophy indicates that it is both. Similarly, Kwame Gyekye is right in asserting that philosophy cannot be viewed as being primarily one of its subfields as Robin Horton and others have attempted to do with logic and epistemology.[1] Such attempts at rigid closures represent little more than the egocentricity and academic politics of professors of philosophy.

Thus, in spite of its preoccupation with the absolute, philosophy is neither an absolute nor a pure discourse. It is an internally differentiated and discursively embedded practice, the boundaries of which will continue to change as work in other fields requires the taking up of new philosophical positions. In other words, there is a consistently significant philosophical substratum to be found in the works of physicists, sociologists, biologists, creative writers, and other knowledge producers. Conversely, there are quite significant literary, religious, sociological, and other discursive substrata in the works of philosophers. This is an interdiscursive embeddedness from which there can be no escape via argument. Like all other discourses, philosophy comes into being as a necessary part of a larger and more diversified discursive field that is a foundation of all human cultural production.

Looked at concretely, Afro-Caribbean philosophy is just such an internally differentiated and intertextually embedded discourse. Its formation and current structure reflect the imperial history of the cultural system that has housed the larger discursive field of Caribbean society. Consequently, many of the original features of our philosophical and other discursive practices have been shaped by the colonial problematics and contours of our cultural history. Within this imperial framework, the original contents of Caribbean philosophy emerged as a series of extended debates over projects of colonial domination between four major social groups: Euro-Caribbeans, Amerindians, Indo-Caribbeans, and Afro-Caribbeans. The discursive productions of the first group were contributions to the creating of hegemonic situations through the legitimating of colonial projects. The productions of the other three groups were attempts at destroying Euro-Caribbean hegemony through the delegitimating of their colonial projects. This was the imperial communicative framework within which Afro-Caribbean philosophy emerged, a framework that always embodied an unequal discursive compromise.

This colonial reframing within the dynamics of legitimacy needs produced a seismic shift in the orientation of Caribbean philosophy. This shift would take it in a very definite politico-ideological direction. In *Black Skin, White Masks*, Fanon argues that the colonial situation created an "existential deviation" in the psyche of the Afro-Caribbean. This deviation was the result of racially induced "aberrations of affect" that relocated the Afro-Caribbean in an antiblack world from which he or she must be extricated. The colonial reframing of Afro-Caribbean philosophy noted above, its reinscription in aberrations of legitimacy demands, produced a discursive deviation that paralleled Fanon's existential deviation.

This discursive deviation was the form that the broader seismic shift took in the case of Afro-Caribbean philosophy. It initiated the foregrounding of

colonial, racial, and national struggles and the backgrounding of classical philosophical issues such as being, truth, spirit, and the nature of the self. Binaries
such as colonizer/colonized, colony/nation, or black/white quickly eclipsed
those of being/nonbeing, spirit/matter, good/evil, and so forth. Classical
ontologies that provided comprehensive accounts of existence, discourses that
plumbed the depths of the self, rapidly gave way to the strategic and ideological productions demanded by the aberrations of legitimacy affect. As a result,
Afro-Caribbean philosophy was relocated to an antiblack, antiphilosophical
world, from which it now has to be extricated.

From the point of view of the creative or world-constituting self, the culture
of a people may be defined as the expression of a distinct consciousness of existence articulated in a variety of discourses. Philosophy is often the discourse in
which we get the most general formulations of that consciousness of existence.
Among Euro-Caribbeans, the consciousness that informed culture and philosophy was one that framed existence as a Faustian/imperial struggle to subdue
all of nature and history. This was an insurrectionary rupture with the established cosmic order of things that inaugurated a new era in the relations
between the European ego and the world. It globalized the European project of
existence, weakened the powers of the gods, relocated Europeans at the center
of this new world, and refigured the Caribbean into one of its subordinate
peripheries. As a result, some of the earliest expressions of Euro-Caribbean
philosophy are to be found in the writings of Hakluyt, Las Casas, Montaigne,
Richard Ligon, Bryan Edwards, Immanuel Kant, Georg Hegel, Thomas Carlyle,
and others who helped to shape the new images of Amerindians and Africans
in Europe's imperial vision of itself. Together, but in very fragmentary forms,
these writings constituted the Euro-Caribbean layer of the imperial framework
that shaped the growth of Caribbean philosophy.

Among the most enduring accounts of the refiguring of Caribbean identities produced by this European/Euro-Caribbean tradition of writing has been
the character Caliban, from Shakespeare's play *The Tempest*. This work was
inspired by the colonizing voyages that Europeans were making to the
Caribbean, particularly the highly publicized wrecks of Thomas Gates and
George Summers off the coast of Bermuda. The play dramatized the new
vision of existence as the global conquest of nature and history. To imperial
Prospero, native Caliban (the Carib) was identical with nature—a cannibal, a
child, a monster without language, and hence a potential slave to be subdued
and domesticated along with nature and history. Much like the raw materials
of nature, the labor of Caliban was there to be exploited for the purposes of
imperial Prospero. In return for his labor, Prospero would give Caliban language and endow his "purposes with words that made them known."[2] But even
with this revelation of purpose, Caliban will only experience a small measure of

humanization. That is, in spite of the gift of language, Caliban remains too heavily mired in nature for its uplifting powers of reason and civilization. So ran one of the most enduring narratives of Caribbean identity to emerge from European literature and philosophy.

With the arrival of slaves from Africa, Caliban became African. As George Lamming points out, "the slave whose skin suggests the savaged deformity of his nature becomes identical with the Carib Indian who feeds on human flesh. Carib Indian and African slave, both seen as the wild fruits of nature, share equally that spirit of revolt which Prospero by sword or language is determined to conquer."[3]

Among Afro-Caribbeans, a corresponding view of our culture and philosophy could be formulated as a consciousness of existence as being the racialization and colonization of Africans and our way of life within the framework of Euro-Caribbean plantation societies. The works of Caliban's reason are Afro-Caribbean philosophy's contributions to the cultural articulation of the problems of this particular existence—and how to respond to them.

The development of this distinct philosophy can be divided into three broad phases: the idealism of traditional African religions, the Christian moralism that combined with or displaced African idealism, and the poeticism and historicism that have dominated both the late-colonial and postcolonial periods. The first phase (1630–1750) is rooted in traditional African thought because from the seventeenth to the late nineteenth century, Africans were forcefully brought to the region to work as slaves in the plantation economies being created as integral parts of European imperial projects. In this phase, Afro-Caribbean philosophy was primarily embedded in religious discourses and could not be separated from the latter's associated practices. These were the primary lenses through which the consciousness of a racialized and colonized existence was articulated. As such, they were at the same time antiracist, anticolonial, and hence delegitimating discourses. Thus, the seismic shift in orientation that marked the development of Afro-Caribbean philosophy was evident in the militant spiritualism of Shango, Vodou, and other religious discourses. Consequently, the idealist characterization of this phase should be taken as an indicator of the predominant role of spirit in this philosophical system. That is, this dominance should not be equated with exclusivity. As we will see in chapter 1, traditional African philosophy incorporates a number of competing themes into well-integrated totalities. Thus in addition to its idealist themes, we also find strong existential, moral, cosmogonic, and empirical ones.

The second phase (1750–1860) is Afro-Christian because of the very asymmetrical processes of interculturation and creolization that were produced by the colonial cultural system. The period is marked by an incredible variety of mixings between African and European religions, as well as other cultural practices. Because the practice of philosophy remained primarily embedded in religion, these are the mixings of most importance for us. They produced the slave narratives such as those of Ottobah Cugoano and Mary Prince. Out of them, slaves and former slaves turned peasants and urban workers also formed popular religious discourses that were delegitimating. Examples of these would include Myalism, Zion, Revival Zion, Vodou, Cumfa, Santeria, and Rastafarianism. The major philosophical consequence of this development was the growth of an ascetic Christian moralism that often challenged the idealist tendencies of traditional African religion. Again it is important to note that this label is not an exclusive one. For example, strong historicist tendencies are to be found in this moral discourse. These are most visible among the Rastafarians. This intermediate phase will not be examined in great detail in this work.

The third phase (1860 to present) that straddles the late- and postcolonial periods cannot be indicated by one major label. It is shared by two major schools within which there are important subdivisions. These are the poeticist and historicist schools. Major representatives of the first would include Claude McKay, Aime Cesaire, Wilson Harris, Edouard Glissant, Derek Walcott, and Sylvia Wynter. Major representatives of the second would include Edward Blyden, George Padmore, Marcus Garvey, C. L. R. James, and Frantz Fanon. Figures like McKay, Cesaire, James, and Fanon bridged to some degree the tensions between these two traditions. This cleavage is one of the major dualities confronting Afro-Caribbean philosophical thought that it has not been able to incorporate into a larger totality and a wider self-understanding.

Rather than achieving this larger unity, the tendency has been toward particularization and fragmentation within these schools. As we will see in chapters 8 and 9, the historicist school tends to divide along Pan-Africanist and Marxist lines with further differentiating of positions within each. For example, within the Pan-Africanist variant we find the racial historicism of Garvey and the providential historicism of Blyden and the Rastafarians. In the Marxist variant we can distinguish between democratic, Leninist, and insurrectionary approaches to a class-oriented historicism. In chapters 4 and 5, we will examine two distinct approaches within the poeticists school, those of Harris and Wynter. In spite of these tendencies toward fragmentation, the texts of these individuals all include the working out of philosophical positions as prefaces to their incorporation in poetic, historical, political, or economic contributions to the debates over European colonialism. The result is the large number of subtextual philosophical positions I've tried to categorize with some difficulty.

In short, Afro-Caribbean philosophy is a complex, multilayered, subtextual discursive formation. Its subtextual, auxiliary status has made it a minor, rather than a major or dominant, discourse. As a minor discourse, Afro-

Caribbean philosophy has remained an open, de-centered field that has been shaped by its diverse intertextual connections. Consequently, it has been without the internally centered forms of organization and the pattern of rapidly changing positions associated with philosophy as a major discourse. In its earliest layers, this minor philosophy was primarily spiritual. It was the intense spirituality of Africa that was the source of its creative responses to the plantation order of Caribbean society. In its intermediary layers, it was also primarily spiritual. However, the discursive order of the spirituality of this phase was an Afro-Christian one in which there was a shift from mythic to moral and historical discourses. In its more current layers, Afro-Caribbean philosophy has aestheticized and historicized its creative and oppositional responses to the neoplantation orders of Caribbean society. The result has been a more secular set of critiques and related philosophical positions.

From this brief portrait at least three general features are worthy of careful notice. First, Afro-Caribbean philosophy is a highly politicized formation whether we are speaking of its predominantly spiritual, moral, or secular phases. This politicization points clearly to its embeddedness in the social and political problems of Caribbean societies. Second, its productions such as racial historicism, Rastafarianism, magical realism, or socialism make it clear that both world constitution and the production of arguments are important features of Afro-Caribbean philosophy. In other words, both the nature of its arguments and of its totalizing strategies are important for its thorough understanding. Third, the formation as a whole has been the work of ministers, doctors, lawyers, historians, economists, political activists, creative writers, and philosophers all working together. This feature points to the intertextual embeddedness of Afro-Caribbean philosophy in the larger Caribbean intellectual tradition. Consequently, by no stretch of the imagination can this philosophy be considered an autonomous one. On the contrary, both its politicization and its production by nonphilosophers points to its origins in the teleological, foundational, and discursive aspects of life projects being undertaken by various groups in Caribbean society.

PHILOSOPHY AND THE CARIBBEAN INTELLECTUAL TRADITION

Because it is not an isolated discourse, the portrait of Afro-Caribbean philosophy that we have developed so far can be effectively supplemented by looking at it from the perspective of the larger intellectual tradition in which it is planted. From this perspective, we can compare the general features of Afro-Caribbean philosophy with those of Afro-Caribbean literature, dance, music, and other cultural forms. Viewed in this comparative way, four additional features stand out.

First, inspite of its importance, philosophy as a whole has been allocated a restricted role in the division of intellectual labor. It has prefatory and auxiliary roles to play but none of its own making. Hence it has carried on a rather subterranean existence with a comparatively low level of visibility within the larger intellectual tradition. However, within this low level of visibility, some traditions of philosophy are more visible than others. By far the most invisible has been the African, a fact that has created significant problems for Afro-Caribbean philosophy.

Second, compared to the other Afro-Caribbean cultural forms, such as dance or literature, Afro-Caribbean philosophy is the least creolized of these important media. That is, the African, European, and Indian elements in it are the least integrated. If we take Afro-Caribbean fiction, Calypso, and Reggae as examples of well-integrated creole forms, then Afro-Caribbean philosophy has a long way to go.

Third and closely related, Afro-Caribbean philosophy was unique among Afro-Caribbean art forms in the extent to which it overidentified with its European heritage and underidentified with its African inheritance. In short, it inherited many of the anti-African biases that have made African thought the most invisible discourse in the Caribbean intellectual tradition.

Fourth and finally, the communicative framework within which Afro-Caribbean philosophy had to make its delegitimating critiques was a particularly unequal one. Communicants were not viewed as equals and arguments were not accepted on merit. As we will see, it was a racially distorted communicative situation that systematically undermined the arguments and the value of Afro-Caribbean philosophy, and thus inhibited its growth.

Although this larger intellectual tradition was necessary for the emergence of Afro-Caribbean philosophy, this tradition also hindered that growth in many ways and was the source of some of the most embarrassing paradoxes and contradictions that have been integral parts of the formation of this philosophy. The most glaring are of course the paradoxes of anti-African biases in an Afro-Caribbean philosophy, its patterns of creolization, and the overidentification with European philosophies in a tradition that is supposed to be critical of the European heritage. The invisibility of black philosophy in the Euro-American tradition has been given very careful logico-political and existential analyses by Charles Mills and Lewis Gordon.[4] At the same time, Gordon has also analyzed the phenomenon of antiblack tendencies in Afro-Caribbean and other black philosophies.[5] Here I would like to supplement the analyses of Mills and Gordon by briefly indicating some of the sociological factors that made it possible for our intellectual tradition to generate such internally contradictory and crisis-ridden discourses.

COLONIALISM AND THE CARIBBEAN INTELLECTUAL TRADITION

From a sociological standpoint, the contradictory tendencies and patterns of communicative inequality that characterize our intellectual tradition derive from the colonial nature of the cultural system that institutionalized it. These colonial roots of the tradition emerge very clearly from its history. This history has been extensively explored by Gordon Lewis and Dennis Benn. In the work of both authors, the dialogical structure already noted in the case of philosophy emerges as a basic feature of the tradition as a whole. In both *The Growth of the Modern West Indies* and *Main Currents in Caribbean Thought*, Lewis describes and analyzes some of the main features and products of the tradition. One of the primary results of Lewis's analysis is the hegemonic position of European texts and discourses within the tradition. Although critical of this hegemony, Lewis is so caught up in its power that he has a very hard time seeing the intellectual contributions of Afro-Caribbeans. So much is he in the grip of the spell of invisibility cast over Afro-Caribbean thought, he is able to suggest that European colonization was capable of creating a "cultural tabula rasa" upon which it could rewrite Caribbean culture.[6] Thus the picture that emerges is one of radical discursive and communicative inequality between Euro- and Afro-Caribbeans. Although not as extreme, much the same pattern emerges from Benn's work.[7] From both authors we can conclude that the colonial cultural system that framed our intellectual tradition established within the tradition a radical inequality between Afro- and Euro-Caribbeans that reflected the politico-economic order of the society.

However, to explain the patterns of creolization, the levels of politicization, the anti-African biases, and the contrasting patterns of visibility and invisibility affecting Euro- and Afro-Caribbean contributions, it is necessary to go beyond this fact of radical inequality. We need to go further and ask what is it about the dynamics of colonial cultural systems that result in the ongoing reproduction of these patterns. From the sociological standpoint, the peripheral dynamics of these cultural systems hold the keys to the explanation of these patterns of politicization, creolization, invisibility, and communicative inequality.

Colonial cultural systems can be subsumed under the broader category of peripheral cultural systems as they share many of the dynamics of the latter. Peripheral cultural systems are historically specific types of cultural formations. They exist only in relation to core or central cultural systems. Both types emerge within the context of imperial or transnational formations such as empires or world economies and disintegrate soon after the collapse of the latter. Between core and peripheral cultural systems there are very definite accumulative dynamics. Core cultural systems must accumulate authority at the expense of peripheral ones. The centralizing or peripheralizing of cultural systems begins with their incorporation into these systematically related patterns of cultural accumulation and disaccummulation. The imperatives of these processes of accumulation and disaccumulation often produce major changes in discursive practices, modes of cultural organization, output, and canonical standards.

Given this mode of formation, peripheral cultural systems are marked by at least five distinguishing characteristics. First, they are plural cultural systems whose integration is achieved by a colonial state with high "legitimacy deficits."[8] Imperial conquest brings with it a new hegemonic culture to the society. Consequently the authority of local cultural elites is replaced by that of the colonial state and a group of foreign cultural elites. This hegemonic shift generates major legitimacy problems for the emerging colonial order, as both the colonial state and its cultural elites emerge as illegitimate formations in local political discourses. Yet the future stability of this order requires that these illegitimate formations be made to appear legitimate. This is the contradictory nature of the legitimacy demands that colonial societies make on peripheral cultural systems. From the point of view of this state, culture is not the consciousness of a distinct existence, but rather a producer and supplier of legitimating symbols and arguments.

Second, the supplying of these legitimacy demands will require differential rates of cultural accumulation in the local and imperial layers of the system. Within the confines of the system, imperial texts, whether religious, poetic, economic, or philosophical will have to accumulate authority at a faster rate, or produce corresponding decreases in the authority of local discourses. These differential rates of accumulating authority or canonicity are important structural characteristics of peripheral cultural systems.

Third, closely associated with these patterns of differential accumulation, have been patterns of discursive competition in which European discourses tend to replace African and Indian ones. In the words of Rex Nettleford, within these systems there has been a "battle for space"[9] between the discourses of their European layers and the corresponding African and Indian ones. As these battles intensify, spatial distributions become more unequal and of increasing significance to the drive to accumulate authority and legitimacy.

As these spatial distributions become more unequal, they institutionalize what Clive Thomas has called a "dynamic divergence"[10] between local centers of cultural production and the primary sites of cultural demand. For the purposes of this study these sites will be the following: (1) ego-genetic processes such as identity formation; (2) sociogenetic processes such as information based economic production; and (3) hegemony producing processes such as the legitimating of state power. As colonization deepens, the cultural demands of these three reproductive sites are increasingly met by outputs from the imperial layer, establishing a "dynamic convergence"[11] between the two. These shifting patterns of divergence and convergence result in significant decreases in the demand for African and Indian cultural production, setting the stages for their decline and underdevelopment.

Fourth, peripheral cultural systems are characterized by a polarized, internal competition between imperial and indigenous sites of production over the supplying of the symbols and discourses that will define and legitimate personal identities in their societies. Like political structures, human identities are in need of cultural legitimacy, and hence are major sites of cultural demand as well as production. These legitimating discourses may be ritualistic, religious, scientific, or philosophical in nature, as long as they provide the ego with the support it needs.

What is peculiar about ego genesis in peripheral cultural systems is that discursive competition over ego-formative needs is not just between qualitatively different discourses such as science and literature but also between local and imperial traditions of the same discourse. In the case of the Caribbean, this competition has been between European discourse such as religion, language, or science and their African and Indian counterparts. Thus here too in the domain of self-formation, Nettleford's battle for space rages on, as indigenous traditions are forced to yield their monopolies over the supplying of identity forming symbols and discourses.

Fifth and finally, peripheral cultural systems are characterized by the racializing of the identities of their different cultural groups. In the Caribbean, this process of racialization turned Africans into blacks, Indians into browns, and Europeans into whites. The process was most extreme between blacks and whites. In the origin narratives, stories of conquest, civilizing missions, and other legitimating discourses of European imperialism, the blackness of Africans became their primary defining feature. In these narratives, color eclipsed culture. The latter became more invisible as Africans were transformed into negroes and niggers in the minds of Europeans. This racial violence shattered the cultural foundations of the African self, causing the latter to implode. Race became the primary signifier of Europeans and Africans and of the differences between them. Consequently, the identities of these two groups were rigidly inscribed in a set of binary oppositions that linked the binary black/white to other binaries such as primitive/civilized, irrational/rational, body/mind, prelogical/logical, flesh/spirit. Similar sets of racialized binaries came to define white/brown interactions and also black/brown ones.

In particular, these perceptions of Afro-Caribbeans amounted to a radical dehumanization that reduced them to the biological level. This biological reduction was also a radical deculturization that shattered both self and world and also made the African's capacity to labor very visible to Europeans. However, this was no ordinary capital/labor relation. Faust, the capitalist developer, was here metamorphosed into Prospero, while his racialized worker was transformed into Caliban. This "Calibanization" of Africans could not but devour their rationality and hence their capacity for philosophical thinking. As a biological being, Caliban is not a philosopher. He or she does not think and in particular does not think rationally. In the European tradition, rationality was a white trait that, by their exclusionary racial logic, blacks could not possess. Hence the inability to see the African now reinvented as Caliban, in the role of sage, philosopher, or thinker. In short, this new racialized identity was also the death of Caliban's reason.

At least in the case of the Caribbean, it should be clear that the above peripheral dynamics profoundly shaped the internal organization of cultural systems, their hierarchical patterns, the nature of discursive output, and the standards and criteria by which this output was recognized and made a valuable part of the heritage. Both individually and collectively, these dynamics pushed Caribbean cultural systems in the direction of producing and reproducing black invisibility, anti-African, and anti-Indian biases.

In the case of the dynamic of differential rates of cultural accumulation, it contributed to the systemic need to devalue African and Indian cultures. Also, the hegemonic need to make an illegitimate state appear legitimate produced strong systemic interests in dogmatic positions and stereotypical misrepresentations of Africans and Indians. The strategic battles for space between imperial and local discourses point very clearly to strategies of control that required the displacing of African and Indian cultural authority. These twin motives of control and displacement are most evident in the struggles over whose cultural definitions of Indians and Africans would be institutionalized as normative. When the Calibanization of the African identity became an integral part of these peripheral dynamics, the Caribbean intellectual tradition was ready for the ongoing production and reproduction of the black invisibility, the patterns of creolization, and anti-African biases that Afro-Caribbean philosophy would inherit.[12]

In sum, to understand this particularly embarrassing set of problems that have plagued Afro-Caribbean philosophy, we have to work our way through these layers of Calibanization, racial othering, discursive competition, dynamic divergences and convergences, legitimacy deficits, and inverse patterns of cultural accumulation that the tradition cultivated in order to make its contributions to the production of colonial hegemony. Also, it was in the midst of the crossfires of these peripheral dynamics that Caliban's reason lost its visibility. These were important sociological conditions and factors in the broader cultural context that shaped the formation of Afro-Caribbean philosophy. Only when we take them into account can we understand the African and creole problems of Afro-Caribbean philosophy.

THE PROBLEMS OF AFRO-CARIBBEAN PHILOSOPHY

The extent of the negative impact of these dynamics makes it unmistakably clear that Afro-Caribbean philosophy has major problems with the contexts of its formation. These problems would certainly make a strong case for its autonomy. With contexts like these, who needs support! However, such an absolute break is not really an option. What is in fact available to Afro-Caribbean philosophy is the option of using its limited autonomy to transform this antiblack context into an epistemic order that is more supportive of its growth.

This option confronts Afro-Caribbean philosophy with the difficult task of trying to change a tradition on which it is dependent and whose antiphilosophical, antiblack, and other negative values it has internalized. Hence it is not going to be an easy undertaking. The dissolution of European colonialism has not produced the end of imperial or antiblack values and constraints. On the contrary, it has resulted in a shift from colonial incorporation into classic empires to peripheral insertion into an American-dominated world economy. Consequently, critiques of doctrines of manifest destiny, of the Caribbean being in America's backyard, and of equally, it not more virulent, antiblack practices, have been important elements in the delegitimating discourses of the region. However, there have been structural changes in the postcolonial period that should make this task easier. First, the shift from a colonial to a nationalist state has changed significantly the legitimacy pressures coming from the political arena. Second, important and stimulating developments have been occurring in African and Afro-American philosophy. These nationalist changes and the developments in Africana philosophy have opened up an effective space in which we can begin to deal constructively with the problems of Afro-Caribbean philosophy.

In addition to these anti-African, antiblack, and creole problems that Afro-Caribbean philosophy has inherited, there are a number of more internal ones for which the solutions may be more creative than reformist. These problems are related to the fragmented state of our philosophy. As a body of thought, it is marked by deep fissures, wide cleavages, and oppositional constructions of binaries or dualities such as spirit/matter, spirit/history, premodern/modern, poeticism/historicism, race/class. Consequently, it is a poorly integrated body of thought that is conscious of itself primarily in part and only rarely as a whole. Some of these divisions can be linked to the peripheral dynamics examined earlier, but they are also related to the existential dynamics of world constitut-ing activities, that is, to conceptions of the ego, its self-creative experiences, and their legitimacy needs.

As noted earlier, Afro-Caribbean philosophy is not just about the making of arguments. It cannot be described as a logicist, analytical, or positivist tradi-tion. The constructing of integrated worlds of meaning is too central a part of its activities for it to fit comfortably under any of these designations. These totalizing strategies have posed unique challenges for Caribbean philosophers and hence have a distinct history and pattern of development that has remained underthematized.

In spite of this uniqueness, the experience of European philosophy with totalizing strategies has been normative in the Caribbean academy. Hence it has shaped profoundly our understanding of these processes of discursive for-mation and change. Wole Soyinka has developed a wonderful metaphor for the European experience that is worth quoting in full:

> You must picture a steam engine which shunts itself between rather closely
> spaced suburban stations. At the first station it picks up a ballast of allegory,
> puffs into the next emitting a smokescreen on the eternal landscape of nature
> truths. At the next, it loads up with a different species of logs which we shall
> call naturalist timber, puffs into a half-way stop where it fills up with the syn-
> thetic fuel of surrealism, from which point yet another holistic world-view is
> glimpsed and asserted through psychedelic smoke. A new consignment of
> absurdist coke lures it into the next station from which it departs giving off no
> smoke at all, and no fire, until it derails briefly along constructivist tracks and
> is towed back to the starting point by a neo-classic engine.[13]

What Soyinka describes so artfully is the rhythm or logic behind the chang-ing of worldviews in the West. It is one of periodically selecting an aspect of reality, an intuition, or a scientific fact and turning it into a separatist and sometimes absolute truth, that is supported and elaborated by proliferating sets of analogies and arguments. For Soyinka, this rhythm is motivated by a search for absolutes in the absence of a symbolic totality that gives a concrete sense of the absolute through integrating humans into the life of the cosmos. Further, such integrating totalities are capable of symbolically reconciling many of the smaller contradictions as well as the more elusive antinomies that accompany everyday human thought.

Given the minor status of philosophy in the Caribbean, our experience with worldviews has been quite different. There is no train puffing out ever-changing constructions of a world that continues to elude the grasp of these attempts. Rather, this forward, linear pattern of worldview development has been contained or counterbalanced by a series of lateral, syncretizing moves, that Edouard Glissant has labeled "transversal."[14] As Wilson Harris has pointed out, the discursive raw material that the creative imagination confronts in the region consists of the damaged bodies of shattered selves and mutually imploded and imploding worldviews.[15] The history of discursive violence in the region has produced high levels of mutual decentering and interculturation between the African and European worlds, the European and Indian worlds, and the Indian and African worlds. This violence has left parts of these systems fairly intact, other parts highly mixed, and others that are damaged beyond repair. This is the heritage upon which creative totalizations must build. These imploded foundations have led to superficial comparisons with postmodern thought that can be misleading. The latter is the latest set of smoke from the Western train now fueled by a technocratic objectification of self and world that is still quite alien to the Caribbean. We consume many of the products of this Western self-objectification, but we do not produce them.

Given this heritage of imploded worldviews, three clear tendencies have emerged in Afro-Caribbean art, religion, and philosophy: (1) reconstructive work within these traditions; (2) synthetic work between them; and (3) transformative projects beyond them. Reconstructive work has taken the form of a search for lost origins that has involved reconstituting aspects of shattered Amerindian, Indian, and African worldviews. Synthetic work has entailed the search for ways to advance the mixed or hybrid parts of these imploded worldviews and the projecting of creole cultural formations as a basis for a new regional identity. Transformative work has centered around the projecting of new national communities that draw on these reconstructed and creolized traditions. In short, there are strong tendencies toward reconceptualizing the fragments of broken traditions, creolizing the differences between them, and projecting transformative alternatives. Both of these hybridizing and reconstructive tendencies are evident in the Afro-Christian and Afro-Hindu syntheses among the masses. These point to a possible creole solution to the problems of this history of cultural division and of the different identities they legitimate. However, these creolizing tendencies exist simultaneously with their opposites, that is, tendencies toward Christian, Hindu, African, or Indian purisms. These neotraditional tendencies are often the result of political manipulation, but they are also related ego-legitimacy needs.

In short, world-constituting activities among both the elite and masses are caught in the pure/creole binary. They oscillate back and forth, never really finding a point of reconciliation or resolution. As the Rastafarians make clear, the Caribbean masses have retained the ability to repair or refashion the integrating totalities of India and Africa, which are able to convey a sense of the absolute and of cosmic integration. This type of spiritual production has been and still is their first line of discursive creativity. Political vision and philosophical and cultural creativity often rest on the categorical foundations of this capacity for spiritual creativity. With this solution to the problem of the absolute, there has been no need among the Caribbean masses for the Soyinkan train.

Among the intelligentsia, the response to the heritage of mutually imploded worldviews has been quite different. This group has lost the ability to be creative in the language of spirit. That is, we have lost the ability to fashion deities and to create classic totalizations based on a spiritual analogy. Instead our first line of creativity has become a bipolar discursive space that is structured around art and history. The first has given rise to the well-established poeticist tradition and the second to an equally strong historicist tradition. The latter has emphasized popular and state-led transformations of colonial/plantation institutions with a view toward creating national and egalitarian communities and corresponding changes in consciousness. In the poeticist tradition, the emphasis has been on the aesthetic reworking of the elements of broken traditions, with a vision toward transforming the consciousness and identity of Caribbean people, whose changed behavior would in turn change their societies. This aesthetic work has kept our intellectual tradition quite close to the traditional African and Indian totalities and their solutions to the problem of the absolute.

However, the totalizations that have come out of this space, whether poeticist or historicist, are qualitatively different from traditional totalizations. Among poeticists, there have been fictional attempts at recreating these earlier totalizations. Such efforts must run into difficulties as they are narrative attempts to create what has been realized only in the language of spirit. The shifts to the languages of art and history mark not only the switch to new creative media but also the emergence of a new phase in the development of primal subjectivity in the region. These changes have brought with them a more assertive role for the Caribbean ego in relation to its spiritual, natural, and sociohistorical environments. While not the techno-instrumental mode of self-assertion of the Western ego, the new Caribbean subject is capable of intervening creatively and practically in its environments. It is ready to rename, revalorize, reimagine, or practically transform plantation geographies, identities, and societies. However, this new assertiveness did not result in projects of total control over spiritual, natural, and social spaces. Rather, it is counterbalanced by strong relations that root the ego organically in an unconscious or spiritual ground. Through these relations the ego is "grown" or constituted more than it creates itself. This rootedness together with the minor status of philosophy have slowed considerably the train on which this group of Caribbean worldviews are traveling.

This new discursive abode of the Caribbean imagination is a large organically unified space, whose contours and strange unity we have not fully explored. That is, the unity of this space precedes, rather than follows, any attempts to thematize or systematize it. Further, intertextually embedded within it are a number of other positions that get formulated in terms of analogies and arguments drawn from its poeticist and historicist poles. However, most of its occupants have been unable to see or thematize this unity. Rather we have only been able to work within its subpositions, or one of the major polar positions. Thus my work has moved primarily within the historical wing and is only now exploring its organic connections with the poeticist tradition that once appeared to be its opposite. This has revealed a unity that has been there all along and that I did not see before. The major exceptions to being trapped in these divisions and binaries have been figures such as Claude McKay, C. L. R. James, Aime Cesaire, Frantz Fanon, Nicholas Guillen, Rex Nettleford, Tim Hector, Orlando Patterson, and the calypsonians Short Shirt and David Rudder, who have all straddled the major polarities of art and history, as well as other oppositions internal to this space. In them we get good glimpses of this underlying but underthematized unity.

As a group, these divisions and dualities constitute the major set of internal theoretical problems of Afro-Caribbean philosophy. The latter's current state of fragmentation reflects the ways in which it has resolved or not resolved, recognized or not recognized, these problems. As we will see, there is still a marked tendency to ignore them, or to see them as not being important. Consequently, both the extent and the quality of the exchanges between the different positions within this space have not been very great. By contrast much more effort has been expended by Afro-Caribbeans on debates in European philosophy that touch on the interests of particular positions. Our contributions to European debates on existentialism, Marxism, Liberalism, and poststructuralism all support this claim. The hidden unity of poeticism and historicism cries out for thematization. So also do the tensions between history and spirit and those between historicism and the African heritage.

Only by taking more seriously these problems that are unique to its own internal formation will Afro-Caribbean philosophy continue to grow and discover its rhythms and patterns of internal organization. These are the regions unknown to Caesar that Caliban must now enter. At the moment we can only guess at some of the answers to these questions. Given the limitations of the poeticist/historicist space we now occupy, even as a whole this must be viewed as a limited affirmation of what we are as a people. But we will not proceed to wider affirmations of ourselves until we have internalized the secret unity of these polarities. Consequently, in chapter 10 and the conclusion, I will return to some of these issues regarding oppositions and polarities.

PROSPECTUS

The arguments of *Caliban's Reason* unfold in three basic parts. In the first, I examine a number of founding texts with the aim of establishing a number of basic themes and concerns. These include the nature of the African philosophical heritage and the primary claims of the poeticists and historicists. The second part consists of three intermediary reflections that take up some important issues in and around Afro-Caribbean philosophy: its relationships to poststructuralism, to Afro-American philosophy, and to Western concepts of rationality. In the third and final part, I focus in-depth on the historicist school and the major problems confronting it.

PART ONE

Sampling
the Founding Texts

The African Philosophical Heritage

U ntil quite recently, to speak
of the African heritage of Afro-Caribbean philosophy would have been to open
myself up to major challenges. In both Africa and the West, the existence of
such a distinct philosophical heritage was in serious doubt among academicians
and professors of philosophy. A cloud of colonial invisibility had descended over
African philosophy. However, thanks to the work of scholars like Kwame
Gyekye, Alexis Kagame, Marcien Towa, Henry Oruka, Tsenay Serequeberhan,[1]
and others, it has been rescued from this awful fate. Consequently, I can proceed with my primary task of outlining the traditional phase of this heritage,
which remains a formative influence on Afro-Caribbean philosophy.

What these scholars have been able to show is that long before there were
professors of philosophy there were philosophers. Gyekye and Oruka in particular have developed for us the role of the African sages who were the producers
and conservers of rich philosophical traditions. Thus in the case of the Akan,
Gyekye has shown that philosophical activity is closely associated with the
Onyansafo, or wise person. This is an individual who exhibits a distinct type of
self-reflective activity that others recognize as both wise and profound. Of such
an individual, it is said: "The wise man is spoken to in proverbs, not in speeches
(or words)."[2]

In this chapter, I will present a systematic outline of traditional African philosophy, particularly those aspects that bear directly on Afro-Caribbean philosophy. Throughout the exposition I make the assumption that the character of

traditional African philosophy has been profoundly shaped by its intertextual relations with the religious, mythic, genealogical, and proverbial discourses that dominate African cultural systems. Indeed, it is a central argument of this book that traditional African philosophy emerged in the philosophical positions that were implicitly taken by sages in these and other important discourses.

This approach to traditional African philosophy will of course differ from those of Robin Horton and the early Paulin Hountondji, who argued that such a discourse did not exist.[3] It will also differ from the position of Marcien Towa, who approaches traditional African philosophy through its intertextual relations with folkloric, rather than mythic or religious, discourses. Focusing on the authoritarian nature of sacred power, Towa argues for a deep opposition between religion and philosophy, and hence against the reconstruction of the latter through its intertextual relations with the former.

Further, in Towa's view, philosophy is essentially a secular discourse, characterized by the making of rational arguments and counterarguments. In African folktales, the implicit philosophical position as Towa demonstrates, is often a secular one. The heroes are usually not religious or mythic figures, but rather crafty animals or humans who challenge all authority and play tricks on everyone including the gods. In developing the philosophical implications of this aspect of African folktales, Towa has made a valuable contribution to the origins of secular thought in traditional societies and their internal bases for rationalization and desacralization.[4]

However, Towa's position is subject to two important criticisms. First, the claim that the authoritarian and dogmatic tendencies of myth and religion void them and their intertextual relations of all philosophical significance is a false one. Dogmatism is not unknown to philosophy. As we will see, much of the phenomenology of both Husserl and Habermas has been directed at the dogmatism of positivism and scientism. Thus, in spite of their dogmatic tendencies, I will take the position that there is much in religious and mythic discourses that is of philosophical importance.

Second, Towa indirectly admits the truth of this position when he begins his discussion of traditional African philosophy with an analysis of Egyptian religion. He demonstrates clearly the philosophical elements in Egyptian religious discourses in spite of the possibilities of finding dogmatic tendencies within them. Hence we can conclude from Towa's own analysis that dogmatism is not an absolute bar to philosophical activity. This conclusion highlights the inconsistency in Towa's approach when he refuses to take a similar view of other traditional African religions. What is it that distinguishes the dogmatic tendencies of Egyptian religion? The specific qualities that reduce their "antiphilosophical"[5] tendencies are never really made clear. An adequate portrait of traditional African philosophy can only be drawn from all of the discourses in which it is implicitly embedded and particularly the dominant ones which include myth, religion, and genealogy.

Thus, I will argue that traditional African philosophy inherited a number of concerns and issues from the basic religious vision it supports. From proverbial styles of thought, it inherited its major mode of expression. In the Yoruba tradition, "A wise man who knows proverbs can reconcile difficulties."[6] According to Igbo tradition, "Proverbs are vegetables for eating speech."[7] From the philosophical positions implicit or explicit in the above discourses, I will develop my outline of traditional African philosophy. In particular, I will show that these positions include cosmogonic ontologies, cosmogonic/communitarian systems of ethics, vitalist and predestinarian systems of existentialism, and epistemologies that are both ego centered and ego transcending. However, before taking up these specific philosophical inheritances, I must provide a brief sketch of the vision of existence created by the religious, mythic, and genealogical discourses of traditional Africa.

THE RELIGIOUS VISION OF TRADITIONAL AFRICAN PHILOSOPHY

The vision that informs traditional African philosophy, that generates its fundamental questions is a religious one. It's a vision that results from a set of religious answers to basic questions about the origin, nature, and purpose of being, particularly human being. As such, this vision rests on origin narratives that parallel Christian, Hindu, and other religious accounts of the origins of existence. Origin narratives are stories of cosmogenesis, of the creation of the world that human groups use to define and legitimate their identities. Among the Igbo of Nigeria, we find several competing origin narratives. One begins its narration by telling how the Supreme Being started creation with the making of Earth and Sky. After these were established, He created two messengers, Sun and Moon, to bring him news of events on earth.[8] Among the Yoruba, the narrating of creation begins with the creator God sharing his *Ashe*, or creative powers, with a group of animals, which included a python, a viper, a snail, an earthworm, and a woodpecker.[9]

In spite of their diversity, origin narratives are not arbitrary or superfluous stories. On the contrary, they are a vital part of the linguistic/discursive infrastructure that complements our biology and makes possible the cultural regulation of behavior that is unique to human orders of existence. They provide important keys to what Edouard Glissant has called atavistic cultures. These cultures were founded on an original imagining of creation. They draw "legitimacy from a Genesis, a creation of the world, which they had intuited and transformed into a myth, the focus of their collective existence."[10] On the strength of origin narratives such as those of the Igbo and Yoruba, atavistic cultures have consistently created "unquestionable genealogies" that linked them to the first day of creation and so confirm their identity and their rights to the land they occupied. Hence the identity-forming and behavior-regulating significance of origin narratives.

In the view of Sylvia Wynter, origin narratives are particularly important for the mythopoetics of human self-formation. The ontogenetic needs of the ego are such that its development requires a mythopoetic mapping of the binary oppositional structure of its language onto significant differences in its environment. These would include differences such as male/female, good/bad, cosmos/chaos, which are vital for the ego's reading of its surroundings. The negative and positive markings of these binary systems of classification must correlate with the plotlines of these narratives to produce desired and undesired modes of being and behaving. These bipolar constructions facilitate acts of ego identification or nonidentification, thus allowing this organ of everyday consciousness to negotiate its self-formation. Later, we will see the importance that Wynter, Harris, Glissant, and Soyinka attach to the mythopoetics of self-formation. For now, what is important is the cosmogonic/ontogenetic significance of origin narratives.

A basic assumption of the narrative visions of African religions is that existence as we know it, see it, and live it is neither self-creating nor self-sustaining. Thus, whether it is the world of material nature, the social world of human interaction, or the ego-centered world of the self-reflecting or cognizing individual, none of these carry within themselves the Ashe, or creative power, that can account for their origin or continued existence. For such explanations, African origin narratives posited a supersensible spiritual world that has both immanent and transcendent relations to the material, social, and individual worlds. In other words, unlike Karl Popper's ontology, traditional African religions posited a four-world model of existence as opposed to a three-world model.[11] The spiritual world constituted the fourth and the most important world in this model of existence. Not only was it the origin and foundation of the other three but also the latter were its manifestations while it remained in the category of the unmanifest. Consequently, the spiritual world could not be grasped by the knowing subject in the same manner that the latter acquired knowledge of the other worlds.

Because of spirit's immanent but also transcendent relations to its manifest worlds, any object, process, or person could potentially become a symbol or locus through which it made itself known. Such revelations of its existence Mircea Eliade has called "hierophanies."[12] For traditional African religions it was the human ego as a symbol or site of hierophanies that was central. In other words, the unmanifest not only bordered the world of the ego but also it transformed the ego's terrain into a symbol for itself. The hierophanies of spirit were the experiences of the sacred that gave African religions their well-known ecstatic qualities and out of which religious worldviews were constructed. Thus, the ego-centered world of everyday life was surrounded by other worlds or orders of meanings that transcended it. Alfred Schutz classified these transcendent orders that border our everyday worlds into three types: little ones like those of earthly time and space; medium ones such as the world of the other person; and the great transcendencies like death, sleep, and dreams.[13] For Africans, the spiritual world was clearly the greatest of the great transcendencies. It was the world beyond (and at the same time one with ego existence) that had the greatest significance for the latter's well-being.

The stories of African origin narratives are about the creative agency of this unmanifested spiritual world, the real hero and sustainer of creation. Although the created and uncreated worlds constituted a unity, the African ego imposed the binary markings of its linguistic capabilities on the difference between the spiritual and material or created worlds. Not surprisingly spirit was positively marked in relation to nonspirit and so came to represent a higher and more desirable order of existence. This binary can be usefully compared to the Platonic binary between the world of being and that of becoming. The former is a spiritual world of eternal ideas, a world that always is. The latter is a world of changing forms that is always becoming but never really is.[14]

Closely related to this privileging of spirit is the primarily symbolic or hierophanic approach of African origin narratives to everyday reality. Objects such as the earth, sun, moon, or stars, social practices such as marriages, sacrifices, or agricultural production, and developmental processes such as health, illness, or human ego genesis were often seen more in terms of their capacities to be symbols of the unmanifest than in their own everyday terms. This hierophanic approach amounted to a spiritual sociology or physiology that subjected the economic, political, cultural, and biological dimensions of everyday life to the spiritual domain. This ordering of discourses is the opposite of the modern one where the spiritual world is subjected to the others or is eliminated altogether. Hence it is more illuminating to call the African approach symbolic or hierophanic, rather than magical.

Given this strong spiritual orientation, the keys to the religious vision of these origin narratives are to be found in the ways they constructed this spiritual domain and the relations they recognized between it and the created or manifested worlds. In these religious narratives, the spiritual world was constructed in both personal and impersonal terms. In the latter case, spirituality was conceived in terms of force or agency, rather than personal qualities. In other words, it was conceived in terms of its enabling capabilities, its creative intelligence and drives. Spirit was like a vast ocean of impersonal creative energy that was capable of realizing the nonspiritual world and of shaping events in it.

Perhaps the best-known ethnographic account of such impersonal views of spirituality among Africans is Placide Tempels's study of the Bantu-speaking Baluba of the former Belgian Congo. For the Baluba, being or existence is constructed in terms of force: "Force is being and being is force."[15] To be is to have force, to not be is to lack force. This force of being resides in the creator God and is the origin of the vital force that gives every creature its being. According to Baluba metaphysics, the vital forces of all creatures are supersensibly in contact with each other and with God. For Tempels, this is the hierarchy of interacting forces that is at the core of Baluba philosophy and religion.

This use of force as an impersonal representation of spirituality is not peculiar to the Baluba. Kagame's work shows that it is also used by other Bantu-speaking groups.[16] We also find it among the Yoruba for whom *Ashe*, the power to make things happen, is the important facility through which God makes and sustains the created world.[17] Among the Akan, Gyekye analyzes their conceptions of spiritual agents and agency in terms of a "metaphysics of potency."[18] However, among both Yoruba and Akan, this concept of force is not as fully elaborated as in some of the Bantu-speaking groups. But in spite of the above differences, these cases all give glimpses of abstract and impersonal approaches to spirituality in traditional African religions.

Existing simultaneously with the above impersonal accounts are the more familiar personalized constructions of the spiritual domain. In these accounts, the spiritual world is constructed in terms of a hierarchical pantheon of gods, goddesses, ancestral spirits, and demons, at the apex of which is the creator God. At the same time that these spiritual agents are personal, they also carry within them the vital force or the power of *Ashe* that is the basis of the impersonal constructions of spirituality.

We can find such spiritual pantheons among the Baluba, the Yoruba and Igbo of Nigeria, the Akan, and the Tellensi of Ghana. Among the Yoruba, the creator God is called Oludamare, among the Igbo, Chineke, and among the Akan, Onayame. The deities or nature gods and goddesses as a group are referred to as the Abosom among the Akan, the Orishas among the Yoruba, and the Mmuo among the Igbo. Below these deities are the souls of the departed ancestors and finally the demons.

Although we can find these hierarchical pantheons in the personal constructions of spirituality that exist in African religions, the relative importance for everyday life of the various categories of beings in these spiritual communities varies considerably. These variations are important because they help us to explain some of the qualitative differences between African religions.

For example, although Tallensi and Baluba religions clearly recognized a creator God and various nature deities, the relations with the ancestors were of paramount importance for everyday life. Consequently, their mythic discourses, which narrated the stories of the deities, were not well developed. However, Baluba and Tallensi genealogical discourses were well developed because they had to narrate the stories of the ancestors. In addition to these narrations, genealogical discourses also situated people, things, events, behaviors, and processes (e.g., ego formation) in relation to lines of patriarchal and matriarchal descent and hence are clearly related to the institution of lineage groups. The kinship system becomes the site of a major hierophany and the founding analogy upon which the constructing of worldviews rests. The authority of these genealogical discourses was grounded in the godlike powers of the ancestors, which derived from their spiritual status. Hence the similarities in the imperative structures of ancestral and divine speech regimes. Thus among the Tallensi and the Baluba, these types of genealogical/ancestral discourses were paramount for everyday life.

In sharp contrast to both were the Yoruba for whom relations with the creator God and the deities were central, with the ancestors a clear third in this hierarchy. Here we have the well-developed mythic discourses that recount the lives of Ogun, Shango, Oshun, Ifa, and the other great Yoruba deities. Kinship systems declined as founding analogies and were replaced by political systems. The Akan and the Igbo fall at differing places between the Yoruba, on the one hand, and Tallensi and Baluba, on the other. In short, the differences in the character and discursive distinctness of African spirituality are closely related to the aspects of pantheons that are thematized and how personal or impersonal the emphasis.

Whether personal or impersonal, genealogical or theological, the crucial problem for religious discourses everywhere is representing and enforcing the regulatory interactions between deities and humans. Often, the point of departure for establishing these behavior-regulating relations with the spiritual domain is a religious ontology of the human self. This ontology asserts that in addition to the social and other factors that help to determine the everyday self or ego, there are important self-deity relations that are fundamental to the process of human self-formation. The authoritative or behavior-determining powers of this relationship derive from the emotions evoked in the human subject by the sacred, creative, and de-creative powers of deities. This is the aspect of myth and religion that in Towa's view make them antiphilosophical. In African religions, this ontology is evident in their conception of the human person and in the relations that such an individual should maintain with the deities.

For example, among the Akan, there are at least three basic parts to the human person, the *Okra*, or soul, the *sunsum*, or ego, and the *honan*, or body.

In Gyekye's view, the individual is "the ontic unity" of these three parts.[19] The *Okra* is the divine spark of Onayame, the creator God, that exists in all human beings. Often it escapes the awareness of the ordinary individual, who is usually conscious of only the *sunsum* and *honan*. In its subconscious depths, the *Okra* carries Onayame's plans for each individual. Hence its relations to the *sunsum*, or ego, are predestinarian. These predestinarian relations are experienced as having formative or determinative powers and cannot be ignored by the ego with impunity. To achieve fulfillment, the *sunsum* must develop within the guidelines encoded in the *Okra*. Gyekye refers to the *sunsum* as "the coperformer of some of the functions of the *Okra*."[20] Thus a successful ego genesis requires cooperative relations with the *Okra*, or soul.

In addition to these predestinarian relations with the *Okra*, and hence the creator God, African religions linked human ego genesis to ongoing relations with the deities, ancestors, and other spirits that made up their religious pantheons. The regulative and ego-constitutive nature of these relations define the paradigmatic situations that generate African religious experiences. They are determined by the sacred character of the deities, their particular personalities, and the tensions between their aims and those of humans.

Not surprisingly, spiritual beings whether deities or ancestors were often seen as ambivalent authority figures with the power to intervene constructively or destructively in the human self-formative process. That is, they had the power to steer and redirect human life in spite of the narrower concerns of the *sunsum*. This guidance had as its aim making humans more aware of the cosmic order of which they were a part, and with which they must seek harmony.

These are some of the important features of the spiritual order that was especially privileged by the binary classifications that informed the origin narratives of African religions. This spiritual order was central to the African religious vision of existence. It shaped desired modes of being and generated norms for regulating human behavior. As such, it raised and answered implicitly a number of philosophical questions, whose explicit thematizing have been foundational for traditional African philosophy.

TRADITIONAL AFRICAN PHILOSOPHY

Although distinct discourses, philosophy and religion overlap at many points, particularly in traditional societies. For example, both are interested in the question of being, the nature and fate of the human self, and questions of ethics and morality. However, in religion the practical problems of moral regulation or the coordinating of divine and human wills assume a priority that is not the case in philosophy. More central to philosophy is the rational truth of the claims we make and less their regulatory or salvific efficacy.

In traditional African philosophy, we have already seen that this type of discursive overlapping was basic. Before setting up a residence of its own, the discursive address of this philosophy was in the small spaces opened up by a variety of religious, genealogical, mythic, and proverbial arguments, claims, and practices. In spite of this dispersal, the philosophical positions that filled these spaces in other discourses were systematically related and hence had a substantive coherence. By examining important ontological, existential, ethical, and epistemological themes in this philosophy, I hope to demonstrate some of this coherence. Also, in contrast to Towa, I hope to show the philosophical importance of intertextual relations with religion, myth, and genealogy.

THE COSMOGONIC ONTOLOGY

The ontological claims of traditional African religions are quite explicit. Both the origin and persistence of being are conceived in terms of the "causality" that binds creature to creator. This image of creative divinity that is analogous to that of the creative individual, becomes crucial for the cosmogonic framing of African ontology. Within this framework, existence is primarily the creative work of deities and ancestors. It is their creative project. The created world is theirs to make, regulate, and unmake. The conceptual and rational elaboration of this idea by sages was the work of traditional African philosophy. The results can be seen in the conceptual elaborations of the notion of the creator.

Among the Akan, Onayame is described by a variety of epithets that give good insight to his conceptual elaboration. Gyekye lists many of these, which include representations of Onayame as Alone, Boundless, Eternal, Absolute, Architect, Originator, Uncreated, Omniscient, and Omnipotent. He is clearly the Absolute reality, "the origin of all things, the absolute ground, the sole and whole explanation of the universe, and the source of all existence."[21] Among the Igbo, the conceptual representations of Chineke are quite similar. Like Onayame, he is described by a number of names, epithets, and proverbial sayings. Among Metuh's list of the latter, we find the following: "God created you and your personal 'Chi' [Destiny]"; "If God removes his hand the world will end"; "If God is not in the plot, death cannot kill a man."[22] Here again the being and persistence of the world is unquestionably the work of Chineke, the Supreme Being.

In tension with such personalized ontological concepts were more matrical conceptions that derived from the impersonal views of spirituality. From this matrical perspective, existence was seen as the result of the careful balancing of a matrix of polar opposites, in which created existence, including the lesser deities, appeared to be enmeshed. Here the image to be conceptually developed is not that of a personal creator, but rather what Soyinka has called a

"vortex of archetypes" or original forms and categories.[23] Among the oppositions in these open-ended matrices are binaries such as being/nonbeing, good/
evil, nomos/wilderness, male/female, and so forth. These are most likely attributes or aspects of impersonal spirituality on which the binary structure of language has been imposed, giving rise to the mythopoetic aspects of Wynter's
origin narratives. As such, these oppositions constitute the primary stuff, the
founding or ontological categories that make existence possible. Again the crucial philosophical work here is the elaborating of these concepts and the
defense of their truth claims.

Whether personal or impersonal, the spatial and temporal dimensions of
these spiritual ontologies are cosmogonic. Time is the durational aspect of the
projects of the deities. It "lasts" as long as they continue the work of creation.
The temporality of divine projects does not follow a linear path. Rather, it
moves in a cyclical path that encompasses material birth from the spiritual
world, death, return to the spiritual world, and rebirth. This eternal cycle
shapes the cosmogonic conception of time in traditional African philosophy.

Like time, the view of space is also cosmogonic. It is the extensive dimension
of the project of creation. Among the Akan, Onayame is the creator of space
and time, but at the same time is beyond both. He is boundless and "cannot be
limited to any particular region of space"[24] or to any particular period of time.
Time and space are thus cosmogonic categories that help to frame the project
of creation, but do not in any way limit or constrain the creator.

Even the ontology of social life was conceived by traditional African philosophy in cosmogonic terms. General conceptions of the nature of society were
based upon cosmogonic analogies. Society was seen as a very fragile normative
order that the great heroes and ancestors created out of the wilderness in ways
that paralleled the creation of the cosmos out of chaos. Thus everyday conceptions of society are supported by an analogy between the binaries cosmos/chaos
and nomos/wilderness. This analogy is what made possible the cosmogonic
readings of the social order.[25]

Finally in this sketch of traditional African ontology is its account of the
being of the ego or self. I've already indicated the religious dimension of this
ontology through the analysis of the relations between the Akanian notions of
Okra and sunsum. In addition to this religious dimension there is also an
important cosmogonic dimension to the African ontology of the self. An
authentic establishing of "the ontic unity" of the self was seen as a cosmogonic
challenge that was analogous to the creating of society out of the wilderness or
the cosmos out of chaos. Thus in many origin narratives and discourses of the
self, the languages of cosmic and self-creation overlap. This cosmogonic coding
of self-formative processes is clear in the origin narrative of the Dogon sage,
Ogotomelli.[26]

The cosmogonic challenge of self-creation is one that humans often fail to meet authentically. Consequently, the ontological status of ego existence is usually that of a subexistence because it often carries within it a far from authentic solution to the challenges of its being. The difficulties in meeting these challenges arise from several sources. First, the ego, or *sunsum*, is often unaware of the divine message and creative intelligence of its *Okra* and so attempts the project of self-creation without its guidance. This must lead to contradictions and blind alleys that will have to be resolved, corrected, or abandoned. Second, as the ego is often unaware of its *Okra*, it is often unaware of claims and obligations it must recognize in relation to deities and ancestors. Without attending to these, there can be no authentic resolution to the ontological problems of ego existence. Third and finally, when the ego defines itself within the binaries of its language, it produces deep fissures and irreconcilable divisions within itself. The figure of Ogun, caught between the binary creativity/destructiveness, illustrates this cosomogonic incompleteness that marks the being of both humans and lesser deities.[27] Genuine ontic unity is impossible when the *sunsum* is caught in these dualities. A ritual path beyond them must be found. For these reasons, the African ontology of the ego contained a cosmogonic challenge that was often unmet and hence saw ego existence as a subexistence constrained by unresolved ontological problems.

Given the spiritual nature of this ontology, a case could be made for describing it as idealist. In spite of clear idealist elements, two objections can be made to the idealist designation. First, the overwhelming metaphorical importance of creation, which has made African ontology a very cosmocentric discourse. Second, the radical separation between matter and spirit that we have in many Western and Indian idealists is largely absent in the African case.

AFRICAN EXISTENTIALISM

In contrast to ontology, which attempts a more comprehensive analysis of being, the existential aspects of a philosophical tradition offer us a more humble and anthropocentric view of existence. It provides a vision of being through the lenses of our lived experiences, rather than those of our more cognitive activities. Consequently, to grasp the existential dimensions of traditional African philosophy it is necessary for us to let go of the magisterial vision of its cosmogony and adopt the perspective of the lived experiences of Africans.

At the core of African existentialism is the difficult cosmogonic challenge inherent in the process of human ego genesis. The ego is our "organ" of everyday consciousness. It mediates our achievement of consciousness, ontic unity, and personal autonomy. Yet we have only partial control over it as we do over the organs of the body. We have as little control over the ego's founding or

defensive activities as we do over the shape of our bodies or rates of our heart-
beat. Thus our egos are externally shaped and determined at least as much as
they prereflectively shape themselves, or we consciously shape them. These
tensions between the ego's experience of itself as being spiritually determined,
prereflectively self-determined, and reflectively self-determined are not easy
for it to assimilate. They are experienced as dualities perpetually in conflict.
Thus the binary, self-determination/spiritual determination, is experienced as
a contradictory opposition that destablizes identity formation. Consequently
the ego tries to understand itself as one or the other. Like most traditional
philosophies, African existentialism resolved this ego-constitutive opposition
in favor of spiritual determination. In the African view, it is the *sunsum*'s successes and failures, its confirmations and disconfirmations by its *Okra*, its
deities, and ancestors that determined the quality of the consciousness, ontic
unity and autonomy it will provide for an individual. It is the lived experiences
of the ego's successes and failures in the face of these challenges that have
been crucial for determining the taste of existence and hence African attitudes
toward it.

As we have seen, the cosmogonic difficulty in these challenges is such that
most of our ego solutions leave us poorly integrated as individuals and subex-
isting, rather than fully existing. This subexistence of the ego suggests less than
perfect solutions to the problems of its being. These imperfect solutions point
to what the great Indian philosopher, Sri Aurobindo, has called "the ignorance" of the ego.[28] That is, the latter's unawareness of its *Okra* and its larger
spiritual environment. In Plato's philosophy, this unawareness is presented as a
result of the ego turning the soul toward the everyday world of becoming and
away from the higher world of being.

In traditional African existentialism, this ignorance or not-knowing on the
part of the ego results in the misrecognition of its *Okra*, its deities and ancestors, and misguided attempts to usurp or replace their creative authority. In
other words, there is an inherent tendency in the *sunsum* to revolt against the
cosmic order of things and subject it to its own creative and self-creative powers. This tendency to revolt on the part of the ego is very clearly captured in the
Dogon myth of the struggle between Yurugu and Amma, the creator God.
Yurugu is a classic figure of cosmic discord, like his Judeo-Christian counterpart, Lucifer. Before Amma was able to give him his female side, Yurugu interrupted the creator and confronted him with the challenge that he could create
a better world. In the grip of this Yuruguan state of misrecognition and blind
rebellion, the ego accumulates debts of recognition to spirit that it will be
forced to pay not in dollars but in ontological currency. We've already seen
that these blind moves made it impossible for the ego to resolve three sets of
self-formative issues: its predestinarian relations with its *Okra*; its regulatory

relations with deities and ancestors; and the dualities in which the ego gets trapped by the binaries of its language. Hence the ego is a spiritually embedded but crisis-ridden site of agency. However, because of its ignorance the full dimensions of this embeddedness remain concealed.

The primary indicators of difficulties on these spiritual levels include experiences of inner resistance to one's self-affirmation, illness, social failure, loss of *Ashe* or vital force, or unusual misfortunes. Primary indicators of good relations include experiences of support for one's self-affirmation, health, social success, and unusual fortunes. The patterns and rhythms of these experiences of spiritual ease or unease are the crucial currents that determine the existential weather in the region around the ego. They are the instruments of the latter's regulation by spirit.

Particularly important for the discursive development of African existentialism are the states of regulatory negativity that individuals in varying states of subexistence will inevitably experience. In the African case, what is distinctive about these negativities is their spiritual nature. They are negations, voidings, sanctionings, or underminings of some aspect of the ego by its deities and ancestors that leave it exposed to experiences of nonbeing. The greater the adversity experienced by the ego, the greater is the spiritual ignorance or the Yuruguan revolt that is internal to its self-creative process. Thus personal failures, ego collapses, and other such difficulties were seen as spiritual interventions whose primary purpose was to shake the ego out of its ignorance or to end its revolt. Consequently, the inner resistance or blockages that individuals encounter in the course of their lives are not seen as arising from childhood difficulties in family relations, as Freud would suggest. Family relations are not the locus of "the primal scene" of ego genesis in African existentialism. Rather, it is to be found in the complex set of relations linking the human ego to its deities. In other words, African existentialism is based on spirituo-analysis, rather than a psychoanalysis of ego-formative problems. These disconfirming experiences constitute some of the tragic possibilities in the cosmogonic challenge of ego existence. Their weight often leaves the ego feeling overpowered and unable to rise and engage in its normal self-maintaining activities. An individual whose ego is in such a state feels an anxious uneasiness about the fate and future course of his or her life that motivates a seeking for help.

However, as important as these spiritual negatives are, they cannot be separated from the spiritual positives. The latter provide the deep joy and ecstatic ethos of African religion and African existentialism. Indeed, the crucial challenge that African existential discourses have undertaken is the attempt to explain the rhythms and patterns of these spiritual negations and affirmations that visit the ego in the various states of its suboptimal existing. These existential currents and related ontic difficulties defined the primary creative spaces inhabited by African religious and philosophical thinkers. These are clearly creative spaces in which the ego is open to its experiences of constitution and deconstitution by spirit. World-constituting activities in response to these currents and difficulties have been given at least three distinct discursive treatments in African existentialism. These activities have produced predestinarian, vitalist, and magical solutions to the patterns of spiritual affirmation or negation that are correlated with the ontic difficulties of ego formation.

The predestinarian analysis takes as its point of departure the predestinarian relationship between ego and soul and develops its implications for noted patterns of spiritual interruption or intervention. This predestinarian reading is particularly common in West Africa. Among the Akan, it is held that every human being has an *Nkrabea*, or destiny, that is fixed before birth. It is implanted in the *Okra* of an individual not long before he or she enters the material world. At this critical juncture "it receives from Onayame the message [*nkra*] that will determine the course of the individual's life on earth."[29] However, ego birth erases from memory much of this prebirth conversation and much of the heavenly realm in which it occurred. This feature of ego existence echoes Wordsworth's well-known claim that "our birth is but a sleep and a forgetting."[30] Similar notions of forgotten prebirth conversations that frame the earthly life of the individual are found among the Yoruba, the Igbo, and the Tallensi. It was the Tallensi notion of destiny that prompted Meyer Fortes's comparisons with the Greek notion of fate. The latter he described as a person's "particular apportionment of good and evil for his lifetime which was decided at birth."[31] Hence Fortes's use of Oedipus as a paradigm for analyzing the workings of destiny in West African societies.

In addition to these prenatal dimensions, African discourses of predestinarian existentialism reserved very important places for deities and ancestors. Both have crucial roles to play in the fulfillment or nonfulfillment of prenatal destinies. For example, among the Tallensi, every individual had an ancestor who served as its spiritual guardian. This ancestor had to be acknowledged as such and allowed to play his or her role. Ignorance or disregard of this ancestor often resulted in misfortunes, the loss of *Ashe*, or the blocking of chosen modes of self-affirmation.

African predestinarian existentialism linked the coming and going of spiritual affirmations and negations to the gaps between the message that was spiritually encoded in the *Okra* and the projects of being that our egos create for themselves. Because this message is not encoded in the ego, the latter may project a person's identity to be hunter even though he may have been spiritually scripted to be a farmer or a sage. Such projections of self will experience spiritual resistance and negation. More often the problem is not so much the particular social vocation, but the blind spots and exclusions that accompany the tendencies to overidentify with such self-definitions. In Platonic language, when the "turning" of the *sunsum* toward the everyday world is such that it effectively eclipses the spiritual world, the corrective negations of the latter will be quite strong. In such cases, being a hunter has been realized at the expense of inadequately acknowledging the claims and concerns of the spiritual agents that have determinate power over one's life. Such an individual would there-fore be unable to recognize and receive their creative contributions that may be necessary for the fulfilling of the person he or she really is.

In all such cases, individuals are at odds with their destinies, or the spiritu-ally encoded messages in their *Okras*. In Sartrean language, we have here the striving of egos to be what they are not, and to not be what they are. Egos in this condition are likely to experience negations of various sorts. Individuals who have missed their destinal tracks by wide margins may experience social and personal failure as a result of resistance from deities and ancestors. Such formative errors cannot be continually compounded without corrective mea-sures. The ego-genetic process must be returned to its destinal tracks. Here we see very clearly, the resolving of the self-determination/spiritual determination binary in favor of the latter. Consequently, as Melville Herskovits has shown in the case of the Dahomeans, the fulfilling of one's destiny is no simple affair. Rather it is a difficult process in which the ego is transformed and the individ-ual educated by the affirmations and negations of deities and ancestors.[32] This education is less about new information and more about reversing the ego's forgetful "turning" away from its *Okra* and the larger spiritual world that accompanied its birth. According to this predestinarian view, the more fully aware one becomes of the whole range of spiritual claims for which one is responsible, the more positive and life facilitating should these spiritual cur-rents become.

This view of African predestinarian thought as a discursive response to the existential anxieties produced by the regulatory powers of the sacred supports a very interesting hypothesis put forward by Rudolf Otto. He suggested that doctrines of predestination arise from the creature consciousness that spiritual regulation of the ego by the sacred powers of deities produces in human sub-jects. For Otto, "the notion of predestination is nothing but that 'creature con-sciousness,' that self-abasement and the annulment of personal strength and claims and achievements in the presence of the transcendent as such."[33] We have seen that this sense of being a creature of the deities is basic to both African ontology and existentialism and, of course, to African religion. Further, Otto's explanation has the advantage over Weber's in that it can account for the emergence of predestinarian views in African and other cultures, and not just European cultures. Further, it encourages us to compare predestinarian views, and not keep them apart.

Vitalist accounts of these spiritual negatives and positives experienced by the ego are systematically related to the more impersonal constructions of spirituality we have already examined. Thus among the Baluba, we find a vitalist existentialism that is free of the predestinarian features so prominent in the cases of the Tellensi, the Akan, and the Yoruba. As noted earlier, Baluba ontology constructed spirituality in terms of vital or creative forces. Consequently, not only being but also nonbeing was conceived in terms of force. Nonbeing was the spiritual negating or diminishing of the vital force that was source of one's being. We also noted that for the Baluba the vital forces of all beings were supersensibly in contact, and that the vital forces of creatures higher up the chain of being could supersensibly influence the vital forces of those below them. It is by way of this channel of "metaphysical causality" that the being of the ego could be negated or affirmed by other humans or higher spiritual agents.

Many of the negatives and positives experienced by the ego are seen by this vitalist approach as coming from the deities and ancestors. Among the Baluba, the nature deities are largely absent, so they are primarily the work of the creator God and the ancestors. The only guide that we humans have to their actions is that they are happy when hierarchy of vital forces is observed and angry when it is disturbed. Thus anyone who behaves like Yurugu, who does not respect the laws and the order of creation, becomes an individual whose "inmost being is pregnant with misfortune and whose vital power is vitiated as a result."[34]

The key difference with the predestinarian reading is the absence of any pre-birth pact or contract that could serve as a basis for a more personal understanding of the actions of the creator God and the ancestors. These spiritual agents are constructed as contractually unbound. Unlike the predestinarians, the vitalists see the actions of these agents as bursting the framework of all contractual constructions. In short, their actions were seen as being more unfathomable. Thus it was the cases of these more inscrutable experiences among the Tallensi that led Fortes to invoke the figure of Job. Here he could have also invoked the work of Otto to thematize this more inscrutable side of divinity that emerges among the Tallensi and is more strongly emphasized by the Baluba. Otto's emphasis on the fascinating yet dreadful, overwhelming but attractive qualities of the powers of the deities are echoed quite explicitly in this vitalist position. But, in spite of this more direct exposure to the existential ups and downs produced by these spiritual currents, the Baluba maintained a positive attitude toward existence through their strong faith in the greater strength of the forces of good.

The magical accounts of existential negations and affirmations are also linked to the more impersonal constructions of spirituality. Here many of the negatives experienced by an individual are seen as coming from demons or other humans, who by magic or sorcery have been able to invoke the vital powers of demons or other spirits. These are used to steal or diminish the vital powers of other humans and to enhance one's own. We find such magical responses to existential anxieties among all our ethnic groups. However they are weak among the Tallensi when compared to the Baluba. Among the latter, *buloji*, or sorcery, is a "perverted will" that annihilates the vital force of humans, who feel an "appalling terror" and "intense repulsion" before it.[35] As Fortes has suggested, this difference could be related to the importance of the predestinarian solution among the Tallensi. Thus much of the anthropological literature on African beliefs that has focused so exclusively on sorcery has missed these existential dynamics and the intertextual connections they establish between sorcery and other existential discourses.

Finally, it is important to note the different patterns of substantive elaboration exhibited by these distinct existential discourses. In the case of the Tallensi where the nature deities are largely absent, predestinarian existentialism is formulated largely in the genealogical discourses that narrate the stories of the ancestors. Among the Baluba where the nature deities are also largely absent, this genealogical pattern is the framework for a vitalist existentialism. In the case of the Dahomeans, the Akan, the Igbo, and the Yoruba where the nature deities are strong, the discursive formulations of their predestinarian existentialisms are much more religious.

Whether religious or genealogical, these existential discourses constitute an important factor in understanding African attitudes toward existence. Because these systems of thought were able to preserve a sense of an ordered cosmos, African attitudes toward existence have been life affirming, rather than life rejecting. There is very little of the radical anticosmism of the Gnostics or some Buddhist and Hindu traditions. There is also no radical rejecting of ego existence in spite of its difficult cosmogonic challenges. In contrast to Indian traditions that call for a dissolving of the ego into the *Atman*, or soul, African solutions to the problems of ego existence call not for its spiritual dissolution, but for each individual ego to recognize its unique spiritually encoded nature and the responsibilities that come with it. This affirmation of ego existence is thus a primary contribution of African existentialism to philosophical anthropology. If the cosmogonic discourses of African philosophy revealed its celestial reach, then its existential discourses reveal its human depths. Between the two, we get a good look at the comprehensive nature of traditional African philosophy.

THE ETHICAL DIMENSIONS

The ethical dimensions of a philosophical tradition are less in need of a general introduction than its existential coordinates. The former are more familiar to us because they deal with our conceptions of right and wrong, good and evil. Because of their regulatory orientation, ethical statements have a distinctive, action-orienting or perlocutionary force, that sets them apart from ontological or existential statements. The ethical dimensions of traditional African philosophy are cosmogonic and communitarian in nature. Their discursive frameworks are cosmogonic, while the object of their regulatory orientation is the human community.

The cosmogonic aspects derive from two sources. The first is that their behavior-regulating powers are often grounded in the higher authority, the cosmogonic, moral, and other concerns of the deities and ancestors. We've already seen the problem of coordination of wills at the heart of religious action. Ethical or moral regulation is one of the primary means through which this coordination in the interest of cosmic order can be achieved.

The second source of the cosmogonic aspects of traditional African ethics is analogical. Earlier, we saw that social ontologies, and hence social ideologies, were grounded in the analogy between the binaries cosmos/chaos and nomos/wilderness. Like the cosmos, the nomos was conceived as an order that was vulnerable to the forces of disorder. To the extent that traditional ethical discourses shared this analogy, they employed cosmogonic categories.

Among the Baluba, we find such a system of cosmogonically grounded ethics. According to Tempels, they recognize "the relationship that exists between cannons of law and rules of morality on the one hand, and the principles of philosophy or ontological order on the other."[36] In other words, "moral standards depend essentially on things ontologically understood."[37] This ontological understanding is of course an understanding of being in terms of force. Consequently, Baluba ethics are grounded in and authorized by the hierarchy of forces that emerged from Baluba ontology.

At the most general level, categories of good and evil are defined in terms of what is consonant or not consonant with the creative order of this hierarchy of vital forces. It is from the sacred aspects of this spiritual order that these ethical categories derive their authority. Human actions that challenge this order are bad, while those that affirm it are good. Thus actions that would either lower or excessively elevate the position of humans in this hierarchy would be bad: "Every act which militates against vital force or against the increase of the hierarchy of 'the *muntu*' [the human] is bad."[38] These are the ontological frameworks of Baluba ethics. In more personal constructions of spirituality, these ontological foundations would be more explicitly cosmogonic.

The communitarian aspect of Baluba ethics becomes clear when these more general onto-ethical principles are applied to individuals and communities. An evil individual is one who vitiates the vital force of another. Thus attitudes of envy, jealousy, and hatred are bad because of their life-destroying effects. In this regard, the sorcerer becomes the extreme embodiment of evil. A good person is one who affirms and increases another's vital force. Consequently, attitudes of love, respect, honesty, and cooperation fall within the category of the good.

At the more collective level, we can observe similar processes of ethical construction and categorization. The Baluba condemn as bad practices such as stealing, murder, adultery, sex in the wilderness, child marriage, and disrespect for elders and ancestors. Those activities that strengthen and affirm the normative order of the community are categorized as good. Here the concerns for the life and stability of the community become evident.

Among the Tallensi, we find a similar cosmogonic/communitarian approach to ethics, but within the framework of a more personal construction of the spiritual domain. In this setting, the cosmogonic aspects of ethical discourses are more explicitly linked to the creative and regulatory activities of deities and ancestors. This is reflected in the perlocutionary force of Tallensi ethical norms.

The most important of the few Tallensi nature deities was the Earth Spirit. She was not constructed as a goddess with a complex mythology as in the cases of the Akan and Yoruba. However, elaborate rituals were performed in her honor as she was seen as being capable of intervening in human affairs, and of exercising the ultimate sanctions of life and death. According to Fortes two distinct types of ethical norms emerged from the interactions with the Earth Spirit. First, there were norms of brotherhood, which enjoined Tallensi individuals to respect the person, property, and rights of fellow members. They especially prohibited them from shedding the blood of a member in conflict. Second, there were strict norms regarding things found on the surface of the earth. They prohibited the taking of articles or stray animals found on the earth, especially near religious shrines. All such objects or animals must be taken to the *Tendaana*, or Custodian of the Earth, who would decide how to dispose of them.

The ethical universe of the Tallensi was further defined by a similar set of imperative regimes in relation to the ancestors. As in the case of the Earth Spirit, the binding or perlocutionary force of these genealogically framed ethical norms was the spiritual authority of the ancestors. To achieve the growth of lineages the ancestors also desired, required the cooperation and obedience of Tallensi individuals. Thus in spite of their smaller portfolios, the ancestors also had the capacity to impose sanctions in the interest of lineage growth and concerns for the larger cosmic order. Ancestors could make pacts with Tallensi leaders in which their good will was conditional upon human cooperation. As Fortes points out, "The moral imperative of a ritual prohibition or injunction a-*kiher*-is connected with the dependence of the lineage on its ancestors goodwill for its survival and welfare."[39]

The ethical norms that emerged from these genealogical discourses were of the type: you must recognize (obey, listen to, make shrines for, give gifts to, and so on) your ancestors; or you must not disregard (disrespect, disobey, reject) your ancestors. The first group of norms fall into the category of good, while the second are instances of the bad. From this brief look at Tallensi ethical norms, whether religiously or genealogically framed, it should be clear that they carry within them analogical links between the cosmogonic and the communitarian.

A possible exception to this pattern is the case of the Akan. Gyekye argues strongly that the ethical discourses of the Akan are communitarian in nature, but without religious foundations. He suggests that the foundations of Akan ethics are humanistic in three important ways: (1) they are established by humans; (2) good and evil are defined in terms of what furthers or hinders the welfare of the community; and (3) that the binding or perlocutionary force of these ethical norms is the welfare of the community.

With regard to the first, Gyekye asserts that goodness in Akan thought "is not defined by reference to religious beliefs or supernatural beings."[40] On the contrary, "what constitutes the good is determined not by spiritual beings but by human beings."[41] On the second claim, Gyekye suggests that among the Akan, "what is morally good is generally that which promotes social welfare, solidarity and harmony in human relationships."[42] With regard to the binding or motivational power of ethical norms, Gyekye suggests that "moral value in the Akan community is determined in terms of its consequences for mankind and society."[43]

Although Gyekye makes a strong case, I am not completely convinced. His case rests upon a downplaying of the harmonizing and regulatory issues that are central to religious action. In his discussion of the problem of evil, Gyekye tells us that within the Akan conceptual scheme "evil stems from the exercise by the person of his or her own free will."[44] However, what exactly about the will of the individual produces evil is not clear. In a later discussion of the behavioral impact of religious sanctions, Gyekye does not relate them to the problem of an errant human will. Consequently, the connections between the tendencies of the will to stray and the regulatory role of sanctions are not developed.

Without such an explicit thematizing, the substantive role of the deities and ancestors in regulating the moral life of society can easily be missed. That Gyekye may have overlooked this aspect is suggested by the following concession he makes on the issue: "Since some of these sanctions derive in the Akan system from religious beliefs, it follows that religion cannot be completely banished from the *practice* of morality."[45] If these regulatory dynamics were more fully developed, the cosmogonic aspects of Akan ethics might have been more visible. If this is indeed the case, then Akan ethics may not be as different from our other cases as Gyekye's analysis suggests.

THE EPISTEMOLOGICAL DIMENSIONS

Like ontological, existential, and ethical discourses, epistemological systems of thought are important dimensions of the field of philosophy. Epistemology is not concerned with the problems of good and evil or the moral regulating of human behavior as is the case with ethics. Rather it is concerned with the problem of knowledge and with regulating the human production of true statements. In contrast to the special perlocutionary force of ethics, epistemological statements draw on experiential, methodological, and illocutionary forces to guarantee the truth of statements.

Like the ethical and other discourses examined above, traditional African epistemologies are most accessible in the cognitive claims made by dominant religious, mythic, genealogical, and empirical discourses. An examination of the epistemic practices employed by these discourses reveals a bifurcated but unified epistemology with different criteria for knowledge about sensible and supersensible realities. Given the priority that African thought gave to the latter, it should come as no surprise that these epistemologies privileged knowledge of the supersensible.

The claims regarding the existence of these two different but connected worlds constitute the foundations of traditional African epistemology. They necessarily raise the question of how knowledge of these domains is acquired. Knowledge of the everyday, sensible world was acquired through the normal functioning of the senses, the emotions and the mind, while knowledge of the supersensible world necessitated their suspension. The normal operations of these faculties can only provide us with knowledge of the material and ego worlds. As such, they can be legitimate bases for empirical, rational, and intuitive epistemologies, but not spiritual ones. The latter required a suspending of normal ego activities and a reversing of the forgetful turn that the ego took at its birth. In other words, spiritual epistemologies included techniques that made possible a recovery of the knowledge of the spiritual domain erased by the worldly turn of the *sunsum*.

In our discussion of destiny, we saw that crises in ego formation are quite often starting points of spiritual knowledge. The experiences of the ego being steered, pulled, or redirected in spite of itself can sensitize an individual to the actualities of spiritual regulation. But in and of themselves, these experiences are not enough to generate knowledge of the deities and ancestors.

This knowledge becomes accessible through direct contacts of a mystical nature and less directly through divination. In African religious traditions, the realm of spirit whether personal or impersonal is mystically accessible to humans. All beings are rooted in the *Ashe*, or creative power of spirituality, even though they may not be aware of it. However, as in so many areas of endeavor, some individuals are better able to make the mystical breakthroughs that will end this ignorance.

As in other mystical traditions, the path of direct access to spiritual knowledge requires a bypassing or silencing of the normal cognizing and world-creating activities of the ego. These must somehow be suspended if the deities and ancestors are to be experienced. These normal activities of the ego often include exclusionary practices that negate and make "invisible" the spiritual ground out of which it arises. It is as though when the ego is caught in but not aware of its normal ignorance, it cannot permit the operating nonego realities in the spaces it creates. Hence the tendency to eclipse the spiritual world along with its deities and ancestors.

The primary technique of interrupting or bypassing the ego used by traditional African religions is the trance state. This is a state of altered or nonego consciousness that is induced by drumming and dancing. Both the behavior and awareness of individuals are different in this state. But most important, the individual's body is open to being "possessed" or taken over by a deity who may speak or act through this person. These spiritual takeovers are resisted by the normal ego, making such direct experiences inaccessible to individuals who are unable to momentarily suspend ego functioning.

This is the mystical practice in which the claims African religions make for the existence of a spiritual world are grounded. The validating of these claims does not presuppose empiricist or rationalist epistemologies. The latter epistemic strategies have their place in the generating of knowledge about the material world. Thus in the herbal, medicinal, and metallurgical lores of traditional Africa, we have discourses that are empirical and rational in orientation. Unlike rational or empirical claims, the validating of spiritual claims presupposes an experiential epistemology that is both mystical and ego transcending.

These epistemological orientations are certainly evident in all of our ethnic groups. In the case of the Baluba, Tempels reports a notion of "metaphysical causality" that links the spiritual and material worlds. Among the Tallensi, Fortes describes a notion of "mystical causation" that binds the spiritual and material aspects of existence. Similarly, Gyekye speaks about a concept of "spiritual causality" among the Akan. Thus in all three cases, we have the positing of a spiritual world and a related notion of spiritual causation.

Trance states as avenues to spiritual knowledge are also well recognized in our groups. Among the Baluba, the spiritually awakened individual becomes what he is only because he has been "seized by the living influence of a deceased ancestor or of a spirit."[46] For this to happen, "the initiate enters into a trance, looses consciousness and becomes as if dead to ordinary human life."[47] Gyekye speaks of paranormal modes of cognition in describing the epistemic strategies used by the Akan in producing true spiritual statements. These strategies include "spirit mediumship, divination and witchcraft."[48]

These cases suggest that what is distinctive about the epistemologies of traditional Africa is their bifurcated spirituo-material nature. However, in its broad categorical outlines, this bifurcated structure is a feature they share with other religiously informed philosophical traditions. Gyekye's summary characterization of the Akan holds for all of our groups: "The acknowledgment of physical (nonsupernatural) casualty indicates a conception of dual casualty, the physical being invoked in consequence of ordinary or regular sequence of events, . . . the spiritual being invoked in cases regarded as extraordinary or abnormal events. . . . Further where as spiritual causality is vertical . . . physical causality is horizontal."[49]

These ontological, existential, ethical, and epistemological systems of thought are some of the major discourses that have defined the core of traditional African philosophy. This survey is by no means complete. We have not examined its idealism, its empiricism, its mysticism, its transcendental presuppositions, or its aesthetics. Earlier in this chapter, we noted in passing the worlds that transcended and bordered the world of everyday life in traditional Africa. The horizons of these worlds, their assumptions, and the ways in which they limited access to each other would constitute the transcendental foundations of this tradition. More specifically, in the constitutive practices of naming and valorizing, of constructing basic categories, of schematically organizing these categories, names, and priorities, in these world-constituting activities of the African consciousness are to be found the transcendental dimensions of the African philosophical heritage. Unfortunately, we cannot go into greater detail here. But in spite of this incompleteness, we have covered enough ground to be able to talk meaningfully about the philosophical heritage that traditional Africa has bequeathed to the Caribbean and the larger Africana world.

TRADITIONAL AFRICAN PHILOSOPHY AND MODERN AFRICANA THOUGHT

Because traditional African philosophy emerged implicitly in the ontological, ethical, existential, and other positions taken in religious, mythic, genealogical, and folkloric discourses, its presence and visibility depended upon the continued vitality and growth of these systems of thought. Their contraction or decay would mean decline and eclipse for traditional African philosophy. Consequently, to understand the heavy cloud of colonial invisibility from which

Gyekye, Towa, and others have rescued traditional African philosophy is to comprehend the modern fate of the religious and other discourses in which this philosophy developed.

The impact of colonization had at least three important consequences for African discourses. First was the devaluation and rejection of their truth claims by Europeans and European-educated Africans. Second was their hybridization as they absorbed European contents and adopted European languages as media of expression. Third, in addition to the Arabic languages, African discourses developed writing capabilities in European languages. In the colonial cultural systems that emerged, African and European cultural practices were locked into Nettleford's " battle for space," with European practices expanding at the expense of African ones.

The developing of writing capabilities radically transformed the African intelligentsia. Starting in late eighteenth century, a literate, hybridized elite emerged that represented various mixtures of African and European elements. Ottobah Cugoano, Anton Amo, Olaudah Equiano, Africanus Horton, Bishop Crowther, James Johnson, Edward Blyden, Henry Carr, Herbert Macaulay, Kitoyi Ajasa, and Joseph Casely-Hayford were some of the major figures of this tradition. Among them were lawyers, doctors, artists, or ministers, but all in varying degrees had been exposed to European education and absorbed many of its biases. Depending upon how these writers were effected by the anti-African biases of European educational institutions, the space and hence the visibility they gave to traditional African thought varied greatly. Thus there were big differences between Blyden and Ajasa in the extent to which traditional African thought and particularly its philosophy were visible in their writing. Similar patterns of a varying eclipse occurred in the Caribbean and in the Americas. It is only in the postcolonial period that these clouds of invisibility have begun to disperse, allowing traditional African philosophy to emerge.

That it has survived this colonial experience is clear from its presence in a number of modern writers. One contemporary African writer in whose work the vision of traditional African philosophy lives explicitly is the Nigerian playwright and essayist Wole Soyinka. He has transformed the traditional Yoruba worldview into a modern dramatic discourse that he uses brilliantly to analyze the social and political realities of contemporary Nigeria and the wider Africana world. Using dramatic master codes, Soyinka has creatively appropriated and reinterpreted the myths and rituals of the Yoruba deities to produce a discursive space that is new and forward-looking.

As a dramatic construct, this new space is aesthetic as opposed to religious. Continuity between old and new is established via Soyinka's retention of the origin narrative or "architectonic unity" as the "basis of man's regulating consciousness."[50] The poetics of drama, particularly tragic drama, become the new categorical framework of Yoruba origin narratives and their behavior-regulating consequences. Also a part of this poetics are traditional themes such as destiny, free will, and the overreachings of the ego. Thus, many of the existential themes that were religiously resolved are here examined and reworked from the perspective of the engaged artist.

The myths and rituals of Ogun, Shango, and Obatala are particularly important for Soyinka's dramatic transformation of the traditional Yoruba worldview. These and other deities become the discursive constructs that keep alive the African view of eternity, with its cycles of birth, death, and rebirth. In addition to being "cosmic extensions of man's physical existence," the deities now become media for communal exploration and recollection of the cosmogonic challenges inherent in human ego genesis: "The dramatic or tragic rites of the gods are, however, engaged with the more profound, more elusive phenomenon of being and nonbeing."[51] The gods are "the means to our inner world of transition, the vortex of archetypes and kiln of primal images"[52] that will remake egos by recoding their binary oppositional patterns. With this notion of the vortex of archetypes through which the self of both deity and human must be periodically reconstituted, Soyinka reproduces the uneasy tension between the personal and impersonal constructions of spirituality that are basic to the religious worldviews of traditional Africa.

In the Caribbean, as we will see in greater detail, traditional African philosophy experienced an even greater eclipse as a result of the rise of colonial discourses and a literate, hybridized local intelligentsia. In some sectors of this tradition, it disappeared completely while in others it remained very much alive. Outside of this literate tradition it remained alive in Afro-Caribbean religions such as Vodou, Santeria, Obeah, and Cumfa. Within the literate tradition, some of the modern writers in whom it has clearly survived include Jamaica Kincaid, Edward Braithwaite, and Wilson Harris.

In Haitian Vodou, we have some of the clearest continuities in the region. Although some of the names have changed, the categorical framework has remained basically the same. At the center is the creator God, Bondye, who is spiritual and hence unmanifest. He is supported in the maintenance of creation by the Lwas, or nature gods, and the ancestors. This continuity also extends to the conception of the human self. Along with its roots in the body, the self consists of two parts, the *gwo-bon-anj* and the *ti-bon-anj*. Like the *Okra* of the Akan, the *gwo-bon-anj* is an offshoot of Bondye, the creator God. According to Leslie Demangles, "the ti-bon-anj is the ego-soul. It represents the unique qualities that characterize an individual's personality."[53] Hence it is comparable to the *sunsum*. Demangles also points out that "Vodouisants believe that throughout life a harmony must be maintained between these two 'compartments' of a person's spirit."[54]

In the case of Kincaid these African survivals are clearest in her first work, *At the Bottom of the River*, a work she has repudiated for its lack of historical and political sophistication. However, it is precisely this containing of the historical within the mythic which points to the spiritual world that the author of this work inhabits. As Diane Simmons points out, Kincaid's work is "about loss, an all but unbearable fall from a paradise partially remembered, partially dreamed, a state of wholeness, in which things are unchangeable by themselves and division is unknown."[55] This paradise beyond the dualities is reminiscent of the spiritual harmony toward which traditional African existentialism has for so long strived.

Culturally, Kincaid inherited access to this world through her parents' belief in and practice of Obeah. As an artist, her ability to reach this spiritual world derived from her ability to silence her ego, and in that silence experience the unconscious spiritual world and artistically reflect its pushes and pulls on her own ego in mythic terms. This ability to displace her ego is a practice she associates with Obeah. Referring to the latter she says: "Instead of going for an hour on the couch, your entire life was on the couch, a world of nervous breakdowns."[56] But in the modern world, "this layer of Obeah life doesn't work any more,"[57] and recedes into inaccessibility. However, before it was lost, Kincaid was able to generate original mythic accounts of the activities of this spiritual world that Afro-Caribbeans have constructed with the aid of this Obeahist discourse. Particularly outstanding are her recreations of the mythic dimensions of the mother image. Kincaid's mother images go way beyond everyday or biological constructions and are distinguished by a mythic coding that is very reminiscent of African mother goddesses. The struggle between mother and daughter bears the mythic imprints of African constructions of the predestinarian struggles between *Okra* and *sunsum*. The failures that so often characterize mother/daughter relations echo the cosmogonic failures that result in the subexistence of the ego that is so central to African existentialism. In her later works, Kincaid achieves the historical sophistication she thought was lacking in this work. However this shift in emphasis demonstrates clearly the tension between poeticism and historicism that has divided the Caribbean philosophical imagination in the postcolonial period.

Thus in Vodou and in the work of both Soyinka and Kincaid, we can see different ways in which traditional African philosophy has entered into modern Africana writing. It has brought to the latter a number of truth claims that it has examined, reworked, and is still reworking. In the remaining chapters of this section, we will use the works of James, Fanon, and Harris to examine more carefully the fate of traditional African philosophy in the historicist and poeticist sectors of the Caribbean philosophical tradition.

C. L. R. James, African, and Afro-Caribbean Philosophy

One of the primary tasks of philosophy has been to analyze the problem of being, conceived as either an absolute or a relative reality. From its beginning in the second half of the nineteenth century, modern Afro-Caribbean philosophy has avoided comprehensive theories of being, such as those of traditional Africa, which begin with creation and end with the dissolution of the cosmos. Rather, Afro-Caribbean philosophy has concentrated its ontological efforts on the poetically or historically constructed nature of social reality, the need to reconstruct elements of its African past, and to project alternatives for the future. These foci have given contemporary Afro-Caribbean ontology its predominantly poeticist and historicist orientations and also reflected its new nineteenth-century creative habitat. As a result, philosophy in the region has largely been social and political in nature and concerned with problems of cultural freedom, political freedom, and racial equality. In the texts of this philosophy, history and poetics assume an ontological status as the domains in which Afro-Caribbean identities and social realities are constituted. The social nature of Afro-Caribbean philosophy, its poetics, and its historical foundations are evident in the works of Edward Blyden, J. J. Thomas, Marcus Garvey, George Padmore, Frantz Fanon, Oliver Cox, Sylvia Wynter, Wilson Harris, and, of course, C. L. R. James.

In this chapter, I explore the links, or the lack thereof, between Afro-Caribbean historicism and African philosophy, primarily through an analysis of the works of James. I argue that Caribbean historicism, including James's, inherited from European philosophy an oppositional construction of the link between modern and premodern thought, which has made premodern African philosophy as invisible in the Caribbean as it is in Europe. At the same time, James and other Afro-Caribbean philosophers have eagerly embraced modern African philosophy when rooted in a comparable historicism.

What are we to make of this bifurcated relationship? Winston James has suggested that it has its roots in Eurocentric tendencies that James inherited from Marxism.[1] Similar views have been expressed by John Henrik Clarke and Yosef ben-Jochannan.[2] Although this reading has some plausibility, it leaves too much unexplained. First, it does not explain the side of James that was critical of so much that was European. Second, it does not account for James's Pan-Africanism[3] or the autonomy he gave to color and race in his approach to racial liberation in both the United States and the Caribbean. Third and finally, the claim that James's Marxism contains Eurocentrism but not the African nationalism of Blyden or Garvey is not only false but overlooks the hybrid nature of anticolonial discourses. Both the Marxist and African nationalist discourses of the region share common Eurocentric themes, in particular the construction of the premodern/modern dichotomy.

Consequently, I argue that a better explanation of James's relationship to African philosophy can be found through an examination of two factors: the historical nature of James's philosophy, and his failure to rework the modern/premodern dichotomy in a way that was more reflective of African realities.

CARIBBEAN HISTORICISM AND EUROPEAN THOUGHT

Historicism has been one of the important generative ontological constructs of modern Caribbean thought. It has provided the philosophical foundations for much of the economic, political, sociological, and literary[4] work undertaken by regional scholars. More than science, historicism has been the discourse through which our consciousness has established itself in the materialism and secular rationalism of the modern period. Consequently, it is a philosophy that understands itself as modern and therefore has distanced itself from its premodern past. The positing of this modern historicist ontology was a discursive response to the radical historicization of our existence that accompanied colonization. This expulsion from myth into history was produced by the near-complete destruction of the precapitalist social orders that supported our prehistoricist ontologies and the totalitarian nature of our incorporation into capitalism. After these experiences, we have come to see ourselves as creatures of history.

Afro-Caribbean historicism mushroomed in a number of varieties: Pan-Africanist, nationalist, religious, culturist, Marxist. This variety resulted from the differing historicist responses of Caribbean thinkers to the intellectual challenges posed by the discursive transformation and delegitimation of African identities, values, and meanings. These transformations were effected by legitimating arguments for capitalism and colonialism. Arguments for colonialism led to racist ideologies of European superiority, whereas those for capitalism included a series of dichotomous constructions that contrasted modern and premodern societies.

These legitimating arguments contained the specific questions and claims that produced the vigorous counterattack by Afro-Caribbean thinkers such as Blyden and Thomas. These questions and claims were answered in European languages and academic discourses because of the colonial context of education. In other words, the impact of colonization on the communicative media was such that Caribbean thinkers had to make their responses in signifying systems that had been semiolinguistically reorganized and deeply influenced by the imperial relationship with European culture.[5] Consequently, whether it was ordinary language, religion, dance, or cricket, the production of counterstatements took place in hybridized signifying systems. This hybridity, as Homi Bhabha has pointed out, is the source of structural or systemic ambivalences because it enmeshes the anticolonial thinker in imperial meanings and values that operate below his or her awareness and volition.[6] It is important to stress, however, that this enmeshment is not primarily linguistic, as Bhabha and other poststructuralists suggest, but also has equally deep social and psychological roots.[7]

The contradictory ambivalences that result from the hybrid nature of colonial languages and other signifying systems have left traces all over the Afro-Caribbean historicist tradition. Some of these traces are embarrassing because they contradict the explicit goals of the authors. Others are useful in that they unintentionally further these goals. The persistence of Eurocentric values and meanings in the thinking of Pan-Africanist or Caribbean Marxist philosophers would constitute examples of embarrassing traces that limit the effectiveness of their critiques.

In spite of their enmeshment, Afro-Caribbean thinkers have effectively countered the arguments that legitimated colonialism and African slavery. This critique of racism and slavery has been sharp and runs consistently through the Afro-Caribbean tradition. By contrast, the critique of the modern/premodern dichotomy has been neither sharp nor consistent. This binary opposition created an unbridgeable gap between the two types of societies, which was homologous to other binary oppositions such as civilized/primitive, colonizer/colonized, forward/backward, and white/black. These oppositions systematically devalued the achievements of premodern societies while inflating those of European capitalism. Not only were these representations false for the European case but also they were particularly inappropriate for Africans, Afro-Caribbeans, and other Third-World peoples with still vital premodern heritages. Yet these constructions of the primitive and the traditional were not dispatched with the same decisiveness as the racist ideologies of European superiority. The discursive liberating of premodern societies, and premodern Africa in particular, from capitalist and socialist misrepresentation has not been as effective as the liberation from colonial racism. Consequently, the meanings and values that crystallized around the modern/premodern dichotomy can be seen all over the critiques of racism and the cases for an African nationalist or Marxist alternative.

James was in many ways proud of this enmeshment in European thought, even though he may not have been aware of all of its ramifications: "I, a man of the Caribbean, have found that it is in the study of Western Literature, Western Philosophy and Western History that I have found out the things that I have found out, even about the underdeveloped countries."[8] A better claim to Caliban's dilemma is hard to find. In this enmeshment, James was confident that he would not get caught, that he could appropriate this tradition and pose alternatives for Caribbean liberation in the language of Prospero. And indeed, James was a master deconstructor of European colonialist thought and an original architect of Caribbean alternatives.

The difficulties that the inherited opposition between modern and premodern created for him become clear in his use of terms such as Negro, primitive, backward, and civilized and in his tendency to claim too great a degree of modernization and Westernization for Caribbean people. An example is the following statement from a 1967 essay "Black Power": "The Negro people in the United States are not a people of a backward colonial area; they are Americans in what is in many ways the most advanced country in the world."[9] The European, capitalist, and colonialist meanings of these terms openly contradict James's explicit intention of affirming black power. Closely related to these smaller embarrassing traces is a larger and more important one: the invisibility of traditional African thought in James's historicism.

As we will see, the consequences of this type of enmeshment were even more embarrassing in Blyden's philosophy of African nationalism. At the same time that he espoused the formation of independent African states, he supported projects of European colonization in Africa because of their modernizing effects.[10] His support of the English language on the grounds that it would modernize the work attitudes of Africans is another embarrassing Euro-centrism in an Africanist discourse.[11] Similar contradictions can be found in Garvey's works. The binary oppositions of European discourses on modernity and race are basic constitutive elements of Garvey's African nationalism. Among the aims of the UNIA was the "civilizing" of the "backward" tribes of Africa.[12] In short, these anti-African biases and structural ambivalences are not peculiar to James, but can be found throughout the Caribbean intellectual tradition. They derive from the peripheral dynamics examined in the introduction and from the existential dynamics of black invisibility which have been so keenly analyzed in the works of Fanon and Gordon.

JAMES'S HISTORICISM

James was an historicist philosopher par excellence. His historicism functioned on many levels. For James, history was the arena of collective action in which individual and group formative projects could be realized. In other words, it was the activist arena in which the projects of individuals, institutions, communities, and nations could be realized. As an Afro-Caribbean philosopher, James's primary concern was the place of Afro-Caribbean people in history and the projects they have undertaken on behalf of their freedom and that of the larger Pan-African community. As a more global thinker, James was concerned with a wider variety of oppressed peoples within the confines of global capitalism and the possibilities for their freedom in a socialist order. This is the discursive context in which James's philosophy is embedded. Hence its primary intertextual relations are with politico-ideological discourses and forms of praxis. If traditional African philosophy rested on a religious vision, then James's philosophy rested on a historical vision. A magisterial vision of progressive movement, of human becoming through collective action. Given this historical vision, it should come as no surprise that the various aspects of James's philosophy—its ontology, epistemology, poetics, philosophy of the self—are historicist in orientation.

For example, James's poeticism is evident in his early writings that are fictional, in his Marxist texts such as *The Black Jacobins,* and of course in *Beyond a Boundary.* In these and other works, images, words, plot, thought, dialectics, projects, and other semantic elements are brought together aesthetically to constitute a powerful poeticist discourse. This discourse stayed with James throughout his life, sometimes in the foreground and at others in the background, but always it was a factor in his world-constituting activities. The historicist orientation of James's poeticism can be seen in his textual readings of historical action, where he often referred to strikes, insurrections, and revolutions as the books, stages, and canvases upon which the masses inscribe solutions to sociohistorical problems. It is also evident in the analyses of the immanent movement of thought and its textual formulations undertaken in *Notes on Dialectics.* Thus any profile of the discursive strategies James used in his world-constituting endeavors must include the poeticist ones.

Similarly, James's epistemology was also historicist in orientation. All existing modes of knowing and their related methodologies were historically rooted. None of them transcended the limits and influences of this historical conditioning. Further, these methodologies were all epistemic formations that were sure to be dated by the movement of history. Yet this was not a reductionist or mechanically deterministic position. James recognized the formal autonomy of epistemic and methodological processes during the historical periods of their flowering. In these periods, they can even eclipse their historical foundations. However, the latter will return to foreground as decline sets in. The consistency of James's self-criticism, or his critiques of Trotskyism, are among the best examples of the historicist orientation of his epistemology.

However, it is through his ontology that James's historicism can be most effectively located. As ontology, history was the primary medium of human self-formation. In its dynamism, James saw the important formative or constitutive powers shaping human development. History and not spirit or nature was the creative womb in which the human dimensions of existence emerged and developed. It was an arena of continuous becoming in which growth was fueled by the conflicts between thesis and antithesis, between projects of group formation and the opposition generated by their internal contradictions.

This ontological status of history in Afro-Caribbean philosophy is not peculiar to James. Fanon gave it its most explicit statement as part of his critique of Sartre's theory of the human self as a dialectic between absolute Being and absolute Nothingness. "Ontology," Fanon wrote, "does not permit us to understand the being of the black man. For not only must the black man be black, he must also be black in relation to the white man."[13] Thus it is the constituting power of the latter historical relationship that Fanon stresses, not the power of the formal, phenomenological relationships between absolute Being and absolute Negativity. It is to the historical relationship that he attributes the emergence of "the Negro" and the new meanings of his or her blackness. In short, for both James and Fanon history performed an ontological function at the same time that it outlawed classical ontological explanations of being. However, it is important to note that both James and Fanon had a healthy appreciation for the poeticism that has been the primary rival of their historicism. Indeed, their omnipresence in regional thought reflects the extent to which they straddled the Marxist, Pan-Africanist, and poeticist divides within our intellectual tradition.

More specifically, James's onto-historicism can be seen in his approach to the human self, particularly the identities of workers and "Negroes." James thematized the self in terms of the creative responses to challenges of the social environment that it permitted individuals or groups to make. The unity or structure of these responses to sociohistorical challenges has the shape of a project or a plan that has to be realized.[14] Both the energy and the codes for these creative projects are assumed to be immanent in the individual. James, however, did not develop these immanent dimensions or make them the basis for a psychological unconscious or a religious soul as with some of the poeticists. Because these dimensions are left implicit, Jamesian projects of selfhood are rooted in an historical ontology and not in the phenomenological ontology of Sartre's projects. In James, the self is radically historicized, which leaves it without mythic or religious dimensions.

As a result, the Jamesian self is very different from the traditional African self. As a modern philosopher, James resolves the binary self-determination/spiritual determination in favor of the former. Here the philosophical subject is no longer capable of mythically understanding itself in terms of its ego's constitution and de-constitution by spirit. Its embrace of both its autonomy and its own self-creative powers is at the same time a break with these mythic patterns of African self-understanding. The only permissible forms of external determination of the ego are sociohistorical in nature. Consequently, the mythic creative intelligence and the special problems that the ego brings to the spiritual arena are not explicitly thematized by James.

Rather the ego's creative and project-forming capabilities were intuitively recognized and invoked, only in the course of articulating the transformative, sociohistorical projects through which James defined modern African peoples. This was an activist mode of self-objectification that eclipsed the mythic dimensions of the Afro-Caribbean identity. This self was not defined in terms of the agency and constraint that is recognized in the mythic compromises between the destinal and Yuruguan struggles of the ego with its spiritual ground. These struggles and compromises disappear from the categorical or transcendental horizon of the Jamesian historical/activist subject. They now occur only in the sociohistorical arena as capitalist and worker, Prospero and Caliban battle with each other. In *Mariners Renegades and Castaways*, and also in *American Civilization*, James's reading of Melville's character Ahab demonstrates this historicizing of Yuruguan and destinal conflicts. Ahab is the American Prospero, determined to conquer both nature and history and to subject all to the demands and logic of capitalist industry. In this industrial setting, the conflicts with Caliban eclipse those with the gods. Consequently, the harmony that James seeks in socialism is one that will overcome the totalitarian tendencies of Faust/Propero/Ahab/Ford and reintegrate the individual into society.

In contrast to this underdevelopment of the immanent and mythic dimensions of the self, James stressed the importance of the social practices, values, goals, languages, and discourses around which identities crystallize. Without these sociohistorical elements there can be no self. James based both individual and group identity on the historical challenges their projects permitted them to undertake, rather than their inherited cultural traditions. This historical approach to the self was at the core of James's fictional writings and deepened as he became a Marxist philosopher. In sum, James never saw the self as a timeless, cultural construct outside of history. On the contrary, it was an agency that moved and had its being in the maelstrom of historical becoming.

Fundamental as this ontological function is, it does not exhaust James's historicism. Equally important as the social practices, values, and discourses around which identities crystallize, was history as an arena of struggle, of domination and the overcoming of domination, of social construction and destruction. These are the more familiar Marxist and Pan-African sides of James's historicism. In spite of its turbulent, dialectical nature, James perceived a progressive trend in history, a movement toward social orders that maximized freedom and self-realization for the masses. This fundamental thesis has consistently encountered antitheses or negations such as constraints on productive capacity, low levels of political consciousness, or strategies of class and racial domination. The latter in particular seek to arrest the historical process at stages of social organization that satisfy their members' desired levels of freedom and material well-being, even at the cost of the slavery or exploitation of others.[15]

A good grasp of James's account of the identity of "the Negro" or the worker requires this dialectical dimension as much as the project-forming aspects of his historicism. To explain the emergence of the "the Negro" identity, James takes us back to the origins of the capitalist world system. Capitalism represented a new and important phase in the historical development of human societies. Although it dramatically increased material production, capitalism still required groups of human beings whose labor it could appropriate and dispose of at will. Consequently, it created a social order in which some, rather than all, would be free. But in spite of this harsh reality, the dominant classes have attempted to legitimate the exploitation, and to present capitalism as the fulfillment of the historical process—the point beyond which a better social order cannot be found.

Among the many groups whose labor was appropriated in the early phases of capitalism, James reserves a special place for the African slaves who were shipped to the Caribbean and the Americas. As a result, James's Pan-Africanism emerges here in the heart of his Marxism. In this New World, African slavery made possible social orders that permitted greater freedom and material well-being, but still for a few. At this historical conjuncture, the traditional African declined and was replaced by "the Negro." The latter emerged when Africans were forced to occupy the necessary positions of coerced labor extraction within European capitalism, at the same time that their racial subjugation was being discursively legitimated.[16] This legitimization produced the discursive transformation of the African into the absolute antithesis of the European. In the European hierarchy of colonial peoples, "the Negro" occupied the zero point.

Whatever Africans were before, they could no longer be the same after their insertion into this particular historical conjuncture. Whatever black meant before, Africans were now black "in relation to the white man." It was the formation of projects of adaptation or emancipation in this new setting of capitalist slavery, European languages, and discourses that made "the Negro" possible. To the extent that these underlying projects were primarily defensive and adaptive in nature, James saw "the Negro" identity as both a sick and a strategic distortion of the African, the Afro-Caribbean, and other New-World Africans. Consequently, James reserved much of his deconstructive fire for those racist constructions and legitimating arguments that made such distorted adaptations possible.

In contrast to these adaptive projects, James's analysis of the Haitian revolution suggests that enslaved and colonized Africans formed revolutionary and insurrectionary projects as responses to the new historical conjuncture. These projects were important for two reasons. First, James saw them as the bases of African liberation from capitalist domination and of the drive for racial equality. He defined these Africana groups on the basis of the specific revolutionary and insurrectionary projects that Africans, Afro-Caribbeans, and Afro-Americans have undertaken, and not on that of their inherited cultural traditions. In other words, the capacity for historical action in the interest of racial liberation defines the modern African, continental or diasporic.

The second reason for the importance of these revolutionary projects is that James saw them as crucial sites of resistance to capitalist attempts to stop the historical process at levels of freedom and self-realization that were appropriate for them. Because capitalism is not a social order in which the masses will find concrete and meaningful freedom, the historical process must be freed from these capitalist constraints and allowed to complete at least a socialist experiment. For James, this socialist experiment had nothing in common with the totalitarianism that recently collapsed in Eastern Europe and what was the Soviet Union. The social order of these societies, James argued, constituted an even more monstrous fetter on the historical push for expanded mass freedom.[17] Only participatory socialism could provide the desired expansion.

James saw the revolutionary and insurrectionary projects of Africans as major contributors to this push for a participatory socialist order.

This, in brief, is James's historicism. It is a multidimensional philosophy, whose poeticist, Pan-Africanist, and Marxist aspects point to the important dualities in Afro-Caribbean thought that needed to be addressed. It is also a philosophy that saw itself as a modern construct and was oriented toward completing an historical project of freedom. It has little room for the premodern past, which it saw as the stage in which nature was the important fetter on the historical process. With the advances of modern technology, these chains have been burst and this stage surpassed. Hence in an era when only human fetters are left to be conquered, these societies were considered "backward." To the extent that James so considered them, his historicism remained enmeshed in European discourses on modernity. And to the extent that this categorization was applied to premodern Africa, it helps to explain the invisibility of traditional African philosophy in James's historicism.

JAMES AND TRADITIONAL AFRICAN PHILOSOPHY

James referred on many occasions to traditional African philosophy and culture, but never developed these references in detail. Of the Afro-Caribbean slave, James observed: "Being a developed person, and with his past, it was natural for him to develop a philosophy and a religion. His philosophy and religion proved to be a combination of what he brought with him and what his new masters sought to impose on him."[18] What philosophy did Africans bring with them to the Caribbean? James never attempted to explain. He usually referred to it when leading up to a discussion of modern African or Afro-Caribbean thought. Consequently, it was an abstract presence that helped James to construct the modern African historically. The attempts of anthropologists such as Melville Herskovits and ethnophilosophers such as Alexis Kagame to reconstuct this philosophy in writing did not engage James. He developed an interest in this literature only late in life.

James's abstract recognition of traditional African philosophy extended to other traditional or premodern philosophies. The traditional philosophies of China, India, and Japan did not engage him. It was not the Greece of the nature gods and the mysteries that interested James but the Greece of the political philosophers who had domesticated the gods and "banished them to the realm of the soul as internalized demons."[19] For James, traditional African philosophy, rooted in the mysteries of the nature gods, clearly fell into the former category, and its truth claims were part of a larger group of premodern claims that James did not feel any necessity to affirm or reject. This attitude toward premodern African philosophy could only have been possible because

James had inherited and, implicitly or explicitly, accepted some European evaluations of premodern thought. These evaluative traces operated in a manner
that made the abstract representation of traditional African philosophy appear
adequate.

Even if James had freed himself from these discursive enmeshments, substantive differences would still have remained between his historicism and traditional African philosophy. It is important that those of us who continue to
work in this historicist tradition not only deconstruct (although not eliminate)
the modern/premodern opposition but also undertake our own independent
assessment of these substantive differences. Only from the results of such a dialogue will we be able to assess the philosophy that Africans brought with them
to the Caribbean. For example, this dialogue should include the differences in
positions on the ontological significance of history, the nature of the self, idealism, and the problem of knowledge. Needless to say, this list could be extended.

As we have seen, traditional African philosophy emerged as an integral part
of the discursive responses of Africans to questions about creation and the significance of human life. These questions were answered from a cosmogonic
perspective that recognized spiritual and material planes of being, as well as
the creative activities of the gods. Most African ontologies, says Wole Soyinka,
recognize four basic stages or areas of existence: the world of the ancestors, the
living, the unborn, and the creative womb or matrix of original forms and energies.[20] Soyinka sees the trials of self-emergence from this matrix as the founding experience of African philosophy and spirituality. The matrices of this
creative maelstrom govern the rites of passage between the various stages or
areas of life and thus between the birth, death, and rebirth of all forms of material life. The African cosmogonic view with its transitions between planes is formulated in mythic discourses whose signifiers represent occurrences on several
planes simultaneously. This analogical style differs significantly from the style
of Caribbean historicism.

Looking at the conceptions of time and history in these African systems of
thought, we encounter our first important difference with Jamesian historicism that needs to be reevaluated. In the cosmogonic perspective of these systems, the ontological or constitutive role of history is severely restricted. Time
is shaped and filled not by human projects but by the creative projects of the
gods. The latter, in fact, eclipse the former. History exists inside cosmology.
Divine creation displaces human self-creation in history. Consequently, traditional African philosophy rooted the analysis of the being of the African in a
cosmic and not a historical context. Self was defined in terms of the place of
humans in creation, the cycle of birth, death, and rebirth, and the relations
that had to be maintained with the gods, the ancestors, the living, and the
unborn. In short, the primary responsibility for selfhood was attributed to the

creative matrix of original energies and not to the self-formative processes of history.

The importance of this attribution can be seen in its impact on the structure of time in traditional Africa. As John Mbiti has suggested, time in traditional Africa was primarily a two-dimensional phenomenon. It had a long and significant past, a present, and virtually no future. Time, Mbiti suggest, "moves 'backward' rather than forward; and people set their minds not on future things, but chiefly on what has taken place."[21] The attractions of the past are the mythic traces of both divine and human life emerging from the creative matrix. These cosmic projects eclipse the social projects of humans, which constitute the contents of the all-important category of the future in the Jamesian structure of time.

What are we to make of these differences in the ontological significance attributed to history? Afro-Caribbean philosophers have accounted for this change in their thinking from the cosmogonic to the historicist primarily by reading it in terms of the modern/premodern oppositions of European discourses. This particularly African cosmogonic view has not been assessed as an independent formation. It has been put in a general category and dismissed as part of the premodern past. But since European categories of modern and premodern have been invested with so many anti-African connotations, these categories need to be reassessed and the questions asked again.

Also, we need to question the limits that historicist discourses have set upon the significance of cosmogonic forces. For example, what does historicism have to say about birth and death? Is a spiritual supplement needed to account for them, as suggested by Cornel West?[22] What are the important differences between the organization of the historicist and the cosmogonic consciousness? How important is the difference in the way they resolve the ego-constitutive binary, self-determined/spiritually determined? Do these differences support or guarantee the progressive claims of historicism? Can we be sure that historicist discourses are not parallel but different discourses that conceal the spiritual while revealing and magnifying the historical? Only when questions such as these have been answered will we be able to make an independent evaluation of the truth claims of the African cosmogonic view of history.

James's opposition to idealism may also account for his failure to engage traditional African philosophy. The primary mark of idealist traditions of thought is their recognition of the supersensible and superconscient reality that we can call spirit. Soyinka's creative matrix constitutes such a reality and occupies a foundational position in traditional African thought. Needless to say, this African vision and experience of spirit is unique, differing from Indian, Japanese, or European spirituality. The roots of African spirituality in "the deep black whirlpool of mythopoeic forces"[23] reveal a turbulent and dynamic picture of the spiritual plane. This picture shows little of the calm of Indian spirituality or the abstractness of Hegelian spirituality.

In spite of this uniqueness, it is the primacy given to spirit that links traditional African thought to global traditions of idealism. Mbiti describes this primacy: "The invisible world is symbolized or manifested by those visible and concrete phenomena and objects of nature. The invisible world presses hard upon the visible world. The physical and the spiritual are but two dimensions of one and the same universe."[24] This conception of reality leads to the view that the universe is not exclusively maintained by scientific and historical laws as James purports. In addition to these, there must also be a place for a spiritual force. Leonard Barret has suggested a hierarchical metaphor to represent this force: "Flowing from the supreme being, it descends to man and through man to all things lower in the scale of life. As long as this vital force which emanates from God is operative throughout the system and in the right proportion, the universe is considered to be in ritual equilibrium."[25]

Assuming that we do not categorically reject the truth claims of African idealism, the crucial question becomes, What could James's historical materialism make of this idealism? At best, it would have permitted James to do a demythologized reading that would have been comparable to his readings of Hegel and St. Paul. Spirit, rather than being the creative demiurge, becomes in these texts a symbol of unrealized human and social potential struggling for fulfillment. Similarly, African spirituality could have been brought down to earth and made immanent in history.

Can we be sure that such a reading is not reductionist? What of the nonreducible remainders that persist after demythologization? On what grounds is this banishment of spirit and the gods justified? These are questions that need to be examined; and to the extent that James overlooked them, we must move to correct the oversight. Without such a coming to terms with the history of our own historicism, Afro-Caribbean philosophy will continue to negate its identity and maintain a problematic dependence on European philosophy.

The concept of the self in traditional African philosophy is also difficult for James's historicism to assimilate. James defined the self not in terms of its immanent dynamics but through the historical challenges that its founding projects made possible. This historical approach to the self can be contrasted to Descartes's rationalist approach in which the self is constructed on the model of the *cogito, ergo sum*. In James, the corresponding formulation could be "I undertake or participate in a historical project, therefore I am." This socially constructed nature of the Jamesian self will find some significant echoes in traditional African thought. In this tradition, the thinking or speaking subject was not conceived on the solitary Cartesian model. On the contrary, as Mbiti suggests, it is more a case of "I am, because we are, and since we are, therefore I am."[26]

In spite of this convergence, it is the divergences that are striking. Going beyond the above social dimension, the traditional African conception of the self developed its immanent dimensions in terms of a spiritual discourse. This spiritual dimension that African discourses gave to the human self was qualitatively different from the world of everyday life and resisted assimilation by the world. It connected the individual to other forms of life, to the nature gods, and to the creative intelligence of spirit. Although very real, these ties remain hidden from the awareness of the normal everyday ego. In other words, the self is not constituted on the rationally and historically restricted model found in James's philosophy. On the contrary, this is a cosmic, expansive construction of the self with deep roots in material nature and extensive connections with spiritual nature.

What is a Jamesian to make of this conception of the human self? Must it be demythologized in the same way as African idealism? Can we understand Afro-Caribbean religions such as Rastafarianism and Vodou without this African conception of the self? Can we understand how we got from one to the other without a more sustained exchange between these two views? Here is another important difference between Caribbean historicism and traditional African philosophy that is in need of reexamination if we are to understand our journey from the cosmic to the historicist. If, as I am suggesting, this journey has been understood in terms of European discourses, then the time has come for us to do it in our own words.

Our fourth and final difference concerns the problem of knowledge. We have looked briefly at James's epistemology as well as some traditional African ones. The first was historicist and the second spiritual in orientation. Given this belief in the spiritual dimensions of the material world, the question arises as to how one acquired knowledge not only of the sensible but also the supersensible world. The latter issue is probably the source of the greatest divergence between James and traditional African philosophy. Like most idealist traditions, we've seen that African idealism derives its spiritual knowledge from religious practices that suspend, displace, or quiet the everyday ego. Once this ego has been displaced, it opens up the possibility for the gods to "possess" an individual and so make their presence real on the human plane. Such hierophanic experiences through possession are the sources of African knowledge of occurrences on the spiritual plane. It is not knowledge acquired through the intellect or the senses. Rather, a primary condition for this knowledge is the suspending of the intellect and the senses as deployed by the everyday ego.

In Africa, we've seen that the suspending or displacing of the ego is effected primarily through drumming and dancing, which facilitate the passing of carefully trained devotees into trance states or states of ego displacement. This use of dancing and drumming can be compared to the use of yoga and meditation in the Indian and Japanese idealist traditions. The aim of yoga, says Sri Aurobindo, "is to enter the divine consciousness by merging into it the separative ego."[27] The vision and role of spirituality in Indian idealism cannot be understood apart from the "merging" experiences that yogic practices have produced. Dancing and drumming play a similar role in the African production of spiritual knowledge.

Clearly there is no place in James's epistemology for this type of knowing. In James, both knowing and the knowing subject are radically historicized. Whether it is knowledge of mind or knowledge of the external world, it takes place within the ego consciousness of a knowing subject who exists in history. For James, there is no transcending of the ego and no transcending of history. They are nonnegotiable boundaries within which human life is lived.

If this is so, then what are we to make of this African epistemology that insists on transgressing these boundaries? How are we to understand its ego-displacing practices? How do they compare with the decentering of the modern subject in poststructuralism? If the gods, the self, and the language of traditional African philosophy must be demythologized, then consistency demands that this strategy be extended to its epistemology. Would this be a satisfactory way to evaluate and reject this epistemology? Again the issue is not the defense of traditional African philosophy, but rather the relevance of the inherited categories through which Afro-Caribbean philosophers have interpreted and rejected its truth claims.

In addition to these substantive philosophical differences, there are some important sociological factors that may have increased the difficulty of a critical assimilation of traditional African philosophy by James and other Caribbean philosophers. Most important is the oral or spoken nature of traditional African philosophy, as it existed in languages that have only recently developed writing capabilities. Writing "technologizes the word"[28] and so opens up discursive possibilities that are restricted in exclusively oral languages. These expanded possibilities permit the complex patterns of argumentation and levels of systematization associated with the "classical period" in the history of a philosophical tradition. African philosophy for the most part never experienced a classical phase in which its ideas were given a written elaboration. Consequently, Africans did not bring written formulations of their philosophy to the Caribbean. This oral confinement certainly made identity maintenance and thematic development in the Caribbean extremely difficult.

The absence of a writing capacity is no doubt related to the nature and comparative brevity of the imperial kingdoms and patrimonial states of the African medieval period. Medieval kingdoms such as Ghana, Mali, and Songhai were

based on tribute-paying modes of production that produced the economic surpluses of patrimonial states. But compared to Egypt, these formations were
short-lived. Consequently, the conditions for producing the "classical civilizations" associated with large patrimonial states were not in place long enough.
The writing of medieval Africa was done largely in the Arabic languages that
came with the Islamic conquest of North Africa. This textual absence, together
with the distorted, animistic accounts of African and Afro-Caribbean thought
that were present in colonial institutions, must be a part of any assessment of
James's abstract relationship to traditional African philosophy.

TRADITIONAL AFRICAN PHILOSOPHY AND THE CRITIQUE OF EGOISM

How do we get beyond these philosophical differences and sociological factors
that have prevented any real dialogue between traditional African philosophy
and Caribbean historicism? How do we transform James's abstract relation
with an almost invisible tradition into a concrete dialogue with a living and
institutionally recognizable tradition? First, we need to look at traditional
African philosophy with eyes that have been freed from European constructions of the premodern/modern dichotomy. Second, we need to look anew at
the problems that traditional African philosophy has attempted to address, and
then define and evaluate it in terms of its contributions to the resolving of
these problems. First among the problems it has attempted to address is the
problem of egoism in the emergence of the self from the matrix of original
forms and energies.

Unlike positivism, which is rooted in the legitimating of scientific projects,
traditional African philosophy is rooted in the legitimating of African religious
projects. The primary project of traditional African religion is the actual transcending of the everyday ego in a search for balance and harmony with the
creative womb or original matrix of forms and energies. Consequently, at the
core of traditional African philosophy we find an existential critique of egoism
that resolves the contradictions of the latter in the idealism of religious
spirituality.

This critique and transcending of egoism establishes quite certainly the
place of traditional African philosophy at the table of cross-cultural philosophical discourse. Clearly it sits very close to the many shamanic and mystical traditions of thought that have been critical of egoism. Distinct in its own right,
traditional African philosophy also shares an ego-critical stance with Asian philosophy but not its degree of ego rejection. Its ego-critical stance can also be
compared to those of Freudian and Jungian psychology, although traditional
African philosophy differs from them on the nature of the forms and forces
that condition and correct the self-formative activities of the ego.

Egoism is the attempt of the ego to ground itself, and so absolutize the reality it has constructed. Ego existence is normally a centered, closed existence with fixed boundaries that define what is and what is not a part of the ego. As Aurobindo suggested, these centering and enclosing tendencies of the ego are "separative," isolating and insulating it from the creative matrix which is its spiritual ground. Ego-critical systems of thought, including traditional African philosophy, question the ability of the ego to genuinely create itself without the constant compensatory and corrective actions of its spiritual ground. Its limited knowledge of its own nature, its hubris, its Yuruguan revolts, its inability to deal constructively with its own existential and psychological anxieties are just some of the problems that critics of the ego have suggested it is unable to solve. This inability of the ego to resolve basic problems associated with its own coming to be is the core of the existential critique of egoism.

In traditional African philosophy, we have seen that this existential critique is grounded in the ego's ignorance of its nature and destiny. As it posits itself, it often makes errors in its selecting and excluding of possibilities for itself. Such errors are usually compounded by its tendencies to center and enclose itself. These errors and their compounding often elicit counteractions from the spiritual ground, which traditional African religion has constructed in terms of gods, goddesses, spirits, and ancestors. The tensions between the ego and its ground often lead to misfortune, illness, or personal failure. This is the dilemma of the ego as it is reflected in traditional African philosophy.

The idealist solution to this dilemma was for the ego to temporarily let go of its self-positing and centering activities and surrender to the correctives and directives of the deities and ancestors. They (e.g., Legba) possess the power to diffuse the polarities that the ego tends to absolutize and so trap itself unnecessarily. Such periodic baptisms in the waters of the spirit are the necessary supplements that exposed the limits of egoism. In chapter 7, we will see the continuing importance of this solution as we examine its contributions to the problem of rationality in modern societies.

Seated among the ego-critical philosophies of the world, traditional African philosophy must be allowed to engage in its own dialogue with other ego-critical philosophies and also with ego-centered philosophies such as empiricism or positivism. As we will see in chapter 10, particularly important for contemporary Afro-Caribbean philosophy is the exchange between this critique of egoism and poeticist and historicist notions of the self. The criticisms of James's historicist approach to the self that would emerge from such an exchange must be taken seriously. On the whole the poeticists have been much more receptive to such exchanges as we will see in the case of Harris. Only in this way will traditional African philosophy regain visibility in the region and find its rightful place at the table of Caribbean intellectual discourse.

JAMES AND MODERN AFRICAN PHILOSOPHY

James's relationship with modern African philosophy stands in sharp contrast to his relationship with traditional African philosophy. The abstract relation that is so evident in the latter becomes concrete and more complex in the former. This reversal points to the bifurcated nature of James's relationship with African thought, which cannot be accounted for in a straight Eurocentric analysis. My aim is not to provide a comprehensive analysis of the modern half of this relationship but the more limited one of showing how James's historicism affected his crucial points of convergence and divergence with modern African thought.

For the purposes of this analysis, modern African philosophers can be put in three broad categories: the political philosophers, the ethnophilosophers, and the pure philosophers. In the first group are figures such as Amilcar Cabral, Kwame Nkrumah, and Julius Nyerere, whose works directly reflect the problems of national liberation and development and for whom ideology and philosophy are inseparable. In the second group are ethnographically oriented philosophers such as Placide Tempels, E. B. Idowu, and Alexis Kagame, who have worked diligently at putting into writing the oral philosophies of traditional Africa. Finally, in the third group are philosophers such as Frantz Cathray, Paulin Hountondji, and Kwasi Wiredu, whose primary concern is for a philosophy governed exclusively by analytic or speculative reason and which conforms to the written canons of modern European philosophy.

James's relationship to these trends in modern African philosophy was complex. He was closest to the political philosophers, a historical step removed from the ethnophilosophers, and furthest removed from the pure philosophers. I shall argue that an important key to these differing relationships was James's historicism.

James approached Afro-Caribbean people in terms of the specific historical challenges that their projects of selfhood permitted them to undertake. He extended this approach to all Africans. His portraits of Afro-Americans were constructed from their slave revolts, their contributions to American agriculture, the War for Independence, the Civil War, the struggle for democracy, and the struggle for socialism.[29] James approached continental Africans in exactly the same manner. He completely historicized their existence, separated them from their cosmogonically grounded identities, and oriented them toward the challenges of postcolonial reconstruction. This historicization was equally radical even though continental Africans were not subjected to the proletarianizing effects of capitalist slavery. James's portrait of continental Africans included the disruptive impact of the slave trade, formal colonization, the revolts against this external rule, and the contributions of Africans to political philosophy and to world literature.[30] In this portrait, although very African, traditional Africa is just about invisible, constituting only the background for these historical developments. In the ongoing debates about African identity,[31] James's historical approach deserves a better hearing.

This historical approach to Africa was the crucial principle that James brought to his appreciation of modern African philosophy. To the extent that these philosophers threw Africans onto the historical stage with revolutionary projects, James was generally very interested, even though he might not have been in agreement with specific truth claims. These were the aspects of Nkrumah, Cabral, Senghor, and other political philosophers that attracted James. But in spite of this area of convergence, traditional African thought had a more concrete representation in the works of these modern African philosophers than with James. This more complex involvement with traditional African thought was the basis for some important divergences between James and these philosophers.

Among the political philosophers, the above patterns of convergence and divergence can be very clearly seen in the case of James's relationship with Nkrumah. Nkrumah's philosophical consciencism was an attempt to find a modern ideology that could unite traditional, Islamic, and Christian Africa around projects of national development. After rejecting European idealism, materialsim, and empiricism, Nkrumah established historical materialism as his basic premise. This was the important point of convergence with James because it stressed both the ontological and dialectical aspects of historicism.[32]

Nkrumah, however, could not escape the reality of having to link his historical materialism to traditional African thought. This led him to make the highly problematic move of linking African spiritualism with radical egalitarianism and socialism. "The traditional face of Africa," say Nkrumah, "includes an attitude toward man which can only be described, in its social manifestation, as being socialist. This arises from the fact that man is regarded in Africa as primarily a spiritual being, a being endowed originally with certain inward dignity, integrity and value."[33] Nkrumah could not simply demythologize traditional African thought, he had to deal with it as a living reality. The solutions he found were unacceptable to James and thus became a significant point of difference.

Another example of this ambivalence in the relationship with Nkrumah can be seen in the role of traditional factors in the organization of the modern Ghanaian state. To combat postindependence disunity and underdevelopment, Nkrumah attempted to create a mass party in a one-party democratic state. These political structures were to be the instruments of transformation. James admired and affirmed Nkrumah's undertaking of this historical challenge, but as a theorist and fervent advocate of participatory democracy, James disagreed with Nkrumah's authoritarian style and his vanguard strategies. "He never understood," says James, "that democracy was a matter in which the official leaders and an opposition were on trial before the mass of the population."[34] The widespread existence of one-party states in Africa, however, suggests that its existence in Ghana was not due solely to Nkrumah's particular outlook. Rather, it points to the persistence of a traditional political culture that included a "grammar" of chiefly or kingly political behavior. Here again Nkrumah succumbed to the pressures of traditionally defined expectations as living realities. Similar sets of problems complicated James's relationships with the other political philosophers.

In the case of the ethnophilosophers, there are no direct links that are comparable to the ties with the political philosophers, although the ideas of the ethnophilosophers greatly influenced members of the negritude movement, which James heartily embraced. For James, historicism was among the factors that distinguished the philosophy of negritude from ethnophilosophy. The negritude philosophers historicized the findings of the ethnophilosophers and redeployed them in the discursive battles against colonialism, racism, and the degradation of the African identity. This was the step that indirectly linked James to the ethnophilosophers and won direct praise for negritude philosophers such as Senghor.

This convergence around historicist themes took place in spite of cultural constructs in Senghor's philosophy that were at odds with James's historicism. Most important was Senghor's idealist reconstruction of the being of Africans, both continental and diasporic. This reconstruction was based on what Senghor saw as the common cultural and spiritual heritage of Africans, which gave them their unique mode of being. This heritage included a distinctive spirituality and the predominance of emotional over rational modes of knowing.[35] These truth claims are difficult to square with James's historicism. Also, they defined Africans in relatively fixed cultural terms that are inconsistent with James's general outlook. But in spite of these differences, Senghor's historicism was strong enough to engage James and win his affirmation.

Finally, James had little or no contact with the pure philosophers for at least two reasons. First, they are the younger philosophers who have followed Nkrumah, Senghor, and others of that generation. Second, their academicism has prevented them from sanctioning the role of ideology in the works of the political philosophers, and makes them highly critical of the ethnophilosophical and negritude schools. In particular, the pure philosophers reject the idealism and spiritualism of these two schools. These critical stances are very clear in the works of Marcien Towa and Paulin Hountondji. The latter in particular has been uncompromising in his rejection of traditional African thought as philosophy. Hountondji defines African philosophy in a very restrictive way, confining it to "the set of texts written by Africans and described as philosophical by their authors themselves."[36] This credo of textual foundationalism clearly defines the oral philosophies out of existence.

In sum, I have attempted to demonstrate some of the complexities and ambiguities that James's philosophy created for his relationship to African philosophy and their implications for Afro-Caribbean philosophy. With regard to the latter, four crucial points emerged. First, there is the need to rethink the costs of its continuing dependence on European philosophy given the latter's discourses on modernity. Second, there is the need for Afro-Caribbean philosophy to undertake an independent dialogue with traditional African philosophy and develop its own arguments for accepting or rejecting its truth claims. Third, in this dialogue, we must also consider the implications of the ego-critical approach of traditional African philosophy for our modern ego-centered practices. Fourth and finally, Afro-Caribbean philosophy must develop its own ethnophilosophy so it can engage critically the thought of Vodouisants, Rastafarians, and Afro-Christians. These traditions of thought are operative in large sections of Caribbean society and continue to shape our creative imaginations, philosophical or otherwise.

Frantz Fanon, African,
and Afro-Caribbean Philosophy

Like James, Fanon is often treated as a writer who can be understood outside of the Caribbean context in which he spent his formative years. These two are usually situated and evaluated in terms of the European influences on their thinking. Seldom have they been examined in terms of the Caribbean tradition of thought that also influenced them and the significance of their work for this tradition.

My aim in this chapter will be to bring the Caribbean intellectual tradition more into focus than I did in the case of James. I will examine its peculiar colonial dynamics, what it passed on to Fanon, and the degree to which he was able to change it. It short, our focus will be the impact of the philosophical aspects of the Caribbean tradition of thought on Fanon and the impact of his philosophy on that tradition.

The Caribbean tradition of thought can be viewed as a series of extended dialogues that arose out of European projects of building colonial societies around plantation economies that were based on African slave labor. For example, both the imperial and enslaving aspects of these projects had to be discursively justified. Also, the identity of the colonial state had to be established and its illegitimate claims to power given the appearance of legitimacy. Such issues and indigenous resistance to them constituted some of the foundational concerns of Caribbean intellectual life. The outcomes of these exchanges were not determined by the better argument or the moral rightness of a cause. Rather, they were determined by political criteria as they directly affected the organization of state power and the strength of economic and political elites.

Given the political framework in which the above issues had to be resolved, it is not surprising that many important truths could not be acknowledged in this tradition of thought. The imperatives of identity and economic and political reproduction were such that many falsities had to be dogmatically asserted as true and many truths dogmatically asserted as false. On the basis of these dogmatic assertions, discourse production was largely an exercise in mythmaking that inflated European identities while deflating African identities. In short, this was a dogma-ridden tradition, in which questions of identity and culture could not be truthfully addressed.

These patterns of necessary misrepresentation are important for understanding the nature and function of philosophy in this tradition. Given the high demand for legitimating and delegitimating arguments, philosophy in this colonial context was largely the handmaiden of ideological production. Hence the social and political nature of philosophy in this region. Answers to cosmogonic, ontological, or epistemological questions remained largely unthematized or were imported from abroad. Not only was philosophy confined in this way, it was further restricted by the overvaluations and undervaluations that the tradition found it necessary to impose on the cultures of Europe and Africa. A central item in the tradition's undervaluation of African culture was the dogmatic assertion that it had no philosophy. That African philosophy did exist could not have been acknowledged by the tradition or truthfully discussed. This disenfranchising of African philosophy established philosophy in the tradition as exclusively European. In short, recognized philosophy in the early phases of the Caribbean tradition of thought was exclusively European in identity and sociopolitical in orientation.

Fanon's assault on this tradition was profound, relentless, and explosive. He grew up at a time when the misrepresenting and alienating powers of this tradition were still very strong, in spite of increasing criticism by Afro-Caribbean writers such as Blyden, Garvey, Padmore, and Cesaire. Consequently, he was profoundly marked by the ambivalences and misrepresentations of this heri-tage. On awakening to his deep enmeshment, Fanon's response was that of the anguished individual who must get out of a nightmare. Hence his vision of the Afro-Caribbean as being "rooted at the core of a universe from which he must be extricated."[1] The goal of this extrication is not just liberation from the practices and institutions of this tradition but also "the liberation of the man of color from himself,"[2] that is, from the misrepresentations of the tradition that had been internalized.

This emancipatory project struck at the heart of the tradition. It violated the strict prohibitions that had been put on the truthful examination of questions of identity. Breaking this taboo was the major impact that Fanon's work has had on the Caribbean tradition of thought. This rupture had two important consequences. Although it did not bring an immediate end to colonial misrepresentations, identity problems would never again be resolved in such dogmatic and racist terms. Second, this opening of the debate on identity necessarily challenged some of the dogmas and prohibitions that sustained the distorted evaluations of African and European cultures. The impact of these challenges on the colonial construction of philosophy was not, however, as explosive as its impact on the racist discourses that legitimated the necessary misrepresentation of identity.

From the standpoint of philosophy in the region, Fanon's work was a bold and original departure. It placed questions of ontology squarely on the table and answered them in existential and historicist terms. These were then carefully linked to analyses of the Afro-Caribbean personality and to the Marxist theories of revolutionary transformation. This synthesis of philosophy, psychology, and revolutionary political theory was both stunning and original, and it is still very potent today. However, it was unable to revolutionize basic conceptions of philosophy in the Caribbean tradition and overturn the valuations placed on European and African philosophy. Fanon's synthesis did not trigger an awareness of a local philosophical tradition whose indigenous identity needed thematizing, even though his work changed dramatically the categories, values, and concerns of the tradition. It remained a case of Caribbean philosophy operating without an adequate awareness of its identity and history. Because of this lack, the equating of philosophy with social philosophy was never really overthrown, nor were the evaluations placed on European and African philosophies. Philosophy continued to function primarily as the handmaiden of political struggle, and its master continued to be European in identity.

The emergence of a vibrant and self-conscious Caribbean philosophy will require the breaking of these colonial fetters. Without such an internal decolonization it will not be able to indigenize itself and affirm its unique identity. As postcolonial recovery proceeds, there is usually a progressive indigenizing of discourses. However, it does not occur uniformly across all discourses. Processes of discursive indigenization have occurred more rapidly in Caribbean drama, folklore, religion, music, political economy, and literature than they have in philosophy. The identities of these cultural practices are distinctly more creole. In these creole formulations, African as well as European elements are visible. By contrast Afro-Caribbean philosophy is unique in the degree to which it has resisted a similar creolizing of its identity. Consequently, the questions raised by the ambivalences in Fanon's relations with African philosophy are quite different from those raised by James's ambivalences. If the latter pointed to problems of recognition and reevaluation, then the former added the problems of surplus repression and cultural accumulation in patterns of creolization.

As we will see, this greater resistance to creolization points to a number of serious problems confronting Caribbean philosophy that even Fanon's explosive writings were unable to remove. These problems suggest that disenfranchisement was greater in the case of African philosophy than in the cases of music or literature. Even more than James, Fanon followed closely the early attempts to rehabilitate traditional African philosophy, but he found them wanting. I will try to show that the constraints, evaluations, and prohibitions that the tradition placed on philosophy were such that they gave Fanon very little but were strong enough to resist his attempt to overthrow them.

THE CARIBBEAN TRADITION OF THOUGHT

As noted earlier, the colonial state needed to establish its legitimacy and so made very specific demands on the discursive outputs of our cultural system. These political demands subjected cultural production to the peripheral dynamics outlined in the introduction. As a result, the institutional framework in which the Caribbean intellectual tradition developed was a very statist one, with opposing patterns of cultural accumulation for its European and African components.

To facilitate these different patterns of cultural accumulation, colonial articulation gave normative priority and state power to European culture, but left African cultural production without similar political support. This unequal allocation of normative and institutional support created the social conditions for the disintegration of authority in the African system and the accumulating of authority in the European system. Accumulation in the latter was therefore at the expense of the former. Such a framework for the rapid accumulation of authority (culture capital)[3] was a pressing need if the discourses produced by the European writers of the tradition were to address effectively the legitimacy deficits of the colonial state, and the slave order it had to maintain.

Whether Spanish, British, or French, such statist cultural systems were established in the Caribbean colonies by the middle of the seventeenth century. They were established by the later generations and new arrivals that followed the first set of colonizers. The basic dialogical structure of the Caribbean tradition of thought was evident as early as the sixteenth century in the Spanish colonies. This structure emerged from the debates over Spanish rights to rule over the indigenous population of Caribs, Arawaks, and Tainos.[4] As it developed more fully in the seventeenth century, the dialogical framework of our Caribbean tradition was determined by three additional issues: (1) the rise of a sugar planter ideology, which included strong positions on property rights, African slavery, European racial supremacy, and white creole nationalism; (2) an imperial ideology of the political elites that stressed imperial authority in local governance, loyalty to the crown, and white supremacy; and (3) the rise of emancipatory counterclaims by enslaved Africans.[5] Because of the oral nature of native Caribbean and African societies, their members were unable to leave behind written accounts of their positions and responses. Good indications of these can be gained, however, from their resistance and from the texts of colonial writers. Thus the early phases of the tradition are quite unequal in the records they have left behind, although not in substance.

Internal divisions are clear among the writers and leaders of groups in Caribbean societies. For example, among Europeans there were differences between those who were Creole nationalists and those who were loyalists, those who were proslavery and those who were antislavery. Political elites were divided on how best to govern colonial territories and on the issue of slavery. Enslaved Africans were divided over the best strategies for ending their oppressive condition. In the Spanish colonies, Victoria, Oviedo, Herrera, Las Casas, José Antonio Saco, and Bachiller y Morales laid the written foundations of the tradition, taking up the issues of Spanish rights, native Caribbean resistance, and African slavery. In the English-speaking Caribbean the writers of the founding texts were Edward Littleton, Dalby Thomas, Richard Ligon, William Young, Edward Long, Bryan Edwards, James Ramsay, and William Wilberforce. And in the case of the French colonies it was Rochefort, Du Tertre, Pere Labat, Moreau de Saint Mercy, Hilliard D'Auberteuil, and the celebrated Victor Schoelcher.[6]

In the works of these writers, the culture and identity of Africans were examined and positions taken on their enslavement. The nature of European imperialism was examined and for the most part "justified." The merits of white creole nationalism versus monarchical government, and economic monopoly versus liberalism were all hotly debated in these texts. Most of these early writers were historians or lawyers, many of whom held social positions. Later, we get the creative writers whose novels will also take up such themes as creolization, slavery, and the tragic fate of the native Caribbeans. The positions defended in these texts constituted the European half of the dialogical framework of the Caribbean intellectual tradition.

The other half of this framework was of course filled with the positions defended by native Caribbeans and Africans. The history of these positions can be divided into two phases: the oral and the written or literate. In the oral phase, the responses of "Indians" and Africans were most visible in the collective actions they took on behalf of these positions. As we have seen, C. L. R. James often reminded us that in their collective actions, dominated groups often work out solutions to real-life problems that equal in creativity the solutions of individual genii. Consequently, collective actions such as strikes, insurrections, and revolutions can be viewed as the media in which an oral population formulates its answer to a social problem.[7] Such actions become the books in which they write and therefore should be read as carefully as the written texts of Labat, Long, or Saco.

On this textual reading of collective action, the slave and former slave uprisings that were led by King Court, Cuffy, Cudjoe, Toussaint L'Overture, Fedon, and others, as well as the actions of the slaves that resisted these undertakings, constituted the early African-Afro-Caribbean responses. By the mid-nineteenth century, the individualist and written phase of this response was established without the abandoning of the collective and insurrectionary options. I emphasize the written text in the transition from oral to literate to facilitate Fanon. The founding texts of this literate phase were authored by Robert Love, Edward Blyden, Marcus Garvey, J. J. Thomas, and H. Sylvester-Williams. By the second and third decades of the twentieth century, this literate Afro-Caribbean tradition began moving in two distinct directions: the historicist, and the poeticist. Among the former were Padmore and James, while Cesaire and Firmin fell into the latter category. A little later, Fanon and Arthur Lewis would join the historicist wing, while the ranks of poeticists would see the addition of Glissant, Harris, and Walcott. From James, Lewis, and Fanon, leadership of the historicist wing would pass to Clive Thomas, George Beckford, Norman Girvan, and other members of the New World group. However, it is important to note that the differences between these two approaches were ones of emphasis and priorities regarding historical action and the creative powers of the human imagination. The positions defended by these Afro-Caribbean writers cannot be separated from those taken by their Euro-Caribbean counterparts. Thus J. J. Thomas's book, *Froudacity* (1889), was a direct response to Froude's *The English in the West Indies*.

This in brief is the dialogical structure of the Caribbean intellectual tradition. It arose within a very definite political framework that helped to shape the unequal relations between the European and African participants in its discursive exchanges. These political constraints were such that the writing of books and the making of arguments found themselves subject to patterns of cultural accumulation and disaccumulation that had more to do with sociopolitical stability than truth. As the political wheels of the tradition turned, African culture increasingly lost value and the identity of the Afro-Caribbean moved slowly from being Akan or Yoruba to the pathology of Caliban. At the same time, European culture increased in value, and the European identity moved from the adventurous Robinson Crusoe or Faust the developer to imperial Prospero.

PHILOSOPHY AND THE CARIBBEAN INTELLECTUAL TRADITION

In the highly racialized and politicized dialogues of this tradition there was very little room for philosophy. The exchanges were not only between Caliban and Prospero, but also between Caliban and Caliban or Prospero and Prospero. What these exchanges needed were legitimating or delegitimating arguments of an ideological nature. Indeed, among the Euro-Caribbean writers, it is accurate to say that ideological production was the primary output of the earlier phases of this tradition. Ideological machines had the biggest contracts with the political economy of Caribbean societies for producing the images and arguments that would sustain Prospero's dominance. As the dominant discourse, its practitioners were able to mobilize selected aspects of other discourses such as philosophy and history. To these appropriations they added large doses of racist dogma to produce the desired ideological outputs.

In a context of such strong ideological hegemony, there was neither the autonomy nor the institutional support for a flourishing philosophy. Consequently, its role in the division of cultural labor was very small. This role was largely auxiliary, supplying the ideological machines with authoritative figures, supporting arguments, and philosophical legitimacy—in particular, providing these services for the production of Eurocentric, plantocratic, white supremacist, proslavery, antislavery, and related kinds of arguments. Hence our earlier characterization of philosophy as the handmaiden of legitimacy-enhancing ideological production.

Commandeered into ideological service, philosophy was of political necessity cut off from religion. Particularly in the early centuries, ideological production was separated from religious production. The notion that all men and women were equal before God was too threatening to the social and political relations that had to be maintained between Prospero and Caliban. Hence the early attempts to limit Christianity and notions of basic political rights to Europeans. Thus to the extent that ideology and religion had to be separated, philosophy as the handmaiden of ideology also had to keep its distance from religion. Ideological service for philosophy also meant that Euro-Caribbeans were unable to develop a distinct philosophy of their own. The cultivating of original analogies and concepts that reflected the spacial and temporal dimensions of the region, its geography, its flora and fauna, and its mythopoetics of self-formation was not encouraged. No such original philosophical foundations were laid, and those used in these production processes were largely European imports. Separated from religion and unable to thematize its own organic metaphysical responses to the Caribbean environment, Euro-Caribbean philosophy was reduced to making available selections of European political philosophy that were useful for local ideological production.

The philosophical selections that informed and augmented the works of the Euro-Caribbean sector of the tradition were concentrated in areas such as conservative monarchism, liberalism, constitutionalism, rationalism, and eugenics. Thus the figures of Burke, Locke, Montesquieu, Rousseau, Diderot, Hume, Hobbes, and Adam Smith loom very large in the tradition. So Bryan Edwards's arguments for more responsible government for Europeans in the colonies are inconceivable without Locke's idea of the consensual bases of government. Similarly, Moreau de Saint Mercy's critical appraisal of Haitian society draws explicitly on the works Diderot and Rousseau. In the case of Saco, British liberalism was used to criticize Spanish mercantilism and to make the case for plutocratic rule in Cuba. In these and many other cases, the universalist and egalitarian tendencies within these imported philosophies had to be compromised if they were to work in societies with enslaved populations. How these tendencies were contained and adjusted to the needs of the local slave order constitutes both the poverty and the distinctness of these ideological productions.

In the case of Edwards, the tensions between his liberal and proslavery positions were resolved by drawing on two sets of stereotypes: the completely uncivilized nature of life in Africa and the inherent lack of capabilities for modern life among African people. On the latter point, he appeals to the authority of Hume.[8] The strategy of resorting to similar stereotypes of Caliban can be seen in Arango, Saco, and many others. Writers such as Schoelcher, Ramsay, and Bachiller y Morales were the exceptions in that they took the universalist implications of these imported philosophies to their logical conclusions.

This containing of universalist tendencies in order to preserve Calibanized stereotypes of Africans greatly affected Euro-Caribbean views of Africans and their ability to philosophize. As Sylvia Wynter has shown, the rise of the European bourgeoisie was accompanied by the metaphorical appropriation of reason for political purposes. The metaphorics of reason replaced those of blood as criteria for distributing political rights and privileges. The possession or nonpossession of reason became a basis for the conferral or denial of political rights.[9] Thus, in his fight against Carib slavery, Las Casas was at pains to point out, against the opinions of his opponents, that Caribs had the capacity to reason and hence the right to self-rule. Within this global deploying of the metaphorics of reason, Africans fared even worse than native Caribbeans. They occupied the zero point on the scale of human rational capability. Africans were seen as being without the capacity for rational thought and unable to develop it even when educated. Given this exclusion from the rational community, it followed that Africans had no philosophy and could not be philosophers. Euro-Caribbean texts of the tradition repeatedly recognized the dancing, dramatic, oratorical, religious, and musical capabilities of Africans but never their philosophical capabilities. African philosophy was completely disenfranchised within the tradition. To be precise, it never existed. Thus in terms of the misrepresentation and the general loss of value that African culture suffered within the accumulative dynamics of the tradition, the case of philosophy was particularly severe.

In the Afro-Caribbean layers of this tradition, philosophy also occupies a minor role in the division of cultural labor. Among the insurrectionists and writers who made this half of the tradition, the pressing need was for delegitimating arguments that would counter European claims to political leadership and racial superiority. Also, there was a need for arguments that would legitimate self-rule and de-Calibanize the Afro-Caribbean identity, just as domination had become the crucial problem that Euro-Caribbeans had to legitimate. In this ideologically polarized setting, the discursive space for philosophy was small with tendencies toward contraction and rigidification.

This close relation between philosophy and ideology was a new development. It was a part of the creolization and adaptation of African philosophy to life in Caribbean plantation societies. By contrast, philosophy in traditional African societies existed in a very close relationship with religion. Philosophy functioned as the handmaiden of religion. It did not grow out of a consciousness of African existences that had been racialized and colonized by Europeans. On the contrary, it grew out of a consciousness of existence as being spiritually embedded and very definitely regulated by deities and ancestors. We've also seen that African philosophy developed largely around the defense of this religious worldview, much as positivism developed around the defense of natural science. Thus the idealism of African philosophy was evident in its defense of the spiritual claims of religion. Its existentialism was in its elaboration of notions of cosmic harmonies, fate, and predestiny to defend its acceptance of world- and life-affirming attitudes. Its ethics were to be found in its defense of religious claims that the gods and ancestors are to be obeyed. Its ontology was in its defense of religious cosmogony, its epistemology in its defense of spiritual knowledge derived from ego-transcending experiences. This was the philosophical heritage that Africans brought to the Caribbean.

However, under the impact of Christianization and the oppressive conditions of plantation slavery, this close relation between philosophy and religion began to dissolve. The demands of ideological production became as strong or stronger than those religions. Consequently, in the genesis of many slave uprisings, large sections of these African religious worldviews were philosophically appropriated and made available for ideological purposes. The figures of Macandal and the later leaders of the Haitian revolutions come to mind at this point. In short, even in the oral/insurrectionary phase of the Afro-Caribbean tradition, the nature and role of philosophy are best understood in relation to the dramatic increase in the demand for ideological production.

In the literate phase of the Afro-Caribbean part of the tradition, the transformation of philosophy under the pull of ideology is ever more marked. First, philosophy becomes less African and progressively more European. Second, it moves from being cosmocentric to being Christocentric and then historiocentric. It loses its connections with the gods of African religion and makes its living by appropriating a variety of European philosophies and making them available for local ideological production. In particular, Afro-Caribbean philosophy appropriated European liberalism, constitutionalism, racialism, and socialism. To these were added heavy doses of black or African nationalism to produce the ideological arguments for decolonization and the return of self-rule. Except for the socialist appropriations, the philosophies chosen were very similar to the selections by Euro-Caribbean writers. However, they were developed very differently by Afro-Caribbean writers such as J. J. Thomas or Garvey. In these writers, the Afro-Caribbean implications of universalist tendencies in the borrowed philosophies were explicitly developed as in the case of antislavery ideologues and married to passionate formulations of black nationalism.

This, in brief, was the role of philosophy in the Caribbean intellectual tradition up to the time that Fanon appeared on the scene. This was the conception and approach to philosophy that Fanon inherited from his teachers. Of particular importance for us was the complete disenfranchisement of African philosophy on the grounds that philosophy was not a practice engaged in by "primitive" peoples. One of the strongest taboos that European discourses placed on themselves was the taboo on the open acknowledgment of their tribal or primitive past. These discourses still like to see their origins in classical Greece (stealing Egypt away from Africa along the way) and not in the "primitive" Celts, Britons, Gauls, Saxons, and other tribal groups that populated Europe.

Euro-Caribbeans hid their intense horror of this past with a compelling necessity to present themselves as always having been "civilized." The primitive past of humanity could be viewed through other people, particularly Africans. Consequently, European discourses contain more about the tribal life of Africans than they do about their own. This powerful binary opposition between primitive and civilized is a polarity that the Caribbean tradition inherited from Europe. There is an unbridgeable gap between the two. Thus within the tradition, one cannot say "African and civilized" or "European and primitive." For the same reason, one cannot say "African and philosophical" or "European and nonphilosophical." In short, the tradition gave Fanon an ideologically restricted conception of philosophy whose European identity excluded its African counterpart because both occupied the extreme points on the powerful underlying binary primitive/civilized. The separating of Caribbean philosophy from this binary would clearly be a necessary cultural condition for the decolonization and reenfranchisement of Afro-Caribbean philosophy.

FANON, PHILOSOPHY, AND THE CARIBBEAN TRADITION

Given these racist features of our intellectual tradition, our next task must be an examination of the impact of Fanon's philosophy on the primitive/civilized binary and related practices that maintained the disenfranchisement of African philosophy. Like James, Fanon's philosophy was both multidimensional and intertextually embedded. It was multidimensional in the sense that it had well-developed ontological, ethical, existential, epistemological, and other dimensions. In other words, it was a qualitatively diverse philosophical field that very ably supported Fanon's primary discursive concerns. This auxiliary role of philosophy points to patterns of interdiscursive embeddedness that are quite similar to the ones found in James. Like the latter, Fanon's philosophy arises out of a consciousness of an imploded African existence that has been racialized and colonized by Europeans in the Caribbean. In articulating the nature of this existence, Fanon employed a variety of discourses. Thus from the start, Fanon's creative responses to the imploded Afro-Caribbean existence embodied both poeticist and historicist themes. His affirmations of the poetry of Cesaire and Keita Fodeba make clear the ways in which Fanon drew not only on Caribbean but Africana poeticism for his discourse of the self. As his explorations of the self developed, Fanon supplemented this poeticism with the insights of psychoanalysis and European existentialism. Thus in contrast to James, the immanent dimensions of the self were explicitly theorized and occupied a major place in Fanon's philosophy.

At the same time that Fanon was developing this profound poeticist/existentialist discourse on the Afro-Caribbean self, he was also working on the sociohistorical forces that were interacting with the immanent dynamics of the self. The analysis of these forces took Fanon's thought in both Pan-Africanist and Marxist directions. These aspects were as well developed as the discourse on the self and hence are strong enough to justify Fanon's inclusion among the historicists. Consequently, his work remains one of the most powerful syntheses of the streams of poeticism, Pan-Africanism, and Marxism that have been moving the modern Caribbean imagination. However, in spite of these strong poeticist and historicist tendencies in Fanon's philosophy, my focus here will be on his existentialism, and the consequences of its ambivalent relations to traditional African existentialism.

Among the historicists, Fanon is unique in the degree to which he explicitly developed a theory of the human self. The more usual pattern among the historicists has been the employing of Cartesian or Marxian notions of the human subject without much question or justification. This holds true for our con-temporary political economists,[10] in spite of the very different notion of the subject that Fanon gave us. Among the poeticists, the subject has been con-structed primarily in mythopoetic terms.

By the time Fanon arrived on the scene, the patterns of cultural accumula-tion and disaccumulation within the Caribbean tradition had begun to reverse themselves. Thanks to the cumulative efforts of Garvey, Padmore, Firmin, Janvier, Cesaire, and others, Afro-Caribbean cultures were accumulating authority while Afro-Caribbean identities were being de-Calibanized. But in spite of these changes, the binary oppositions, the stereotypes and dogmatic arguments of the tradition, were still strong enough to continue the reproduc-tion of white superiority. It was this continuing ability of the tradition to repro-duce black inferiority, in spite of criticism, that engaged Fanon. Thus the primary targets of his attacks were the racist strategies and discourses of the tradition and, only secondarily, its philosophical practices.

Fanon's point of departure was the impact of these racist discourses on the formation of the Afro-Caribbean psyche. The internalizing of their "imago of the Negro," produced what Fanon called "aberrations of affect." At their worst, these aberrations produced in black Caribbeans a desire to be white and European. These aberrations were both psychological and existential in nature, creating a "psycho-existential complex" that imploded and dramatically altered the personality of the Afro-Caribbean.

The existential dimensions of this complex are to be found in the "zone of nonbeing" that it opens up within the Afro-Caribbean psyche. Fanon also describes the psychological exposure to this zone as an existential deviation that now becomes a problematic constraint that conditions Afro-Caribbean ego genesis. By the zone of nonbeing, Fanon is referring to "an extraordinarily sterile and arid region, an utterly naked declivity where an authentic upheaval can be born."[11]

We encounter this zone of nonbeing in extreme states of ego collapse. Because such states of ego dissolution are terrifying, we normally do everything we can to avoid them. But, as Fanon points out, they can also be the occasions for genuine rebirths. Egos can collapse because they are internally divided, or because they are being recreated or integrated into a larger psychic formation. However, these are not the sources of ego collapse that interest Fanon. Rather, he is concerned with the negative reflections and distorted images of them-selves that Afro-Caribbeans saw in the eyes of the colonial other and in the dis-courses of the intellectual tradition. Fanon assumes that genuine recognition and affirmation from significant others are necessary for healthy ego genesis.

Knowing well the condition of ego collapse and the zone of nonbeing that it opens up, Fanon takes us there several times in *Black Skin, White Masks*. Let us look at two of these instances. The first is clearly an instance of ego collapse brought on by the negative reflections of blackness produced by the tradition.

"Dirty Nigger!" or simply, "Look, a Negro!"

I arrived in the world anxious to make sense of things, my spirit filled with desire to be at the origin of the world, and here I discovered myself an object amongst other objects.

Imprisoned in this overwhelming objectivity, I implored others. Their liberating regard, running over my body that suddenly becomes smooth, returns to me a lightness that I believed lost, and, absenting me from the world, returns me to the world. But there, just at the opposite slope, I stumble, and the other, by gestures, attitudes, looks, fixed me, in the sense that one fixes a chemical preparation with a dye. I was furious. I demanded an explanation. Nothing happened. I exploded. Now the tiny pieces are collected by another self.[12]

Here Fanon is moving painfully back and forth between projecting his ego out into the world and its explosion and collapse into the zone of nonbeing. The description reveals the fragility of the ego in this state and its dependence on the movements, attitudes, and glances of the other. It also reveals an ego that is unable to launch and stabilize itself. Each time it attempts to constitute itself, the effort ends in a collapse followed by another attempt. In Fanon's language, this is an ego that has no ontological resistance to the look and evaluation of the white.

Our second visit to the zone of nonbeing reveals more of the creative possibilities of this region and the expanses beyond it.

I feel in myself a soul as immense as the world, truly a soul as deep as the deepest rivers, my chest has the power to expand without limit. I am a master and I am advised to adopt the humility of a cripple. Yesterday, awakening to the world, I saw the sky turn upon itself utterly and wholly. I wanted to rise, but the disemboweled silence fell back upon me, its wings paralyzed. Without responsibility, straddling Nothingness and Infinity, I began to weep.[13]

This instance of ego collapse gives Fanon more than just exposure to nonbeing with its paralyzing silence. It also gives him a glimpse of the infinity that includes but extends beyond the zone of nonbeing. This infinite oceanic consciousness can genuinely transform any complex-ridden ego, if only it can conquer its fear and creatively negotiate its way in the zone of nonbeing.

By exploring these zones beyond the borders of the ego, Fanon had taken the analyses of the Afro-Caribbean psyche to new philosophical depths. His uniqueness within the historicist school is largely determined by the extent to which he fearlessly explored these regions. His explorations exposed for us the ground out of which the Afro-Caribbean ego emerges and against which it must secure its everyday existence. This ground conditions the normal process of ego genesis, which requires the support of positive interpersonal relations for it to have a stable existence above the ground. Without such cultural and interpersonal support, egos tend to collapse into their ground under the pressure of its "gravitational" pull. This vulnerability is the existential deviation that Calibanized images and evaluations of the tradition produced in the Afro-Caribbean psyche.

The complex associated with this deviation was psycho-existential in nature. Consequently, Fanon's theory of the self was not exclusively existential. In fact, the existential was only one of its dimensions. Ego formation for Fanon was also conditioned by the many defense mechanisms and neurotic strategies identified by Freud. Hence the strong Freudian elements in Fanon's theory. Third and most important, ego genesis is also conditioned by the system of binary oppositions, values, discourses, and practices that a culture or tradition imposes on its members. Fanon conceptualizes this layer as the logical equivalent of Jung's collective unconscious. But, unlike Jung's collective unconscious, Fanon's is not the result of "cerebral inheritance." On the contrary, it becomes a part of an individual through "the unreflected imposition of a culture."[14]

In addition to the more scholarly works that constituted a part of this layer, Fanon also emphasized images and values internalized from movies, magazines, jokes, and other forms of popular expression. This emphasis on the sociocultural layer over the existential and the psychological points to Fanon's historicism. This layer is for Fanon thoroughly historicized. Traditional as well as colonial orders of discourse rise and decline as the historical process moves ever onward. Consequently, personality structures and the psycho-existential complexes that shape them are necessarily historicized by this changing of cultural orders. This penetration of the existential by history and culture explains Fanon's provocative claim that "ontology . . . does not permit us to explain the being of the black."[15] This requires culture and history. Fanon's historicism is here asserting itself in the heart of his existentialism.

To complete our analyses of Fanon's existentialism, we must return to the zone of nonbeing. We have already noted Fanon's suggestions that it could be the locus of a "genuine upheaval," of a rebirth. But he also added without explanation the following caution: "In most cases, the black lacks the advantage of being able to accomplish this descent into a real hell."[16] Fanon is here suggesting that the discourses of the Afro-Caribbean tradition were not able to navigate the individual across the difficult waters of this zone. Hence Fanon's turn to European existentialism for the language and concepts with which to explore the existential depths of the Afro-Caribbean psyche.

From European existentialism, Fanon inherited the basic concept of nonbeing that he used to describe the conditions of aridity and paralysis that often follow ego collapse. This is an abstract philosophical representation of these states that could have been described differently in the languages of myth, religion, or ritual.

From this tradition, Fanon also inherited the distinction between the in-itself and the for-itself. Logically, the former was the equivalent of Fanon's infinity and the latter of the existential aspects of his model of the self. For Sartre, the for-itself represented the basic emergence and growth of structures of self-consciousness that are conditioned by the zone of nonbeing. The "gravitational" pull of the latter establishes a basic lack in the existence of the for-itself. It attempts to overcome this lack through a compensatory project of being. The goal of this project is to establish the for-itself (consciousness) as a full positivity by restoring the being negated by the zone of nonbeing. In other words, the goal is to be a for-itself with all the powers of consciousness, and at the same time possess the full positivity of the in-itself. For Sartre, this project of being an in-itself-for-itself is a necessary but impossible one. Hence the anguish of the for-itself. Nonetheless, this dialectic between being and nothingness and the projects it necessitates are inescapable. It conditions ego formation by imposing upon it the structure and dynamics of its problematic projects.[17]

This language and its related concepts find their way into Fanon's analysis of the zone of nonbeing in the Afro-Caribbean psyche. He also borrows from Hegel, Kierkegaard, and Jaspers. The following passage shows us the way in which Fanon used this language and redeployed some of its concepts:

> Thus human reality as in-itself-for-itself can be achieved only through conflict
> and through the risk that conflict implies. This risk means that I go beyond
> life toward a supreme good that is the transformation of subjective certainty
> of my own worth into a universally objective truth.[18]

Here the influences of Hegel and Sartre are unmistakable. However, Fanon is here employing the language and concepts of this tradition to articulate a possibility for the Afro-Caribbean that neither had imagined. In other words, the language is that of European existentialism, but the experience is Afro-Caribbean.

FANONIAN, AFRICAN, AND EUROPEAN EXISTENTIALISM

By incorporating these existential dimensions, Fanon revolutionized the treatment of black identity within our intellectual tradition. He opened up questions of ontology that hitherto had gone unaddressed. Compared to the dogmatic and stereotypical treatment of Afro-Caribbean identity in the European layer of our tradition, this was a revolutionary counterstatement that de-Calibanized blackness. Like the counterdiscourses of J. J. Thomas, Garvey, Padmore, and Cesaire, Fanon's work was a major contribution to reversing the patterns of cultural accumulation and disaccummulation within the tradition.

In addition to its impact on patterns of accumulation, Fanon's revolutionary approach to the self had two important consequences for philosophy in the region. First, it provided Caribbean philosophy with a new model of the self. This was not the rational, solitary, and enclosed model of the subject that the tradition had inherited from Hume or Adam Smith. Fanon's model was less closed and less securely centered. It opened the self to possibilities of collapse, to its rootedness in a collective unconscious, and beyond that to its grounding in infinity. This remains an unsurpassed achievement in Caribbean philosophy.

The second important consequence of Fanon's approach to the self was that it established a solid link between the zone of nonbeing in the Afro-Caribbean psyche and the existential tradition of European philosophy. It was a new move within the tradition. This existential coding liberated the zone from its invisibility and nonrecognition in dominant discourses of the tradition. It supplemented the emancipatory appropriations of European liberalism, socialism, constitutionalism, and surrealism that was evident in the works of Garvey, James, Cesaire, and other Afro-Caribbean writers. At the same time, it was in sharp contrast with the repressive use to which many of these same philosophical appropriations were put by Euro-Caribbean writers.

In spite of these important contributions to Afro-Caribbean philosophy, Fanon's analysis of black identity did not revolutionize the basic position or the overall functioning of philosophy in the Caribbean intellectual tradition. This was so for two reasons. First, it did not change the intertextual location of Caribbean philosophy. Fanon's work linked it primarily to the production of an emancipatory political theory. Thus it remained very much the handmaiden of ideology. In the polarized colonial context it was difficult for it to be otherwise. Separated from art, religion, and its own original vision, the intertextual location of philosophy remained the same.

The second reason why Fanon's contribution did not revolutionize regional philosophy was that his existentialism left the identity of Caribbean philosophy as European and as white as it found it. At the same time that it was helping to destroy racist discourses, the linguistic coding of Fanon's existentialism reinforced Caribbean philosophy's overidentification with Europe and underidentification with Africa. This is the underlying pattern that needs to be changed. Fanon's decision to appropriate the language and concepts of European existentialism while excluding African ones presented no major challenge to this pattern. This choice left African existentialism and African philosophy as a whole still unrecognized and still under the spell of that powerful binary opposition, primitive/civilized. Consequently the European identity of Caribbean philosophy remained essentially unchanged.

This is not to suggest that Fanon was unaware of the above problem of overidentification, or that he did not make original contributions with his appropriation of the language and concepts of European existentialism. As indicated above, it was an Afro-Caribbean experience that he analyzed with this language. Although I am of the view that Caliban can say something new and original in the language of Prospero, my point is that Fanon's specific philosophical formulations did not have the weight or critical mass to break the underlying binary that disenfranchised African philosophy and inhibited the emergence of a distinct regional philosophy. This failure says nothing about the quality or originality of Fanon's philosophy, but it says a lot about the discursive authority that it had to overcome.

Fanon did not turn to European existentialism because there was no African or Afro-Caribbean existentialist discourse. Rather, it was because he was unable to break the spell of Calibanization that the tradition had cast over it. If African and Afro-Caribbean cultures have supported viable egos, then they must have found discursive solutions to the "gravitational" pulls of nonbeing. Fanon's failure to recognize and appropriate these discourses was indicative of the power of the tradition.

Earlier, we noted that Fanon's existentialism was grounded in experiences of ego implosion or collapse that were brought on by the negative reflections of blackness that pervade our tradition. The existentialism of traditional Africa also derived from experiences of ego collapse or displacement. However, these experiences were of a spiritual and not a racial origin. Conscious and controlled exercises in ego dissolution or suspension are spiritual practices that many societies cultivate. In Africa techniques of ego transcendence center on the rhythms of the drums and getting into trance states. In the East, these techniques center on the practice of meditation. In traditional Africa, the vision of reality that anchored cultural life was in large part derived from states in which the ego had been silenced. As we've seen, Africans were experienced explorers of the borders of the ego. More important, they had developed the discursive ability to code those supreme existential moments in which the human self is confronted with the conditions of its possibility or nonpossibility.

The realities discovered by African explorers were not coded in the impersonal language of being and nonbeing, in-itself and for-itself. On the contrary, they were coded in the more personal language of gods and spirits who were in charge of various aspects of creation, including the process of ego genesis and hence ego performance. In the crucial notions of *fate* and *destiny*, *sunsum*, and *Okra* we had the hidden instruments through which human self-formation was subjected to the control of the gods. The individual's relation to his or her destiny was made problematic by two factors: the relative autonomy of the human will and the fact that the *sunsum*, our organ of ego consciousness, was often in the dark about our real destiny.

These factors set the stage for the African to be at odds or in harmony with his or her destiny, that is, with the forces beyond the borders of the ego. To the extent that the individual is not in accord with the gods, he or she will experience the "gravitational" pull of nonbeing or the anger of the gods, both of which can result in personal failure or ego collapse. To the extent that the individual is in harmony with the gods, he or she will experience confirmation, guidance, and help in personal projects. The individual will experience the upward, "heliotropic" pull of the power of being or the blessings of the gods. Both of these will lead to ego affirmation and personal success. The pushes and pulls of these "gravitational" and "heliotropic" forces on the individual are very reminiscent of Kierkegaard's descriptions of being "educated by anxiety."[19]

As we've seen, this discourse of fate is an important foundation of African existentialism.[20] It is beautifully portrayed in Chinua Achebe's *Things Fall Apart* and ethnographically reproduced in the works of scholars such as Fortes[21] (1959) and Rattray[22] (1923) on the Tallensi and the Ashanti. It contains the language and concepts that Africans have used to describe the relationship between the ego's self-formation and its expansive ground. Africans brought this discourse, with its gods and practices of ego transcendence, with them to the Caribbean. In the colonial context of Caribbean societies, this discourse was forced to historicize and Christianize itself. In making these adaptations, it incorporated secular ideologies of liberation and syncretized itself with the more ritualized and ego-transcending aspects of European Christianity. Thus with the passage of time, personal fate came to be understood either in Afro-Christian, primarily Christian, terms or through secular ideologies of historicism.

Since this discourse existed, why didn't Fanon include it in his existential explorations? It was certainly not because he was unaware of it. He was too close to Cesaire and other poeticists for him not to know about it. Even more than James, Fanon followed closely the developments that were taking place in African ethnophilosophy. References to them can be found throughout *Black Skin*. Given these facts, it must be that in spite of being there, Fanon did not find them capable of meeting the challenge he was confronting.

This challenge was to break the power of European discourses to negate or neutralize the counterdiscourses of colonized Afro-Caribbeans. Fanon was in search of a philosophy that could repel the discursive bullets, even the physical bullets, of European colonialism. "What use are reflections on Bantu ontology," asks Fanon, "when striking black miners in South Africa are being shot down?"[23]

Or, "When a bachelor of philosophy from the Antilles refuses to apply for certification as a teacher because of his color, I say that philosophy has never saved anyone."[24] Fanon is clearly in search of a philosophy that can counter "the lived experience of the black" as it had been construed in the tradition.

Like the negritude discourses of the poeticists, Fanon did not find the discourse of fate really capable of restoring an African meaning to "the lived experience of the black." It could not neutralize the "primitive" images with which blackness was associated, or counter the existential deviations and ego implosions that these images produced in the Afro-Caribbean psyche. It couldn't because the discourse of fate carried the same markings of blackness. These markings Calibanized it, robbed it of objective value and its capacity to counterpunch. Consequently, for Fanon, to use it in an argument against Europeans was to lose the argument before it began. This loss would have nothing to do with logic, evidence, or truth, but with the authority European philosophical discourses had accumulated at the expense of African ones. The power differential between the two was still so wide that Fanon experienced the latter as having little or no ontological resistance in the face of the former.

This becomes clear as Fanon matches various black counterarguments against white stereotypes and devaluations, using his own ego genesis to test the ontological strengths of both. Here is Fanon testing the ability of a negritude argument to support his ego:

> I rummaged frenetically through all of black antiquary. What I found there took my breath away. In his book, *L'Abolition de l'esclavage* Schoelcher presented us with compelling arguments. Since then, Frobenius, Westermann, Delafosse—all of them white had jointed the chorus: Segou, Djenne, cities of more than a hundred thousand people; accounts of learned blacks (doctors of theology who went *to* Mecca to interpret the Koran). All of that, exhumed from the past, spread with its insides out, made *it* possible for me to find a valid historic place.[25]

Feeling as if he had "put the white man back into his place," Fanon experiences a moment of contentment and ego stability. But then the white man responds:

> Lay aside your history and your research on the past, and try to put yourself into our rhythm. In a society such as ours, industrialized to the extreme, scienticized, there is no longer any place for your sensitivity. It is necessary to be strong to be allowed to live. What matters now is no longer playing the game of the world but subjugating it with integrals and atoms. . . . When we are tired of our lives in our buildings, we will turn to you as we do to our children— to the innocent, the ingenuous, the spontaneous.[26]

The negritude argument did not hold up against this response. Fanon experiences ego collapse; his reasons were countered by "real reasons," his arguments by "real" arguments. The fact that Fanon did not explicitly mention the discourse of fate is not really important. It would have failed his ontological test just like the others, leaving Fanon with another experience of ego implosion. Like the negritude argument, it would have been countered by "real" reasons and "real" arguments—real because of the authority European existentialist discourses had accumulated in relation to this discourse of fate.

FANON, CREOLIZATION, AND AFRO-CARIBBEAN PHILOSOPHY

Fanon's failure to change the European identity of Caribbean philosophy was clearly the result of his inability to liberate it from its enmeshment in the values and markings of our tradition. This failure to liberate Caribbean philosophy from its colonial complex is all the more striking, as such emancipations were taking place in literature, dance, music, and other media of expression. This points to the special situation of Afro-Caribbean philosophy: the extreme degree to which it was disenfranchised from the community of discourse.

Given this persistence of the European identity, it is not surprising that Fanon's philosophy did not lead to a creolizing of Caribbean philosophy in the way that the works of George Lamming, V. S. Reid, Wilson Harris, Sam Selvon, and others led to the creolizing of Caribbean literature. Caribbean philosophy is yet to undergo a similar change. Given the increases in authority that Afro-Caribbean discourses have accumulated since Fanon, the key question for us is whether or not such a change is now possible. That is, with the corresponding loss of authority by Euro-Caribbean discourses, will Afro-Caribbean philosophy now be able to claim its rightful place in the community of discourses? I think this is not only possible but also highly desirable.

Creolization is an active project that would indigenize Afro-Caribbean philosophy and end its state of Calibanization and limited activation. The existence of more advanced states of creolization in other discourses points to the uneven rates at which recovery has been taking place in the various dimensions of the Caribbean imagination. These differential rates also indicate the problem areas in our capacity for symbolically representing local realities. The limited capabilities of areas such as philosophy must affect our performances in stronger areas such as literature.

Edouard Glissant has suggested that these differential rates of recovery have left our postcolonial imagination with limited vision and an inability to see the whole. In areas such as myth and philosophy, Glissant sees a continuing failure of mythopoetic and discursive processes to root themselves in local experiences of time and space, flora and fauna, work and play.[27] These areas of symbolic immobilization have created fissures, blanks, and nonfunctioning spots on the Caribbean imagination as a whole. Because of these cleavages, it is unable to produce comprehensive pictures of itself, or adequately reflect its national and social environments.

This absence of comprehensive pictures of ourselves points to our limited capacity to philosophically represent ourselves. By its nature, philosophical discourse tends toward the systematically integrated view. Glissant suggests that the prevalence of the folktale as a medium of collective self-representation is indicative of this reluctance to form comprehensive pictures of ourselves. Folktales deal with particular events and therefore generate stories that cannot be generalized.[28] I think the use of the novel as our primary medium of self-exploration sends a similar message. If we are to have comprehensive pictures of ourselves, we must remove the blocks on the philosophical and other dimensions of the Caribbean imagination. Philosophy is an indispensable practice in our division of cultural labor. Without the full functioning of its African, Indian, and European dimensions, our vision will be narrowed and our capacity to understand ourselves limited.

To free the philosophical and other underperforming spots on the Caribbean imagination, Glissant suggests a project of creolization, one in which intellectual workers would reenter the long-concealed areas of our imagination and undo the binary oppositions and negative evaluations that block African and European elements from creatively coming together. These subterranean voyagers should strive to open blocked arteries and channels so that rates of creolization would synchronize and capacities for discursive representation would increase more uniformly. Such changes would make more operational the underlying unity of our imagination and reconnect philosophy, folktales, literature, and so forth, to the unconscious patterns, rhythms, and images that make this unity possible. In short, creolization is a process of semio-semantic hybridization that can occur between the arguments, vocabularies, phonologies, or grammars of discourses within a culture or across cultures. This is the context in which we can envision the reenfranchising of African and Afro-Caribbean philosophies, the reestablishing of their ability to accumulate authority and their capacity for ontological resistance.

Such a creolizing of Caribbean philosophy must begin with subterranean plunges of the type suggested by Glissant. At these depths, African and Afro-Caribbean philosophies must be freed from the legacy of invisibility and entrapment in the binaries of colonial discourses. With their visibility and legitimacy restored, this philosophical heritage must be allowed to find its own equilibrium in the processes of semio-semantic hybridization that have creolized other discourses. In this creole framework, the African discourse of fate should find a place in any discussion of Afro-Caribbean existentialism.

However, this inclusion would be related to its ability to reflect the existential realities of Afro-Caribbean people. In other words, its inclusion would not be the result of the repressive authority it had accumulated over other discourses.

Such a creole philosophy means going beyond the philosophical models we inherited from James and Fanon. In their models, Caribbean philosophy recovered a knowledge of itself and its society by drawing on the discourses of the Western tradition. Given the nature of the colonial situation, such a period of philosophical dependence is probably a necessary phase. If postcolonial reconstruction is to proceed, then this pattern of dependent borrowing must give way to processes of philosophical indigenization. The levels of philosophical dependence inherited from James and Fanon are not consistent with our modern aspirations and national self-projections. Paradoxically, to move closer to its own modernity, Caribbean philosophy must creolize itself by breaking its misidentifications with European and African philosophies and allowing them to remix within the framework of more organic relations with local realities.

In sum, Fanon's overall philosophy displays many of the features outlined in our general characterization of Afro-Caribbean philosophy. It is multidimensional, interdiscursively embedded and indelibly marked by the peripheral dynamics of Caribbean cultural systems. As a result, it shares many of the orientations, strengths, and contradictions of James's philosophy. Even though we did not examine its Pan-African and Marxist dimensions, these were well-developed features of Fanon's philosophy, making it one of the exemplary dialectical syntheses of Afro-Caribbean philosophy. Although explicit by Caribbean standards, Fanon's philosophy remained politico-ideologically embedded. Finally, because of his greater awareness than James of traditional African philosophy, Fanon's ambivalences toward the latter have raised more directly questions regarding patterns of creolization and the surplus of repressive authority that shapes them.

CHAPTER 4

Wilson Harris and
Caribbean Poeticism

With Harris, we leave behind the world of Caribbean historicism and move to the center of the region's poeticist tradition of thought. Harris's work is rooted in the creative space of this tradition and often attempts to make this unconscious background an object of explicit thematization. If James represents the transformative aspects of Afro-Caribbean philosophy, then Harris exemplifies its reconstructive and transversal tendencies. Harris's focus is the particular type of symbolic world that can be created out of the imploded worldviews of the Caribbean colonial experience. In this undertaking, Harris's point of departure is the self, its creative dynamics and their relations to practices of world constitution. Thus like Fanon, the immanent, creative dynamics of the self are explicitly thematized in Harris and occupy a central place in his philosophy. However, raising more than issues of recognition and creolization, Harris's philosophy points the way to a contemporary dialogue with traditional African philosophy.

Author of seventeen works of fiction and four works of criticism, an imaginative writer of the highest caliber, Wilson Harris is also an important Caribbean philosopher. The philosophical aspects of his work have been clearly recognized by his critics, even if it has been with some bewilderment. In his introduction to the 1954 collection of poetry, *Eternity to Season*, A. J. Seymour observed: "to an unusual degree, the poetry of Wilson Harris is intermingled with philosophy. As he writes his verse, he is also creating a flux of thought in which he is probing ultimate matters and asking questions of life."[1] With characteristic brilliance, C. L. R. James wrote: "Harris writes his fiction and his philosophy and his dramatic episodes all in one book."[2] Coming early in Harris's career, Seymour's remarks were particularly on target as the philosophical aspects Harris's creative writing have only continued to grow.

Several attempts have been made to identify the philosophical position that supports and informs Harris's writing. Two in particular have established themselves in the literature: an existentialist and a Hegelian reading of Harris's philosophical position. C. L. R. James has made the strongest case for a Heideggerian reading of Harris's philosophy, while Gregory Shaw has made the case for a Hegelian reading.

The key point on which James rests his case is that central to both Harris and Heidegger is the distinction between authentic and inauthentic existences, and the conditions under which an individual moves from the latter to the former. James often developed this point by thematizing Heidegger's ontology of the inauthenticity of everyday life and comparing it with Harris's. For Heidegger, the ontology of everyday life was being-for-others. In the condition of everydayness, the individual "belongs to" and "stands in subjection"[3] to others. To live exclusively in such a state of everydayness is to live an inauthentic existence. It is an escape, a distraction from the many unsolved problems of ego formation, that can only be authentically addressed when the individual is able to engage his or her depths that go beyond the level of everydayness.

In Harris's unrelenting attempts to shatter the realism, closure, and self-assuredness of the everyday ego, James sees a similar dynamic at work. Thus in the experiences of Donne and his crew in *Palace of the Peacock*, James reads a movement from a condition of everyday closure and inauthenticity to a state of openness and authenticity that is brought on by encounters with spiritual forces suppressed by the limits of everydayness.[4] Hence the connection with Heidegger.

Gregory Shaw objects strongly to this existential reading of Harris's philosophy. He suggests that James has wandered "off-track in speaking of Heidegger and Jaspers and has sent quite a few scholars on a wildgoose chase trying to connect Harris to the phenomenological school."[5] Instead of an ontological dynamic between inauthentic and authentic existences, Shaw sees in Harris's philosophy dialectical movements of the Hegelian type.

> The Harrisian word, the Harrisian image, tend to possess a peculiarly dialectical quality of negating themselves. . . . As it is with word and image, so it is with character. The Harrisian world is a world of "doubles," his nature, a nature of mirrors, opaque streams, dark pools, eyes in which the double springs to life.[6]

Like James, Shaw sees Harris's work as disrupting everyday realities, a "dismantling of history and society, of object and even the word."[7] However, this work is the work of a Hegelian dialectic with its dissolving and superseding capabilities. Thus in contrast to James, Shaw draws a parallel between the achievement of absolute self-consciousness by Hegelian spirit and the arrival of Donne and his crew at the Palace of the Peacock.

What are we to make of these two different interpretations of Harris's philosophy? I shall argue that Harris is the quintessential creole thinker in whose work a very large number of influences converge. However, in spite of his ability to engage a wide array of thinkers, I take the position that the key to Harris's philosophy is his own original encounters with the depths beyond the everyday ego. To get to these depths, Harris needs neither Hegel or Heidegger. What indeed he does share with them is the ability to explore firsthand the nature and role of consciousness in human life. Thus, in spite of being very real, I see these Hegelian and Heideggerian themes as useful appropriations that Harris has included in a larger discourse of his own making, that he has used to report the original findings of his explorations of consciousness. In contrast to both James and Shaw, I shall further argue that the most important discursive key to Harris's philosophy is his roots in the philosophical tradition of Caribbean poeticism. As a result, Harris's unique poeticist discourse offers us a very different analysis of consciousness from both Hegel's and Heidegger's.

First, through this discourse, we are given a quantum mechanical reading of consciousness. This reading shows consciousness to be a universal creative force that supports all forms of created existence, including the ego and its mode of self-consciousness. Second, the unique transforming power of the universal consciousness for Harris does not take the form of Hegel's absolute spirit or Heidegger's being-towards-death, but the possibility for what I shall call an *archetypal life*. Third and finally, Harris's philosophical approach to consciousness is indeed phenomenological. However, it is not the conceptual phenomenology of Heidegger or Hegel. Rather it is an imagistic, mythopoetic phenomenology in which Harris's dazzling ability with images takes precedence over conceptual representations of the movement of consciousness, hence the strong poeticist orientation.

I will develop these arguments in four basic steps: (1) I will locate Harris in the philosophical tradition of Caribbean poeticism; (2) I will examine in detail his ontology of consciousness; (3) I will outline the specific place of poetics in this discourse on consciousness; and (4) I will undertake a brief historicist engagement of Harris's poeticism. The chapter concludes with some of the implications of this engagement for Caribbean philosophy.

HARRIS AND THE CARIBBEAN INTELLECTUAL TRADITION

The Caribbean intellectual tradition emerged from the discursive attempts by Africans, Amerindians, and Indians to delegitimate European colonial rule, to preserve traditional identities and to legitimate their attempts at racial and national liberation. Arising in response to claims of white supremacy and other arguments used by Europeans to legitimate colonial rule, the Caribbean intellectual tradition can be seen as a series of contentious dialogues between Europeans and the above groups. These exchanges began in the sixteenth century and continue into the present. The specific problematic that links Harris to the poeticist wing of the Caribbean intellectual tradition is the role of the self in the project of postcolonial reconstruction. It is an issue that poeticists and historicists have treated very differently. The poeticists make the recovery of the postcolonial self an important precondition for institutional recovery, while the historicists tend to see recovery of self as following institutional recovery. Harris has been strongly influenced by the first of these positions, and with Derek Walcott, Edouard Glissant, Sylvia Wynter, Rex Nettleford, and others has contributed greatly to its establishment in the region.

The special problems associated with reconstructing the postcolonial Caribbean self received their classic formulation from Fanon as he transitioned from the poeticist to the historicist school. For Fanon, the key to the postcolonial Afro-Caribbean self is the implosion its African predecessor experienced under colonialism and the self-preservative strategies it adopted. In Fanon's view, internalizing the colonial experience divided the Afro-Caribbean psyche, leaving it with a Duboisian "double consciousness" of itself. As we've seen, this division was created by the "imago of the Negro" that European colonization implanted in the Afro-Caribbean psyche. Thus Afro-Caribbeans had both an African and European image of themselves. These contradictory self-images left the Afro-Caribbean psyche divided, vulnerable to ego collapse, and thus open to experiences of the "zone of nonbeing."

This "existential deviation," as Fanon called it, had to be addressed in some way. One could withdraw in despair, wear "white masks," engage in compensatory self-assertion, resist violently, or use this deviation as a gateway to the re-creative possibilities that lie beyond the ego. For the most part, historicists like Padmore, Garvey, James, and Fanon have opted for the fourth response of violent resistance. Fanon described in dialectical fashion some of the offensive and defensive moves that the Caribbean ego has made against its existential deviation. He examined its attempts to establish physiological, rational, black, and other models of Afro-Caribbean selfhood, to compensate for the lack produced by the internalized imago. These all prove to be inadequate before the institutional power of the imago. Hence the turn to revolutionary resistance that would destroy the institutional foundations of the imago.

In contrast, Harris has consistently opted for the fifth position: recovery through the creative affirmation of the colonial trauma and its existential deviations. For Harris, the worst response would be to conceal this trauma or its deviations beneath compensatory or even oppositional projects. These moves would cut us off from vital sources of mythopoetic creativity that have the power to renew and refashion identities. In his view, "such fortress ornamentation consolidates itself until it blocks a descent into complex and hidden forces of truth; it becomes a ritual, a wall or a curtain, a ritual dead-end, a ritual journalese that paralyzes creativity in the name of fact."[8] This blocking of the path to mythopoetic creativity must be avoided at all costs.

To keep it open Harris insists that we build our recovery upon the existential deviations, "upon the real reverses the human spirit has endured, the real chasm of pain it has entered, rather than the apparent consolidation, victories and battles it has won."[9] If we are able to subsist with hope in this location of loss and anguish, unpredictable movements of creativity will start the reconstruction process. This power of mythopoetic action to regenerate the self together with the claim that this regeneration is a condition for postcolonial institutional recovery constitutes the core of Harris's poeticism. It is a position he shares with other members of this school, although their formulation of it may be different.

In short, Harris has been very much a part of the Caribbean poeticist school. As we will see, he has been active in its internal debates and its exchanges with the historicists. This involvement in the debate over the developmental significance of the postcolonial self is in my view the most important discursive influence on Harris's work. It is the specific creative matrix out of which comes the original view of consciousness that distinguishes him from both Hegel and Heidegger. Thus the ontology of consciousness that I will discuss next, is best seen as one of the most original philosophical developments in the poeticist tradition.

ONTOLOGY AND CONSCIOUSNESS IN HARRIS

Harris's philosophy is difficult, if not impossible, to present systematically because the basic containing category of his thought is fluidity and not systematic coherence. In spite of this refusal of systematic coherence, it is still possible to isolate and develop certain basic philosophical positions that in fact support the fluidity of Harris's thought. For example, it is possible to identify very definite ontological, epistemological, existential, and ethical themes in

Harris's writings. So, once again Afro-Caribbean philosophy emerges as a multidimensional, qualitatively diverse field that permits the asking and answering of different but related types of questions. However, the most important of these subfields for the originality and distinctiveness of Harris's poeticism is his ontology, which gives to consciousness a very special and unique place.

The fluid character of Harris's philosophy derives from his very complex and expansive view of consciousness and from the unpredictable ways in which it penetrates and interacts with the worlds of self, society, and nature. Thus he shares with traditional African philosophy a four-world model of existence. For Harris, consciousness is a universal living medium whose activities are necessary for the emergence and sustenance of all life forms. Consciousness is a universal dimension that embraces all existence, but remains an absent or unconscious presence for most of these life forms. In speaking of a consciousness that can be the unconscious of material life forms, Harris is not speaking only of humans: "When I speak of the unconscious I'm not only speaking of the human unconscious but of the unconscious that resides in objects, in trees, in rivers. I am suggesting that there is a psyche, mysterious entity that links us to the unconscious in nature."[10] This conception of the unconscious existence of consciousness is clearly quite similar to the behavior of Hegel's spirit. However, it also echoes the spirituality of traditional African religion. The major difference is that Harris's spirituality is radically immanent and does not have the permanently externalized and projected features of African spirituality.

The primary goal of Harris's ontology is to reveal the active, creative side of consciousness. He is highly critical of discourses that conceal the creative, constitutive, and life-sustaining powers of this universal consciousness. Harris is uncomfortable with discourses that recognize only the passive shaping of consciousness by material forces, or its role in knowledge production. Thus at the heart of his ontology is the attempt to demonstrate the founding capabilities of consciousness, the ways in which it creates the worlds of self, society, and nature, how it holds them in its hands and shapes them.

In this pursuit of the ontological significance of consciousness, Harris confronts head-on the difficulties created by the refusal of consciousness to fit within our intellectual grasp. For him, there can be no final or total grasping of consciousness. At their best such attempts will produce only revealing traces or fragmentary revelations of its vastness, its unending creativity, and its ability to mask and unmask itself. Given that only these fleeting and partial images of it are possible, it is not surprising that Harris has a large number of word-images that he uses to represent consciousness. Thus he refers to it as "that deep organism that presently moves away from and eludes our grasp," or as a "groping spirit that leaves behind a trail of archeological witnesses."[11] Other word-images include an absent presence, a photographic negative, authentic rhythms with great creative power, the ground of reality, the dimension of depth, or with Jung, the collective unconscious.

A final set of very important metaphors that Harris uses to describe universal consciousness in relation to the worlds of self, society, and nature are derived from quantum mechanics. Each of these is treated as a quantum layer with its own laws, while consciousness holds the keys to their unity, interpenetration, and transcendence. This quantum view of consciousness is most systematically developed in *The Radical Imagination*. There Harris stresses the connections between quantum levels that are available to consciousness but often remain hidden on specific levels. Thus on the ego level, a rose is a rose is a rose. From the perspective of consciousness, "a rose is a particle is a wave." Or, from the point of view of the ego, a table is an object we put books on. But from the quantum perspective, a table becomes a tree, the tree becomes the forest and the forest "is the lungs of the globe and the lungs of the globe breathe on the stars."[12]

In spite of its elusiveness, Harris thinks that consciousness leaves behind enough traces to support his expansive view of it. For example, he suggests that its creative impact on the social world is strong and clear enough to refer to it as an "objective process." This objective process takes the form of a unique tradition of images, symbols, and practices through which consciousness "yields itself, fragmentarily perhaps, but decisively as time goes on."[13] In other words, the unique traditions of a people are not just human creations but also manifestations and mediations of a unique relationship with universal consciousness.

From the above, it should be clear that Harris approaches consciousness through a very careful threading together of the archetypal traces and images of itself that consciousness leaves behind as it penetrates or temporarily interrupts the accustomed order of life on other quantum planes. His work is filled with detailed portrayals of such eruptions of consciousness on the quantum planes of ego, society, and nature. By far the richest of these portrayals occur on the plane of the ego. Hence it shares a hierophanic orientation with traditional African philosophy. Here Harris's ability to generate images in which we can see consciousness moving in and out of the world of the ego is truly awesome. From this carefully threaded field of traces and images emerges a magisterial view of consciousness that is immemorial in its temporality and infinite in its creative possibilities. Consequently, Harris's view of the ontological significance of consciousness is most accessible through its relationship with the ego. Thus the additional development of his ontology below will take place through a closer focus on the hierophanic ego/consciousness relationship.

CONSCIOUSNESS AND THE ONTOLOGY OF THE EVERYDAY EGO

As the "photographic" but spiritual negative that makes the existence of the ego possible, the most basic relationship of consciousness to the ego is a relation of self-concealment in which consciousness transforms itself into an absent presence. It is a relationship of self-suspension in which consciousness voids the codes of its existence and in this void allows the intentionality of the ego to emerge. As an intentional structure, the ego has self-creative powers that are in part dependent upon a variety of social stimuli. Consciousness further allows itself to be eclipsed by these socially stimulated onto-poetic processes by which the ego posits and auto-institutes itself. The more completely the ego is able to institute itself, the more absolutely it believes in the reality it has created, and the less it is able to experience consciousness. The ego thus comes to believe in its self-sufficiency, and in the paramountcy of the everyday world from which its slice of reality was cut.

These tendencies of the ego to house itself and to build walls around its house are prereflective. That is, before the ego has achieved a mature reflective capacity, it has inherited an intentional structure whose information codes and creative intelligence allow it to carry out egocentric offensive and defensive actions. The codes and creative abilities that sustain these Yuruguan tendencies are more centered, analytic, and less mythopoetic when compared with the decentered and mythopoetic code of consciousness. This semiotic capacity allows the ego to recode and reorder the activities of consciousness, thus bringing them partially under its control. Thus, quantum connections or binary opposites (male/female, good/bad) that exist side by side in consciousness are separated and made analytically distinct by the ego. This is also consciousness cooperating in its own displacement. Without this prereflective awareness, the ego would be unable to define, recognize, and respond to internal and external threats, including actions from the universal consciousness. Because of its limited coding, this prereflective capability is extremely error prone and often shuts the ego's doors on consciousness when there is really no need. This tendency toward error in its self-creative endeavors parallels the cosmogonic difficulties of the ego in African existentialism, which we examined earlier.

This enclosing of the ego around its own self-sufficiency and the realism of everyday life, sets up the basic conditions for Harris's ontological dynamic between the ego and consciousness. Although consciousness initially cooperates in its exclusion from the world of the ego, it resists its complete exclusion. Its resistance increases the closer the ego gets to effecting such a closure. A battle ensues as this point is approached. This dynamic is ontological in that it effects the ego's capacity to complete its project of being. At the same time, it is also a dynamic of closure and openness, concealment and disclosure, non-recognition and recognition, consolidation and fulfillment.

Harris has several terms for this state of ego closure. In clearly Heideggerian terms, he often refers to this state as an ontic tautology. At other times he refers to it as a tautology of facts, a state of embalmed facts, a straitjacket, or a claustrophobic state. These terms all describe conditions of rigid or extreme ego institutionalization that give rise to illusions of self-sufficiency and self-completion. The ego now believes exclusively in its own ontology. Of its living relationship with consciousness it is clueless.

For Harris, such states of ontic closure and ego confidence are inauthentic. They are inauthentic irrespective of whether closure is around being a doctor, a worker, a parent, a writer, or a revolutionary. This inauthenticity derives from at least three sources: first, the ego's refusal to recognize the resistance of consciousness; second, the one-sidedness that these self-enclosures require; and third, the ego's blindness to what its illusions must exclude. Such exclusions often lead to splits in the ego as in the case of the character Donne. These splits can result in situations of internal nonrecognition, banishment, or protracted struggle to maintain the illusion of unity or self-sufficiency.

Although such conditions of premature ontic closure are largely the work of the ego, these consolidating activities are reinforced by similar hardening tendencies in the institutions and social practices that maintain the reality of the social world. This reality is also an inauthentic, rigidified one and is maintained by "mechanical institutions." Harris rejects the thesis of the ontological paramountcy of the world of everyday life; he sees it as involved in the same ontological struggles with consciousness as the ego. Thus the specific degree of inauthenticity an ego experiences will vary also with social conditions.

The ego's drive toward inauthentic ontic closure opens it up to the unmaking or disestablishing powers of consciousness. This dynamic of making and unmaking bring us to the heart of Harris's ontology of the everyday ego. One is here reminded of Sartre's ontology of the human self (the for-itself), which is distinguished by its tendency to remain suspended between being and nonbeing. We are also reminded of the regulatory negations by which the ego is shaken out of its spiritual ignorance in African existentialism. Harris views the unmaking actions of consciousness as the latter reclaiming the void out of which the ego emerged, and filling it with rhythms of its own. In other words, it will no longer cooperate passively in its own eclipse. A point of egocentric closure has been reached beyond which it will no longer continue its voluntary sleep of concealment.

Consciousness disturbs the ego by voiding or de-intentionalizing an area of its self-activity, preventing it from completing its prereflective goal of closure. The ego now experiences itself as partially grounded, blocked, and hence unable to be. It is now in the Harrisian void or abyss. The conception of a de-intentionalized state is the best philosophical translation I can make of Harris's void. It can be viewed as a state in which the ego's intentional coding has been superseded by consciousness thus making prereflective activity extremely difficult. This makes it similar to Fanon's "zone of nonbeing," that is experienced in cases of severe ego collapse. The ego is frightened by such acts of de-intentionalization. Hence it is anxious before its voiding by consciousness. In responding to this anxiety as the sign of a mortal danger, the ego takes anxious flight into compensatory activity or makes anxious withdrawals into closed defensive postures. In either case, we have a form of additional straitjacketing. But in responding to its anxiety, the ego misreads consciousness. Thus it has a hard time realizing that the goal of consciousness is not to keep it in this voided state. On the contrary, in Harris's view, it is to reintentionalize the ego at a lower level of prereflective egocentricity. Unable to recognize this intent, the relation between ego and consciousness becomes antagonistic.

Awakened in this disestablishing way, consciousness can be a very terrifying presence or an unwanted intruder for the ego. As the latter resumes its now interrupted existence, it is shaken to the core. Forced to confront realities other than its own, the ego experiences blockages and new anxieties. These eruptions of the concealed consciousness into the life of the ego are the primary materials for both the art and the philosophy of Harris. In Jungian language, Harris tells us that "the unconscious can erupt through the conscious (the ego) and address one in a startling way that strikes at one's presuppositions. So that one's presuppositions, which are so dear to one, are dislodged."[14] Such eruptive addresses from the concealed universal consciousness are basic to the relationship with the straitjacketed ego. They break its patterns of compulsively consolidating its limited reality and open possibilities for what Harris calls "fulfillment."

This construction of the universal consciousness as an unwanted intruder illuminates a key concept in African magical discourses, especially those of the Baluba. This concept is the theft of an individual's vital force by an intrusive deity, ancestor, or human being. The concept describes an experience of loss or negating of intentionality that occurs against the will of the individual. Harris's voiding is coded here as the taking or stealing of the ego's vital force by what appears to be a terrifying and predatory presence. The major difference is that with the aid of the archetypal apprenticeship, Harris absorbs the intruder in a radically immanent fashion. In the case of the Baluba, the intruder is partially externalized and projected onto humans. However, in both cases, we are dealing with similar moments in the oppositional relationships between ego and spiritual ground.

Throughout his work, Harris provides us with many examples of consciousness breaking through the circular walls of the ego. These occur through dreams, visions, visits from one's fictional characters, states of possession, or moments of ego collapse. The case of visits from one's fictional characters is a favorite of Harris's and is most systematically developed in the *Radical Imagination*. In this work, Harris is taking a critical look at some of his own fiction. What is really engaging about the overall structure of this work is the existential distance that Harris is able to establish between himself and his works. This distance is achieved by convincing us that the main characters in these novels are their real authors. Thus Anselm becomes the real author of *The Four Banks of the River of Space*. He becomes a living persona with his own creative vision, while Harris is reduced to being "the editor" of Anselm's book. "The Four Banks is Anselm's book, one of those troublesome characters, who visits one occasionally in the park or wherever, who will come upon one and intrude and make their demands."[15] This description in particular calls to mind the disruptive and intrusive visits of deities and ancestors to which the African ego is subject.

Fascinating as these cases are, the most dramatic visit is clearly that of Aunt Alicia, also a character from *The Four Banks*. She intrudes upon Harris while he is in his study and proceeds to shred the lecture he was preparing. As she destroys the lecture, she declares: "That's no good. No sort of formal essay for you. No oversimplifications. Speak out of your vulnerability. Speak from within your creative experiences."[16] These visits from fictional characters effect a radical decentering of Harris's everyday ego. The spell of ontic closure is decisively broken, bringing clear revelations of creative activities that were not its doing.

Another of Harris's favorite examples of intrusive addresses that disturb and fulfill the ego are those in which consciousness makes rocks talk and whole landscapes come alive. In describing the people who have influenced his writing, Harris includes the landscapes of his native Guyana as real interrogating presences with whom he had an ongoing dialogue. "It was a dialogue in which I sensed that I was being tested very deeply about the nature of reality, how I viewed reality, and not just by the people but by the landscape, which for a long time people had accepted as passive. . . . But landscape is not a passive creature because it has rhythms, it has complexities, it has dimensions, that address one in terms of all sorts of faculties that one has eclipsed in oneself."[17] In Harris's fiction, inauthentic characters are constantly having intrusive experiences in which they see the world from the perspective of the universal consciousness. In *Palace of the Peacock*, the narrator has a vision in which he sees the world through an eye he "shared only with the soul, the soul and mother of the universe."[18] In this vision, "I saw the tree in the distance wave its arms and walk when I looked at it through the spiritual eye of the soul."[19] In the world of consciousness landscapes are not permanently fixed as passive, silent matter. They can come alive in new ways by stepping out of such molds and addressing the ego in ways that challenge it to move from consolidation to fulfillment.

Such intrusions of consciousness into the world of the ego do not necessarily dislodge the latter's commitment to closure and self-sufficiency. As we have seen, they often lead to anxious flights or withdrawals, which usually reinforce existing straitjackets. This denial or concealing of the involuntary presence of consciousness is for Harris an inauthentic move. In fact, it represents the hubris of the ego. Authenticity requires the recognition of voidings and the decision to live out of them and the vulnerabilities they create. If the ego is able to accept these realities, it will discover an ability to digest certain kinds of traumas that are particularly fulfilling. This fulfillment is Harris's answer to the problems of closure and inauthenticity. It is here that we see important differences with both Hegel and Heidegger. Harris's authenticity does not come from Heidegger's being-towards-death, or Hegel's philosophical intuiting of absolute truth. Rather, it is to be found in the archetypal life that the ego can have with consciousness.

For Harris fulfillment is the opposite of consolidation. It is the growth that follows the clear recognition and acceptance of a voiding. This growth is a product of an archetypal life. To start on this path, the ego must be able to conquer the anxiety or dread it feels before these voidings by consciousness. We must be able to arrest the tendency for this dread to propel the ego into more egocentric consolidation. This hardening only blocks the path to fulfillment, which lies through the abyss and into the archetypal life. As long as the ego is struggling to conceal or reestablish its shattered world, the last thing it will want to do is experience and go through the void. But in this refusal, it cuts itself off from inflows of creative energy that are regenerative and fulfilling.

Like Fanon, the power and originality of Harris's ontology derives from his ability to navigate the voids in his life, the "zone of nonbeing" that the everyday ego strives so desperately to avoid. Fanon clearly recognized the regenerative potential that came from being able to navigate these states of nonbeing. Harris's archetypal life can be viewed as a mythopoetic filling out of the creative possibilities of voids that Fanon left unthematized, as he turned to the life of a revolutionary historical actor.

The foundation of the archetypal life is the honest facing of the challenges that a voiding poses for the ego. A void confronts the ego with a paradoxical challenge it initially finds overwhelming: it has been given the prereflective creative intelligence to constitute itself as an ego, but the void appears to be a blocking of the execution of this project. The launching of the archetypal life requires the acceptance of this challenge, this apparent defeat, as a first step in recognizing the legitimacy of voidings. With this legitimate recognition, the goal of the archetypal life becomes the exploring and understanding of the significance of a particular void for the growth, transformation, and fulfillment of the ego. This is what Harris means by the digesting of trauma.

For this digesting to proceed, the ego must slowly come to the realization that dread is not the meaning of the voidings or intrusive addresses by consciousness. It must also clearly recognize that its tendencies to flee or withdraw from consciousness are misguided and inappropriate responses. Much more appropriate would be the building of a relationship of trust. In this relationship the ego must learn to live in the void "with hope." In particular, the hope that consciousness, which had so generously voided itself so that the ego could come into being, would not abort its creation in this fashion. Rather, that beyond the void new intentional structures, new registers of creative intelligence will be available that will radically transform the ego's prereflective tendencies to premature closure.

Such transformations in the prereflective capabilities of the ego require a direct and extended apprenticeship of the ego to consciousness. Hence its voiding or involuntary silencing. In the course of this apprenticeship, the ego learns about life on another quantum plane. It learns of the archetypal order and textuality of this world that exists beyond its borders. While retaining its own quantum identity, the ego learns to think archetypally and to speak the archetypal language of consciousness. It develops the capacity to see itself from the archetypal perspective of consciousness. This shift in perspective slowly transforms the ego's view of itself, particularly its blind commitments to ontic closure and self-sufficiency. Only the assimilation of the lessons from this archetypal apprenticeship supplies the ego with a sense of alternatives that empowers it to conquer the dread that drives it toward the compulsive reinforcing of its closure. This compulsive dynamic must be arrested if fulfillment is to be realized.

During the ego's apprenticeship, it is exposed to the mythopoetic logic that governs the archetypal perspective of consciousness. Mythopoetic logic is paradoxical and partial, rather than syllogistic and universally sovereign. "Myth teaches us that sovereign gods and sovereign institutions are partial, partial in the sense that they are biased, but when they begin to penetrate their biases, they also begin to transform their fear of the other, of others, of other parts in a larger complex of wholeness."[20] Exposed to this mythopoetic logic, the straitjacketed ego is made to encounter the internal contradictions it is concealing, or experience new dimensions of reality that break the spell of its circular self-sufficiency. In other words, in the mythopoetic light of consciousness, the ego discovers the partial nature of its most sovereign universals.

The appearance of Aunt Alicia breaches the universal polarity that the ego has established between fiction and reality. Another of Harris's favorite examples is the figure of Tiresias from Greek myth. As punishment for striking two snakes while they are mating, Tiresias is turned into a woman and later changed back into a man. Here the universal consciousness transgresses the firm divide that the ego has established between male and female. With the fact that Ulysses descends into the world of the dead to consult him, Tiresias also breaches the ego's conventions separating life and death. Thus the ego's apprenticeship to such a figure exposes it to the logic of a different quantum layer that has the effect of revealing the partiality of its absolutes. From the Tiresian perspective, male and female, life and death are "related as diverse rooms, capacities expanding or contracting within the one field of consciousness"[21] that also supports the separative ego as another of its possibilities.

Fulfillment depends upon how much the prereflective core of the ego can learn from this mythopoetic recoding of its universals into partials. Only a substantial assimilation of these lessions will increase the ego's capability to be calm in the face of dread and hence its ability to interrupt and weaken its compulsive tendencies to reinforce closure. Such reduction in levels of egocentrism is the goal of the voidings by consciousness; the more profoundly the ego realizes this during its first apprenticeships, the smaller will be its problems with voidings. Prereflective centrism or narcissism on the part of the ego will always elicit resistance from consciousness. Thus Harrisian fulfillment is always in permanent opposition to ontic closure. It is the forever incomplete completing of the being of the ego, which is always an unfinished process.

These ego-fulfilling aspects of the archetypal life parallel in important ways the reconciliatory aspects of the destinal life of African existentialism. In both, the binary opposition self-determination/spiritual determination is resolved in favor of the latter. In other words, in both cases the philosophical subject is open to its spiritual ground and to its experiences of being constituted or voided by the latter. Consequently, when Harris invokes the African heritage, he is often drawn to its images of the ego in moments of spiritual intrusion that echo the dynamism of his archetypal life.

As a result, the African spaces in Harris's ontology are not modern, literate, and Pan-African as in the cases of James and Fanon, but rather traditional in orientation. African thought is represented in Harris's poeticism primarily through Afro-Caribbean creole formations such as Vodou and limbo. In Vodou ceremonies, Harris sees the dancers as "courting a subconscious community."[22] When the dancers enter the trance state, they become "a dramatic agent of subconsciousness."[23] These views of the ego in the light of its spiritual displacement are the primary contributions of the African heritage to Harris's poeticism. Both are ego-critical discourses in which the ego/spirit relationship is not only explicitly thematized but also serves as a founding analogy.

I consider the above outline to be the core of Harris's ontology of the everyday ego. It is an ontology that establishes the active, ongoing place of consciousness in the ego's project of being. Relying solely on its own creative intelligence, the ego is unable to complete its attempt at self-creation. Similar relations hold between consciousness and other domains of existence such as nature and society that are included in Harris's general ontology. What is distinctive about this ontology is the way in which Harris cybernetically maps and ranks the mutual founding and shaping of life forms on the various quanta of existence. Although Harris clearly privileges the level of consciousness, what is important is the relativity, the mutuality and interpenetrability of quantum-based ontological activities. Thus the ego can mold consciousness and vice versa. A similar relationship exists between nature and consciousness. The result is a decentered ontology in which quantum worlds merge seamlessly into each other, establishing and relativizing each other at the same time. These decentered features of Harris's ontology make it difficult to define it as idealist. It is clearly not materialist nor historicist. Because of these open-ended and fluid dynamics in his ontology, it is difficult to characterize Harris's philosophy by the domain to which he gives priority. A less obtrusive way to characterize his philosophy is through the method by which he approaches consciousness—a mythopoetic phenomenology.

POETICS: THE DISCOURSE OF THE ARCHETYPAL LIFE

To be effective, Harris's archetypal response to the ontological problems of the everyday ego requires an additional feature that we have not yet made explicit: a discourse that would give us access to the deeper unity of life that transcends the specific quantum levels of his general ontology. For Harris, this discourse is poetics, or what he often refers to as the "arts of the imagination." It is a discourse in which the quantum connections denied by the everyday realism of ego are taken seriously and creatively repaired when and where they are broken. The reestablishing of these severed ties is an important step in cultivating the archetypal life.

Poetics usually refers to strategies of symbolic and textual production, in particular to the ways in which concept, word, image, trope, plot, character, and other structural components of a work of art are brought together to create new meanings. But, for many authors, poetics is much more than the strategies by which meanings are produced in texts. It is also an ordering of meanings that is capable of shaping human behavior. In other words, when poetically constructed systems of meaning are internalized, their rules of formation, transformation, and deformation become a grammar of human self-formation and motivation. This action-orienting potential of poetics has been important for the Caribbean poeticist tradition. Harris shares this emphasis, and hence it is not the distinguishing feature of his poetics.

Harris's poetics can be distinguished by two of its important features. The first is the explicit way it incorporates consciousness into the system of meanings by which it orders human behavior. The second is the imagistic phenomenology through which it approaches consciousness. With regard to the first of these, it is the mythopoetic activity of consciousness that Harris's poetics incorporates into its register of meanings. Thus consciousness is incorporated as a site of agency that is not bound by the rules of ego existence or its patterns of textual production. Consciousness has its own distinct textuality. In fact the textuality of the ego depends upon and is often corrected by the textuality of consciousness. Indeed the goal of Harris's poetics is the mythopoetic recoding of the analytically oriented codings that the ego imposed on both consciousness and its own self-formative process. It is this decentered, fluid textuality of consciousness that shapes the distinctive action-orienting capabilities of Harris's poetics. It also determines the place of action, plot, character, and those incredible sliding metaphors in Harris's projects of literary production.

What is philosophically important in Harris's inclusion of consciousness in his poetics is the notion of a deeper unity to life that becomes operative in it. This is the unity of the world as a continuum that transcends the specific levels of the general ontology and the unities of the ego level in particular. This unity derives from the creative role that consciousness plays in the genesis and maintenance of all life forms. From playing these diverse creative roles, consciousness must possess the ability to translate and transcend the intentional codes and mechanical laws that make distinct forms and planes of existence possible. When Harris speaks of the "texts of nature, spirit and being,"[24] this is the archetypal textuality he has in mind. Its codes constitute the unwritten book of life, the unstruck music of the universe, and the unargued philosophy of our world.

Harris refers to the unity of this textuality of consciousness as the "fabric of the imagination."[25] This notion implies that "there has been a genesis of the imagination somewhere within the interstices of unrecorded time, that the unique—indeed inimitable—force of such a genesis imbues the human psyche with flexible and far flung roots in all creatures, all elements, all worlds and constellations, all sciences, all spaces susceptible to visualization."[26] In other words, the imaginative textuality of the ego is threaded into the fabric of the imagination, the unity of the textuality of consciousness.

Harris's poetics requires of us the ability to engage discursively the larger unity that is implicit in the imaginative fabric of consciousness. This is necessary if the archetypal life is to be sustained and represented. But through ontic closure, "we have been conditioned to freeze such an awe-inspiring and wonderful notion of the genesis of the imagination into an obsession with binding and homogenous archetype."[27] Through this important notion of unity, Harris's poetics here incorporates and reflects the dynamics of his ontology. Hence its importance to the prescriptive or action-orienting side of his poetics.

The second distinguishing feature of Harris's poetics is the imagistic phenomenology through which it approaches consciousness. As noted earlier, Harris's archetypal life requires a mythopoetic return of the ego to consciousness. This problem of getting the ego to reopen to consciousness leads, however guardedly, to a methodology of some sort, that is, a method of how to approach consciousness from the plane of the ego. In the religious and philosophical literatures, there are a wide variety of models for repairing broken relations between the ego and consciousness, the latter being conceived in widely differing ways. In traditional African religions there is the method of spiritual possession. In the religions of Asia, it is yoga and meditation. In Western phenomenological philosophy, the method of the phenomenological and eidetic reductions were used to disclose a transcendental consciousness that was not visible to the everyday or "natural attitude." Harris's method differs from all of these, but in their terms could be best described as a combination of the African religious and the Western phenomenological approaches.

If by phenomenology we mean a reflective description of the activities of consciousness following the bracketing of the natural attitude by some ego-displacing technique, then Harris's method can be described as phenomenological. It reflects on consciousness and employs two techniques for bracketing the natural attitude of the everyday ego. The first is what I shall call a *de-intentionalized reduction*; and the second is the technique of quantum reading, or reading creative images from the mythopoetic perspective of consciousness.

I use the concept of a de-intentionalized reduction to capture the way in which Harris converts voids, traumas, or de-intentionalized states into "gateways" that reveal what is beyond ego awareness. In other words, the digesting of voids that immobilize ego genesis becomes a methodological device when they are conceptualized as gateways. As one goes through these portals, it becomes necessary to change one's attitude toward the inherited world of the ego. It becomes possible to bracket it in ways that phenomenologists do and proceed with the describing of the activities of consciousness. This consciousness will of course be a very different one from that of the phenomenologists. The de-intentionalized reduction is different from the eidetic and phenomenological reductions of transcendental phenomenology although it performs a similar function. It is much closer to the use of negative ego states by existential phenomenologists. However, the latter don't always let these states be gateways to the world beyond the ego.

The second technique Harris's poetics employs for bracketing the everyday world is the quantum reading of creative images. In quantum readings, we make or reestablish connections between planes of existence or between binary opposites on the same planes, that are suppressed by the everyday attitude. The rose becoming a particle and wave, and the table becoming tree and lungs of the globe are cases in point. Here, Harris wants to do this kind of reading with creative images. Creative images are the carriers of codes and meanings from both ego and consciousness. The textuality of both meet in these images. As noted earlier, the mythopoetics that the ego uses in self-formation is different from that used by consciousness. The more centered, analytic, and reductive codings of the ego tend to tone down the polyvalent, "contradictory," and decentered codings of consciousness. However, in the mythopoetic registers of the ego many of the connecting threads between creative images that exist in the imaginative fabric of consciousness are "broken" or concealed. Thus creative images can be read from the perspectives of these two sites of agency. The quantum reading takes the point of view of consciousness and seeks to reestablish broken ties between creative images or to discover new ones between them.

Harris often does quantum readings of the creative images in his own work. Thus he is constantly making connections between images in different works of his own fiction and between these creative images and those of writers in different cultures and different times. For example, Harris discusses the image of sailing vessels in three of his novels, *Carnival*, *The Infinite Rehearsal*, and *The Four Banks of the River of Space*. In the last of these, the image is linked to the image of the city of God. Harris goes on to suggest that this chain of connections was not a chance occurrence or the result of deliberate action on his part. Rather, it was the result of "a surrender to the intuitive element in the images."[28] In other words, there is an objective process involved in these intuitive connections, that one surrenders to and learns how to access discursively.

To take another example, in *Carnival*, Herman Melville's Bartleby "metamorphoses into a woman called Alice Bartleby."[29] Dante's Beatrice becomes Amaryllis, the hero's wife, while Everyman Masters is his Virgilian guide. For Harris, these are not intellectual propositions. On the contrary, they are cross-cultural connections thrown up by a different mythopoetic logic of consciousness, which is connecting these images in ways that are different from those made by the ego. This is the logic that counters the logic of the ego and helps the Harrisian phenomenologist, in conjunction with the de-intentionalized reduction, to bracket the everyday world.

Given this imagistic phenomenology of consciousness, it should come as no surprise that Harris's poetics reserves a very special place for the artist. The role of the Harrisian artist is to dissolve and overturn the straitjacketed condition of the ego; to break open the cells of subjectivity in which the ego imprisons itself when voided by consciousness. In the case of the Caribbean, the artist is also confronted with straitjacketing that derives from the implosive traumas of colonization discussed earlier. Harris sees these traumas as similar to voidings by consciousness. Thus they can result in closures that conceal voids, blockages, and anxieties. Hence these closures also become the terrain of the artist. The disruption of both sets of closures must lead to new and more expansive relations with consciousness, nature, and society. Harris's goal is nothing short of a new architecture between the Caribbean ego and consciousness, or a whole new set of "subconscious alliances." This is the Harrisian revolution.

The primary agent of this revolution is the insurrectionary artist. He or she directs firepower not at overt political and economic structures, but rather at the inauthentic, onto-existential connections between ego and consciousness that run much deeper than the circumstantial political or economic situation. The immediate focus of the Harrisian artist is not the being of the economy, but "the economy of being." Such is the clear ontological mission of this artist. In this revolution, the power he or she mobilizes is not that of the party or the masses but the "re-visionary" powers of an imagination that has been schooled in the quantum literacy of consciousness.

Harris attributes the persistence of the postcolonial crisis of Caribbean society to our failure to take seriously this kind of revolutionary poetic praxis. We've ignored the mythopoetic ways of treating our voids whether their origins were in acts of consciousness or of colonizers. Instead, we followed the paths of consolidation, resistance, and compensatory action. These are inauthentic moves, which can only result in the premature exhaustion of creativity. This exhaustion can only be avoided by creating out of the paradigmatic situation of the Caribbean ego, which for Harris is the void. The "subject which is being approached exists in a void and therefore one needs to participate in it, I believe, with an art of fiction, an imaginative fluidity that is as close as one can possibly come now, with immediacy, in a form that has already been broken in the past."[30] Thus Harris's poetics eventuates in a critical imaginative praxis that aims at transforming the ego into a more authentic and genuinely creative agent of postcolonial transformation. Harris regards this ontological transformation of the Caribbean ego as a precondition for the vision and creativity necessary for successful postcolonial reconstruction.

HARRIS AND CARIBBEAN HISTORICISM

Given the expository nature of this chapter, this is not the place for a detailed critique of Harris's philosophy. Rather I've envisioned my task as the gentle resisting of Aunt Alicia's injunction against formal essays that explicitly thematize Harris's philosophy. However, this chapter would not be complete without a clearer situating of Harris in relation to the tradition of historicist writing in the region. Unfortunately, these two schools have not really understood each other, nor have they dialogued sufficiently. As a long-standing historicist, I am very aware of these misunderstandings and the poor quality of our dialogue with the poeticists. Thus one of my primary goals in doing this philosophical translation of Harris is to relocate him in an intermediary discursive space that may facilitate a more constructive dialogue.

After this engagement with Harris, I am convinced that much of the tension between these two schools is rooted in an implicit difference that has never been made explicit and fully discussed: a difference over the ontology of the Caribbean ego. In the case of Harris, it becomes a difference between a phenomenological ontology and the sociohistorical ontology of the historicists. This is the underthematized philosophical issue that has blocked constructive dialogue between Caribbean poeticists and historicists. The blockage is further complicated by the fact that poeticists differ significantly among themselves in their conceptions of consciousness and the nature of its mythopoetic activity.

For example, in Sylvia Wynter's poeticism, a categorical unconscious takes the place of Harris's consciousness. She shares with Harris the position that ego transformation is a precondition for postcolonial reconstruction. However, the nature of this ego transformation is very different. In Wynter's case, the unconscious mythopoetic dynamics, which auto-institute the ego and which are in need of change, are the prereflective, centered, comparatively more analytic and reductive symbolic capabilities of early ego formation. They are not supplemented or corrected by anything that corresponds to Harris's consciousness. These symbolic capabilities of the ego are grounded in what Wynter calls "epistemes." These are founding or onto-epistemic categories of the ego that are prereflectively and "autopoetically instituted." The problems that these prereflectively instituted epistemes create for the ego are the focus of Wynter's concern, and not ontic closure.

The failure to put squarely on the table these differences in poeticists approaches to the ego and their differences with the historicist approach has led to talking past each other. A good example is James becoming incensed at Harris's observation that "it is one of the ironic things with West Indians of my generation that they may conceive of themselves in the most radical political light but their approach to art and literature is one which consolidates the most conventional and documentary techniques in the novel."[31] Responding to this "political matter," James proceeds to lecture Harris on the nature of political radicalism and the sociohistorical significance of Caribbean literature, including Harris's fiction. Of particular interest is James's defense of Naipaul, asserting that A House For Mr. Biswas "was the finest study ever produced in the West Indies of a minority."[32] It is precisely the sociohistorical determination of Naipaul's characters that James likes. By contrast, it is this determination that leads Harris to describe the novel as conventional, with its characters never asking "revolutionary or alien questions of spirit."[33] The underlying difference here is clearly the ontology of character in the novel, which reflects differences over the ontology of the human ego.

Historicists find three positions of Harris's poeticism particularly difficult to recognize: (1) the priority that the ego/consciousness relationship takes over the ego/society relationship; (2) the suggestion that the traumas of colonialism are to be read on the model of a voiding by consciousness; and (3) that the transformation of the postcolonial ego is a precondition for postcolonial reconstruction.

The displacement of the ego/society relationship by the ego/consciousness relationship reflects very sharp differences in views on the nature of consciousness and the ontology of the ego. Historicists have operated with a much more restricted view of consciousness than either Harris or Wynter. We have also operated for the most part with a largely nonproblematic view of the ontology of the everyday ego. For most historicists, the term *consciousness* refers to ego consciousness, the capacity of the ego to be aware of itself and its surroundings. It is a unique feature of human life. As such, it provides the framework for the reflective levels of our lives, particularly our discursive activities. Consequently, there is no equivalent to Harris's universal consciousness or Wynter's categorical unconscious among the historicists. The closest parallel is the concept of history as dynamic becoming. The major exception to these claims is clearly Fanon, who is an important bridge figure, but he has seldom been treated as such. As a historicist, he retained a concept of consciousness that is comparable to those of Harris and Wynter.

Similar patterns mark the differences between these two schools over the ontology of the ego. When it is problematic, historicists have seen this ontology largely as a social issue, resulting either from poor institutional support, systematic oppression, or destructive personal interactions. Beyond these considerations, the ontology of the ego is an issue that we have treated as a nonproblematic given, which could be put on hold and addressed in the future. The ego's capacity for effective action is thus not the result of good ego/consciousness relations but good ego/society relations. An effective ego, one capable of creative historical action, was a consequence of good social interactions on the formation of the human individual. History is thus the ontological medium par excellence, not language or consciousness. These ontological differences have never really been put on the table and discussed. We've never really gotten past the polemical phase of ideologically defending the ego/consciousness position or the ego/society position. These ontological differences deserve a more serious philosophical hearing.

The second position of Harris that surprises the historicist is his suggestion that we read our postcolonial dilemmas on the model of a voiding by consciousness. If the first position pointed to serious differences over the nature of consciousness, then this points to equally significant differences over foundational issues: that is, history and consciousness as referential finalities and how we are to handle differences over these special points of reference. Further, this second position raises some very important questions concerning the consequences of the ontological dynamics of the ego for historical action. Here Harris is insisting that anxious relations and unresolved problems with consciousness make for an inauthentic, uncreative, and poor performing ego. Unresolved problems with consciousness are often dealt with inauthentically by seeking ontological supplements in compensatory activities such as dominating others or demanding conformity from them that is ego supportive, in other words, a form of primitive ontological accumulation that covers the nonperforming spots in one's "economy of being." Thus unresolved ontological problems can impose an alien accumulative logic on the creative action that would solve a problem, thus undermining the ego's performance capabilities. Hence it is important to deal with these ontological issues on their own terms if historical action is not to be invaded by alien demands that exhaust its creativity and abort its projects.

This I think is an excellent point that historicists have not given sufficient consideration. At the same time, it raises the question of whether or not Harris is here conflating two quantum levels in a way that reduces the agency of history. In the traumas of colonial societies, voiding by consciousness and voidings by imperial violence meet, interact, and recode each other. What is different in Harris's position is his prioritizing of the mythopoetic recodings of the ego by consciousness over the politico-economic recodings by imperialism. For Harris, this ordering of priorities is particularly important for postcolonial societies like those in the Caribbean. These societies do not have the option of covering up their nonresolution of ontological problems with imperial activity, excessive capital accumulation, or compensatory consumption. In Wynter, we find a similar prioritizing of the mythopoetic over the politico-economic. She emphasizes the uprooting of the liminal categorizing of Caribbean people (Fanon's imago?) as "the other" that helps to sustain "the we" of the imperial West. Thus in both cases, we have changes in the mythopoetic coding of the Caribbean ego, being made the primary conditions for postcolonial transformation.

Like many historicists, I sense here a displacement that unnecessarily compromises the relative autonomy of political economy. Particularly in the case of Harris, the mythopoetics of the ego/consciousness relationship replaces a historicized political economy as the grammar of human self-formation. The latter is given such a secondary status that it becomes incorrect to view the current Caribbean crisis in strategic economic and political terms, rather than mythopoetic ones. Instead, we should be viewing it as a de-intentionalized state with surrender and the appropriate mythopoetic recoding of the ego as our first and most important response. This seems to me an unsatisfactory conflating of the mythopoetic and the politico-economic, where a more dialectical linking should be. This unsatisfactory nature of the links between consciousness and history as referential finalities or founding analogies points once again to the need for a more serious philosophical hearing.

Our third and last of Harris's positions is his claim that ego recoding and transformation must be preconditions for postcolonial reconstruction. This is the exact opposite of the position that historicists have taken. Our precondition has been the structural transformation of basic institutions, particularly the state and the economy. These are clearly prescriptive or policy differences that reflect the different stances taken on the two previous issues. Given the importance Harris attaches to consciousness, it follows that he would make the resolving of ego/consciousness relations a precondition for successful developmental action. Similarly, given our view of history it certainly makes sense to us that changes in the institutional foundations of historical action are preconditions for successful postcolonial development. Thus it should be clear that differences over this problem cannot be resolved without addressing the deeper issues upon which they rest. So once again the need for a philosophical dialogue becomes very apparent.

Needless to say, what poeticists find unacceptable in historicists is our prioritizing of the ego-society relationship and the way in which we work out its implications for creative transformation. This is clear in Harris's discomfort with the social realism of James's *The Black Jacobins*. Harris is uncomfortable with James's attempts "to smooth a number of cracks in building his portrait"[34] of Toussaint L'Overture. According to Harris, James sees these "flaws" as resulting from a secretive mentality, while he sees in them L'Overture "groping towards an original vision, an alternative to conventional statehood."[35] For Harris, L'Overture emerges from James's text "not because he fits where James wants him to stand, but because he escapes the author's self-determination in the end."[36] In other words, L'Overture escaped the net of James's social ontology.

I will not develop this side of the debate in great detail. That I think should be done by the poeticists. However, the above sampling can serve as clear testimony on behalf of its existence. What is important for us here is that sources of this conflict are on both sides. It is my view that the responses of the Caribbean imagination to our social crisis have been both historicist and poeticist, not one or the other. These discursive responses belong together, not apart. Together they constitute the total Caribbean response to the trauma of colonization. They have appeared together in so many of our major thinkers only to separate in one direction or the other. Thus they have appeared together in James, Fanon, Aime Cesaire, Edward Kamau Brathwaite, George Lamming, Orlando Patterson, Rex Nettleford, and V. S. Naipaul. These writers with varying degrees of success have been able to forge some measure of unity between these historicist and poeticist traditions that have been so basic to thought in the region. Hence the need to get beyond the above impasse that currently separates them is very real. The concerted contributions of both are, no doubt, necessary for the developmental tasks that still lie ahead of us. Our failure to bring these two traditions into a more creative unity reflects our failure to give them the philosophical hearing they deserve. This in turn reflects the fragmented and underthematized state of contemporary Caribbean philosophy.

In sum, I've tried to demonstrate the originality and distinctiveness of the philosophy that exists implicitly in Harris's fiction and critical essays. I've suggested two primary sources for this originality. The first was Harris's ability to explore firsthand the world of consciousness that lies beyond the ego. The second was his creation of a unique poeticist discourse for reporting and fictionalizing the results of his explorations. Consequently, in spite of sharing insights and positions with the Hegelian and existential traditions of the West, I've argued that Harris's philosophy is best understood as a bold and breathtaking move within the tradition of Caribbean poeticism.

Further, I argued that the specific ontological claims of Harris's poeticism and its archetypal practices separate his philosophy quite sharply from Hegel's or Heidegger's. I agree with James that Harris's and Heidegger's philosophies converge around the dynamics of authenticity and inauthenticity. James is absolutely right when he suggests that Harris is concerned with issues of being, time, dread, and consciousness. But James's analysis fails to deal adequately with the divergences. In particular, divergences such as Harris's approaching of these issues through the colonial question and his focus on the archetypal life.

Similarly, I agree with Shaw that in the fluidity of their categories, the philosophies of Harris and Hegel converge. Further, as Shaw suggests, there is a definite convergence between the spiritual trajectories of *The Phenomenology of Spirit* and the *Palace of the Peacock*. But again the convergences are not enough to make Harris's philosophy Hegelian. Harris's words and images are much more fluid than Hegel's. Their logic is not always dialectical, but often mythopoetic. Thus they move and change in ways that Hegel's dialectic would not predict.

What of the African religious themes in the *Palace*? What of the radical divergence between the spiritual trajectories of *The Secret Ladder* and *The Phenomoenology*? The spiritual trajectory of this novel is definitely not

Hegelian. As the figure of an African Poseidon suggest, it is much closer to the spiritual trajectories of classical Greek or African religion. These divergences force us to recognize the distinctiveness of Harris's poeticism. It has opened very real gateways to African, Amerindian, Indian, and European spirituality, but none of these individually can capture or erase its originality.

Finally, in engaging Harris's poeticism, my strategy has been to follow closely his quantum readings, but emphasizing the conceptual rather than the imagistic elements in his intuitive connections. This was for me a very stimulating and creative experience. It has permanently changed my historicism. Conceptually read, Harris's imagistic connections constitute an inexhaustible source of Caribbean philosophical ideas, particularly in relation to the ontology of the ego. With all due respects to Aunt Alicia, this gold mine/mind should not be overlooked by philosophers.

Unity, Rationality, and Africana Thought

PART TWO

Sylvia Wynter: Poststructuralism and Postcolonial Thought

FOR SYLVIA WYNTER ON HER 66TH BIRTHDAY.

Then the foaming rabid maw of the tidal wave swallowing Port Royal, and that was Jonah.

—DEREK WALCOTT

Know that at this stage of world history and your own history there can be no progress in the West Indies unless it begins with you (the masses) and grows as you grow.

—C. L. R. JAMES

The samples of Afro-Caribbean philosophy examined in the previous section have made clear not only the nature of this body of thought but also some of its major problems. Our focus on Wynter, Habermas, and Afro-American philosophy in this section of the text represents a shift away from exposition and toward issues in and around the field of Afro-Caribbean philosophy. One of the major problems that emerged from our sampling of Harris's work was that of potential unities that have remained unrealized. In particular, we focused on the duality that has inhibited richer exchanges between historicists and poeticists. This chapter examines the attempt of Sylvia Wynter to bridge this divide. Wynter's attempt is a part of her larger effort at rethinking the problems of postcolonial reconstruction in the region, following the collapse of both liberal and socialist projects of transformation. Wynter's primary instrument for building this new bridge is poststructuralist theory.

An outstanding novelist, playwright, and critic from Jamaica, Wynter's creative and world-constituting activities have been both reconstructive and transformative. Their primary focus has been the practical problems created by the internal contradictions of the postcolonial ideologies of the region. The originality of Wynter's contribution derives from her invitation to both historicists and poeticists to make an epistemic turn.

This turn challenges us to focus more closely on the founding categories of our intellectual and political discourses and a little less on the social situation to be changed or the ontology of the everyday self. This categorical focus is an orientation that she shares with poststructuralists. Thus it is not surprising that Wynter makes extensive use of poststructuralist theory, particularly its concern with chains of signification, the metaphorical play within these chains, and how they are grounded. Wynter makes both brilliant and playful use of these semiotic appropriations, producing strikingly original ideas, which are elaborated with virtuoso performances of metaphorical play. Wynter's playful elaborations of very serious ideas can only be compared to the exquisitely decorated notes of Sarah Vaughan's singing. She is in so many ways "the Divine One" of Caribbean letters.

I will argue that three important results for Caribbean thought have followed her epistemic turn. The first is that she departs from an important poeticist philosophy of history that the early Wynter shared with writers such as Wilson Harris, Derek Walcott, and Edouard Glissant. The second is that she also departs from historicists like Frantz Fanon and C. L. R. James, who constitute the other important Caribbean approach to historical change. Third, Wynter's attempt to establish a poststructuralist bridge between these two philosophies of history reveals very clearly both the limitations and possibilities of poststructuralist thought in relation to the problems of postcolonial reconstruction in the Caribbean. Wynter's bridge shows not only the capabilities of poststructuralist thought to deal with categorical and mythopoetic issues but also its limitations in dealing with the institutional and ego-genetic issues related to postcolonial transformation.

The overall result of Wynter's contribution is a very constructive engagement between poststructuralism and postcolonial thought in the Caribbean. Unlike the poststructuralism of Michael Dash and David Scott, Wynter's engagement does not create new dualities between historicism and poeticism or reinforce old ones. In Dash's work, most of the standard poststructuralist dualities between language and its others (subject, spirit, history) are very present. Consequently, in spite of his rejection of discursive totalities, language as founding analogy is totalized and hardened into the analytic position from which all texts are interpreted and evaluated. The result is an almost sectarian deployment of poststructuralism in which writers like Fanon and Cesaire are othered because of their nonlinguistic approaches to textual production.[1] As we will see in chapter 9, a similar essentializing of language occurs in the case of Scott, in spite of essentialism being a cardinal sin in poststructuralist thought.[2] In Wynter's more dialectical engagement, these essentializing tendencies are contained by poststructuralism's supplementary relations with Marxism and Pan-Africanism.

POSTSTRUCTURALISM AND POSTCOLONIAL THOUGHT

Poststructuralism is a special type of cogito-critical philosophy, as opposed to an ego-critical one. Like other critical philosophies (e.g., Kant, Hegel) its aim is a self-reflexive examination of the cogito-conditions of knowledge production. What distinguishes it from other critical philosophies is the special type of reflexivity it brings to the task of analyzing the foundations of knowledge. In the place of the reflexive philosophical cogito, it puts the reflexivity of language as theorized by semiotics and concretized by the modernist or nonrepresentational text. This displacing of the subject, by the play of systems of signifiers, positions the poststructuralist for new critiques of ego or subject-centered systems of thought. The latter (e.g., structuralism Hegelianism, or Marxism) tended to be carefully constructed closed systems, whose closure in large measure resulted from their being centered or grounded in what was taken to be an absolute presence.

The critical or deconstructive strategies of poststructuralism are aimed precisely at the discursive mediations between posited centers and the closed systems that philosophical subjects have produced. As in a modernist text, the aim is to expose the discursive strategies and maneuvers, the epistemic violence that make closed systems possible. This is the practice of deconstruction. It is marked by a refusal to accept at face value all positive or determinate discursive formulations, denotative representations, fixed constructions, or essentialized formulations, however brief or provisional. These must be dissolved into the play of the signifiers of which they are effects.[3] In this dissolving aspect, deconstructive critiques are similar to but also different from dialectical critiques. Here the model of ever-moving, de-centered systems of signifiers that produce and destroy texts is the basis for critique.

Needless to say, the impact of poststructuralist thought has been far-reaching. It has not only decentered philosophical discourses but also social discourses such as Marxism and nationalism. The tension between poststructuralism and postcolonial thought has been sharpest where the former attempts to de-center or displace the theoretical and ideological discourses that supported the anticolonial struggles of Third-World peoples. These discourses were largely nationalist, antiracist, and Marxist in nature, with specific historical projects of postcolonial reconstruction. In spite of their differences, the fulfillment of these projects centered around state-led actions. From the poststructuralist point of view, all of these projects employed essentialized notions of history and the state.[4] Poststructuralist critiques have not only challenged these ideologies and essentialized notions but also have attributed to them many of the tragedies and crises of postcolonial transformation. Thus Homi Bhabha and Paul Gilroy have tried to separate postcolonial transformation from these ideologies and notions.

The tension between poststructuralism and postcolonial thought in the Caribbean derives in part from different approaches to history. One of the consequences of European colonization has been that Caribbean people have had no other option but to seek their postcolonial future through historical action on the national and international stages. Postcolonial reconstruction has meant leaving behind the comforts of a mythopoetically ordered society and undertaking the task of building a modern technologically ordered one. This experiment in societal reorganization has not been an evolutionary, but rather an historical undertaking. That is, with the state as chief executive agent, this reorganization must be undertaken consciously and collectively.

For writers like Garvey, Padmore, James, and Fanon, this historical immersion became the basis for an historicist reading of the Caribbean experience and an equally historicist projection of its future. Through populist and state-led collective action, Caribbean people would liberate themselves and build a new society through either a proletarian, nationalist, or African revolution or some combination of these. Because history was the medium in which this transformation would take place, it acquired an ontological or formative status in these writers. It was the medium in which Caribbean identities and social structures would experience redefinition and reconstellation.[5]

In contrast to this onto-historic response to the colonial thrust into history is the poeticist response. This approach seeks to replace the special constituting position given to history by the historicists with the task of reassembling the mythopoetic fragments of our shattered premodern world. History as the medium and place of postcolonial recovery is replaced by the creative powers of mythopoetic self-determination. This ontological positioning of mythopoetic processes is strongest in Caribbean writers like Derek Walcott, Wilson

Harris, Edouard Glissant, and Alejo Carpentier. For Walcott, history is any-thing but the primary medium of self-creation or redefinition. Like the Irish novelist James Joyce, history is for him an "insomniac night" in spite of which he must continue the real creative work of "renaming and finding new metaphors"[6] with which to fashion the desired postcolonial reconstruction.

Colonial histories are particularly nightmarish for Walcott in that they attempt mythopoetic redefinitions of the identity, space, and history of a people. For the poeticist, this mythopoetic framing or reframing is founda-tional. Before objects, persons, or events can be historicized they must be mythopoetically named or semanticized in some way. This original naming is the work of poets and mythmakers. Within these frameworks, names are not fixed forever. Very often objects, persons, or events need to be re-presented or resemanticized. The primary locus of these naming, formative, and transfor-mative activities is not history but "that self-astonishing elemental force,"[7] the mind.

As we've seen, the displacing of the historicist position is very strongly devel-oped in the works of Wilson Harris. Harris is concerned not only with the unnaming and renaming tendencies of colonial histories but also with the dif-ficulties he associates with all ego-centered historical projects. In Harris's view, historical action is often the product of the surface layers of an ego-centered mind. The problem with ego-centeredness is that it is achieved through the radical suppression of the gods, which are mythological representations of the formative powers of the unconscious mind. The corresponding phenomenon in Wynter is the "degodding of nature."[8] Cut off from the guidance and sym-bolic inputs of the universal consciousness by its tendencies to ontic closure, the conscious ego imprisons itself in partial and limited appropriations of real-ity. For Harris, these necessary but problematic centralizing tendencies can only be balanced or compensated by the actions of a de-centered agent such as consciousness. Like Glissant, Harris rejects all totalized views of history—Marxist, nationalist, or Hegelian—that are ego centered and cut off from the compensatory mythopoetic influences of consciousness. The emancipatory projects of these totalized views of history are fragmentary truths that consti-tute poor guides for historical transformation. Without the countertendencies of a de-centered agency, these ego-centered historical projects can only result in tragedy and betrayal of promises.

Thus in Harris's works, a vertical "drama of consciousness" competes with or displaces the horizontal historical dramas of nationalism, proletarian libera-tion, or societal reorganization. A similar theme of periodic mythopoetic bap-tisms in the sea of consciousness can be found in Walcott. In his poem, "The Sea is History," Walcott uses this theme to establish the sea as both the womb and tomb of ego-centered history: "\Where are your monuments, your battles,

Martyrs/ Where are your tribal memories? Sirs,/ In that grey vault. The Sea/The Sea has locked them up/The sea is History."⁹ These "vertical" encounters between the historicized ego and consciousness are parental, corrective, and redemptive in nature. They are to facilitate growth through the ego's integrating of parts of itself that were repressed or unknown.

This onto-poetic response to the historical challenges of postcolonial reconstruction contains a view of history and its relation to the constituting activities of the mind that prefigured or anticipated many of the views of the poststructuralists. Thus it should come as no surprise that writers like Glissant and Wynter found significant echoes in the works of these philosophers. Earlier, we saw that the goal of poststructuralism was to produce a modernist philosophy—that is, a philosophy that showed and examined its own strategies of textual production, and which also sought to expose the textual strategies of other philosophies that had an interest in concealing their own textuality. These constructive and deconstructive projects required that the de-centered but reflexive agency of language replace the reflexive subject as the innovative and revolutionary starting point of critical philosophy. This textual/linguistic turn in philosophy and social theory was also the starting point for a new understanding of history in the context of an advanced capitalism that seemed capable of seducing or neutralizing all opposition. It was an understanding of history as a text. As text, history loses its finality, determinism, and the paramountcy of its reality. These qualities of objectivity, permanence, unity, telos, and totality were all inscribed effects, written into being by the discursive strategies of ideological production. As inscribed effects they could as easily be undone by pulling apart the fabric of their textuality. History thus becomes an essentialized and totalized ideological construction that should be deconstructed and reconstellated on the model of a modernist text. From this perspective, the goals of history are both relativized and reinterpreted as the play of partial possibilities.

This emphasis on the play of possibilities brought with it new conceptions of freedom, of the political actor, and of politics. Freedom was no longer defined in opposition to institutional and physical domination. Instead, it became a communicative practice that was defined largely in opposition to the centralizing and essentializing tendencies in discourses we normally use. The free-floating signifier that moves beyond the constraints of a closed system of thought became the new image of freedom. Wynter defines this new freedom as "the autonomy of human cognition" from the imperatives of overrepresenting its social and cultural formations.¹⁰ The new political actor is distinguished by his or her ability to de-center and expose the founding categories and discursive strategies of his or her ideology or emancipatory project. Politics thus becomes a twofold communicative process. On the offensive side, the enemy to be overthrown is discursive authoritarianism. On the defensive side, efforts must be made to deal with the multiplying but undecidable discursive plural- ism that results from the abandonment of discursive authoritarianism.

Some of the similarities between the poststructuralist and the poeticist approaches to history should now be clear. Both dissolve the objectivity of his- tory by exposing its totalized ideological forms to their polar opposites in the de-centered agencies of either language or the universal consciousness. These totalized projections then appear as illusory halves, fragments or artifacts of either an uncompensated ego-centeredness or an uncompensated discursive authoritarianism. However, in spite of the shared tendencies toward the de- centering of ego-based historical projects, the differences in de-centering agents make for significant differences in how de-centered projects are viewed. Poststructuralist de-centering (deconstruction) often brings a collapse of belief in historical projects, which has produced a lot of talk about the end of his- tory.[11] Poeticist de-centering tends to rescue historical projects by supplement- ing their partial realities and lessening the hostility and resistance from the gods that they generate.

In the historicist tradition, this concern with the vertical drama of the de- centering and recentering of ego consciousness is eclipsed by the focus on praxis, the activity of making and implementing conscious decisions aimed at realizing emancipatory projects. A strong emphasis is placed upon the political economy of praxis by historicists and hence the importance of popular and state transformations of modes of economic production. History is the medium or stage upon which we engage in praxis. De-centering plays a more limited role in this philosophy of history. Consequently, it is not characterized by as sharp a categorical turn as the Wynterian or the poststructuralist philoso- phies of history. De-centering is employed almost exclusively to unmask strate- gic misrepresentations of self and others that are motivated by interests in group exploitation. The vertical dramas of ego consciousness are therefore con- tained within the historical dramas of transforming societies. In short, an important difference between the historicists and the poststructuralists is that the latter erase most of the difference between praxis and deconstruction.

The tensions between these three philosophies of history are crucial for understanding Wynter's reformulation of the colonial problematic. Wynter's work has always been characterized by attempts to bridge the historicist and poeticist traditions. It is from this bridge that she attempts to reformulate the postcolonial problematic in the Caribbean. What has changed over the years is the nature of the bridge she has placed between them. As we will see, this is the task for which she appropriates poststructuralist theory.

SYLVIA WYNTER: HISTORY AND THE LIMINAL CATEGORY

Whereas Derek Walcott's view of history echoes Joyce's, Sylvia Wynter's view of history echoes Walter Benjamin's. Although committed to working-class liberation in history, Benjamin's view of the historical process was not the familiar Marxian one of ordered progressive development through praxis. Rather history is a maelstrom in which we struggle with our backs to the future, and whose piles of wreckage keep getting higher.[12] A similar ambivalence marks Wynter's conception of Caribbean history. She is committed to the liberation of the colonized and racialized African through historical action, but sees historical projects leading more often to Benjaminian piles of wreckage than to liberation. These wreckage's and their betrayals void or interrupt the more progressive or teleological constructions of history that we find in James and Fanon.

Wynter's primary intellectual concern has been to account for this tendency of Caribbean historical projects to produce more blindness than insights, more error than truth, more destruction than growth, and more repression than liberation. Her point of departure is the poetics of knowing, the semiotic and mythopoetic processes that establish our categories of knowing. By focusing so directly on our cognitive categories and away from the self or the universal consciousness, Wynter makes a very definite epistemic turn within the poeticist tradition. With this turn, her answers to the above concerns focus more on the error-proneness of the cultural categories and discursive strategies with which our historical projects are constructed. In particular, it is to the systemic errors of what Wynter calls the liminal categories of totalized discourses that she attributes the additions that postcolonial societies are making to the rising piles of historical wreckage. Here liminal categories would be the categories that are diametrically opposed to a core or founding category of one of these ideological discourses. The regressive dialectics generated by liminal categories Wynter uses as a discursive check on the progressive dialectics of class, race, and national liberation that drive the Jamesian and Fanonian philosophies of history.

THE EARLY FICTION

This error-prone view of the totalized projects through which we construct history is evident in Wynter's early fiction, although it shares the stronger psychological orientation of the poeticist approach. In *The Hills of Hebron* she examines the historical fate of the Jamaican urban underclass at the turn of the twentieth century. Three liberating projects were formed by this class fraction in response to its social position: the Garvey movement, the labor movement, and small utopian communities. Wynter's focus is on a case of the latter: the community of New Believers, who left the urban jungles of Kingston to set up a "New Canaan" in the hills of Hebron. The novel chronicles the decline and collapse of this attempt at self-liberation.

In the unraveling of this historical project, two factors stand out in Wynter's portrayal. The first is that most of the New Believers at one point or another found it necessary to resort to madness as an escape valve or coping strategy. "They had a respect for madness," says Wynter. "It was a private nirvana a man could reach when he was pushed beyond the limits of human endurance."[13] The distinguishing mark of their leader, Moses Barton, was that his nirvanic escapes were not private, but rather public in nature. They included a failed trip to heaven in golden chariots, which was aborted when Moses fell from a tree instead of flying up to heaven to get the chariots for the remainder of his flock. This widespread intimacy with madness made more erroneous than usual the ideological construction and political execution of their historical projects.

Second, there was the mental colonization of the educated members of the group: "In exploring the symbols of power that their rulers had trapped in books, they had become enmeshed in its complexities, had fallen victims to a servitude more absolute than the one imposed by guns, whips, chains and hunger."[14] Trapped in the language and categories of the colonizer, these individuals were unable to imagine and execute genuinely new historical alternatives.

This focus on our cognitive categories of historical construction, the realities they establish, the possibilities they define, the distortions they introduce, and the limits they set, point to Wynter's cultural orientation and its focus on the systemic errors of cultural categories. Both of these are important points that link Wynter's early fiction with her later work as a critic. This ontological or founding role of epistemic categories becomes the point of departure for examining the textuality, crises, and betrayals of historical projects, whether postcolonial or otherwise. It also becomes the basis for a new vertical drama of ego (cogito) consciousness, a corresponding decline in the psychological orientation of the fiction years and a greater distance from her onto-poetic roots.

THE *EPISTEME* AND CRITICISM

Wynter's shift from fiction to criticism was bridged by her search for a theory of textual and, in particular, literary production. Early explorations led to experiments with the critical theories of Adorno and Lukacs, before the more sustained engagements with poststructuralist theory. This turn to poststructuralism produced two important tendencies in Wynter's philosophy of history. First, drawing on Foucault's notion of the *episteme*, Wynter developed an onto-epistemic approach to history that is close to, but quite distinct from, the poeticist and poststructuralist approaches. Second, this epistemicist position inverts in Baudrillardian fashion, the Marxian relations between culture and political economy. It suggests that the original naming and semanticizing capabilities of the Marxian mode of production is part of a larger symbolic totality grounded in our *epistemes* and conceptual schemes. In other words, if the mode of economic production is currently dominant, then it is because it has been culturally (i.e., mythopeotically) coded to be dominant. Hence it is in these cultural codes that the crucial revolutionary transformations are located.

In explaining the crisis-ridden nature of the categorical processes and discursive totalizations by which we construct our historical projects, Wynter's point of departure is the semiotic nature of the epistemic spaces in which our categories and concepts arise. The semiotic nature of these spaces is determined by the sign systems that we use to represent ourselves and the world around us. With this semiotic element in the foreground, Wynter asks anew the Kantian questions concerning the conditions that make knowledge possible. What are the rules that govern these sign systems? What are the processes by which they represent objects and so shape our perception of them?

The first and most important rule that Wynter examines is the rule of indirect representation. That is, symbolic representation always takes place within already established *epistemes*, or discursive frameworks. *Epistemes* have very definite transcendental characteristics, which are shaped by the organization and orientation of the analogies, categories, concepts, symbols, and rules of statement formation that constitute them. The organization and orientation of these elements are in turn shaped by the behavior-orienting imperatives of understanding, controlling, and relating to the social and natural environments. These goals or behavior-orienting imperatives function like Habermas's "knowledge-constitutive interest" to construct and adapt the *episteme* to the production of the kind of knowledge that is relevant to the goals. However, Wynter's knowledge-constitutive goals are more fluid and variable than Habermas's three knowledge-constitutive interests because they are to serve not only the sciences but also the humanities.[15] This fluidity makes it more explicit in Wynter that knowledge production is always guided by the imperatives of representing social goals or interests at least to the degree that the latter have shaped the *episteme* in use. The discourses of the knowing subject are always grounded in such organized epistemic spaces and hence are incapable of representing objects in frameworks that are not biased toward group survival.

In their relations with the environment, a group may have a superordinate goal or a set of related subgoals that serve as the more immediate source of epistemic organization. For example, Wynter suggests that maintaining the flow of creative energy between all life forms was the knowledge-constitutive goal shaping the founding *epistemes* of Aztec religious and philosophical thought. For medieval Europe, she suggests that the corresponding goal was religious redemption through the church. In our age, it is the search for rational redemption through the state and the economy.[16] It is within *epistemes* shaped by such knowledge-constitutive goals that symbolic representation and knowledge production always take place.

Developing further the semiotic elements of this epistemic analysis, Wynter focuses next on the binary characteristics that *epistemes* inherit from language and other sign systems. One result of the formation of *epistemes* around transcendental or knowledge-constitutive goals is the developing of conceptual schemas whose primary functions are to order and classify perceptions.[17] Like her knowledge-constitutive goals, Wynter's classificatory schemas are quite variable and reflect the influence of these goals. Thus schemas may be cosmogonic, sociohistorical, political, or salvific. In other words, the organization of an *episteme* was never just a matter of the formal relations between analogies, concepts, schemas, and arguments. In addition to such relations, overall epistemic unity and the specificity of discursive practices were also profoundly shaped by knowledge-constitutive goals.

The emergence and development of such schemas are achieved through the establishing of boundary markers. These markers define and police what is inside the schema and what is outside. "Inside" and "outside" are important knowledge-constitutive features of conceptual schemas. Inside these schemas we have the classifying of objects, persons, or events on the basis of sameness or identity and outside on the basis of difference or nonidentity. In a salvific schema, saving activities constitute the inside while damning activities fill the outside. In a truth-oriented schema, what is considered true constitutes the inside, and untruth the outside. Consequently, the discursive elaboration given to objects, persons, or events within the categories of these schemas will definitely be affected by whether they are on the inside or outside of boundary markers.

These binary oppositional characteristics of conceptual schemas derive from the binary nature of linguistic and other signs. Once a binary relation (e.g., sacred/profane) has been imposed on a set of objects, the grammar of symbolic representation is such that a whole series of related or homologous oppositions can be derived to reinforce the constructions of objects that are inside the schema, and also on its outside.[18] Thus from the sacred/profane opposition, we can derive light/dark, good/evil, and much more. Whether explicit or not, conceptual schemas have these binary characteristics and may or may not have conscious strategies for policing these boundaries of sameness and difference. The criteria of sameness will determine the variety of discourses that can be on the inside of the schema. Thus the rational schema of politico-economic salvation has been able to support a wide variety of ideological discourses, while at the same time excluding an equally wide variety of spiritual discourses.

In short, Wynter views the *episteme* as a knowledge-constitutive field whose schemas and concepts are also shaped in part by the imperatives of adapting their representational capabilities to specific social and natural environments. It is important to note that the ontological or founding status of *epistemes* does not derive from the specific contents of knowledge-constitutive goals. As in the case of Walcott, it derives from the immanent symbolic processes that are spontaneously triggered by these goals. In Wynter's language, this founding status of the *episteme* is "auto-poetically instituted."[19] This auto-instituting of *epistemes* is what Wynter wants to interrupt, decenter, and make conscious as part of the new vertical drama of cogito consciousness.

EPISTEMIC CHANGE

The next important step in grasping Wynter's approach to history is to understand her position on how *epistemes* change and the relationship between epistemic change and social transformation. This relationship is a major point of disagreement between Wynter and Marxian historicists. Epistemic change is the process by which any individual or group moves beyond the *episteme* of its day and thinks new thoughts in new discourses and disciplines. Wynter employs two distinct models of change to account for such epistemic shifts.[20] The first is an energistic model, while the second is a model of categorical and schematic reorganization. The energistic model plays only a supplementary role and is never explicitly developed for its own sake. The secondary role of this model further evidences the break with the psychological orientation of the poeticist approach. Hence our focus here will be on the model of categorical and schematic reorganization.

The key to this model of epistemic change is the magnitude of the systemic errors that are compounded in representing what is outside of the *episteme*'s conceptual schema. These errors are greatest with objects that occupy the point that is most antithetical, most radically other, to the core of the schema. This antithetical point, Wynter labels the liminal category of the *episteme*. Such a point constitutes an external "transgressive chaos," that threatens the internal order of the *episteme*. The misrepresentation generated by liminal categories is systemically related to the semiotic aspects of *epistemes* and only indirectly to the specific contents of their knowledge-constitutive schemes. Because objects or persons represented by the liminal category are systemically assigned negative values, the resulting distortions and misrepresentations are highly resistant to discursive criticism or attack. This tendency toward systemic misrepresentation is for Wynter the Achilles' heel of *epistemes* and the primary source of epistemic shifts. Gross misrepresentation makes an elaborated discourse and its founding *episteme* vulnerable to the contrary signals that continue to emerge from the misrepresented object, person, or event. The greater the misrepresentation, the greater the vulnerability of the *episteme*.

As a case in point, Wynter analyzes the liminal misrepresentations of medieval Christian geography that made it vulnerable to the voyages and vision of Christopher Columbus, and the growth of humanism and scientism that they encouraged.[21] Wynter suggests that one of the binaries that inscribed the Christian schema of spiritual salvation through the church was the opposition, within the redemptive grace of God/outside the redemptive grace of God. Grace was the uplifting, heliocentric force that sustained and protected all life above the earth's surface from the downward pull of gravitational forces. However, it operated only within the boundaries of medieval Christianity. These grace-related characteristics of geographical space gave rise to a closely related opposition: habitable versus uninhabitable areas. The latter signified transgressive chaotic regions that were beyond the uplifting power of God's grace. Consequently, there could be no land in the Western Hemisphere or the torrid zone, as it would naturally sink below the waters of the ocean without the unnatural support of divine grace. This misrepresentation of the Western Hemisphere and the torrid zone via the liminal category is the systemic source of errors that made the discourses of medieval Christianity vulnerable to Columbus's geography. His voyages would demonstrate to medieval Christians the existence of land above the water in regions outside the grace of their God. It is the breaking through of such countersignals that force major changes in the organization of categories and schemes that make up *epistemes*.

Vulnerability via the necessary misrepresentation of liminal categories is the dynamic principle of epistemic change for Wynter. Because of these categories, discourse production is accompanied by the creating of a shadow that will eventually lead to the downfall of the discourse. Wynter's new vertical drama of cogito consciousness is to make explicit this process of shadow creation through the analysis of the liminal categories of *epistemes*. By making discursive shadow production explicit, Wynter hopes to introduce a qualitatively new type of *episteme*, one that would give us greater control over the misrepresentations that have undermined horizontal projects of emancipation.

THE DIALECTICS OF LIMINAL CATEGORIES

This analysis of epistemic change is important because it is the foundation of Wynter's philosophy of history. *Epistemes* do not exist apart from societies and their transformation. They provide societies with the founding categories, the classificatory schemes of sameness and difference, the mythopoetic processes of original naming, the language, and the variety of discourses through which the aspects of everyday life are made available in an ordered and meaningful way. That is, epistemes not only provide the underlying "order of things,"[22] but also the order of knowledge (sciences, disciplines, discourses) through which we know and interpret objects. It is the job of scholars to preserve the *episteme* and its order of knowledge by using it and encouraging their students to think and write within it. In this role scholars become what Wynter likes to refer to as the grammarians of the order of knowledge. In short, the orders established by *epistemes* extend into the social organization of knowledge and thus to the framing and legitimating of social life. Consequently when *epistemes* change their effects are far-reaching—changing dramatically these symbolic processes and legitimating arguments upon which the social order rests.

A glimpse of the epochal dimensions of a major epistemic change was provided by our example of the impact of Columbian geography on the Christian order of knowledge. The latter was a religiously legitimated order of knowledge that was grounded in an epistemic goal of religious redemption through the church. This order of knowledge rested on a particular ordering of things, and a pattern of disciplinary/discursive organization that was anchored in the theology of the clergy. On the other hand, Columbian geography was an early expression of a new order of secular knowledge that was grounded in the epistemic goal of national redemption through economic and political action. This order of knowledge was founded on a different order of things and a pattern of disciplinary/discursive organization that would eventually be anchored in the Western university system. The grammarians of the above religious *episteme* were the primary obstacles to the new secular *episteme* that was emerging in response to religious misrepresentations of world geography—the *episteme* that would bring us the humanities and later the social sciences. Similarly, it is Wynter's view that our current humanist/social scientific order of knowledge and its grammarians are the primary obstacles to the new *episteme* that emerged in the struggles of the sixties. She sees this epistemic shift as a response to the misrepresentation of dominated groups (e.g., African Americans, women, Native Americans, and so on) in the humanities and social sciences. These misrepresentations have produced a liminal dialectic that parallels that produced by the earlier religious misrepresentations of world geography. Thus the challenge of the moment is the overthrowing of the grammarians of our order of knowledge so that the discourses of the humanities and social sciences can be reinscribed and reorganized in the new *episteme* that appears to be oriented toward the more accurate representing of human differencies.

This revolutionary significance that Wynter attributes to epistemic change is a major source of difference with the Marxian dialectic. It opposes the mode of epistemic production to the mode of economic production as the locus of crucial revolutionary change. Wynter sees this liminal dialectic of the former as both encompassing and surpassing the Marxian dialectic. The practice of exploitation within a mode of economic production along with its overthrow must be referred back to the conditions of liminal domination and the epistemic changes necessary for the latter's removal. This is the core of Wynter's philosophy of history and the liminal dialectic that moves it. In this philosophy, the historical process is not driven by class or racial conflict, but rather by the epistemic and liminal dynamics in the mythopoetic constructions of groups in conflict.

COLONIALISM, POSTCOLONIALISM, AND THE LIMINAL DIALECTIC

This liminal as opposed to a Marxian dialectic can be seen in Wynter's analysis of colonial and postcolonial problems. Here, patterns and practices of politico-economic domination are consistently related to the gradual changes that shifted the Western *episteme* from religious to secular salvation. These changes were the result of pressures to represent more accurately not only new world geography but also more broadly secular knowledge and activities. The pressure to assimilate these new realities produced a partial displacing of the schema of spiritual salvation. It now had to share its knowledge-constitutive status with the schema of rational salvation through the state and economy, as European capitalism continued to grow at home and colonize abroad. In short, the Columbian period was a transitional one in which two distinct schemas found a temporary hybrid unity. This epistemic hybridity is Wynter's key to the liminal categories through which Columbus and his followers would reconstruct the peoples of "the new world."

To the extent that Columbus remained a Christian, the new world, although above ground, was a non-Christian world. As such it had to fall into the liminal category of the Christian part of his hybrid schema. Through this category, the people of the new world became idolaters and had to be devalued, negated, and Christianized. This position of being outside the Christian kingdom determined their value as human beings and what could or could not be done to them by Christians. Most important for Wynter is that the liminal label of idolaters made it possible to construct the people of the new world as a group that could be used for the well-being of Christendom.

However, this reconstruction as idolaters did not complete the mythopoetic rewriting of the identity of new-world peoples. It also had to be reshaped by the categories of the rational, politico-economic schema of salvation. For Wynter, this schema had been triggered by the liminal misrepresentations of the material world in Christian discourses. Thus, the latter were the source of an alternative politico-economic discourse within Christendom that gave capitalism its founding categories and ideological legitimacy. This discourse not only defined and justified the transforming capabilities of state power but also legitimated the rewarding of individuals by their sovereigns for extending the boundaries or territorial holdings of the state. Wynter suggests that the liminal categories of this discourse were also important for the rewriting of the identity of new-world peoples. These categories made them non-Europeans and therefore could be used to further the well-being of European states.

For example, in Spain this politico-economic discourse developed the status of natural slaves in its rewriting of the identity of new-world people.[23] A group's estimated degree of rational capability determined whether or not it fell into this liminal category. Spanish estimates of the level of rationality among the "Indios" were used to justify their liminal redefinition as natural slaves.

In short, within the hybrid schema that supplied the founding categories and ideologies of early capitalism, the Caribs, Arawaks, Tainos, and other new-world peoples were redefined as idolaters and natural slaves. Wynter suggests that this schema allowed Columbus to see these people "only in terms of securing the good of himself, the state and Christendom."[24]

Thus, in spite of correcting Christian geography, Columbus ends up making a similar error of misrepresentation. Just as Christians had distorted the geography of the Western Hemisphere, so he distorted the people of the region. This is the cycle of liminal violence that must be stopped if historical projects are not to end in betrayal. It is the new vertical challenge that cogito-consciousness must overcome.

The enslavement of the Indios was just one liminal tragedy of the colonial projects of Christendom and capitalism. The others Wynter links to further changes in the hybrid *episteme* that supplied early capitalism with its peculiar order of knowledge. These changes reflected the growing importance of the rational and statist elements, which continued to displace the spiritual elements. Wynter's concern with such shifts is how they affect processes of liminal construction and the sociopolitical consequences of such projections. She suggests that one of the major results of subsequent changes in the schema of early capitalism was the displacing of the concepts of idolaters and natural slaves by race as the most extreme point of its liminal category.

This shift occurred in the context of determining the place and role of Africans in the expanding empires of Christendom and of modern European states. The black skins of Africans, their estimated levels of rational capability, and their non-Christian religions made them the new polar opposites of white, rational, and Christian Europe. In the Spanish view, the above features of Africans placed them below the category of natural slaves, and into the category of civil slaves.[25] The lower value of civil slaves justified their complete commodification as disposable items on the labor market. Here we see the importance of onto-epistemic constitution for Wynter. Race as a social force does not function by itself, nor does it have its genesis in the legitimacy needs of economic and political institutions. On the contrary, it is the mythopoetic inscription of race in the liminal dynamics of the schema of early capitalism that gives power and social reality to race.

This liminal redefinition of Africans Wynter links directly to the tragic experiences of poverty, racism, and colonialism that have been the lot of Africans within "the Enlightenment" and wealth-producing projects of liberal capitalism. Wynter is particularly interested in the connections between the freedom and wealth of European elites and the domination and devaluation of groups such as workers, Africans, Caribs, Jews, Arabs, and Indians. These connections are for her systemic, grounded in the semiotic relation between the founding categories of *epistemes* and the dialectics of their socially deployed liminal categories.

This problem of liminal distortion and its relation to social domination is not just a European problem; it haunts and makes vulnerable all human discourses. Thus Wynter uses it to analyze not only the colonial phases of Third-World societies but precolonial and postcolonial phases as well. A good example of its operation in the precolonial phase is Wynter's discussion of identity construction among the Congolese people of Africa.[26] In these societies, identity was grounded in lineage schemes. Belonging to a lineage group was the basis for social inclusion and recognition as members of human communities. The outside of this schema was to be lineageless. To be without a lineage identity was to be different, other. It was to be liminal, that is, part of the transgressive chaos of the outside. Thus it is not surprising that slaves in Congolese societies were lineageless men and women. Such individuals could be legitimately enslaved and made to serve the well-being of lineage-based social orders.

More important for us is the liminal analysis of the crises of postcolonial societies. We've already seen that colonialism and its relatives, slavery and racism, are liminal shadows cast across the globe by liberal and neoliberal capitalism. The tension between the misrepresentation of the colonized and the contrary signals they continued to transmit, was the basis for a new or postcolonial phase in this dialectic. Between the 1930s and the 1970s, the volume and intensity of these countertransmissions reached unprecedented levels. In Africa, Asia, and the Caribbean, these countersignals gave rise to a chorus of political, economic, ideological, and other discourses demanding national liberation from the chains of European colonialism. These anticolonial discourses inscribed historical projects of postcolonial reconstruction that were to be realized collectively through the steering powers of a national state. However, in

Wynter's view, these efforts did not introduce a new *episteme*. They did not fundamentally change the capitalist order of things or its order of knowledge. On the contrary, these counterdiscourses were formulated within the Western *episteme* and its humanist/social scientific order of knowledge. Hence Wynter's perception of the region as currently being more epistemically colonized, than militarily or politico-economically. Today we live in the wake of these poorly fashioned projects, the wreckages they have produced, and a major loss of faith in the postcolonial state. Regimes such as Nkrumah's in Ghana, Kenyetta's in Kenya, Burnham's in Guyana, whose aims were freedom and development, produced new forms of domination and underdevelopment. The disappointment that has followed this collapse of postcolonial projects has found its most searing expression in the works of the Ghanaian novelist Ayi Kwei Armah.

Wynter's approach to this postcolonial crisis is to subject its development ideology to an epistemic analysis, exposing in the process its counterproductive entrapment in the liminial categories of the Western *episteme*. This analysis suggests that the constructing of development projects in the language and discourses of the colonizer places severe limits on their originality. In Wynter's view, this enmeshment of development thinking in the *episteme* and culture of the colonizer blocks the emergence of new social orders in these societies. To achieve such new orders, it is necessary to reject not only specific ideologies but also the founding *episteme* of the colonial project. Without such an epistemic break, the capacity for original and independent thinking will remain severely limited. These constraints on originality are further compounded by the fact that within the epistemic schemes of European colonial projects the colonized were redefined through the liminal categories. Inheriting these schemes also means internalizing liminal modes of self-definition and misrepresentation, which can only inhibit new attempts at self-definition and self-realization.

In Wynter's categorical perspective, development as a signifier is semiolinguistically linked to underdevelopment as a binary opposite.[27] The latter is a signifier of lack or absence, while the former signifies a desireable presence. Although it may be hidden, this semiotic connection inscribes and institutes a relationship of domination and dependence between those labeled developed and underdeveloped. Wynter insists that the current instituting of this relationship is further secured through the continuities and references it can establish with other binary oppositions that have inscribed similar relations of domination and dependence between the advanced capitalist societies and the areas of the world they control.

As we saw earlier, some of these oppositions have been Christians/idolaters, Europeans/natives, colonizer/colonized, civilized/uncivilized, and self/governing/nonself-governing. The opposition development/underdevelopment is thus the latest (postcolonial) mutation in a series of such binaries that have inscribed and maintained the liminal divisions within the capitalist world order. Appearances to the contrary, this opposition does not stand alone. Its reality defining hegemony is supported by its hidden semiotic connections to its predecessors. As the latest mutation, it's able to change and re-present images of absence and presence that are more appropriate and contemporary. In Wynter's view, underdevelopment is a new inscription of an old form of lack: the categorically determined inability of the idolaters, slaves, colonized, natives, and now the underdeveloped to overcome a supposed universal human subjugation to a condition of natural scarcity.[28] The internalization of this lack by the leaders and masses involved in postcolonial reconstruction is necessarily self-defeating.

What happens when native individuals or groups bring categorical frameworks of this neocolonial nature to the task of postcolonial reconstruction? Wynter suggests that when such inadequately transformed categorical frameworks are redeployed by the class fractions that replace colonial rulers, the results are disastrous.[29] This new class surrounds itself with the surplus of positive representation provided by the founding categories of the revised schema, while projecting its liminal categories onto new groups or the same groups of the colonial period. It is the automatic functioning of this neocolonial schema below the consciousness of economic and political elites that for Wynter explains the collapse of postcolonial projects. Better results will require a change in this underlying schema that frames the larger epistemic and discursive totalities of which development projects are a part. For Wynter, this means that the deepening crisis of "we the underdeveloped" is "not primarily an economic one,"[30] but is really epistemic in nature. Even though it manifests itself most visibly in economic terms, it is a crisis that stems from our failure to institute a new *episteme* in which we are not defined by a category of lack whose symbols and conditions of fullfilment are elsewhere. In other words, postcolonial crises stem from a failure to radically decolonize *epistemes* along with ideologies, institutions, and economic practices. This is the epistemic difference that marks Wynter's position.

Further, it is not only capitalist projects of postcolonial reconstruction that have been defeated by these liminal dynamics. Wynter sees the state socialist alternative as also having succumbed to them. Thus the tragic collapse of the 1979 revolution in Grenada, after only four and a half years, she sees as an echo of the same liminal dynamics that led to the worldwide collapse of state socialism.[31] For Wynter, the crisis of state socialism is summed up in the following question: Why did the emancipatory project of nationalizing property generate gulags and finally end in collapse? Her answer is not Stalin's personality or Soviet political economy, but the absolutizing of the founding category of nationalized property. This produced an equal but negative absolutizing of its opposite: the dissidents who insisted on private forms of property. They became the categorical equivalents of the Jews in Nazi eugenic projects or Africans in the capitalist project. For Wynter, this suggests that the Marxian "mode of production" is a subset of a larger epistemic totality whose constitutive schema (statist redemption) includes uncontrolled founding and liminal categories. In Grenada, the brutality with which the Coard faction murdered Maurice Bishop and his colleagues, signaled for Wynter the same blind violence that liminal categories have triggered around the world. In short, socialist projects of postcolonial reconstruction are no freer of the problems of liminal categories than are capitalist projects.

TOWARD A NEW *EPISTEME*

Given the categorical (i.e., vertical) crises of both capitalist and socialist projects of emancipation, Wynter insists that Caribbean people make a radical break with the *episteme* of material redemption through the state and economy that has supported these projects. The starting point of such a break must be "the socio-existential" experiences of liminal groups. It is from the perspective of its liminal victims that access to the truth of the order can be had. For Wynter, capitalist projects have produced multiple points of liminality. The poor of the inner-city ghettos, of Third-World shanty towns, women, and ethnic minorities are all liminal victims of advanced consumer capitalism. These are all points of resistance with different liminal perspectives on the capitalist order that are potentially capable of overthrowing its governing *episteme*. What these perspectives share is their origin in a "transculturally applicable systemic category,"[32] the liminal category. Borrowing from Fanon, Wynter labels this wide variety of liminal victims, "the condemned of the earth."[33] From their perspectives the new *episteme* must emerge. This retention of an insurrectionary and transformative dimension to her thought is an important overlap with the historicists.

However, it is not enough for us "to marry our thoughts" to those of the condemned.[34] The other big challenge that new movements must confront is that of increasing the conscious control over the operations of their own liminal categories. In other words, they must adopt a new vertical project in the field of consciousness-raising. The unconscious operating of liminal categories in new movements would only result in new piles of wreckage. Hence the importance of fighting discursive authoritarianism in the social movements that started in the sixties. A significant increase in our ability to de-center founding categories, recognize liminal opposites, and control their social impact is a necessary condition for the success of new historical projects. This new model of discursive freedom must become an integral part of new movements. In short, the way out of the present crises of postcolonial reconstruction is the projecting of new emancipatory narratives that are rooted in a new *episteme*, but whose auto-poetic functioning is consciously exposed as are the discursive strategies of a modernist text.

THE ADVANTAGES OF WYNTER'S REFORMULATION

Wynter's primary achievement is that she succeeds in theorizing more explicitly the negativities of history without succumbing to them as in the case of V. S. Naipaul or the early Armah. In this respect she also departs quite sharply from the poststructuralists. Her task is not to mourn or minimize the failures of the past, but rather to place them at the center of her theoretical agenda. In foregrounding the negatives of postcolonial Caribbean history, Wynter rejects explanations of historical failures that emphasize difficulties such as the immaturity of the masses, poor leadership, powerful external actors, or technical obstacles. She places the emphases on the oppositional categories that our historical projects silently generate and carry within their epistemic foundations.

If in the case of Harris the key differences with historicists centered around the ontology of the everyday ego, then with Wynter they are over the ontology of the cogito. As poeticists, Harris and Wynter share a focus on the creative and world-constituting powers of the everyday ego and the cogito. However, they differ significantly in their views and approaches to these two sites of conscious agency. It is the importance that Wynter attaches to the shadows and dualities created by the transcendental workings of our cogito that sets her apart from Harris, James, or Fanon. In contrast to Harris who emphasizes the correcting and compensatory aspects of the universal consciousness on the ego, Wynter's focus is on sociopolitical consequences of the negative categories that are a part of the formative process of the transcendental ego. Although this shadow phenomenon is central to Fanon's work, it is more psychological than categorical in nature.[35] Liminal categories are inverted and projected onto the colonizer who becomes the embodiment of evil during the period of decolonization. Outside of this particular conflict, the shadow phenomenon disappears as the class aspects of Fanon's analysis gain ascendancy. In James, the shadow phenomenon is addressed in Hegelian terms. Particularly in his *Notes on Dialectics*, James uses Hegel's theory of discursive logic to establish several connections between the categories of Stalinist thought and the gulags. At the same time, he also subjected Trotskyism to a similar kind of critique. However, this recognition of a categorical shadow probem in no way displaced the centrality of political economy in James's thinking. The centrality of the categorical shadow is the distinctive mark of Wynter's philosophy of history. It is her special move, and her thought rests on it in ways that are not true for Harris, Fanon, or James.

Although she shares this categorical turn with the poststructuralists, there are no apocalyptic, end-of-history themes in Wynter's philosophy. Rather, the effects of her categorical analysis on historical projects are much closer to those of the poeticist approach. For her, the problem is not just the formulation of new historical projects. It is also their redemption or rescuing from unconscious entanglements with their liminal categories. However, Wynter's redemption is not from the angry or jealous gods of Harris, but rather from entrapping semio-linguistic forces that push us to betray our intentions.

There are at least three important advantages that follow from Wynter's reformulation of the issues of postcolonial reconstruction. The first is a more explicit thematizing of the deeper layers of our cultural universe. This level of explicitness was achieved through Wynter's microscopic use of semio-linguistics to reexamine the formation and deformation of *epistemes*. The primary result of this reexamination is Wynter's positing of an encoded "corre-lation between our notions of human emancipation . . . the founding Origin Narratives that inscribe and institute them, and the rules governing our laws of thought."[36] Thus the level of cultural analysis from which Wynter operates is not that of specific discursive formulations, but rather the correlation estab-lished by founding narratives between knowledge-constitutive goals and the way we think. Consequently, we learn a great deal about the ways in which lan-guage and collective goals constitute and polarize the frameworks within which we think. Because these categorical processes operate so silently, this knowledge-constitutive level of our cultural heritage is extremely difficult to thematize. Wynter's repositioning of the shadow problem gives us a new model and new tools with which to thematize more explicitly these elusive but foundational aspects of discourse production.

The second advantage that Wynter's reformulation offers is increased access to the links between the categorical and the political. This adds a new layer of complexity to existing formulations of the links between culture and politics. Two links between the categorical and the political are particularly important. The first is the problem of the discursive authoritarianism. This phenomenon signals not only certain centralizing and essentializing tenden-cies but also serves as a metaphor for political and other forms of authoritari-anism. In other words, the epistemic violence encoded in the centralizing strategies of discourses can be transcoded into violence on the political level. As a consequence, Wynter suggests that we will not eliminate political author-itarianism until we are able to control the authoritarian elements encoded in the categorical foundations of our discursive practices.

The second important link between culture and politics is of course that between liminal categories and sociopolitical domination. This particular link clearly displaces the institutional links to sociopolitical domination established by Marxist and Pan-African approaches. Here liminality displaces the exploitation of labor as a primary locus of sociopolitical devaluation and domination. Thus in Wynter's view, changing or inverting colonial ideologies and overturning colonial institutions are not enough. In addition, the semio-linguistic processes that govern the formation of the founding and liminal categories that frame these ideologies and institutions must be brought under more conscious control.

The third and final advantage offered by Wynter's reformulation is the possibility of reducing some of the pluralism that has paralyzed oppositional groups since the collapse of more unifying grand narratives. The persistence of racism and sexism within working-class movements, of classism and racism within feminist movements, and sexism and classism within racialist movements have been major sources of the fragmentation that has characterized these movements since the mid-seventies. Wynter's concept of transculturally applicable liminal categories of domination may be helpful here. These categories and their processes of formation can indeed serve as common points of reference for understanding the domination experienced by women, Africans, Jews, the poor, and other oppressed groups. The use of these categories as nonreductive common points of reference, could be a significant alternative to forcibly subsuming one struggle under the ideological banner of another.

THE DISADVANTAGES OF WYNTER'S REFORMULATION

Wynter's reformulation is open to questions from both the poeticist and historicist traditions. For reasons of space and familiarity, I will restrict my critical remarks to questions from my own historicist position. To see some of the implications for the historicist position, we need to ask ourselves the following question: What would be the costs to Caribbean postcolonial thought if it made this shift from the politico-economic to the categorical? At least three major costs will be incurred.

First, it would require replacing the "Marxian key of the mode of production" as the one that explains domination and poverty.[37] Its place would be taken by the auto-poetics of founding schemes that include the mode of production in a larger symbolic totality. Two problems arise from this suggested replacement. First is the imprecision of this epistemic totality compared to the mode of economic production. Wynter uses several terms to refer to this larger totality—the forms of social life, the mode of domination, the order informing systemic code, or the *imaginaire social* of Corneluis Castoriadis. Throughout my exposition for consistency I used the expression—an *episteme* and its order knowledge. The differences in nature and generality of these terms point to the imprecision of Wynter's concept. To replace the Marxian mode of production, she will have to specify her oppositionally coded totalities more precisely.

Second, for societies struggling so desperately with issues of economic development in an increasingly competitive world, this may indeed be a difficult shift to make, even with a more precisely defined epistemic totality. The importance of political economy to Caribbean postcolonial thought is indicated by the wide influence of political economists from James through Arthur Lewis to Clive Thomas. A radical turn toward the categorical would significantly increase the distance between social theory and processes such as labor extraction, plant closings, lobbying, and IMF adjustment programs that are seen to be the moving forces of political life. This long and complex route from the categorical to the economic and the political is not sufficiently recognized by Wynter. It needs to be mediated in a way that recognizes more specifically the relative autonomy of the economic in spite of its original mythopoetic naming. This semiotic priority of the cultural Wynter translates into a consistently higher (almost absolute) cybernetic ranking, which restricts both the autonomy of the economic and its ability to resist or reinscribe its original cultural construction. This results in an underrepresentation of the economic, in particular, and an underestimation of its importance. This is evident from the manner in which her critique of development economics moves exclusively on the level of its cultural inscription and bypasses the specific findings and projects that have emerged from its concrete practice.

The systematic underrepresenting of the economic introduces the second difficulty with Wynter's position: the relationship between categorical processes and institutional structures. They are blurred in a way that is similar to the poststructuralist erasure of the difference between praxis and deconstruction. In theory, Wynter's position is one of equality and mutuality, but in practice this is consistently violated. For example, in the legitimacy needs of institutional systems of power, Wynter sees "the equiprimordiality of structure and cultural conceptions in the genesis of power."[38] In other words, "the cultural aspects of power are as original as the structural aspects; each serves as a code for the other's development."[39] However, the above repositioning of political economy is not in line with this position of equiprimordiality. This gap suggests that in actual practice Wynter has not been able to control the discursive tendencies toward overrepresenting founding categories. The underrepresenting of economic and other institutional structures is systematically related to the overrepresentation of language, sign systems, and discursive processes in Wynter's approach. These factors take on both a centered and determinate significance that is inconsistent with the call for de-centered discourses.

This tension between categorical processes and institutional structures raises the question of the autonomy of the latter. There is little in Wynter's texts that supports a higher cybernetic ranking for epistemic and categorical processes. On the contrary, the evidence suggests a much greater degree of autonomy for institutional structures than her ranking would entail. The differences in the temporalities of categorical/discursive processes and institutional structures constitute a good case in point. There are many instances in which institutional structures (e.g., racism or capitalism) continue to grow long after their legitimating arguments have been deconstructed. There are also cases (e.g., African religions in the new world) where categorical foundations continue to exist long after their institutional support has been removed. These differences in temporality suggest that categorical processes have only limited influences over institutional structures and that the latter possess self-preservative dynamics of their own. This autonomy means that there is no simple route from the categorical to the economic or political.

The consequences of this underrepresenting of institutional structures are very evident in Wynter's analyses of state socialism. In the cases of both Grenada and the Soviet Union, the examination moves exclusively on the categorical level. It fails to address or adequately recognize the patterns of state domination of other institutions that were related to processes of economic and political accumulation. The principle of equiprimordiality disappears in these analyses as emphasis is placed on domination generated by the liminal status of owners of private property. If we take a glance at the long and violent struggle for democracy in Haiti, the need for a stronger institutional analysis is again quite clear. While the persistence of the Noirisme/Mulatrisme opposition in Haitian society provides good grist for Wynter's categorical mill, there can be no getting around the hegemony of the military as an institution, and the totalitarian manner in which it penetrated the judiciary, the church, the schools, the press, and other institutions of civil society. The categorical (onto-epistemic) deconstructing of the above opposition and its deeper epistemic structures could at best weaken but not overthrow this military hegemony. In short, greater attention to the institutional dynamics of Caribbean societies is needed if Wynter's reformulation is to adequately address the postcolonial crisis.

Our third and final concern with Wynter's position is its reformulation of the vertical drama of ego consciousness as one of cogito consciousness, that is, whether or not as human beings we will be able to increase significantly our consciousness of and control over the auto-poetic processes that ground our discursive practices. For historicists, this reformulation raises an important question: Can this drama be mastered sufficiently and in time to improve significantly the quality of historical action? Earlier, we noted Wynter's inability to control the overrepresenting of her own founding categories. Failure to control these tendencies suggests that underrepresentation and liminal definition are also not under conscious control. Yet this type of control is a necessary condition for Wynter's new emancipatory project. The latter requires increasing our consciousness of the processes by which the socioexistential perspectives of liminal groups are ideologically established. Such a goal would require an increase in consciousness and control that goes beyond the levels made available by dialectics and other forms of categorical self-reflection. More specifically for Wynter, it will require "the autonomy of human cognition" from the historical projections (emancipatory or self-preservative) and collective goals to which they have so far been auto-poetically connected.

It is only in the natural sciences that Wynter sees the securing of significant measures of cognitive autonomy. A comparable autonomy must be secured for the humanities and the social sciences. These Wynter suggests will come from two sources: the growth and development of a science of signs, and long-term evolutionary changes in our cognitive relations with social worlds.[40]

The major problem with these roads to cognitive autonomy is that they belong to the distant future while Wynter needs the conscious instituting of *epistemes* right now. This is a practical problem with real political consequences. Because cognitive autonomy is not presently available, new projects of postcolonial reconstruction will continue to be formulated in states of semiconscious awareness. Semiotics (a candidate for Wynter's science of signs) has no doubt supplemented the categorical awareness produced by dialectics and other critical philosophies. But in spite of these semiotic supplements, the desired level of cognitive autonomy remains very much a future reality. This must certainly affect the feasibility of Wynter's reformulation.

Finally, I am sure the poeticists will have their own concerns with Wynter's reformulation. Two in particular strike me as being important. The first is the relation between the transcendental level and the psychological unconscious, or Harris's universal consciousness. Are the latter adequately represented in Wynter's transcendental analyses of the cogito, or is there between them a tension comparable to that between categorical processes and institutional structures? Wynter's focus on the poetics of founding schemes and categories emphasizes the cognitive, discourse-producing aspect of the self as opposed to the ontic and psychological aspects that are so important to Harris and Walcott. The consequences of this refocusing need to be carefully examined.

Second, the categorical reformulation of Harris's vertical drama of consciousness raises the question of whether or not the specific kind of ego integration and correction that Harris wants from the archetypal life is covered by Wynter's push for a science of mythopoetic processes. Is there enough room for Walcott's formative sea that invades the ego with tidal waves of creation and destruction? I would argue that these are very different dramas of consciousness. Hence there is a real need for Wynter to situate her reformulation in relation to this poeticist tradition. Indeed only such a situating in relation to both the historicist and the poeticist traditions will give Wynter the hearing her work deserves.

In spite of these problems with Wynter's position, it is a major attempt at rethinking Caribbean history and politics in the wake of our postcolonial crisis. Also, her strategy of using a poststructuralist bridge between the historicist and poeticist philosophies of history as the framework for this rethinking remains a revealing and challenging project. It clearly reveals both the strengths and weaknesses of poststructuralist thought in the Caribbean context. It suggests that poststructuralist thought can be useful in the analysis of categorical issues, but is of more limited value in relation to the institutional and identity issues confronting postcolonial reconstruction in the region. Wynter reminds us often of James's call for Caliban to enter into regions that Caesar never knew. Her reformulation challenges us to enter these new regions, to found new *epistemes*, and to inscribe them consciously. Only then will we be able to enter the historical maelstrom with our faces instead of our backs to the future.

Afro-American Philosophy: A Caribbean Perspective

F rom within the Afro-Caribbean intellectual tradition, it is difficult not to see Afro-American philosophy as a brother or sister discourse with Africa and Europe as our parents. Further, from this vantage point Afro-American philosophy also appears to be an interdiscursively embedded auxiliary discourse. Hence it shares the open, de-centered, and multidimensional features that mark Afro-Caribbean philosophy as a minor discourse. Even a cursory look at their major thinkers and patterns of development reveal important overlaps and similarities.

But in spite of these significant areas of convergence, the nature and importance of these fraternal ties have not been adequately thematized. Are they strong enough to ground Africana identities for Afro-American and Afro-Caribbean philosophies? Or, are they of such minor significance that we can regard these two as separate and distinct philosophies? In this chapter, I will argue for the first of these positions, drawing on the role of African symbols in the ego-genetic processes of Afro-Caribbean and Afro-American philosophers, as well as similarities in patterns of discursive development.

For most of its history, Afro-American philosophy has existed outside of the mainstream academic institutions of America. It has existed as a parallel discourse that only touched the dominant Euro-American philosophical tradition at certain crucial points. Given its recent recognition by the academic guardians of the latter tradition, it is not surprising that several attempts have been made to specify the nature of Afro-American philosophy and the path it should take within the American academy. Like Afro-Caribbean philosophy, Afro-American philosophy is a hybrid discourse in which European, African, and American philosophical traditions are locked in Rex Nettleford's "battle for space." Thus it should come as no surprise that there are several competing positions on how we should approach the identity and substantive themes of this philosophy.

In this literature on Afro-American philosophy, two positions in particular have gained significance. The first is an approach that suggests an American reading of Afro-American philosophy, while the second suggests an Africana reading. The American readings have stressed the connections between Afro-American philosophy and the American pragmatist tradition. On the other hand, the Africana readings such as those of Molefi Asante, Marimba Ani, and Maulana Karenga have stressed the connections of Afro-American philosophy to traditional African philosophy and to the discourses of the global struggles of African peoples for liberation from colonialism and racial domination.

In this chapter, I will offer an Africana reading of Afro-American philosophy. In particular I will review the attempts of Lucius Outlaw and Lewis Gordon to thematize this notion of an Africana philosophy. Building on their work, I will outline in detail my own view of this important notion. My approach will be one that brings together phenomenological and discursive strategies, as well as insights drawn from the Caribbean philosophical experience. I will begin with a brief look at the American readings of Afro-American philosophy through the work of Cornel West. Next, I will examine the Africana readings of Outlaw and Gordon and then present my own.

CORNEL WEST

Two excellent examples of American readings of Afro-American philosophy can be found in the works of Johnny Washington[1] and Cornel West. In spite of important differences, both develop the identity of Afro-American philosophy with detailed references to Euro-American pragmatism and little or no reference to traditional African philosophy. However, for reasons of space, we will here examine only the case of West.

For West, "Afro-American philosophy is an expression of the particular variation of European modernity that Afro-Americans helped to shape."[2] It is primarily an American philosophy that is rooted in the life worlds created by American modernity: "The life-worlds of Africans in the United States are conceptually and existentially neither solely African, European nor American, but more the latter than any of the former."[3] This American identity of

Afro-American philosophy leads West to a clear rejection of an African model of Afro-American philosophy: "While it might be possible to articulate a competing Afro-American philosophy based on African norms and notions, it is likely that the results would be theoretically thin."[4]

As with Washington, West sees an important convergence between the Afro-American and pragmatist conceptions of philosophy as forms of engaged cultural criticism. These engaged views West opposes to the more "epistemology-centered" conceptions of philosophy that have come out of Europe. Consequently, Afro-American philosophy is seen as "a textuality, a mode of discourse that interprets, describes, and evaluates Afro-American life in order comprehensively to understand and effectively to transform it."[5] Afro-American philosophy is not concerned with foundations and transcendental grounds, but with being "a material force for Afro-American freedom."[6]

It is within such a pragmatist conception of Afro-American philosophy that West identifies its primary tasks. These include two important dialogical engagements. One between Afro-American Christianity and Marxism, and the other between Afro-American Christianity and Euro-American pragmatism. The primary convergence that West sees between Afro-American Christianity and pragmatism is a shared commitment to social changes that enhance personal agency and increase democratic practices. In both, the commitment to change is ethically motivated. For West, one of pragmatism's important achievements is that it "dethroned epistemology as the highest priority of modern thought in favor of ethics."[7] This position on ethics points to an important polarization in West's thought: that between epistemological and ontological concerns, on the one hand, and ethically motivated activism, on the other. West associates the former with "the subjectivist turn" in modern European philosophy, which in his view attempts to locate the grounds for truth in the transcendental activity of the cogito or thinking subject, and "outside of politics and power."[8] Hence this turn is associated with a possible weakening of the activist thrust. Both Afro-American Christianity and pragmatism avoid this threat to their activism by the priority they give to ethically motivated action. Further, this polarization points to a more centered and monothetic organization of the diverse field of Afro-American philosophy than its highly varied textual embeddedness would suggest.

In addition to the case of Afro-American Christianity, West also argues that the work of W. E. B. DuBois is another important instance of the convergence between Afro-American philosophy and pragmatism: "DuBois seems to have been attracted to pragmatism owing to its Emersonian evasion of epistemology-centered philosophy, and his sense of pragmatism's relevance to the Afro-American predicament."[9] Even DuBois's poeticism is seen in terms of its Emersonian resonances: "Like Emerson, DuBois always viewed himself as a poet in the broad nineteenth century sense, that is one who creates new visions and vocabularies for the moral enhancement of humanity."[10]

However, West is clear that this pragmatist reading of Afro-American philosophy does not imply a perfect fit. Thus he notes pragmatism's neglect of the self, its veneration of science, and its refusal to take seriously racial and class struggles. These are important divergences, the full implications of which are not developed by West. In spite of these limitations, pragmatism provides an American context for Afro-American thought, a context that imparts to it both a shape and a heritage of philosophical legitimacy. In this pragmatist setting, West sees no need for any special dialogical engagements with traditional or modern African philosophy.

LUCIUS OUTLAW

In contrast to West and Washington, Lucius Outlaw and Lewis Gordon are strong exponents of Africana readings of Afro-American philosophy. Here the dialogical engagements with pragmatism are replaced by exchanges with traditional African thought and the discourses of the global struggle for African liberation. For Outlaw, the core of Afro-American philosophy is to be found in the socially transformative discourses that Afro-Americans have produced. Thus the accommodationist position of Booker T. Washington, the assimilationist position of Frederick Douglass, the integrationist positions of DuBois and King, and the nationalism of Malcolm X are all vital expressions of an Afro-American philosophical tradition.

However, Outlaw does not link this activist orientation to American pragmatism. In his work, it is thematized in relation to European traditions of hermeneutic, critical, and poststructuralist theory, but primarily in relation to an Africana tradition of resistance to European imperialism and racism. One of Outlaw's most pressing concerns about contemporary Afro-American philosophy is that it "is conducted with little or no knowledge of, or attention to, the history of philosophical activity on the African continent, or elsewhere in the African Diaspora."[11]

In developing this Africana reading, the major problem Outlaw takes up is the specifying of common or unifying contents and the professional norms that would justify his claims for a field of Africana philosophy. At the most general level, Outlaw resolves the first of these two problems by seeking unity and commonality in "third order organizing, classificatory strategies"[12] directed at the lived experiences and second-order classifications of continental and diasporic Africans. However, the concrete implementing of this general solution turns out to be quite problematic as Outlaw's examination of Molefi Asante's Afrocentric strategy makes clear. Outlaw remains skeptical about the existence of a set of underlying principles or common contents that could unify the diverse practices of peoples of African descent. Consequently, the identity problem remains unresolved, but it is indirectly addressed as a part of Outlaw's solution to the second problem regarding professional norms.

Given this absence of any clear third-order unifying principle, Outlaw suggests that unity and Africana identity can only come from the discursive practices of Afro-American philosophers: "The presentation of commonality is a function of my discursive agenda. But not mine alone."[13] Thus the Africana identity of Afro-American or Afro-Caribbean philosophy would not be rooted in a set of shared symbols, but rather in the agendas, norms, and practices that these and other philosophers have set for their fields.

This solution to the problem of a common Africana identity reflects Outlaw's view of philosophy as an activity grounded "in socially shared practices."[14] This collectively oriented philosophy is mediated by rules of discourse in the Foucaultian sense of the term. Like West, Outlaw rejects the subjectivist turn of modern European philosophy: "There is no timeless essence shared by any and all forms of thought call 'philosophy.' . . . There are no transcendental rules a priori that are the essential, thus defining features of 'philosophy.'"[15]

Although very important, Outlaw pushes these discursive factors too far. For example, this extreme discursivist solution to the problem of commonality does not allow Outlaw to resolve his very important problem of "Africans-becoming-Americans as instances of philosophy."[16] It does not, because this solution entails a radical displacing of the subject, or ego, that puts the problem of identity beyond adequate reach. To keep identity within reach, a more interpenetrating, dialectical relationship between self-formation and discursive formation is required. This greater visibility of the self is one of the distinctive marks of Gordon's approach.

LEWIS GORDON

In the work of Lewis Gordon, we find an existential-phenomenological approach to the problems of an Africana philosophy that is quite different from the discursivist approach of Outlaw. Gordon embraces the subjectivist turn in modern European philosophy, and does not see it as a threat to black activism the way West does. On the contrary, like Fanon, he uses the ontological spaces it opens up to ground an activist philosophical position. Gordon uses the subjectivist turn to thematize more explicitly than West or Outlaw the problems of black self-formation and, in particular, its racialization in the white societies. Consequently, he grounds the Africana project in the Pan-African task of reconstituting this racialized self in the wake of the "phenomenological disappearance"[17] of its humanity and its African heritage.

In his explicit foregrounding of the self, Gordon's focus is the ontology (not the psychology) of everyday black and white egos, the interactive dynamics between these ontologies, and their relations to the origins and maintenance of antiblack racism. The interactive dynamics between these ontologies have trapped black and white ego formation in classic imperial battles for ontological space. By ontological space, I mean space to be, to posit oneself and realize that self-positing. The imperial nature of this battle derives from the fact that Europeans and Euro-Americans have defined the ontological space of white ego genesis in a way that requires the evading of the humanity of Africans. This evasion is effected through the racial redefining of Africans as blacks, Negroes, or more pejoratively as "niggers." The result is an imperial ontology that restricts the space of black ego genesis and appropriates its ego-formative resources in the interest of white self-formation.

To come to terms with this battle for ontological space, Gordon focuses even more closely on the source of these predatory and extractive relations that exist between white and black egos. These relations are motivated by the easy solutions they provide to the blockages, contradictions, polar divisions, and unacceptable tendencies that are integral parts of white ego genesis. Their predatory transformation, Gordon theorizes with the aid of the Sartrean notion of bad faith.[18] In bad faith, human beings in all cultures deal inauthentically and evasively with the specific blockages and obstacles that stand between self-positing and self-realization. These impediments may be political, racial, or economic. But for both Gordon and Sartre, they are also ineliminably ontological. The ego that executes the project of being always falls short of making the self conform to the projected ideal. How we deal with the less than perfect selves we inherit from the structural limitations of the ego will determine the extent to which we live in bad faith.

In bad faith, we feign or assert greater degrees of self-integration and completion than our ego has in fact achieved. The full extent of the failure of the ego to create a well-integrated, autonomous self that goes into its ideal without remainders, must be concealed through some type of compensatory, evasive, or accumulative activity. For Gordon, white racism with its diminutive stereotyping of blacks is one such accumulative activity. It is a set of discriminatory attitudes and practices toward blacks that provide whites with counterfeit solutions to the problems and anxieties of incomplete self-formation. The black self thus becomes a zone of ontological struggle as colonized states become zones of political conflict. Racism is thus linked directly to the ontology of white egos, as it becomes a form of existential exploitation that leads to the accumulating of counterfeit solutions to ontological problems.

This practice of existential exploitation entails a "projective nonseeing"[19] that enacts "the phenomenological disappearance" of black humanity.

Invisibility, absence, displacement, anonymity, physicality become the constitutive acts through which white ego consciousness reconstructs the meaning of black existence. Although routinized institutionally, this invisibility is clearly not a stark social or physical fact. It is also fundamentally phenomenological, that is, an absence that is constituted as a meaning in the white consciousness. This spell of phenomenological invisibility is an important contribution of the European and Euro-American philosophical consciousness to the clouds of nonseeing that veil the humanity of Africans caught within the peripheral dynamics of European imperialism. Consequently, as long as blacks and whites continue to share social and ontological spaces the removal of this invisibility must include a calling to task of the white philosophical consciousness for this particular expression of bad faith.

The philosophical aspects of the task of restoring visibility would require an Africana-oriented phenomenology that is capable of dissolving the defensive formations and layers of meaning that have enacted black invisibility in the consciousness of both blacks and whites. Among whites it would have to identify the blockages in self-formation, disrupt the defense mechanism of projective nonseeing, thus helping to restore sight. Among blacks, it would have to uproot white images of blacks that the latter have internalized, thus restoring visibility, presence, and ontological space to African elements of black identity. These once more visible African elements will of course not be the original ones. Noticeable or not, these symbols and discourses have been undergoing significant changes in response to European imperialism and racism. Yet, it is precisely in this shared task of reconstituting the racialized black self in the wake of the phenomenological disappearance of its African heritage that Gordon roots the Africana identity of Afro-American philosophy. In doing so, he has established phenomenological reflection on the existential dynamics of the black self as a philosophical practice that is indispensable for an Africana philosophy.

I would like to build on this phenomenological solution to the identity and core of an Africana philosophy. I think it will be extremely helpful in the philosophical examination of Outlaw's problem of Africans-becoming-Americans, Africans-becoming-Caribbeans, or modern Africans. I will argue that the phenomenologically significant similarities and differences between these processes of becoming are capable of establishing the common core of an Africana philosophy. However, to do this, we need to expand Gordon's analysis in two important ways.

First, we need to expand the analysis so that it includes more systematic phenomenological analyses of the traditional African ego. That is, we will need phenomenological accounts of the self-positing activities, the defensive formations, and creative practices by which this ego created self and world. In addition, we will also need to know how this set of ego activities differs from those that followed its racialization as analyzed in the work of DuBois, Fanon, Mills, and Gordon. Second, these expanded phenomenological analyses need to be dialectically linked to many of the discursive formations, emphasized by Outlaw, that have shaped the development of Afro-American philosophy. In other words, although extremely important, the dynamics of black self-formation cannot by themselves establish the identity of Afro-American philosophy as an ongoing discourse. These dynamics must be supplemented by the specific processes of publishing, writing, argumentation, debate, institutional recognition, or nonrecognition that have shaped the formation of Afro-American philosophy. In the next section, I will make use of such a dialectical synthesis in outlining my view of an Africana philosophy.

AFRO-AMERICAN PHILOSOPHY: AN AFRICANA PERSPECTIVE

Although my approach to an Africana philosophy is indeed a synthetic one, for purposes of presentation I will separate the phenomenological and discursive components that make up the dialectal synthesis. Space does not permit the elaborating of a case study that would clearly illustrate the ways in which they work in concert.

The Phenomenological Foundations

The phenomenological aspects of my Africana project are rooted in the racially oriented self-reflective practices that Gordon and others have established. In general terms, we can define phenomenology as self-reflective activity in which a conscious agent comes to a greater awareness of the constitutive determinants of the self-formative process that makes its everyday life possible. Because we are usually unaware of many of these determinants, phenomenological self-reflection often results in a transcending of everyday levels of awareness that can change the conduct of an individual life. However, strategies of self-reflection vary widely, leading to different types of phenomenologies. Hence we need to specify some of the particulars of an Africana phenomenology.

In Descartes and Kant, European self-reflection was directed at the knowing activities of the cogito. Shaped by these concerns, self-reflection came to know itself as epistemology, rather than phenomenology.[20] European phenomenological self-determination came with Hegel, where the growth in consciousness produced by self-reflection was linked to a larger theodicy and to a philosophy of identity between spirit and nature. Although focused on spirit's loss and subsequent recovery of identity, the epistemological issue is still very present in Hegel's concern with absolute knowledge.[21] The stronger "epistemology-centered" orientation of Descartes and Kant returns in Husserl, whose phenomenology included the search for an absolute ground for the practice of self-reflection.[22]

In Heidegger and Sartre, there is a clear break with this type of transcendental or epistemology-centered phenomenology. Self-reflection is linked to the ontology of everyday egos, thus establishing the European tradition of existential phenomenology.[23] In Habermas, European self-reflection regains somewhat its earlier epistemological focus. As we will see, it takes the form of self-reflection on the methodologies of the sciences and on Habermas's angst over the technocratic impact of these sciences on modern democratic life. The result is a socioepistemic phenomenology in which Habermas articulates a theory of knowledge that is at the same time a theory of society.[24]

As in the case of Harris's mythopoetic phenomenology, the Africana phenomenology emerging from the work of Gordon does not fit neatly into any of the above phenomenologies. It shares with them the centrality of self-reflection, but links it to a different set of concerns. As West clearly suggests, Afro-American self-reflection has not made cognitive activities its point of departure. The same is true of Afro-Caribbean philosophy. As we have seen, the major exception here is the work of Sylvia Wynter. However, in both philosophies, self-reflection has given high priority to the "existential deviations"[25] that colonialism and racism have inserted into the self-formative processes of Afro-Caribbeans and Afro-Americans. This direct link between self-reflection and black ego genesis has given Africana phenomenology its existential orientation.

However, this existential orientation is defined by sources of ego negation that are *both* social and ontological in nature, although the latter are extremely important for Gordon. Consequently, as in the case of Habermas's phenomenology the second site of self-reflection in Africana phenomenology is also social in nature. However, the contents of these two social points of departure are quite different. In the place of Habermas's angst over technocratic colonization, Africana phenomenology reflects on black anguish over and resistance to racial colonization. The discursive elaborations that have arisen from these existential and social sites of Africana self-reflection, meet, and engage each other in a philosophical space that can be labeled a theory of the racialized self as a theory of society. Consequently, in contrast to Habermas's socioepistemic phenomenology, Africana phenomenology can be described as socioexistential. Thus rather than attempting to fit Gordon's phenomenological analysis into any of the above European models, I think it will be better if we place it alongside them as the expression of a distinct type of self-reflection.

The first modification of Gordon's analysis that we must undertake is the suggested expansion of its phenomenological analyses to include the constitutive activities of the traditional African ego.[26] In particular, the mythic and religious discourses that have been integral to its formation and stability over time. Phenomenological reflections on these ego-genetic cultural constructs will enable us to examine the different ways in which they were made to "disappear," as the African self was racialized on the continent and in the diaspora. They will also permit us to focus more effectively on the different ways in which these traditional constructs are being incorporated by continental and diasporic Africans, into postcolonial and postracial identities that now occupy less-cramped ontological spaces. In other words, to address the problem of Africans-becoming-Americans or Caribbeans as instances of philosophy, we will require a comprehensive phenomenological history of Africana subjectivity.

This question of a phenomenological history, and in particular its extension to the traditional African ego, raises some difficult methodological problems. Specifically, it poses the problem of the phenomenological study of the ego activities of predecessors. The work of Alfred Schutz demonstrates that this difficulty is not an insurmountable one. He shows that from the perspective of the meaning-constituting activities of the ego, it is possible to divide the social universe into three domains: (1) the world of consociates with whom we are in immediate face-to-face relation; (2) the world of contemporaries with whom we are in mediated, nonface-to-face relations; and (3) the world of predecessors with whom we are in similarly mediated relations, but whose lived experiences do not overlap in time with ours.[27] Shutz demonstrates that phenomenological analyses of all three subuniverses are possible, although the last is clearly the most difficult.

The latter is possible because we can reach the world of predecessors through records, monuments, artifacts, and other expressions of their subjectivity that they have left behind. We can also approach this world through a living person who may have known a predecessor. These are all indirect relations that lack the reciprocity of face-to-face relations. However, Schutz points to one possible reciprocal relation to predecessors. That is, a relation in which the behavior of an individual is oriented toward an act of a predecessor. This one reciprocal relation for Schutz was the bequeathing of property.[28] It is certainly a relationship through which predecessors continue to influence our behavior. If we take the notion of property to include cultural heritages, then such bequests can constitute another set of important phenomenological links to the worlds of predecessors.

The nature of the links to the worlds of consociates, contemporaries, and predecessors will determine the methods that our phenomenological history will employ. Because of the predominantly oral nature of the traditional African heritage, the data on our traditional African predecessors will clearly be ethnographic in nature. The ethnophilosophical data from these analyses will be qualitatively different from the historical, conversational, and self-reflective data we will gather on more recent predecessors, contemporaries, consociates, and from our individual lived experiences. Thus, in spite of the controversy that has raged over the practice of ethnophilosophy, I think it is a necessary component of not only African philosophy but also all Africana-oriented philosophies. Although with great caution, Anthony Appiah has argued for the viability of such an ethnophilosophical component for Afro-American philosophy.[29] In chapter 2, I suggested a similar component for Afro-Caribbean philosophy. Thus the approach in this phase of our phenomenological history will be ethnophilosophical.

Given this possibility of phenomenologically analyzing the world of our traditional African predecessors, we need to specify more precisely why their cultural symbols and discourses are so important for our project of an Africana philosophy. How will these cultural constructs help to define the identity of this philosophy? How will they help to establish its core? I will discuss two reasons why the traditional African heritage is extremely important for both of these concerns.

First, for many African, Afro-American, and Afro-Caribbean philosophers, these cultural constructs are invaluable properties that our traditional African predecessors have bequeathed to us. This Shutzian property relation helps to constitute the complex, phenomenologically significant ties that bind us to this African heritage. Because of the meanings associated with this reciprocal relation, expectations (particularly of continuity), obligations, and constraints are imposed on us. This legacy is our responsibility in ways that it cannot be for non-African groups. The reciprocal nature of our relation to these African symbols and discourses links us more directly to the wishes and expectations of the predecessors who created and nurtured them. In short, unique ties of kinship and inheritance have given Africana philosophers a special responsibility for a shared set of symbols and discourses. To fulfill the obligations of this responsibility, Africana philosophers must preserve and develop this heritage by examining it ethnophilosophically, by reflecting on it in their own lived experiences, or collectively with contemporaries and consociates.

Second, African, Afro-Caribbean, and Afro-American philosophers are not only in unique proprietary relations with the symbols and discourses of traditional Africa but also they are in unique ego-genetic relations with them. These relations establish certain common cultural or mythopoetic elements in the formation of African, Afro-American, and Afro-Caribbean egos. The formative or ego-genetic role of these cultural elements will establish them as common elements in the self-reflections of Africana philosophers on their own ego-genetic processes. This will also be the case whether these reflections are ethnophilosophical in nature, or more conversational with contemporaries and consociates. In other words, because of the critical importance of traditional

African symbols and discourses to the ego formation of African philosophers—continental and diasporic—they are crucial for the identity of an Africana philosophy. Let's develop this claim more fully.

By the nature of its formative process, the human ego is reproductively tied to a culturally specific set of symbols, or to a number of them. These cultural constructs help to define, sustain, and legitimate the ego. More than any other factor, it is the self-reflection of philosophers on the symbols and discourses of their own ego formation that gives a philosophy its cultural identity. Thus the similarities and differences that emerge from the self-reflections of African, Afro-American, and Afro-Caribbean philosophers will be extremely important for their cultural identities.

In spite of its universalistic and transcultural claims, philosophy shares the above cultural birthmarks with literature, music, dance, and other discourses that affirm a national, collective identity. The rational orientation of philosophy does not in any way negate this moment of cultural rootedness, or filial ties with the arts. This cultural moment is indispensable for examining the Africana dimensions of Afro-American philosophy, because it forces us to confront the cultural identity of this rationally oriented discourse. This identity is the necessary moment of prior cultural definition and mythopoetic instituting that the philosophical cogito must inherit. It is the latter's necessary encounter with time-bound symbols and discourses. The philosophical cogito can ignore this cultural identity or affirm it through a phenomenological reconstruction of its self-formative process. In other words, the philosophical cogito can and should make its prephilosophical or inherited identities and their changing discursive registers the objects of a self-reflective philosophical analysis.

Ultimately, the possibilities for an Africana philosophy rests upon our ability to affirm the operating of African cultural registers in the ego genesis of African, Afro-American, and Afro-Caribbean philosophers. Without claiming the status of timeless essences, such affirmations would allow us to identify specific philosophical cogitos whose unique features are in part determined by the formative influences of African symbols and discourses. These formative experiences are ones that philosophers of African descent do not share with other philosophers. They are responsible in part for our uniqueness and our original voice. Again, these symbols and discourses are not timeless essences. On the contrary, they have been changed by different processes of hybridization and creolization. But like so many other sets of ego forming symbols, they have a long half-life.

To the extent that these hybridized identity-legitimating constructs shape or influence the work of African, Afro-American, and Afro-Caribbean philosophers in comparable ways, to that extent do African-derived symbols and discourses constitute important foundations for the Africana identity of

Afro-American philosophy. If, for example, we are able to reconstruct their influence on the Afro-American philosophical consciousness over time and compare it with similar reconstructions in the African and Afro-Caribbean cases, then the Africana project will be on solid foundations. On the other hand, if we are not able to recognize the common influences in the ego genesis and work of philosophers of African descent, then the basis for an Africana philosophy will be severely weakened. This I do not think is the case.

This phenomenological history of Africana subjectivity is not the kind of project that one person can complete. Rather, it is an open-ended collective project to which many must contribute chapters. It should encompass comparative phenomenological analyses of ego formation, deformation (racialization), and transformation among continental and diasporic Africans. The existential analyses of the African ego presented throughout this text, as well as those of Gyekye and Soyinka, are important contributions to the African phase of this phenomenological history of Africana subjectivity. The works of DuBois, Fanon, Richard Wright, James Baldwin, Harris, and Gordon are important founding chapters on the period of racialization. They have all focused on the deformation (double consciousness) that accompanied the racialization of African identities and their subjugation to the ontological needs of white ego genesis. With regard to the continuities and discontinuities between these two periods, the works of Harris, Wynter, and Soyinka are particularly important. In the case of Harris, direct comparisons between his archetypal life and the destinal life of traditional Africans should be very helpful in articulating some of the similarities and differences between the two major periods of our phenomenological history. In other words, it should be a history that allows us to enter not only the poeticist/historicist spaces we currently inhabit but also the African and Afro-Christian ones we either formerly inhabited or continue to inhabit. This phenomenological history will of course be both existential and transcendental, descriptive rather than scientific, social as well as individual, its claims falsifiable rather than absolutely certain. The special value of our phenomenological history is that it will add a unique philosophical perspective to the study of African symbols and to the identities they continue to reproduce.

The Discursive Foundations
Important as these phenomenological foundations are, we've already accepted the importance of Outlaw's suggestion that we take into account the discursive processes that have been vital to the formation of Afro-American, Afro-Caribbean, and African philosophies. In this section I will argue that in addition to intentional acts of bad faith, "the phenomenological disappearance" of the African heritage in Africa, the Caribbean, and the United States was enacted by Europeans with the aid of a corresponding set of arguments,

debates, and practices of institutional exclusion. In short, it was enacted in all three cases by similar sets of discursive dynamics. The arguments against the existence of an African philosophy, and the exclusion of African religions from the table of religious dialogue are cases that reveal these similarities in discursive strategies.

Equally important to the arguments of this section is the fact that the resistance of African, Afro-American, and Afro-Caribbean philosophers to this discursive invisibility was also carried out with the aid of internally similar counterdiscourses and struggles for institutional recognition. This is important for the project of an Africana philosophy. The similarities in these counterdiscourses were not accidental, but rather the result of historical contacts and textual exchanges. Thus the level of invisibility that surrounded the African heritage at a given point in historical time and social space was in part the result of the nature of the discursive compromise produced by these contentious exchanges. The greater visibility of African philosophy today is in part the result of important reverses in the terms of these exchanges that have produced a new discursive compromise. The changing degrees of invisibility that have accompanied these compromises, and the struggles to emerge from beneath their veils, are shared experiences of crucial importance for an Africana approach to Afro-American philosophy. These experiences point to at least three sets of discursive facts that strongly support these broader Pan-African dimensions to the identity of Afro-American philosophy: (1) similarities in patterns of development with African and Afro-Caribbean philosophy; (2) the large number of scholars shared by the three traditions; and (3) their current emergence from more restrictive discursive compromises. I will briefly examine each of these with an emphasis on Afro-American and Afro-Caribbean philosophies.

Afro-American philosophy did not develop in an intellectual vacuum. On the contrary, it developed as an integral part of a larger intellectual tradition. Like its Caribbean counterpart, the Afro-American intellectual tradition has its roots in the discursives responses of Africans to the existential, political, economic, and other challenges of the new-world environment. These challenges came via the institution of slavery that framed the life of Africans in the Caribbean and the United States. The discursive responses that founded these two intellectual traditions were critiques and rejections of the racist and imperialist arguments used by Europeans to justify the practice of slavery. In short, both traditions can be viewed as being rooted in two distinct series of contentious, delegitimating dialogues with European slaveowners and white supremacists.

The initial set of counterchallenges must have been formulated primarily in the discourse of traditional African religions, and ably supported by responses in the more auxiliary discourses of African magic, ritual, song, and philosophy. These were the discourses that sustained African ego formation and hence the ones that Africans were able to reproduce in America and the Caribbean. However, surviving instances of this type of religiously coded resistance by Africans are much harder to find in the United States than in the Caribbean.

Drawing on Caribbean religions such as Shango, Santería, and Vodou, we can suggest two basic responses. First is a politicizing of religious cosmologies that gave greater visibility and power to the gods of war and strength as is clear in the cases of Vodou and Shango. Here the appeal was to gods like Shango and Ogun for the strength to fight enslavers and colonizers. Self-reflection recognized itself as angry, anguished, and religious. In the second response, resistance was less direct. The experience of slavery was placed in the providential category of divine punishment and thus a form of redemptive or expiatory suffering. Self-reflection comprehended itself as religious fate. However, those who were the immediate cause of this suffering would in time also get their taste of divine punishment. In other words, liberation from slavery and colonialism would be by the hands of the gods. Responses of both types were a part of the first discursive compromises Afro-Caribbean and Afro-American thinkers were able to achieve vis-à-vis their European counterparts. In these compromises, the role of philosophy was clearly to supplement religious and ideological responses to slavery.

Over time, these primarily African religious responses changed their discursive registers and became predominantly Christian. Although rooted in the great Protestant revivals of the 1700s the processes of Christianization in the Caribbean and Afro-America were quite different. In the main, Caribbean Christianity was the product of classic colonial churches that did not become independent until the 1960s.[30] By contrast Afro-American Christianity emerged from black churches that were autonomous by the start of the American Civil War.[31] In the Caribbean, we have the two extremes produced by these processes of Afro-Christian syncretism: the survival of predominantly African religions such as Shango and Vodou, on the one hand, and highly Europeanized churches, on the other. The latter are products of centuries of colonial control during which pastors were predominantly European. In Afro-America, there has been a more uniform and intermediate pattern of syncretism that has produced a distinct Afro-American Christianity. This Christianity is more African in tone than the classic colonial churches of the Caribbean, but less so than religions like Shango or Vodou.

The discursive impact of these processes of Christianization is evident in the earliest published writing of Afro-Americans and Afro-Caribbeans. Richard Allen, Lemuel Haynes, Jupiter Hammond, Phyllis Wheatley, and David Walker are Afro-Americans whose work clearly reflect this change of religious registers. In the Caribbean, similar changes are evident in the works of Ann Hart (1804), Jean-Baptiste Phillipe (1824), Mary Prince (1831), and Michel Maxwell Phillip (1854).[32] This shift introduced important changes in the dramatis personae of Afro-American and Afro-Caribbean writing. Satan, Jehovah, Mary, Jesus Christ, his disciples, and the saints replaced Legba, Obatala, Shango, Erzulie, Oshun, Damballah, and other African deities.

But in spite of these and other significant discontinuities, there were also important continuities. Slavery and colonial domination were still understood in terms of two basic categories: situations to be resisted forcefully with the aid of divine power, or providentially conceived cases of divine punishment from which they would be relieved after a necessary period of expiatory suffering. The insurrectionary activities of Denmark Vessey in Afro-America and Paul Bogle in Jamaica are instances of the first. Evidence of the second can be seen in the works of Hammond and Walker. Walker explicitly links the experience of enslavement to punishment for the disobedience of our African forefathers.[33] As we will see, this belief can still be found among the Rastafarians of Jamaica.[34] In short, the basic characteristic of self-reflection as religious fate survived the change of registers.

The fact that these older arguments were now being made in Christian, rather than African religious terms significantly altered the role of philosophy in this set of discursive compromises made by Afro-American and Afro-Caribbean thinkers. Instead of legitimating the African religious frameworks of these arguments, Afro-American and Afro-Caribbean philosophies were now legitimating their newly adopted Christian frameworks.

However, this change in religious registers was a particularly difficult one for these two philosophies. Blinded like other European discourses by hegemonic concerns, the new Christian register was already deeply involved in the peripheral dynamics of European imperialism and hence in the discursive production of African invisibility. Binary oppositions were being specially marked and discursively mobilized on behalf of this effort. The new register made its contributions by using these binaries to maximize the differences between African and European religions. The former was labeled and evaluated through categories such as primitive, pagan, black, evil, and polytheistic, while modern, Christian, white, good, and monotheistic were the categories used to evaluate the latter. A greater inequality between religions would be difficult to construct. This chasm became the basis for excluding African religions from the American and Caribbean communities of religious discourse. In spite of the difference in patterns of religious creolization, both Afro-Caribbean and Afro-American Christianity inherited this radical disenfranchising of traditional African religions. A similar deployment of binaries led to European/Christian denials of the existence of an African philosophy.

These anti-African biases entered the philosophical and religious thought of Afro-Caribbeans and Afro-Americans with this shift in religious registers. It was the shift that lowered the veil over African philosophy in both traditions. In this state of self-alienation, the Afro-American and Afro-Caribbean philosophical cogitos were overtaken by cases of DuBoisian double consciousness. This lack of public recognition should not be equated with the nonexistence of traditional African philosophy, but rather with a discursive illegitimacy that made it disappear. With this submerging of their African heritages, Afro-American and Afro-Caribbean philosophies entered a long contradictory period in which they were marked by underidentifications with traditional African thought and overidentifications with modern European thought. In other words, philosophical versions of Fanon's black skins wearing white masks. In this state, Afro-Caribbean and Afro-American philosophies were forced to legitimate Christian critiques of slavery at the cost of contributing to the invisibility of traditional Africa. Only with the shift to the currently emerging discursive compromise has this contradictory dynamic shown real signs of reversal. The full recovery of traditional African philosophy from a life beneath veils and masks must be a central concern of an Africana philosophy.

From this predominantly Christian phase, the Afro-American and Afro-Caribbean intellectual traditions moved into more secular and ideological phases in the second half of the nineteenth century. In the former case, this shift was marked by the rise of figures such as Frederick Douglass, Booker T. Washington, Alain Locke, Zora Neale Hurston, W. E. B. DuBois, and others. In the latter case, it was inaugurated by writers such as Edward Blyden, J. J. Thomas, Robert Love, Marcus Garvey, C. L. R. James, George Padmore, Aime Cesaire, Frantz Fanon, and others. However, in many of the transitional figures such as Douglass and Blyden, the impact of the earlier Christian phase is still evident. In this more ideological phase, slavery and racism were seen primarily in terms of the motivations and historical practices of Europeans. Receding into the background were the religious explanations, particularly the providential ones of divine punishment. This shift in perspective is clearly captured in DuBois's reflections on the period: "A way back in the days of bondage they thought to see in one divine event the end of all doubt and disappointment; few men ever worshipped Freedom with half such unquestioning faith as did the American Negro for two centuries."[35]

These shifts in the dominant patterns of argument in their larger intellectual traditions had important consequences for both Afro-Caribbean and Afro-American philosophies. In both traditions, it led to dramatic increases in the importance of historicism and poeticism. However, with these philosophical shifts, Africana self-reflection did not recognize itself as phenomenological, but primarily as poeticist. It came close in DuBois and James, but really only assumed an explicit phenomenological identity in Fanon. Consequently, the philosophical positions of historicism and poeticism assumed much greater prominence than positions of empiricism, scientism, or transcendentalism. Poeticism became the philosophical discourse for analyzing the motives and mythopoetics of white and black subjectivities. Historicism became the philosophical discourse for analyzing institutions of racial domination and the conditions for their political transformation. In some cases, both of these philosophical positions were embodied in the same person in a complementary or oppositional fashion. Thus, DuBois, Jean Toomer, Zora Neale Hurston, Cesaire, James, and Fanon were all important individuals who embodied strong historicist and poeticist tendencies. Indeed, as a short characterization of the philosophies that emerged from the more secular discursive compromises of the late nineteenth and early twentieth centuries, I would suggest the label, between poeticism and historicism.

It is in these third compromises that the politico-ideological orientation of the Afro-American and Afro-Caribbean philosophical traditions really becomes explicit. Also more visible is the auxiliary role of philosophy within the discursive formations of the larger intellectual traditions. Even a cursory examination of the role of philosophy in the works of Locke, DuBois, Garvey, or James should make this clear. It is particularly evident in the case of Locke. Although he was formally trained in philosophy, he very often used it as the minor text in his culturally oriented writings. Locke's philosophy often took the form of a subtextual poeticism, which was used to discursively mobilized the rising power of Afro-American aesthetics in struggles against the racial stereotypes that created and sustained double consciousness.[36]

Finally in this brief account of the similarities in patterns of development, it is important to note that the philosophies associated with these compromises were also marked by high levels of invisibly with regard to traditional African thought. This was a characteristic they inherited from their larger intellectual traditions. As we have seen, this was an inheritance of the Christianizing of these traditions that the first secular philosophical formations were not able to reject effectively.

Closely related to these parallels and similarities in the historical development of these two philosophies is the second discursive factor that is crucial for the broader Africana identities of African, Afro-Caribbean, and Afro-American philosophies. This factor is the large number of important philosophical and other writers that these three traditions share. From Afro-America, the three traditions share the figures of Douglass, DuBois, Washington, Hurston, King, Malcolm X, West, bell hooks, Angela Davis, and many others. From Africa, we share the heritage of traditional African religions, as well as figures like Kwame Nkrumah, Leopold Senghor, Julius Nyerrere, Amilcar Cabral, Samir Amin,

Paulin Hountondji, Wole Soyinka, Anthony Appiah, Kwame Gyekye, and many others. From the Caribbean, we have the figures of Edward Blyden, Marcus Garvey, C. L. R. James, Frantz Fanon, Aime Cesaire, Edouard Glissant, Wilson Harris, Derek Walcott, Sylvia Wynter, Stokeley Carmichael, Jamaica Kincaid, Hazel Carby, Lewis Gordon, and many more.

These historical and intertextual connections are important as they point to common problems and shared solutions between these three intellectual traditions. In particular, these connections must have influenced the nature and pattern of development of philosophy in all three cases. Consequently Afro-American philosophy has not developed in complete isolation from either African or Afro-Caribbean philosophy. These connections, which are embedded in its larger intellectual tradition, constitute important foundations for its Africana identity.

The third and final discursive factor that is important for my Africana project is the current move toward a fourth compromise in both Afro-American and Afro-Caribbean philosophy. In both of these traditions, philosophy has been shaped by the discursive demands of religion, literature, history, music, and sociology. Work in these fields generated demands for philosophical arguments and transformative visions that would inform and support their creative productions. Given the politically charged nature of the issues that occupied scholars in the above fields, the philosophical demands they generated were largely ideological in nature. This ideological orientation was clearly visible in our earlier review of the works of West, Outlaw, and Gordon.

However, as I've argued in the case of Afro-Caribbean philosophy, this ideological orientation has its limitations.[37] In this position, philosophy remains a subordinate discourse in intellectual traditions that have been dominated by religion, literature, history, and so on. In both traditions, philosophy has ably supported the work done in these fields, but really has not had an agenda of its own. Its existence has been a subtextual one, providing infrastructural support for more dominant texts. This comparatively weak presence may be what Deotis Roberts had in mind when he described Afro-Americans as "reluctant philosophers."[38] From these specific ideological/subtextual positions, it has been quite difficult to establish substantive connections with traditional African philosophy. These weaknesses are reflections of the cramped spaces in which Afro-American and Afro-Caribbean philosophies developed.

In the less-cramped spaces of the contemporary period, both philosophies have been moving out of the subtextual roles they have occupied in their respective divisions of intellectual labor. They have also been moving away from their near exclusive politico-ideological foci and have begun engaging a broader range of issues. This is evident in the growing relations with traditional and modern African philosophy, the contacts with Euro-American pragmatism and various branches of European philosophy. These new engagements together with the changing realities that constitute the lived experiences of Afro-Americans and Afro-Caribbeans, should dramatically widen the scope of these philosophies and increase their presence in the emerging discursive orders. The above forces have already moved these philosophies from their earlier states of delicate suspensions between historicism and poeticism. The divisions between these positions will continue to decline as they are forced to establish new balances with a wider variety of philosophical positions.

The engagements with traditional African philosophy should help to make more explicit the largely implicit ethnophilosophical components in both Afro-Caribbean and Afro-American philosophies. Because of the greater retentions of African religions, this ethnophilosophical component may be stronger in the Afro-Caribbean case. In short, the increased contact with both traditional and contemporary African philosophy should bring these two diasporic traditions closer in form and spirit to continental philosophy.

The engagements with European, Euro-American, or other traditions of philosophy we should expect to vary more widely. These variations will reflect difference in the lived experiences of Afro-Caribbeans and Afro-Americans. For example, the national experiences of the two groups, the ways in which these experiences have colored problems of class, race, gender, and economic development have already and will continue to make for differences in patterns of engagement. I suspect that differences in the struggle for economic development account for the greater visibility of economic thinking in Afro-Caribbean philosophy and its less enthusiastic response to the poststructuralist turn in European thought.

Finally, as it shares societal space with a large Indo-Caribbean population, Afro-Caribbean philosophy will have to engage in more systematic dialogues with Indian and Indo-Caribbean philosophies. To a lesser degree, the latter have also been victims of the phenomenological and discursive invisibility mobilized by European racism and imperialism. Yet both groups have inherited much of this blindness and have not been able to see each other's philosophies. Hence the urgent need for dialogue.

In spite of these important differences, current trends indicate that Afro-Caribbean and Afro-American philosophies are both moving from similar points toward new discursive formations. The latter are likely to be similar in their African components, but dissimilar in their non-African components. If realized, these are changes that will take both philosophies out of their earlier ideological and subtextual roles. These similarities and continuities, which are clearly integral parts of this new phase, constitute important bases for the broader Africana identity of both Afro-American and Afro-Caribbean philosophies.

My case for an Africana philosophy that embraces African, Afro-American, Afro-Caribbean, and other diasporic African philosophies rests on the above three discursive pillars. It rests as well on the prospects for a comparative phenomenological history of ego formation in the precolonial, colonial, and postcolonial periods among continental and diasporic Africans. The discursive pillars would establish the important interchanges, parallels, and similarities necessary for a shared discursive field. The phenomenological history would establish the common ego-genetic symbols that are necessary for this field to share an Africana identity and a distinct Africana tradition of philosophical self-reflection. To the extent that our comparative phenomenology reveals the continuing ego-genetic relevance of African symbols, and our discursive analyses reveal continuing patterns of textual exchange and shared patterns of discursive development, to that degree will we have a firm basis for an Africana philosophy.

As the above account of the contemporary phase suggests, the pursuit of such an Africana approach to Afro-American philosophy does not exclude engagements with its European or Euro-American heritages. The Africana approach is an extremely important possibility within the emerging discursive conjuncture of Afro-American philosophy. As noted earlier it is quite possible for philosophers to ignore the cultural identity of their discourse and completely immerse themselves in its technical problems and its universalistic or transcultural claims. I am sure there will be Afro-American and Afro-Caribbean philosophers who will adopt such positions.

However, in spite of being a possibility that philosophers can ignore, our Africana project remains extremely important for the futures of African, Afro-American, and Afro-Caribbean philosophies. I will conclude this chapter with three reason why this is the case.

The first concerns the retaining of traditions of activism. If these philosophies are to retain their traditions of activism in the new conjuncture, then an Africana project that takes seriously the cultural identities of these philosophies becomes extremely important. In their respective societies, devalued ego-genetic African symbols have been reproducing devalued or illegitimate black existences. An intellectually honest revalorizing of these symbols is thus an urgent task, as the self-worth of many African peoples depend upon it. As our Africana project takes this challenge seriously, it would commit these philosophies to contributing to this critical task of revalorization through their own independent revaluing of the cultural symbols of their inherited identity. In doing so, these philosophies will be contributing to increases in the value of the lives that depend on these symbols. This is an important form of personal empowerment that enhances the courage to resist invisibility, discrimination, sexual abuse, and other forms of domination.

The second reason our Africana project will be important for the futures of African, Afro-American, and Afro-Caribbean philosophies is related to the place and status of African mythic discourses in these systems of thought. It is likely that our comparative phenomenology will reveal patterns of exit from the traditional worlds of African myth and religion into the modern period that are very different from European patterns of exit. Indeed, an important dimension of a distinct modern identity is the extent to which members of a cultural group have been able to represent symbolically the uniqueness of their path to modernity. Can contemporary appropriations of Oedipus, Electra, Prometheus, and other members of the Greek pantheon adequately represent the African paths to modernity, or will we require modern appropriations of Ogun, Erzulie, Shango, and other members of the African pantheon? The paths of Africans, both continental and diasporic, have been marked by the survival of strong mythic elements into the modern period. They have also been shaped by territorially limited enclaves of patrimonial or feudal social organization and colonization by an imperial Europe that was transitioning from feudal to capitalist forms of social organization. The specific discursive shifts and changes in registers that mark the paths by which Africans have become modern Americans or Caribbeans are important prerequisites for any accurate account of the uniqueness the modern Afro-American or Afro-Caribbean identity. To the task of assessing this uniqueness our comparative phenomenology can make a valuable contribution. With the results, Afro-Caribbean and Afro-American philosophies will be able to gauge more carefully the future of their current practices.

Third and finally, is the significance of our unique paths out of the world of myth for the broader problem of human modernity, an issue which we will examine more fully in the next chapter and the conclusion. Are there distinct perspectives or special philosophical lessons indigenous to our paths that might throw new light on the crises threatening this global project? Next to the problem of the color line, the biggest challenge with which modernity has confronted African philosophies is the problem of science and technology, their marriage to commodity production, and the imperial scientism that has been their offspring. Because of the priority given to historicism and poeticism, neither Afro-American or Afro-Caribbean philosophy has dealt adequately with the challenges of science or scientism. As we have seen, these philosophies have been practice and not epistemology oriented. Self-reflection on knowledge production has not been for them a primary point of departure. To meet this modern challenge, these philosophies will have to engage in new modes of self-reflection and bring original and indigenous symbolic resources with which to reframe and recode scientistic problems.

For example, scientism requires the "phenomenological disappearance" of myth, religion, and other nonscientific discourses. European phenomenology has been unable to stop the march of this science-driven invisibility that has overtaken many of these discourses. Can an Africana phenomenology be of help here? We certainly need to find out. By bringing different attitudes toward myth and science, by establishing interesting parallels between black invisibility and mythic invisibility, Afro-American and Afro-Caribbean philosophies could make important contributions to empowering the critical impulses against scientism. Consequently, it is important that Afro-American philosophy express not only European modernity as West suggests but also African modernity. Through the latter, Afro-American philosophy will be able to bring unique symbolic resources that are not only important for its future as a modern discourse but also for the project of modernity itself.

Habermas, Phenomenology, and Rationality: An Africana Contribution

In earlier chapters, we examined the peripheral, categorical, and existential dynamics that produced the negation and invisibility of Caliban's reason. In this chapter, I will continue to trace the return of visibility by identifying some important philosophical contributions that have emerged from Caliban's thought. I will take up the problem of rationality in contemporary Western societies from the perspective of the most liminalized of Caliban's discourses: the traditional African heritage. I will address two sets of problems from this African perspective: first, the blind and excessive growth of technocratic rationality in Western societies; and second, the difficulties these societies have experienced in renewing certain types of meaning- and world-constituting practices that are vital for their ethical and normative foundations.

I will approach these problems through an Africana critique of Habermas's communicative response to the problems of Western rationality. First, I briefly take up Habermas's relations with Husserl's phenomenological response. Second, I examine the originality and uniqueness of Habermas's approach. Third, I critique this response from the perspective of the mythic discourses of the Africana philosophical tradition. This critique is developed in three stages.

In the first, I argue that Habermas does not adequately address the connections between the one-sided development of Western rationality and the exclusionary practices through which it has consistently produced conceptual others. Second, I show that in the case of Habermas, the other of his communicatively expanded model of Western rationality is mythic thought. Drawing on the work of Frantz Fanon, Sylvia Wynter, Lewis Gordon, and Atu Sekyi-Otu, I examine the relation of this excluding of myth to Habermasian communicative rationality. Making extensive use of Wynter's work, I argue that this relation is liminal in nature and has very little to do with the formal properties of mythic thought. Third, I argue that such patterns of liminal exclusion constitute important bases of support for one-sided patterns of self-assertion such as those we find in the cases of modern scientistic or technocratic reason. I substantiate this claim by demonstrating the existential bases for practices of othering and one-sided self-assertion that cannot be adequately reached from Habermas's communicative perspective. In addition, I suggest that addressing the problems associated with these existential dimensions will require discourses of a reconciliatory nature, such as myth. Consequently, I end with the suggestion that Habermas's discursive mobilizations against technocratic rationality need the reconciliatory rationality of mythic thought as an ally, rather than an irrational other.

HUSSERL AND THE CRISIS OF THE SCIENCES

The incorporation of the sciences into the everyday life of Western societies has created a number of problems that continue to challenge the best efforts to resolve them. As new expressions of the life of reason, the universalism of the sciences provided new norms for identity formation, and the regulation of several areas of social life. However, the social deploying of these new norms and regulatory principles quickly exposed their differences with the norms of philosophical reasons and the one-sided patterns of development with which they were associated. In the late nineteenth and early twentieth centuries, Max Weber and Edmund Husserl produced two classic analyses of this crisis that had overtaken these attempt to integrate the sciences into Western societies. In the present period, Habermas has offered us an equally comprehensive analysis of this crisis that draws extensively on these two earlier attempts.

It is an understatement to say that the problem of rationality is central to the work of Habermas and Husserl. Both are deeply rooted in the rational project that Western societies have been struggling to realize. In fact, much of their philosophizing is motivated by an anxious concern that factors closely related to the rise of the sciences and their institutionalization as forces of economic production and bureaucratic control, seriously threaten the future of this project. As the technical successes of sciences led to their wider institutionalization in the nineteenth century, the latter has produced a technocratic narrowing of the guiding concept of reason. This abridged conception has mapped itself onto the meaning-constituting practices of nontechnocratic discourses, particularly the philosophic and scientific narratives of universalism that have defined rational conceptions of "Western Man."

For Husserl, this fall from the philosophic to the technocratic conception of reason constituted "the crisis of European man."[1] It eclipsed the domain of spirit, impoverished the everyday life world, and displaced the goal of absolute knowledge through a scientifically rigorous philosophy as the self-defining project of "European man."

For Habermas, the ascendency of technocratic reason has resulted in "the colonization of the lifeworld"[2] by systems of instrumental action. This domination has brought with it the technocratic colonization of identity, raising the cybernetic automaton or cyborg as the real model of the human that will emerge from Western modernity. Habermas argues that this conquest of "the lifeworld" and personal identity has destroyed the conditions necessary for the renewal of ethical and other traditional cultural practices upon which Western societies depend for motivation. As a result, they "are being nonrenewably dismantled."[3] In Habermas's view, cultural traditions "remain alive as long as they take shape in an unplanned, nature-like manner or are shaped with hermenentic consciousness."[4] As the instrumental orientation of modern societies is particularly hostile to the first of these conditions, the traditional heritages of these societies are being nonrenewably eroded.

Husserl's response to these tendencies was a careful phenomenological analysis of the foundations of the sciences with a view toward finding the source of this decline into technocratic rationality. He located this source in the tendency of sciences-in-action to conceal the meaning-constituting activities of the creative center or ego upon which their presuppositions and basic categories rest. Further, scientific routines tend to exclude the self-reflective practices by which scientists could recognize this ego and its founding activities.[5] This tendency to close off the transcendental domain was not unique to the sciences. Husserl observed similar patterns in logical and historical discourses and, hence, was as critical of logicism and historicism as he was of scientism.[6] Using a distinct type of phenomenological self-reflection, Husserl was able to recover this ego and its transcendental domain that had been closed off by the objectivistic or scientistic outlook of the sciences. Indeed, Husserl would attempt to ground problems of objectivity in the knowledge-constitutive activities of this recovered ego. Because knowledge of the activities of this transcendental ego was not the result of scientific cognition, Husserl saw in phenomenology a mode of philosophical rationality that did not fit within the confines of scientific or technocratic reason. Hence it could be mobilized as a countervailing force on behalf of the project of Western rationalism.

With these goals of phenomenologically reopening the transcendental domain and philosophically reexpanding the contracted notion of Western rationality, Husserl sought to establish phenomenology on a rigorous and universal basis. However, this foundation would have to be different from that of the sciences. Since phenomenology's primary task was the examination of the foundations of the sciences and all other discourses, it could not rest on unclarified presuppositions as was the case in the sciences. On the contrary, it required a presuppositionless foundation, or one whose presuppositions had to be clarified to the point of transparency.

Husserl thought he had secured such a presuppositionless foundation in the original intuitions of the transcendental ego in action that arose spontaneously in practices of self-reflection.[7] These are of course the self-reflective practices in which we are aided by the eidetic and phenomenological reductions. The latter procedures aided the thinker in eliminating the contingent and arriving at the pure phenomenal forms in which things are immediately given to or intuited by consciousness. In Husserl's view, the immediacy of these intuitions gave them an apodictic certainty that obviated the need for any further grounding. Consequently, phenomenology was not founded on the certainty of empirical generalizations, or the necessities of inductive or deductive reasoning. On the contrary, they were rooted in the apodictic clarity and certainty of immediately given intuitions of our transcendental ego doing its knowledge-constitutive work. With phenomenology established on this universal but non-scientific foundation, Husserl could then mobilize its distinct philosophical rationality in the struggle against the dominance of technocratic rationality.

In short, Husserl's response to the crisis of scientific objectivism plaguing Western rationality was a phenomenological reexpansion of both the notion of rationality, and the identity of the rational subject. Along with this transcendentally enlarged vision of rationality, Husserl wanted to revive some version of the Greek practice of *theoria* through which this rational, in contrast to technocratic, model of the human could be cultivated. In his words, "The crisis of European existence requires for its solution a heroism of reason that will definitely overcome naturalism."[8] In playing this heroic role, reason would have to wear the costume of phenomenology. Thus the life of reason would be restored through its cultivation on the transcendental plane and in turn the life of Western humanity.

THE HABERMASIAN CRITIQUE

Habermas's eager embrace of the project of rescuing self-reflective rationality and its transcendental domain from scientistic eclipse establishes a primary area of convergence with Husserl. The importance of rescuing self-reflection is clear in Habermas's early works.[9] But in spite of this important convergence, Habermas departs from Husserl on just how self-reflective rationality is to be mobilized in the modern period. There are three crucial differences motivating this departure.

First, Habermas is not persuaded by Husserl's attempts to give his phenomenology an absolute ground and hence a rigorous formulation. Habermas inherited this critical stance from Adorno's rejection of Hegelian and Husserlian phenomenologies in favor of immanent critique. The latter employs as its motor the reflexivity and power of the dialectical negation in Hegel's phenomenology, while rejecting its claims to absolute truth.[10] From the perspective of immanent critique, Habermas argued that the Husserlian immediate is always mediated, whether it is a given for the everyday or the transcendental ego.[11] In other words, Habermas is skeptical about phenomenological immediacy and hence its ability to provide absolute foundations.

Habermas's second difference with Husserl is over the possibility of reviving Greek *theoria* as a model for linking theory and praxis in the modern period. This model employed a view of philosophical theorizing as the disinterested (presuppositionless) contemplation of the cosmos in which, through mimesis, the individual brought his or her life into harmony with the rhythms and proportions of the cosmos. For Husserl, the important condition for the generating of this type of life-orienting theory was the attitude of disinterestedness. Habermas objects to this conflating of disinterestedness and presuppostionlessness.[12] The former does not translate easily into the latter. Also he is not convinced that phenomenological self-reflection can take the place of the mimetic aspects of the classical model without a considerable loss of action-orienting power. Hence Habermas's skepticism about this particular way of mobilizing self-reflective rationality in the modern period.

The third important divergence between the early Habermas and Husserl is the different roles they assign to self-reflection in the constituting of the "I," or the self-conscious ego. Because of his commitment to a self-reflectively accessible transcendental domain, Habermas's conception of the rational subject overlaps but does not coincide with Husserl's. In the latter, the scientistic conception is philosophically expanded by a phenomenological knowledge of the knowing subject as it relates to itself, and not as it relates to others or to its objects of cognition. In other words, the "I" is primarily the unity of the transcendental ego as it is constructed in self-reflection. In Habermas, self-reflection does not play such a crucial role in ego determination. His view of ego genesis is much closer to the conception of human subjectivity found in Hegelian phenomenology. Here the constituting of the "I" is theorized not in terms of the unity of its relations with itself, but through the dynamics of reciprocal recognition between itself and other communicating subjects.

Habermas distinguishes five different versions of this communicative model of ego genesis in Hegel. For example, (and important for this chapter) the third version is centered on a dialectic of misrecognition and separation in which ego growth includes a phase of inflating its fragment of reality into a false totality, which it substitutes for the real totality. This false absolutization gives the ego room to grow, but at the same time separates it from the genuine whole. After a period of resistance, the ego exchanges this formative separation for a reconciliation in which it sublates its absolutist claims and recognizes itself as a fragment of the real totality. This version is important for us because it echoes Harris's archetypal life and the destinal life of traditional African existentialism. All three share the theme of a *Yuruguan* revolt against the cosmic order as a phase in the ego-genetic process that is followed by a reconciliation.

However, it is the fourth version of the communicative model of ego genesis that Habermas chooses. It is of course the version with the three interrelated dialectics that are rooted in the distinct practices of symbolic representation, work and interaction. In these dialectics, subjects lose and subsequently find themselves through the media of language, instrumental action and communicative action. As a medium of self-formation, language—particularly its powers to name and represent—makes possible a discursive interrupting of the prior continuity between the emerging ego and the world of nature. Like language, instrumental action inserts a technical mediation between the immediacy of human needs and their satisfaction from the natural environment. Finally communicative action disrupts the immediacy of interactive needs by the discursive insertion of a dialectic of mutual recognition between them and their satisfaction by other human beings. For Habermas, it is these three discursive/communicative disruptions of states of continuity or immediacy that make possible the emergence of the ego and give it the capacity for agency and autonomy.[13] Given this conception of ego genesis it is not surprising that communication plays a more prominent role than self-reflection. The Husserlian ego that is unified by self-reflection is seen as an abstraction from this more concrete communicative framework. Thus, it is within the latter that self-reflection finds its proper place in Habermas.

THE HABERMASIAN REFORMULATION

These three differences with Husserl go a long way in explaining the different ways in which Habermas will mobilize self-reflective rationality in the struggle against technocratic domination. First, self-reflection will be mobilized not as phenomenology, but as critical theory. Second, it will be linked and subsequently delinked from the Marxian project. Finally, replacing the Marxian project as partner in the struggle against technocratic domination will be the power of communicative rationality. Let us look briefly at these three aspects of Habermas's response to the crisis of Western rationality.

FROM IMMANENT CRITIQUE TO CRITICAL THEORY

Earlier we noted that Habermas inherited the position of immanent critique from Adorno as a way of preserving the self-reflective elements in the phenomenologies of Hegel and Husserl. Immanent critique rejected the absolutist claims of both phenomenologies. Hence it is a form of negative dialectics in which self-reflection is without an absolute ground and thus unable to name the origins or final goals of its continuous movements. Habermas is just as uncomfortable with this ungrounded aspect of Adorno's dialectics as he is with the absolutist claims of Hegel and Husserl. Thus he will attempt to formulate a position in which the negative reflexivity of self-reflection is transcendentally grounded by a concrete interest and not by disinterested or presuppositionless intuitions.

Habermas's critical alternative to Husserlian immediacy rests on the claim that knowledge, including phenomenological knowledge, is always motivated by an interest of some sort.[14] Hence it cannot be free of presuppositions and standpoints. For Habermas, the interest that mediates the transcendental intuitions, categories, and epistemic orders that ground self-reflection is an emancipatory one. It is an interest that helps to shape the categorical framework in which objects of cognition are constituted, and the perspective from which they are seen. In other words, an emancipatory interest helps us to frame people, objects, events, and resources from a perspective that maximizes popular freedom and autonomy. A critical theory is one whose categorical foundations are shaped by such an interest in freedom. For example, increasing freedom may require making people more aware of inhibiting influences on them. The categorical framework, internal organization, and propositions of critical theories are such that they will trigger processes of self-reflection in their addressees regarding these inhibiting influences. The result is a raising of consciousness that may produce new forms of practical, as opposed to technical, action.

For Habermas, the discourses of Kant, Hegel, Fichte, Marx, Freud, and Husserl all share this critical dimension. Their insight-yielding and consciousness-raising powers derive from the categorical organization of people, objects, and events made possible by this interest. However, they are not quite critical theories in the Habermasian sense as their epistemological self-understanding is rooted in a metaphysical, rather than a postmetaphysical, conception of philosophy. For Habermas, the impact of the sciences has been such that all metaphysical approaches to knowledge production have become nonviable in the modern period. Thus, for self-reflection to survive in the modern period, its epistemological claims, although different from those of the sciences, must be consistent with them. This normative pressure for consistency with the sciences is absent in the attempts of Adorno, Horkheimer, and Marcuse to specify the notion of a critical theory. Hence it constitutes a sharp difference between the epistemology of Habermas's critical theory and the epistemologies of these three important critical theorists. Similarly, Habermas's choice of critical theory over Husserlian phenomenology has much do with the interested and more scientifically consistent nature of the former's epistemological grounding.

These aspects of the epistemology of critical theory become even clearer when we take into account Habermas's broader reforms of the whole transcendent terrain. He has attempted to restructure it around three primary knowledge-constitutive interests. Thus in addition to the knowledge-constitutive interest in emancipation, Habermas recognized an interest in technical control, and an interest in mutual understanding. The interest in technical control shapes the categorical framework of the empirical sciences, while the interest in mutual understanding shapes the categorical frameworks of the hermeneutic sciences. With these interests, there is now both diversity and equality on the transcendental plane. All of the recognized forms of knowledge production have their prior constituting activities rooted in an interest, without their truth claims being automatically invalidated or compromised. Critical theories can now stand on their own grounds when challenged by scientistic arguments. In short, as critical theory, self-reflection acquired legitimacy as a nonscientific discourse in this era of scientific hegemony. Hence it is in the form of critical theory, and not phenomenology or immanent critique, that Habermas will mobilize self-reflective rationality in the struggle against a "one-dimensional"[15] technocratic reason.

CRITICAL THEORY AND MARXISM

As critical theorist, Habermas did not restrict the immanent philosophizing of self-reflection to the reopening of the transcendental domain that had been closed off by scientistic practices. On the contrary, he wanted to extend its powers to the social arena. Social demands for self-reflection arise whenever specialized (particularly scientific) knowledge is being incorporated into the everyday world with its already established meanings. However, the specific set of the social demands that linked critical theory to Marxism were those arising from the ideological distortion of social groups and from exploitative practices produced by the pressure of hidden or suppressed social interest. Thus in works such as *Towards a Rational Society*, *Theory and Praxis*, and *Legitimation Crisis*, the students, workers, and intellectuals who are resisting capitalist domination become the addressees of critical theory. In these oppositional endeavors, self-reflective rationality is being mobilized against certain fixed ideological constructions, in addition to the closure of the transcendental domain. It is precisely in this area of ideology critique that critical theory joined the Marxian project of overcoming the capitalist order of domination. However, Habermas has two important differences with Marx. The first is phenomenological, while the second is sociological.

The phenomenological differences center around the restrictions that Marxism places on the transcendental domain. These restrictions obscure self-reflection and blur the differences between the natural sciences and critique. Marxism obscures self-reflection because it organizes the transcendental domain in terms of the instrumental activity of labor. In Marxism, labor replaces not only the transcendental ego but also obscures the distinct cognitive interests in emancipation and mutual understanding. Consequently, labor's functions are not just social but transcendental as well. It shapes the crucial meaning-constituting activities that inform both discursive production and identity formation. Given Habermas's tripartite restructuring of the transcendental domain, Marxism's laborist formulation is clearly too narrow. It explicitly recognizes only the interest in technical/instrumental work. Hence it tends to obscure or reduce self-reflection to the level of instrumental action.[16] In other words, self-reflection is conceived according to the model of production. For Habermas, this is not good enough. It restricts the "unconditional phenomenological self-reflection of knowledge"[17] necessary to counter the one-dimensional rationality threatening the modern project. In short, Marxism unnecessarily limits the mobilizing of self-reflective rationality.

The sociological difference is over the proletariat, the Marxian agent of social change. Habermas shares Marx's basic analysis of class domination in capitalist societies, but argues that the growth of science and technology as forces of production has significantly eroded the transformative power of the proletariat. Hence the need to reformulate this aspect of Marxism. In Habermas's view, the more the sciences transform liberal capitalism into technocratic capitalism the more the primary site of resistance shifts to the life-world and its communicative rationality. Consequently, the struggle between technical and communicative rationality replaces that between capital and labor. Socialism for Habermas is the social order that is able to contain the imperialism of technocratic rationality: "What constitutes the idea of socialism, for me, is the possibility of overcoming the one-sidedness of the capitalist process of rationalization . . . in the sense of the rise to dominance of the cognitive instrumental aspects, which results in everything else being driven into the realm of apparent irrationality. My criticism of Marx is that he failed to see that capitalist production methods ushered in not only a new political form of class domination, but a new level of system differentiation."[18]

As the hegemony of these social systems of instrumental action over the life-world increases, the mobilizing of communicative rationality takes precedence over the critical mobilizing of proletarian resistance. In short, critical theory as a self-reflectively expanded notion of rationality was linked to the Marxian project as a move in the struggle against technocratic domination. However, as the grip of this domination continued to tighten, this Marxian link weakened as priority was given to mobilizing communicative rationality.

CRITICAL THEORY AND COMMUNICATIVE RATIONALITY

As noted earlier, communicative action was originally an integral part of the existential dimensions of Habermas's thought, particularly his theory of ego formation. However, with the failure of the transcendental and Marxian mobilizations to effectively multidimensionalize Western reason, the rationality of communicative action assumed an increasing normative importance for Habermas. A drive to increase the visibility, legitimacy, and the discursive production of communicative rationality now replaced the earlier drive to increase the production of self-reflective rationality via the Marxian and transcendental routes. Thus it is in works such as *Communication and the Evolution of Society*, *The Theory of Communicative Action*, and *Moral Consciousness and Communicative Action* that we really see the roles of communicative rationality in Habermas's response to the deepening crises of Western modernity. With this communicative turn, Habermas takes his response beyond the phenomenological inheritances from Husserl and Adorno.

The above communicative works are marked by a major shift in categorical foundations. The paradigm of consciousness as the creative and organizing center assumed by self-reflective rationality is replaced by the paradigm of language in which the latter's illocutionary forces become the new creative and organizing center. As McCarthy notes, "Habermas's response to the decline of the paradigm of consciousness is an explicit shift to the paradigm of language —not to language as a syntactic or semantic system—but to language-in-use or speech."[19] In other words, although Habermas makes the linguistic turn, it is not that of the poststructuralists.

The appeal of communicative rationality is quite similar to that of self-reflective rationality. Both are "resistant to cognitive instrumental abridgments of reason"[20] and are thus capable of providing alternative models of rationality. But, in spite of this similarity in appeal, the internal structures of these two rationalities are quite different. In addition to the declining fortunes of the paradigm of consciousness, or subject-centered reason, Habermas's turn to the paradigm of language was also motivated by the greater access it provided to the rational potential of communicative action. The paradigm of consciousness obscured this potential by subordinating it to the creativity of the conscious subject. For Habermas, the rational potential of communicative action is to be found in its relations to the internal structure of language, particularly the latter's procedures for arriving at an understanding. This is the rational potential that Habermas will attempt to mobilize with the aid of Austin's theory of the illocutionary powers of speech acts.

Drawing on speech act theory, Habermas establishes the unique rationality of communicatively coordinated social action. For him, it is the most general category of action. Thus, with appropriate qualifiers it includes instrumental, expressive, and everyday interactions. These different types of action are conceived in terms of speech acts and examined in terms of the validity claims associated with these speech acts. Everyday actions are analyzed through imperative or normatively regulated speech acts, expressive actions through expressive speech acts, and instrumental action through constative speech acts. Together, these speech acts construct the social universe in terms that expose its roots in the coordinating capabilities of language.

The essence of communicative rationality is its "power to rationally motivate acceptance" on the basis of internal connections between validity, validity claim, and the redemption of a validity claim.[21] Ordinary language offers its speakers the opportunities of contesting at least three types of validity claims in their attempts to make a rational decision or to rationally motivate another speaker. They can contest the truth of a claim, its normative correctness, and the authenticity of the speaker's presentation of the self. These are the universal pragmatics of speech. The contesting of the claims embodied in these universals is carried out with the aid of the Husserlian lifeworld, which ordinary language makes available to speakers. Among other things, the lifeworld contains a stock of linguistically organized knowledge that speakers draw on when contesting validity claims.

For example, a professor standing unusually close to a student makes the following assertion: "Habermas is a sociologist." In doing so, he or she is not only making claims to truth but also for the normative appropriateness of his or her distance and for authenticity or truthfulness in self-presentation. In this case, the student could easily contest the claim to truth given Habermas's philosophical writings and the normative appropriateness of the distance from the student. A rational agreement from the student would then require satisfactory responses to these two contestations.

Such contesting and redeeming of validly claims to the satisfaction of speakers constitutes the rationalizing of the illocutionary forces through which linguistic communication coordinates social action. These communicative practices make possible a rationally motivated "yes" or "no" to an offer. The large-scale production of such rationally motivated affirmations and negations is what Habermas wants from his mobilizing of communicative rationality. In particular, Habermas would like to see such affirmations and negations ground a communicative ethics, as the most promising alternative to the traditions that are being nonrenewably eroded. Such a development would make possible a communicative extension of the technocratic model of societal rationalization.

The above are brief accounts of the three dimensions of Habermas's response to the crisis of Western modernity. Together they constitute the most sustained effort to come to grips with this crisis since Husserl. To Husserl's phenomenological mobilization of self-reflective rationality, Habermas has added both a Marxian and a communicative component. Our concern in the remainder of this chapter is an evaluation of this response primarily from the perspective of Africana philosophy. In particular, this will require a closer examination of why traditions have become nonrenewable in modern societies, and how effective a substitute is a system of discourse ethics.

HABERMAS AND AFRICANA PHILOSOPHY

In Habermas's account of the one-dimensionality of technocratic reason, the explanatory principles are primarily socioepistemic. That is, this one-sidedness is the result of the incorporation of the sciences into everyday life and the absolutizing of their epistemic outlook. Within the Africana tradition, this exclusionary one-dimensionality has been explained in more socioexistential terms. Even in Wynter, who is the most socioepistemically oriented, ego-constitutive dualities play a prominent role in accounting for such self-enclosing one-sidedness.

From this socioexistential perspective, Habermas's communicatively expanded version of rationality shares an excluding/self-enclosing feature with the technocratic and other constructions of Western reason. This self-enclosing feature produces the need for a shadow or an other against which reason defines itself. Habermasian reason is thus an internally divided or "metastable" discursive formation. In spite of its efforts to achieve a stable, positive identity, it has not been able to define itself exclusively in terms of the specific structures of argumentation it sets up as its ideal. On the contrary, self-definition in terms of self-reflective and communicative structures of argumentation has been supplemented by exclusionary practices that contradict the norms of these two types of rationality. Consequently, it shares this feature with earlier constructions of Western rationality. These oppositional dynamics suggest that Habermas's reason is still subject centered and that the commu-

nicative turn has not liberated it from the ontic difficulties identified by traditional African existentialism or Harris's ontology of the everyday ego.

The specific contents of this category of the other of Western rationality has
of course changed with the different attempts at self-definition. Because
Westerners have consistently othered African thought and identity, this category of the other has been the liminal point of departure for many Africana
thinkers. For Fanon, the othered African had been transformed into the irrational and hence "phobogenic" possibility that the rational Westerner must
struggle to suppress. For Wynter, to be othered is to be liminalized or associated with the chaos category of the reigning system of order. For Gordon, to be
othered is to be the victim of a "projective nonseeing." It is to be made to disappear phenomenologically. As Sekyi-Otu points out, the othering of Africans
by such strategies resulted in categorical structures of heterogeneity that repudiated all communicative paradigms of reciprocal recognition and mutual
understanding. In these situations, human interaction is not regulated by a
principle of reciprocal recognition that supports the realizing of self-projected
possibilities. On the contrary, it is regulated by a principle of nonrecognition
that arrests such possibilities at their very foundations.[22] When it does not
arrest in such a manner, this principle results in what Habermas would call
"forms of systematically distorted communication." As Fanon suggests, without counterviolence this antidialectic of nonrecognition does not return to the
communicative paradigm of reciprocal recognition.[23] In short, the practice that
accompanies discursive othering is violent, noncommunicative suppression.

Given this concern with the liminal, phobogenic, and noncommunicative
dimensions of Western rationality, it is not surprising that the Africana tradition sees this rationality very differently from Habermas or Husserl. At the
same time that this tradition recognizes Western efforts to define itself in
terms of structures of argumentation, it also recognizes the dualistic impact of
European ego genesis on these definitions. The othering strategies of this genesis have consistently produced domains in which these structures of argumentation are suspended. As we will see, even in Habermas's case, interactions with
subjects in these domains are not negotiable and communicatively rational.
On the contrary, the responses of these addressees are determined in advance
by liminal elements in Habermas's logic. Thus we are confronted with the con-
tradiction of instances of systematically distorted communication in a communicative theory that is committed to overcoming them. This paradox can only
be explained by the continued enmeshment of Habermasian reason in "the
ignorance" of the ego discussed in chapter 1.

For Western technocratic reason, this othered domain, as Habermas pointed
out earlier, subsumes all forms of noninstrumental discourse including the self-
reflective and communicative varieties. As these discourses are affiliated with

its chaos category they exist under a cloud of phenomenological invisibility, which produces systematic distortions in communications with technocratic rationalists. For both Husserlian and Habermasian reason, this conceptual other is mythic thought. Husserlian reason sees itself as distinctly European, and has its roots in "the telos of European man."[24] Husserl shared the Faustian view of European man as for him this telos "lies in infinity."[25] European man is defined by a *Yuruguan* insurrection of infinite proportions that will establish his control over the universe. This revolt has inaugurated a new epoch in the history of European humanity, the epoch in which it lives by "the free fashioning of its being and its historical life out of rational ideas and infinite tasks."[26] Sustaining this infinite vision and complete autonomy is philosophy as the universal science.

In spite of defining itself in terms of this infinite ideal, Husserlian reason must also grasp itself as European through putting quotation marks around all non-Western philosophies. Thus the telos of the Indians and the Chinese can only produce "philosophies." We can only guess at what the telos of Africans has produced. What separates European philosophy from "philosophies" is that the latter rest on a "mythico-practical attitude"[27] as distinct from the theoretical attitude of the former. This mythical/religious attitude "brings those other philosophies into being."[28] As a result, their cosmic insurrections are not of infinite proportions. The more limited and practical aims of "the other philosophies" are evident "to the extent that the whole world is looked upon as dominated by mythical powers and to the extent that human destiny depends immediately or mediately on the way these powers rule the world."[29] In short, it is the triumph of European science and philosophy over these mythic powers that gives them their infinite vision and separates them from non-Western philosophies.

In Habermas, myth plays a similar negative role in the construction of Western rationality. It is the category of human thought that Habermas has refused to rescue from scientistic and technocratic oblivion. It constitutes the liminal, irrational category against which communicative rationality is defined. Although smaller than the liminal category of technocratic reason, it functions in similar ways. The resulting systematic distortions in communication parallel those between technocratic and noninstrumental discourses. This exclusionary or boundary-maintaining stance opens *The Theory of Communicative Action* and puts Habermasian rationalism in need of the kind of critique that he carried out against scientism in *Knowledge and Human Interests*. Yet, in spite of Habermas's insistence on excluding mythic thought, I will argue that only in the rationality of mythic thought is it possible to find models for the type of discursive interventions that could internally transform the project of technocratic reason and address the problem of nonrenewable traditions.

Given the foregoing, the best place to begin our Africana critique is clearly Habermas's analysis of mythic thought, whose primary examples are African. Like Husserl and Weber, Habermas wants to establish the universality of Western reason while at the same time preserving its cultural specificity. Consequently, the primary reason for the comparison between mythic and modern Western thought is to demonstrate the latter's justifiable claims to universality in contrast to the nonjustifiable claims of the former. In Habermas's view, "mythical worldviews are far from making possible rational orientations of action in our sense. With respect to the conditions for a rational conduct of life in this sense, they present an antithesis to the modern understanding of the world. Thus the heretofore unthematized presuppositions of modern thought should become visible in the mirror of mythical thought."[30] In other words, through its liminal status and nonrational nature mythic thought should make visible to modern thought its rational nature.

The data that Habermas then selects to construct his portrait of mythic thought all cohere around this prior assigning of myth to the role of polar opposite. The result is a very liminal and highly distorted picture that is unable to bring myth within the communicative paradigm of reciprocal recognition and mutual understanding. Habermas establishes this liminal exclusion on five basic arguments.

The first is the totalizing strategies of mythic thought. These strategies establish problematic connections between widely varying aspects of reality on the basis of matrices of similarity and difference. Second, because of its totalizing strategies, myth is a mode of thought that does "not penetrate the surface of what is grasped perceptually."[31] Hence Habermas describes mythic thought as "concretistic."[32] Third, the totalizing strategies of mythic thought lead to a confusing or leveling of different aspects of reality such as nature and culture. Fourth, the categories of mythic thought "originate in domains of experience that have to be analyzed sociologically."[33] That is, they are not to be analyzed epistemologically, but rather in terms of social systems of kinship. Fifth and finally, mythic thought is the most centered and closed form of thought. It is incapable of separating its linguistically constituted worldview from the objective world order. Consequently, its view of the world "is dogmatically invested with a specific content that is withdrawn from rational discussion and thus from criticism."[34]

With regard to the first of these points, it should be clear that the urge to totalize is not peculiar to mythic thought. Modern Western philosophy is inconceivable without it. Sartre's analysis of the problem of totalizing strategies clearly demonstrates their presence in the modern West.[35] As Habermas himself has pointed, even positivism carries within it a totalized view of the world.[36] Hence this cannot be a legitimate criterion for excluding mythic thought from the domain of rationality. We will return to this problem of totalization.

Habermas's second point makes the claim that mythic thought does not penetrate the surface of what it perceives. This is a claim that could only be made from an external view of mythic thought. It is the equivalent of looking at the thought of a discipline like physics from the perspective of its analogical extensions to the social world, while completely ignoring its core cognitive practices in relation to natural processes. As we saw in chapter 1, the core of mythic thought is a discourse of the ego, particularly its origin and fate, whose founding concepts can be appropriately or inappropriately extended to domains outside of the ego. This discourse penetrates the surface of the ego and reaches its existential depths. In principle, analogical extensions of mythic discourses of the ego are no different from the analogical extensions of semio-linguistic discourses that are so characteristic of the present period in the West. Consequently, the latter are subject to similar kinds of errors that will vary with the level of research capability and the social stock of knowledge. These errors have not created insurmountable barriers to depth for semio-linguistic discourses, so why should they for mythic discourses?

Habermas's third point is that mythic thought confuses or levels different domains of existence such as nature and culture. This confusion is clearly a result of inappropriate extensions of its discourse of the ego to the world of objects. However, as suggested above these types of errors are not peculiar to mythic thought. At the paradigmatic level, it is the same kind of error that characterizes the one-dimensionality of modern technocratic reason. Instead of imposing a discourse of the subject onto objects, it imposed a discourse of objects onto subjects. In the process, significant differences between these two domains are leveled. Objectivist discourses often remain on the surface of the ego and seldom reach its existential depths. Those dimensions of subjectivity that resist assimilation are declared illusory and hence nonexistent. These "fatal prejudices" were at the core of Husserl's explanation of the eclipse of spirit by scientific objectivism. Moving in the opposite direction mythic thought tends to subjectivize and hence conceal the technical dimensions of objects. In both cases, the errors of paradigmatic overextension are of the same type. If Habermas wants to exclude mythic thought from the domain of ratio-nality on these grounds then he will also have to exclude technocratic and sci-entistic discourses.

Fourth, the claim that mythic thought should be analyzed sociologically reveals Habermas's liminal urge to determine in advance the responses of his mythic addressees. Their speech acts with their claims to authenticity and truth cannot be addressed directly. First, they must be sociologically inter-preted by modern Westerners in terms of kinship systems. This move is strikingly inconsistent with Habermas's epistemological approach to knowledge production and is clearly a case of systematically distorted communication. After so brilliantly critiquing Marx's attempt to explain knowledge in terms of the system of social labor, there is no nonliminal way in which Habermas can explain mythic knowledge in terms of social systems of kinship. This exceptional treatment can only be explained by the liminal need to maximize epistemic distance given the designation of mythic thought as the irrational other of modern thought.

Imagine for a moment that this categorization had not been made, and that Habermas had indeed looked at mythic thought in the way he looked at self-reflective or instrumental thought. He would have asked about its knowledge-constitutive interests, its distinct approach to appropriating language, and its substantive domain of discursive intervention with which it has a long history of feedback relations. Out of these would have come an epistemological analysis of mythic thought that paralleled self-reflective or instrumental thought. Instead, we are offered a sociologically reductionist analysis that caricatures mythic thought. Consequently, to make clear the distinctive rational potential of mythic thought, it will be necessary for us to supply this missing Habermasian analysis of myth.

Fifth and finally is Habermas's claim that myth is the most closed and rigidly centered form of thought. Drawing on Robin Horton's contribution to the debate on Azande witchcraft, Habermas wants to distinguish the opened and de-centered nature of modern thought from the closed and centered nature of mythic thought. In particular, the closed nature of mythic thought is indicated by its refusal to let go of beliefs that are contradicted by evidence.

I will briefly raise three objections to this Habermasian position. First, the refusal to let go of a theory or a belief in spite of contrary evidence is certainly a widespread phenomenon in the history of modern thought. The history of science is replete with examples of theories being defended in spite of contrary evidence.[37] These examples multiply rapidly when we include the histories of modern Western religious, philosophical, ideological, and magical discourses. Even the most cursory examination of these histories will reveal the persistence and normality in the modern period of the practice of holding to beliefs in spite of contrary evidence.

Second is Habermas's failure to see the same resistance to evidence in Horton and other anthropologists upon whom he relies. The blindness and intensity of Horton's attachment to scientific rationality is an exact parallel to the Azande attachment to mythic rationality. But according to Habermas's liminal logic, one is rational, while the other is not. Like the Azande, Horton is unable to think outside of his categorical (scientific) framework and defends it passionately, rather than leaving its fate open to the outcome of experiments or tests. The alternatives that supposedly make modern thought more open are all alternatives that are possible within the paradigm of scientific rationality. The Azande are characterized as closed for not being responsive to the technical possibilities and alternatives that scientific rationality routinely embraces. On the other hand, modern Westerners are characterized as open when they are unresponsive to the spiritual possibilities and alternatives routinely embraced by mythic thought. From their respective transcendental domains, mythic and scientific thought have difficulties reaching each other. Indeed both are here liminalizing each other in comparable ways. The closure and the blind spots are on both sides and point to the enmeshment of both in similar processes of dualistic construction.

Third and finally, the association that Habermas claims between modern thought and the "decentration of an egocentric understanding of the world" is spurious. Two points will make this clear. First, the poststructuralist critiques of modern Western thought have focused on their centered nature. At the same time, Marxist and phenomenological critiques of poststructuralism have pointed to its centeredness in semio-linguistics. In short, as Harris has made clear, the problems of centered thought and their tendencies to closure are still very much with us. Second, by far and away the most radically de-centered traditions of thought are not to be found in the modern West. They are to be found in the meditative traditions of India. There the grounding of thought in the ego-displacing practices of yoga surrounds the ego with a spiritual consciousness that de-centers its desire for closure in ways that poststructuralism or scientific rationality have been unable to do.

Together, the above criticisms point to the illegitimacy of the five grounds upon which Habermas excludes myth from the domain of the rational. The exclusion rests on an ego-constitutive opposition between myth and reason that is subsequently rationalized. This illegitimacy was made clear by the inconsistencies in the evaluation of similar practices by mythic and modern thought. The same practice would be evaluated as rational or open in one and irrational or closed in another. These systematic distortions are liminal in nature. What are we to make of these liminally distorted moves in Habermas's exchange with mythic thought? Is there a connection between them and the liminal elements of technocratic thought? I will argue for an affirmative answer to this question, but first, the missing analysis of mythic thought that Habermas should have performed.

THE INTERESTS AND RATIONALITY OF MYTH

Earlier, I suggested that the substantive core of myth is its discourse of the ego. Consequently, its distinct rationality is not to be found in its practices of magic and witchcraft. Rather, much like the modern discourse of psychoanalysis, it is to be found in its capacity to discursively intervene in the production of a certain kind of subjectivity. The domain of intervention with which mythic discourses have feedback relations is clearly the connection between the ego and its unconscious or spiritual ground. Consequently, they make little sense when they are forced to operate in any one of Habermas's three epistemic universes. Mythic discourses require a fourth epistemic world, whose primary interest is the domain of spirit or inner nature. This domain is the spiritual parallel of outer nature and is distinct from the subjective life of the ego and the social world. Like other domains, inner nature is for myth an arena in which human agency confronts the conditions of its possibility and nonpossibility. Hence agency must be maintained in spite of the unique negativities of this plane. The resistance of these negativities can only be overcome through discursive interventions that decode and recode this spiritual order in ways that enhance human growth within the framework of a larger cosmic whole. This is the context from which traditional worldviews emerge, and in which their renewal is very possible.

In traditional Africa, the world of inner nature was discursively constructed in both personal and impersonal terms. In the impersonal model, spirituality was conceived as an inexhaustible ocean of energy into which all life is inserted. In the more familiar personal models of inner nature, the spiritual ground of the *sunsum*, or ego, is constructed as a hierarchical pantheon of gods, goddesses, and ancestral spirits. These deities and spirits are sites of agency capable of affirming or negating human actions. Given these constructions of inner nature, African mythic thought located its importance in the way in which it supported, regulated, constrained, affirmed, or negated the *sunsum*, the organ of human agency. Because the deities were experienced as beings of a higher order, their relations to the ego were often read as analogous to those with parents and monarchs. Reductionist sociological readings of these analogies become necessary because rationalistic or scientistic closure requires in advance the nonexistence of this spiritual domain.

The discursive interventions of mythic thought into the domain of inner nature are not motivated by an interest in technical control or the communicative reaching of an understanding between equals. Rather they are motivated by an interest in restoring harmony and achieving reconciliation between an errant, overreaching ego and its deities or subconscious allies. Mythic and religious action is action that is oriented toward harmony with the deities. Mythic and religious thought make possible the discursive interventions that generate conditions for harmony and reconciliation after the ego-genetic phase of cosmic revolts. Consequently, the knowledge-constitutive interest of mythic thought is indeed this concern with harmony and reconciliation between ego and cosmos.

In traditional Africa, this need for knowledge motivated by an interest in cosmic harmony stemmed from its view of the *sunsum*, or ego. In its phase *Yuruguan* revolt, the latter suffers from a case of congenital blindness with regard to its capacities for self-determination and world constitution. On this score it is always overreaching its specific capabilities and getting in the way of creative work that its deities must perform on its behalf. Thus there is the great likelihood that the exercise of agency on the part of the ego is likely to generate significant measures of ego alienation and cosmic discord. Hence the need for restorative discourses. This suggests that the insurrectionary tendencies that Husserl made his basis for the distinctiveness of European man are seen in the African tradition as basic to a normal ego genesis. Thus the real difference here is their empowering by science in the West. As we've seen, this problematic view of the ego can be found in traditional African views on fate and destiny, and it clearly bears some interesting similarities to the third version of Hegel's communicative model of human ego genesis.

Finally, we need to point out that this knowledge of the ego in relation to its spiritual ground is not accessible through the senses and the practices of science as in the case of outer nature. The primary condition for this accessibility was and still is the suspending of such cognitive practices and the silencing or displacing of the everyday ego in more radical ways than the phenomenological reduction of Husserl. This suspending of the self-determining ego should make visible the conditions of its spiritual determination. In this state of ego dissolution, inner nature and its connections to human consciousness become visible, much like the unconscious becomes visible in psychoanalysis through dream imagery.

From this brief alternative sketch, the interests and rationality of mythic thought should now be clear. We can recognize the rationality of myth in the specific discursive practices by which it intervenes effectively in the relationships (particularly the *Yuruguan* struggles) between the ego and its spiritual ground. This is the domain in which its claims are tested on the basis of trial and error. The transcendental framework supporting these claims is a distinct one that discloses reality (particularly the ego) from the perspective of its creation and moral ordering by deities. These interests and orientations link mythic thought to the praxis of cosmic harmony, just as the technical interests of the sciences link them to instrumental action. Finally mythic rationality is distinguished by the epistemological criterion of radical ego transcendence as a condition for knowledge production.

This in my view is the epistemological portrait of mythic thought that is implicit in and should have emerged from Habermas's restructuring of the transcendental domain. It would have been more consistent with his earlier work and provided a better complement to the brilliant discussion of the "linguistification of the sacred" that opens the second volume of *The Theory of Communicative Action*. As they presently stand, the two treatments of mythic thought in the opening sections of this two-volume work contradict, rather than support, each other. Instead of developing such a portrait, myth was liminally barred, its identity distorted, and its truth claims devalued in advance. These systematic distortions in Habermas's cognitive offers to his mythic addressees can only be removed by a qualitative change in epistemological perception and getting past the ego-constitutive oppositions in which his communicative rationality is still caught. These oppositions have created a mythic hole in Habermas's discursive economy. This is why the mythic critique of Western rationality carried out by Adorno and Horkheimer in *Dialectic of Enlightenment* still echoes strongly in spite of Habermas's critique of this work. If my liminal explanation is correct, it suggests that the exclusionary practices behind the one-dimensional tendencies of Western rationality could also be liminal in nature, that there is indeed the possibility of a parallel between the technocratic exclusion of self-reflective or communicative rationality and Habermas's exclusion of mythic rationality.

MYTH, EXISTENTIAL PHENOMENOLOGY, AND ONE-SIDED SELF-ASSERTION

On the basis of the arguments of the last two sections, I would like to suggest that mythic, technocratic, and Habermasian communicative rationality all have liminal blind spots. That is, each has systematically generated an other of its own that it is unable to recognize in spite of evidence. The categorical dimensions of this blindness suggest that it cannot be understood at the levels of methodological procedures or everyday communicative practices. Such liminal interactions fall outside of Habermas's model of communicative action because they violate the presuppositions of the pragmatic universal truthfulness. They violate it because the liminal speaker deceives not only others but also himself. In Habermas's view, "anyone who systematically deceives himself about himself behaves irrationally."[38] To meet the presuppositions of communicatively rational discourse, such a speaker would have to go through a therapeutic exercise of the psychoanalytic nature. In other words, the sources of liminal blindness are to be found at the ego-genetic, and not the communicative, level.

However, this possible psychoanalytic referral leaves many questions unanswered. Are liminal practices always the result of some pathology? Are these mythic problems? Do we find them in modern, everyday communicating subjects? Is it possible for a normal person to deceive herself while behaving rationally with regard to the truth of statements and their normative correctness? In Habermasian terms, this would clearly be the model that best fits our three cases of liminal blindness. However, Habermas is not clear on these issues, and they cannot be deduced from his theory of communicative action.

There are times when Habermas catches the global and historic dimensions of the problem of liminality, but then he returns to being inscribed in it via well-established European responses of denial and projection. For example, he makes the following observations: "The caesurae between the mythical, religious-metaphysical and modern modes of thought are characterized by changes in the system of basic concepts. With the transition to a new stage the interpretations of the superseded stage are, no matter what their content, *categorically devalued.* It is not this or that reason, but the kind of reason which is no longer convincing" (emphasis in original).[39] In other words, these devaluations are forms of discursive violence, of exclusion in advance. They do not respond constructively to the older discourse's rules of evidence and argumentation, as we saw in the case of self-reflective rules versus technocratic ones. Habermas suggests that these categorical devaluations may be necessary for "socioevolutionary transitions to new levels of learning."[40] However, in spite of being cases of liminally distorted communication, he does not examine their implications for communicative practice. Consequently, we cannot satisfactorily account for these liminal practices using Habermas's communicative model in spite of their visible presence in his categorical devaluation of mythic thought.

Implicit in our critique of Habermasian rationality has been its failure to thematize the countercommunicative impact of the dualistic and exclusionary dynamics of its own grounding in an ego-centered subject. It is time to bring these ego-genetic dynamics into the foreground and to thematize explicitly their relationship to one-sided modes of self-assertion and to nonrenewable traditions. As these missing dynamics are onto-existential in nature they can be thematized in a number of existentialist traditions. However, the works of Fanon and Gordon on race suggest that our three instances of "projective nonseeing" can be most broadly theorized with the aid of the Sartrean ego-constitutive concept of the project in bad faith. To establish the connections with conditions for cultural renewability and nonrenewability, I will supplement this concept with a number of insights from the African existentialist tradition.

Following Sekyi-Otu, I will argue that although an ego-generative concept, the project and its dynamics also constitute a transcendental horizon for everyday cognitive and communicative practices.[41] Thus in Sartre's existential model of action, it is the dynamics of the project, and not the interest in mutual understanding, that provides the transcendental norms for interaction, or what he calls "concrete relations with others."[42] With the project in this universal and action-orienting role, it is much easier to recognize the global nature of the problem of liminal exclusion, and Habermas's error in projecting it onto mythic thought.

For Sartre, the project is the prereflective, totalizing set of self-generative acts through which the ego establishes itself.[43] Unlike Hegel and Habermas, language, work, and interaction are not the primary media through which the ego effects its revolt against and separation from the "in-itself" or the totality of being. Rather it is the totalizing capabilities of its self-projections that unify and individualize ego formation. This rupture disengages the emerging ego from the universal determinism of existence and relocates it in the determinism of the possibilities contained in the project. From this reframing, the ego will derive both its identity and new bases for engaging and participating in existence. Consequently, it is the focus on the totalizing dynamics of the ego's prereflective capacity for self-projection that distinguishes Sartre's explanation of blind resistance to evidence from Habermas's.

The aspect of self-projection that relates directly to this phenomenon of liminal blindness is its metastability. A metastable subject is one whose existence emerges as the result of an anxious choice over competing possibilities. The projected possibility is therefore not an object or a pure positivity like a stone, or a table. Rather, it exists as the chosen possibility in "the scandal of the plurality of consciousness,"[44] and in spite of resistance from the other possibilities that constitute the plurality of consciousness. Hence its ontology always includes the anxious possibility of being displaced by a competitor, even if the project is imagined to be an infinite one.

Given the chaos of this founding, competitive plurality, self-projections always include affirmative as well as defensive moves. On the defensive side, the emerging project can only be secured through the active suppression of those possibilities that represent its negation. Consequently, the unity of the project is established in opposition to these contending possibilities. Thus dualities and exclusionary practices are rooted in project formation, and not the semiotic aspects of founding categories emphasized by Wynter. From this point on, the ego supported by this oppositional project will be unable to recognize these excluded possibilities. An antidialectic of reciprocal nonrecognition is established between them, cutting off all forms of rational communication. In short, the ego-genetic sources of the antidialectic of liminal othering are to be found in the metastable nature of the projects through which the ego asserts itself.

For example, the ego may project itself forward through a prereflective identification with the abstract rationality of the laws of the cosmos as opposed to the mythic deities asserted to be responsible for its order. The realizing of this projected model of the self would require the categorical devaluing of the deities and relations of reciprocal nonrecognition with other possibilities in the plurality of consciousness that maintain prereflective identifications with the deities. Such bad faith exclusions of other possibilities of being constitute the bases for what Kierkegaard called "disrelationships between the self and itself."[45] These inner disrelationships make it impossible for the self to attain and remain in equilibrium and rest by itself. Hence the metastability of the above self-projection and others like it. This metastability is a more general formulation of the unease of the ego before its deities in African existentialism.

However, for such an ego to feel a satisfactory level of security about its realization of this rational identity, it has to conceal from its conscious awareness the repressing of its mythic possibilities. Awareness of these exclusionary practices would undermine the necessity and objectivity of its choice. This systematic self-deception regarding such necessary repressions is precisely why the projects of normal everyday individuals are in bad faith. The everyday ego is in bad faith because it conceals from itself the truth of its other possibilities. The truth of these possibilities must be known if they are to be effectively concealed. Hence deceiver and deceived are one.

In these characteristics of bad faith, we find important instances of the resistance to evidence that Habermas attributes to mythic thought. Sartre notes, "Bad faith does not hold the norms and criteria of truth as they are accepted by the critical thought of good faith. What it decides first, in fact is the nature of truth. . . . Consequently a peculiar type of evidence appears: nonpersuasive evidence. Bad faith apprehends evidence, but it is resigned in advance to not being fulfilled by this evidence, to not being persuaded and transformed into good faith."[46] These practices regarding evidence are integral to the projective and totalizing dynamics of the modern subject. Thus when Sartre refers to the "primitive" nature of bad faith, it is not the mythic thought of the Azande or other premodern people he has in mind. Rather it is to the blind positings and violent repressions that flow from the metastable nature of the projects through which modern Westerners assert themselves.

What do these existential dynamics, which are internal to the ego, have to do with everyday cognitive and communicative practices? As Sekyi-Otu has suggested, the former are connected to the latter because these metastable dynamics of self-projection constitute the transcendental horizon of Sartre's existential model of human interaction. In Kierkegaard's language, the inner disrelationships associated with metastability in turn become normative bases for outer disrelationships in interaction with others. For Sartre, these interactive disrelationships are primarily sadistic and masochistic in nature. However, these are concepts that Sartre formulates in terms of seeing, not seeing, being seen, and not being seen. Consequently, the transcendental/normative impact of projects on patterns of interaction are very different from those produced by language, work, and communication.

On Sartre's transcendental horizon, we see first the prior conditions of self-constitution as opposed to those of knowledge production in the cases of Husserl and Habermas. However, we also see the prior conditions of knowledge production, because for Sartre the cognitive and communicative functions are not isolated from the conditions of ego formation. On the contrary, they are as existentially conditioned as the self produced by the project affects their mode of operating. Because of the existential conditioning of these two functions, the dynamics of the project also supplies transcendental norms for everyday cognitive and communicative practices.

The norms supplied by the project do not result in models of action that are communicatively coordinated. Rather they lead to existential models of inter-action or "concrete relations with others" that are motivated by an interest in ontological supremacy. The values or norms supported by this interest are centeredness, absolute totalizations, forced coincidence between ego and projected ideal, one-sided modes of self-assertion, the exclusion, categorical devaluation, and nonrecognition of the possibilities that radically challenge a project's supremacy, centeredness, or totalized state. Hence existentially normed inter-actions are more agnostic, they routinely make use of "nonpersuasive evidence" in their exclusionary practices, and operate within an antidialectic of reciprocal nonrecognition. In short, the normative impact of the metastable dynamics of self-projection is the routine production of liminally distorted forms of communication. The systematic nature of the liminal distortions are not peculiar to a type of discourse or society. On the contrary, Sartre links them to the dynamics of modern ego formation, which I am suggesting echoes the dynamics of ego formation in traditional African thought.

From the African existentialist tradition, we could have derived a similar set of norms for an interactive model of reciprocal nonrecognition, if it had thematized more explicitly the nature of projects of self-definition. These patterns of reciprocal nonrecognition are most fully developed in the relations between the ego and various characters chosen to represent its spiritual ground. The metastability of the Sartrean project corresponds with the cosmogonic challenge of African existentialism that the ego routinely fails. Both portray the ego as oppositionally excluding possibilities as a part of its formative process and not being able to recognize these excluded possibilities.

Thus the destinal life of traditional Africans would be inconceivable without similar types of disrelationships and distorted communications between the ego and its spiritual ground. These set the stage for the corrective actions of the deities, which the ego may never come to recognize. In spite of this possibility, the primary purpose of these actions is to disturb the ego's premature ontic closure and open it to relevant possibilities that it has excluded. This is the beginning of the process of reconciliation. This is the framework within which the antidialectic of reciprocal nonrecognition is thematized, and not the internal dynamics of projects. In many ways, the two formulations complement one another as in Sartre the in-itself remains a rather abstract reality to which the ego is never reconciled.

As the in-itself of traditional African existentialism, spirit is much more of a living, accessible reality. It is not the abstract domain of Sartre's in-itself. Consequently, there are important qualitative differences in the ego's relationship with the in-itself in these two cases. In the African case, there is more give and take, which in turn makes the destinal life possible.

These qualitative differences derive in part from the different choices legitimated by traditional and modern societies in regard to the ego-constitutive binary self-determination/spiritual determination. Modern societies encourage the resolution of this binary in favor of its first term. Consequently, they also encourage projects that deny in bad faith the ego's possibilities for spiritual determination. Cut off from these possibilities, the modern ego (including the Sartrean) must find ways to ground and create itself. To realize this antonomy, it must attempt to create its reality and its ideals out of itself and to deny the creative inputs of the in-itself. Thus high levels of unreconciled egoism tend to be a feature of modern modes of self-assertion, whether technocratic or not.

In traditional societies, members are encouraged to resolve the above binary in favor of its second term. As a result, they often devalue in bad faith the ego's capabilities for agency and self-creation. Hence the tendency to routinely defer explanations of occurances to the gods, and not the ego. The resolution of this binary in favor of spiritual determination counters egoism and encourages the reconciliatory practices of destinal life. These are the practices, and not those of linguistic agreement, that are capable of transforming the liminal and exclusionary tendencies of human ego genesis into communicative patterns of mutual recognition. As long as the ego remains in the unreconciled state, its antidialectic of reciprocal nonrecognition will prevent it from reaching such Habermasian communicative goals. This is traditional African philosophy's answer to the Sartrean problem of authenticity and to Habermas's concern over the deepening one-sidedness of Western rationality. However, it is important to note that this reconciliatory resolution does not automatically solve the difficulties that traditional societies have with ego agency.

Further, these different positions on this binary bear directly on a society's capacity to renew its traditions or to keep its ego-genetic process open to the creative and regulatory inputs of spirit. When the ego affirms and thematizes its possibilities for spiritual determination, it experiences its growth more as an organic process than one of willful projection and continuous consolidation. It is around this type of ego growth that cultural traditions "can take shape in an unplanned, nature-like manner." This naturelike manner corresponds to

Harris's "objective process" through which the universal consciousness "yields itself" to the ego in a variety of images, symbols, and practices. These yieldings establish both the creative and moral authority of spirit, as well as the bases for ethics that are more than communicative, that is, ethics that participate directly in the power of the sacred. These are the ego-based processes through which ethical and cultural traditions both emerge and renew themselves. As long as the ego is unable to experience itself as a legitimate site for such hierophanies and intrusive addresses from the universal consciousness, the renewal of traditions will be a problem.

In *Legitimation Crisis*, Habermas suggested that sociocultural systems cannot experience input crises. The crises of these systems are always "output crises."[47] From the reconciliatory perspective of African mythic discourses, this does not appear to be correct. The input crises of sociocultural systems arise whenever their ego-formative processes are significantly closed to Harris's objective process. To have a living tradition is to have discourses that, among other things, thematize the yieldings of spirit and keep the ego open to them. The renewals that come with these yieldings will continue as long as the ego does not succeed in absolutizing any idea or image from this stream. Its flow is interrupted when we refuse to let go of such partial selections. As Harris artfully notes: "In confessing to partial images . . . we come abreast of both bias (the bias of aging institution) and potential (the capacity within all of us to be born anew) in all regimes and civilizations."[48] African existentialism reveals these modes of openness to spirit that have become hidden undersides of the modern ego. Thus from its perspective, projects of cultural renewal must include a change in relations with these undersides. Through reflective strategies, their powers of renewal can be mobilized against technocratic one-dimensionality in much the same way that Husserl and Habermas have mobilized powers of self-reflective and communicative rationalities.

Given these existential perspectives on liminality, we can now return to the blind spot of technocratic reason—its one-dimensional mode of self-assertion. Technocratic reason understands itself through a blind identification with specific modes of knowledge production. However, the larger projective dimensions that help to shape it as a discursive formation are for the most part unacknowledged. These dimensions are evident in its orientation toward expansive cognitive claims that are to be realized in the future. They are also evident in its exclusionary practices that Habermas earlier described as driving all forms of noninstrumental knowledge into the realm of the irrational. This affirmation of itself against other forms of rationality exposes the metastable nature of its existence and the scandalous competitive plurality over which it is attempting to establish ontological supremacy. These exclusionary, competitive, and supremacist practices suggest that although technocratic knowledge may be piecemeal in nature, it is nonetheless informed by a totalized vision that shows all the marks of being normatively conditioned by the existential dynamics of ego-constitutive projects. Consequently, arresting the one-dimensional self-assertion of technocratic reason must include discursive interventions that are capable of reaching the existential aspects of its projective dimensions and recoding them in a more reconciliatory direction. It is at this point that the existentialism of African myth complements the Sartrean analysis of the project.

In sum, the crucial point that emerges from this liminal underside of Western rationality is that Habermas needs the reconciliatory rationality of myth as an ally. He needs the special powers of this rationality to overcome the bad-faith strategies that empower the blind one-sidedness of the project of technocratic reason. This existentially empowered one-sidedness is an important source of the exclusionary practices of technocratic reason that Habermas wants to explode. Reconciliatory rationality disrupts and transforms the immediacy of the bad-faith strategies of the ego that produce these countercommunicative results, hence Habermas's need to transform this liminal other into an ally. Finally, even with self-reflective and reconciliatory rationalities as allies, the institutional powers of technocratic reason would enable it to resist these challenges. Consequently, there remains the need for a countermobilization of the Marxian type that is institutionally oriented.

PART THREE

Reconstructing
Caribbean Historicism

Pan-Africanism and Philosophy: Race, Class, and Development

So far, our analyses of Afro-Caribbean philosophy have focused on two major fissures within the field as a whole: first, the deep cleavages between the African heritage and the remainder of the field; and second, the opposition between its historicist and poeticist wings. We are not through with these issues yet and will return to them in chapter 10. Now it is time to focus more intensely on the historicist school, the divisions within it, and the crises that have overtaken its praxis.

As we saw in the case of James, Caribbean historicism has been one of the major philosophical responses to the imperialism and practices of class/race domination that have plagued Caribbean societies. Because of the multidimensional nature of this domination, Caribbean historicism has developed in two major directions that quite often have been at odds with each other. First was the Pan-Africanist tendency, which placed the emphasis on racial liberation and the cultivating of strong ties with Africa and Afro-America. Second was the Marxist tendency that stressed class liberation and solidarity with proletarian and other class-dominated groups.

These two tendencies emerged within the class/race order of the plantation societies that European imperialism established in the region between the sixteenth and nineteenth centuries. This was a three-tiered class/race order dominated by European planters, the class that owned the major plantations on which the agricultural staples were produced. At the bottom were large numbers of African laborers, who were the actual producers of the staples. These two were the major antagonistic classes of Caribbean societies, whose conflicts were the primary source of class violence. Between the planters and workers there were various strata of intermediary groups, who were primarily mulatto and engaged in small-scale agriculture, retailing, and various professional activities. Because of the size and distinct socioracial status of mulattos, this was tripolar construction of race as opposed to the bipolar American construction or the multipolar Brazilian construction. This was the framework in which cultural differences and identities in the region were racialized and whose color hierarchies and white-supremacist values the two wings of Caribbean historicism would delegitimate.

Today both the Marxist and Pan-Africanist variants of Caribbean historicism find themselves in the grip of major crises. We will examine the crises confronting the Marxist variant in the next chapter and devote this one to problems of the Pan-Africanist variant. The latter has found confirmation for many of its claims in the persistence of racism in the postcolonial period of Caribbean societies and in the neosegregationist tendencies that have emerged in the post–civil rights era in the United States. These tendencies have emerged under the ideological cover of the antistate and antiregulation arguments of neoliberalism. The result has been the rise of market-legitimated forms of racism. In other words, the neoliberal turn has not only deregulated industries and restructured them on market principles but also attempted to do the same for race, class, and other intergroup relations. The resulting increases in urban, residential, and educational segregation has made the neoliberal period one of rising, rather than declining, racial significance.[1] Hence its importance for the Pan-Africanist school.

On the other hand, the rise of the women's movement and the inadequate performances of black political elites in Africa, the Caribbean, and Afro-America have confronted the black nationalism of the Pan-Africanists and its ideas of African repatriation with serious challenges. The crises of African economic and political development must be of particular concern to Pan-Africanists. The descent into genocide in Rwanda must be one of those extreme reference points that this tradition must internalize as it reconstructs itself.

In the light of these concerns, my aim in this chapter is a limited but necessary one: to review this wing of Caribbean historicism emphasizing its philosophical foundations, rather than its more familiar ideological and political positions. From the philosophical standpoint, this wing has been shaped by the providential historicism of Blyden and the Rastafarians, the racial historicism of Garvey, the class/race historicism of James, Fanon, and Rodney, the racial semioticism of Paul Gilroy and the later Stuart Hall, the existentialism of

Lewis Gordon, and the political logicism of Charles Mills. Here we will examine the positions of Blyden, Garvey, the Rastafarians, Rodney, and Gilroy. In the course of this examination, I will point out the difficulties in politico-nationalist practices that have led to the current postnationalist turn in Pan-Africanist thought.

EDWARD BLYDEN'S PROVIDENTIAL HISTORICISM

Born on the island of St. Thomas in 1832, Blyden made Liberia his zone of liberation, and from there emerged as the major nineteenth-century theorist of black liberation. Largely self-taught, Blyden was a student of theology and understood both self and world in Christian terms. In 1858, he was ordained a Presbyterian minister, while he was also the principal of his high school in Monrovia. In 1862, he was appointed professor of classics at Liberia College. A man with a mission, Blyden entered the world of politics in 1864, serving as Liberia's secretary of state. Later, he would serve as the country's minister of the interior and its ambassador to England. But in spite of these academic and political achievements, it is for his advocacy on behalf of African nationalism that Blyden is best remembered.

Blyden's advocacy was distinguished by two important traits: a particular style of leadership and a very explicit racial ideology. As a political leader Blyden emerged out of the racial uplift tradition of postslavery black leadership. This was a reformist tradition of leadership by an Afro-Christian, educated elite. Their primary goal was to modernize and improve the conditions of blacks and their African homeland through racial mobilization and appeals to influential but sympathetic whites in local power structures. The reforms initiated were primarily educational and religious in nature, which left in place the oppressive structures of class domination that governed the lives of the agro-proletariat and the landless former slaves. This style of leadership Blyden shared with Edward Vickars and Robert Love in the Caribbean and Frederick Douglass and Booker T. Washington in the United States.

Like his style of leadership, Blyden's racial ideology drew on the larger Pan-Africanist response that emerged in the second half of the nineteenth century. Rooted in an Afro-Christian tradition of thought, some of the major contributors to this position included the African Majola Agbeke, and the Afro-American Alexander Crummell. In Blyden's formulation of Pan-Africanism, the problems of African peoples were analyzed in terms of patterns of conflict and domination that defined the relations between different races. The oppressed state of blacks was the result of their devaluation, exclusion, and exploitation that came with their racialization in the modernizing societies of the West. Consequently, there were four distinct concerns in the praxis of

Blyden's African nationalism: (1) abolition of slavery; (2) Western education for Africans; (3) emigration to Africa; and (4) modern nation building on the continent. Blyden developed these positions with great erudition, brilliant argumentation, and unflagging courage, hence his towering figure.

However, as Blyden began to put this plan into action, the clarity and simplicity of his solution quickly disappeared. What emerged in the heat of action was a complex nationalist discourse whose liberatory project carried within its discursive structure a number of contradictory ambivalences and anti-African positions. Among the more glaring of these contradictions were Blyden's inclusion of the American Colonization Society in his work on national reconstruction, his advocacy of British and French colonization in West Africa, and his early insistence that westernized Africans lead the process of African nation building.

These contradictions derived in large part from the fact that Blyden's ideology drew its concept of race from European race theory and hence reproduced many of the Eurocentric and anti-African biases of that discourse. His concept of race shared many of the biological assumptions and claims of European race theory. For example, he accepted the claims that there were innate differences between the races, that each had their own "race instincts,"[2] talents, and destinies, that there was a mutual antipathy between races, that racial purity was necessary for building strong nations, and that race mixing was unnatural because it destroyed the purity of the "race instincts." What Blyden did not accept in European race theory was the claim of inequality between the races.

In short, Blyden's discourse was a classic case of Caliban's reason being deeply enmeshed in that of Prospero. All of the liminal dynamics of this enmeshment that Wynter analyzed applies to Blyden. Thus the early Blyden found himself in the liminal and contradictory position of advocating the elimination of traditional African religions and languages, and their replacement by Christianity and European languages.[3] Because of these liminal dynamics, Blyden's was a liberatory black nationalist discourse whose Eurocentric and anti-African tendencies made its implementation a difficult one. In addition to these dynamics there were also limitations that derived from the uplift strategy, which did not address the class dimensions of black oppression. But in spite of these difficulties, Blyden's personal courage, eloquence, and erudition made him one of the founding figures of the Pan-Africanist tradition.

These aspects of Blyden's thought have been examined in great detail by scholars such as Hollis Lynch and V. Y. Mudimbe. What has not been adequately addressed is the discursive formation that made it possible for Blyden to hold these contradictory positions together. Here, I will argue that it was his implicit and auxiliary philosophy of providential historicism. In other words, it was Blyden's philosophy of history that provided the underlying unity that contained his many contradictory positions. His nationalist solution for the racial problems that European modernity had created for African peoples was clearly situated in the field of historical praxis. As in the case of James, Blyden made history both the medium and the arena in which the modern racialization of Africans would be transformed from something negative into a positive. In these transformative undertakings, the state was an indispensable steering mechanism. Thus, as far as African identities and societies were concerned, history had constitutive or ontological powers.

However, in spite of these areas of convergence, Blyden's historicism differed from James's in at least three important ways. First, the historical process was not perceived as being driven by the motor of class conflict. On the contrary, the history of all hitherto existing societies is the history of racial conflict, of the mutual antipathy between races. Race becomes the primary human key to history and to the historical activity of nation building. Second, change and transformation do not derive from the insurrectionary activities of the masses. It is the result of informed historico-political decision-making on the part of educated elites. As a strong proponent of elite leadership, Blyden's historicism was far from being insurrectionist. Third, although a modern subject, Blyden did not invert the self-determined/spiritually determined binary in a fashion that excluded its second half. Consequently, Blyden's historicism did not make the denial of spirit that is common to many materialist philosophies. In addition to racial conflict, history was also driven by spirit. Encompassing and often using racial conflict were the providential activities of God. History for Blyden was providentially guided and consequently was seen as fulfilling a higher purpose. Thus within Blyden's providential historicism it was possible to move between the worlds of the sacred and the profane, between spirit and history.

Blyden's concept of a providentially guided history is one that developed in the early phases of Afro-Christian thought both on the continent and in the diaspora. In this regard, Blyden's work can be usefully compared to those of the African Americans David Walker and Alexander Crummell. The Afro-Christian tradition of thought registered a clear move away from African cosmogonic and predestinarian constructions of the relation between spirit and history to the Christian notion of the providence of God. The concept of providence becomes the new way of conceptualizing God's active participation in the historical process. Thus it represents both a break and a continuation with the traditional African view. Rooted in his Christian self-understanding, Blyden made the notion of providence the foundational concept of his philosophy of history. As such, Blyden used it to fill in and legitimate some of the more troublesome and contradictory areas of his thought.

For Blyden, there were two ways in which God spoke to people and so became active in their history. The first was "by his word and the other by his providence."[4] In the case of Africans under the weight of racial domination, God did not send "any Moses, with signs and wonders, to cause an exodus of the descendants of Africa to their fatherland."[5] However, Blyden was certain that through His Providence, God had "loudly spoken to them as to their duty in the matters."[6] His providential call to them was evident in at least four crucial events in the lives of Africans: first, God's allowing them to be brought into the Western Hemisphere "where they would receive a training fitting them for the work of civilizing and evangelizing the land from whence they were torn, and by preserving them under the severest trials and afflictions"[7]; second, in spite of their service to Western societies, allowing them "to be treated as strangers and aliens, . . . and to make them long for some refuge from their social and civil deprivations"[8]; the third, providential event through which God spoke to Africans was His "bearing a portion of them across the tempestuous seas back to Africa"[9]; and finally by "keeping their fatherland in reserve for them in their absence."[10]

These events illustrate the way in which Blyden used the concept of divine providence in his construction of the world of African nationalism. He used it to bridge gaps in this world and to grasp some of the more difficult and perplexing areas of the black experience. Thus he employed it to explain the original forced departure of Africans and their enslavement in the Western Hemisphere. This explanation gave a meaning to these events that transcended the everyday racial motor of history and also opened up the possibility for a providential solution to this dilemma. This was the larger framework of providential historicism within which he saw the repatriation of Africans from the West and the building of African nations. Thus the facts of slavery and the opposition to it are explained by the notion of providence and so too are both the exodus and the return of Africans. In this providential spirit, Blyden proclaimed that an African nationality is our great need, and God tells us by his Providence that he "has set the land before us, and bids us go up and possess it."[11] Blyden made this call to Africans in the Caribbean, the United States, Canada, and other parts of the Western Hemisphere.

This was Blyden's providential historicism. Like other Afro-Caribbean philosophies, it helped to construct a world out of the shattering of African existences by European colonialism and attempted to legitimate it through a series of providential arguments and claims. As a type of world-constituting activity, it was both reconstructive and historically transformative. In spite of these complexities, it remained an implicit, underthematized philosophical formation that was intertextually embedded in Blyden's larger ideological discourse, which is a pattern we have encountered in Fanon, Harris, and other Caribbean philosophers. However, it performed important foundational tasks and provided Blyden's ideological discourse with much-needed unity.

As we will see in the case of Garvey, Blyden's nationalist solution has clearly been a legacy that others in this tradition picked up and carried forward. However, his providential historicism has not fared as well. In the history of Caliban's reason, providential historicism has occupied a rather prominent place. It is older than Blyden and has continued long after him. For example, it is very much alive among the Rastafarians and in the thought of the contemporary African-American theologian Josiah Young. Thus before moving on to Garvey, it will be necessary to point out what is problematic in this approach to history.

The category of spirit has been a central one in the history of Caliban's reason. We've seen throughout this text that the full range of Caliban's thought cannot be appreciated without recognizing the analogical importance of the ego-spirit relationship. This relationship has served as both transcendental and ego-formative horizons and its knowledge-constitutive interests are of a reconciliatory nature. However, not all claims and arguments (including providential ones) generated in this ontoepistemic space are automatically correct. Neither are they automatically false. Like other human epistemic spaces, this too is caught in the dualities and liminal dynamics that limit our grasp of the truth of existence. Consequently, we must have objective criteria and feedback relations to help us determine the truth or falsity of providential arguments and claims.

Particularly in the case of Blyden, the primary problems are methodological and epistemological. It is not clear what events or combinations of events carry providential significance. What are the criteria by which such events can be determined with a reasonable degree of consistency? Without a more rigorous methodology, there remains an element of arbitrariness that leads to opposing or contradictory readings of the same events. Such outcomes have led to the rejection of providential arguments as discursive strategies.

Closely related to these methodological problems are the epistemological ones. Even after systematizing the events that carry providential significance, how do we know that we are accurately reading from them the intentions of God? What or where is the concrete or experiential domain of feedback relations in which the truth claims of providential explanations encounter confirmation or disconfirmation? Without reference to such a domain, we have no checks on the fallible arguments we make about the providence of God, who may in fact be infallible.

In response to this epistemological issue, let me suggest that this domain of feedback relations is the ego-spirit axis; that is, lived experiences of the ego being guided by forces outside of it, as in the destinal life of traditional Africans, constitute the analogical bases for providential arguments. However, the move from experiences of the ego being guided to the guiding of history is effected by an unacknowledged leap. The concealing of the latter obscures the identity and nature of providential arguments and makes possible their abuse or overextension. With their unique analogical structure concealed, Blyden deployed them in the same way one would deploy logico-historical arguments, making the everyday world their domain of feedback relations. Such misapplications can only result in claims that are often disconfirmed by history and hence lead to the questioning of providential strategies. To be viable in the modern period, the users of providential arguments must recognize their specific analogical structure and impose on their truth claims the necessary epistemic constraints that go with such a figurative projecting from one domain of experience to another.

MARCUS GARVEY'S RACIAL HISTORICISM

Although better known than Blyden, Garvey's African nationalism is inconceivable without the contributions of Blyden. Indeed, the broad outlines of Garvey's nationalist solution to the racial problems of African peoples are quite similar to those of Blyden's. Like Blyden, Garvey emerged as a political leader within the reformist uplift tradition of postslavery black leadership. His debt to this tradition was very evident in the early programs of his Universal Negro Improvement Association (UNIA) in Jamaica, an organization that was greatly influenced by the work of Booker T. Washington. Like the latter, Garvey went through a phase of eschewing politics and focusing primarily on educational and industrial uplift.

The more political and aggressive Pan-Africanist solution for which Garvey is remembered came with his exposure to changes that were taking place in African-American political leadership. In opposition to the tradition of Booker T. Washington, two others had emerged. First was the integrationist and anti–Jim Crow tradition of the NAACP and the National Urban League. Second was the socialist/trade union oriented tradition of A. Phillip Randolf and Chancellor Owen. Closely related to the latter were Hubert Harrison's Liberty League and Cyril Briggs's African Blood Brothers, both of whom were Caribbean immigrants. These organizations made more explicit the tensions between class and race, as the various rising working men's associations were also doing in the Caribbean. Garvey was closest to those who emphasized the primacy of race and would later come out strongly against the socialists. His return to politics was galvanized by the debate over the fate of Germany's African colonies, particularly the proposal they should be governed by a political committee that included Afro-Caribbeans, Afro-Americans, and Japanese.

The uniqueness of Garvey's Pan-African solution was that it combined in an original way the strategies of Washington and Blyden. Thus in the early American phases of the UNIA, Garvey's focus was on economic mobilization much in the tradition of Washington. The formation of the Black Star Line was the most important expression of this drive for racial uplift through economic organizations. But equally important to Garvey's solution was "the redemption of Africa," through the building of strong black nations on the continent. As in the case of Blyden, this goal led to Garvey's interest in Liberia.

The failure of both these drives were major blows to Garveyism and to Pan-Africanist praxis. These failures were largely due to organizational mismanagement, factional infighting, and the opposition of both black and white elites outside of the UNIA. In addition to these strategic and organizational factors, there was the fact that the UNIA was unable to improve land and other conditions of class formation for the bulk of the black population who were agro-proletarians. The same was true for policies toward Africa. There, international black leadership was not strong enough to resist the establishing of plantation and mining economies and the reduction of racialized Africans to impoverished agro-proletarians and miners. In short, it was the imploding of another Afro-Caribbean project by the contrary interests of Western capitalism.

However, before the collapse of the Black Star Line, Garvey had succeeded in pulling together the active support of large numbers of urban blacks, the black church, sectors of the educated elite, and white bankers into the most dramatic attempt to realize the Pan-African project. This spectacular politico-ideological undertaking was not without its intellectual and philosophical foundations. Like Blyden, Garvey was largely self-taught. In particular, he worked at mastering European nationalist, racial, and Christian discourses, the American gospel of success, and African history, including the work of Blyden. The result was Garvey's own nationalist discourse of racial uplift and liberation. Given its similar patterns of European embeddedness, it should come as no surprise that many of its racial positions and political stances contained contradictions that echoed those in Blyden's thought. For example, Garvey's attempt to reach an understanding with the Ku Klux Klan as part of this southern strategy was reminiscent of Blyden's alliance with the American Colonization Society. However, in spite of these overlaps, they differed significantly in their philosophical views of history, which gave overall unity to their vision and strategies of transformation.

The crucial differences in their philosophical approaches to history was that Garvey openly rejected the providential view. However, this rejection did not include the denial of spirit often found in materialist philosophies. Indeed Garvey was often quite critical of twentieth-century materialism.[12] His philosophy included an understanding of self and a broader philosophical anthropology that was primarily Christian. This self-understanding together with his secular view of history produced a racial historicism that was quite different from Blyden's providential historicism.

For Garvey, "history is the land-mark by which we are directed into the true course of life."[13] In other words, it is the arena in which human beings make and fulfill themselves. This is also true at the collective level: "The history of a movement, the history of a nation, the history of a race is the guide-post of that movement's destiny, that nation's destiny, that race's destiny."[14] Thus, like for James and Blyden, history was of ontological significance for Garvey. It was the self-formative but also conflicted arena in which Africans lost their freedom and in which they had to regain it. Further, history was a distinctly human sphere of activity from which God had withdrawn: "After the creation of the world . . . the Creator relinquished all authority to his lord . . . all that authority which meant the regulation of human affairs, human society and human happiness was given to man by the Creator, and man therefore became the master of his own destiny and the architect of his own fate."[15] Consequently, the sociohistorical fates of individuals, communities, races, and nations are in our hands. God cannot be held responsible for historical formations like slavery or for their elimination. Divine providence is real for Garvey, but it is not directly active in history. Thus he was highly critical of black leaders who "flatter us into believing that our future should rest with chance and with Providence, believing that through these agencies will come the solution of the restless problems."[16]

Although Garvey's ontology of history overlapped with James's, they differed sharply on the concrete nature of the historical process and the factors that kept it in motion. Like Blyden, Garvey saw the historical process as one that was primarily driven by racial conflict. Race for Garvey was the primary category of collective identity. He accepted the color and other biological criteria of European racial discourses that divided the world into black, white, brown, red, and yellow races. Unlike classes, which were human creations, Garvey believed the races were created by God.[17] He often declared his belief in racial purity in terms of these discourses: "I believe in a pure Black race just as how all self-respecting whites believe in a pure white race, as far as that can be."[18] He was opposed to miscegenation and all strategies of racial integration within white-dominated nations. Garvey saw "universal suspicion" and distrust as necessary outcomes of racial self-assertion.[19] These in turn were sources of the racial conflicts that drove the historical process, creating cyclical patterns of racial rise and decline. He situated the crisis confronting African peoples within such ongoing processes of racial formation and deformation. These historical cycles took the place of providential actions in Blyden's thought:

> This race of ours gave civilization, gave art, gave science, gave literature to the world. But it has been the way with races and nations. The one race stands out prominently in the one century or in the one age; and in another century or

age it passes off the stage of action, and another race takes its place. The Negro once occupied a high position in the world, scientifically, artistically and commercially, but in the balancing of the great scale of evolution, we lost our place and some one, other than ourselves occupies the stand we once held.[20]

Garvey's African nationalism was aimed directly at the downswing of this racial cycle in which Africans were caught. His goal was to reverse this downward movement by getting blacks on a racial upswing and so returning them to the center of the historical stage. However, initiating such an upswing would require the accumulating of technological, economic, and political power in independent African nations. Racial cycles and racial hegemonies were very closely linked to accumulating these types of powers. They were also abstract ways of representing the outcomes of the almost Darwinian struggles between races that accompanied these processes of accumulation. However, these accumulative tendencies did not result in a class dynamic systematically interacting with these racial cycles as in the case of James.

The Darwinian aspects of Garvey's racial discourse were often stated in some of his most hyperbolic language. Garvey declared, "Power is the only argument that satisfies man. Except the individual, the race, the nation has POWER that is exclusive it means that the individual, race or nation will be bound by the will of the other who possesses this great qualification."[21] He often repeated that the "prejudice of the white race against the Black race is not so much because of color as of condition, because as a race, to them, we have accomplished nothing; we have built no nation, no governments."[22] Here we can see the differences between Garvey's historicism and the racial existentialism of Fanon and Gordon. Garvey went on to suggest that this prejudice and its transformation into domination cannot be curbed by law, only "by progress and force."[23] History was thus a racial battle of wills in which the accumulating of power in nation-states made all the difference. Hence the importance of strong African nations for getting blacks on the upswing of a historically constituted racial cycle. This is the core of Garvey's racial historicism.

However, our analysis of Garvey's philosophy would not be complete if we did not examine more closely its philosophical anthropology. At the everyday level, Garvey saw individuals in racial terms. However, at a more originary level, his discourse of self becomes religious. As Randall Burkett has pointed out, Garvey's view of the human self rested ultimately on "the doctrine of the *imago dei*."[24] That is, to be human is to be modeled on the image of God. In the important essay "Christ," Garvey takes this idea further by arguing that "what we [Afro-Caribbean people] call the spirit" is the Holy Spirit of Christianity, and that it dwells in all people.[25] This is one of the few references that we find in Garvey to the ego/spirit relationship of traditional African religions. But it remained underdeveloped. Through this spirit, God is active in the human self. It is here that Garvey locates the providence of God, and not in history.

This philosophical anthropology serves two important functions in Garvey's racial historicism. First, it grounds his claim for the equality between different races; and second, it provides him with a model of individual development. For Garvey, the ultimate grounds for racial equality were religious. He often asserted, "God almighty created all men equal, whether they be white, yellow or Black and for any race to admit that it cannot do what others have done, is to hurl an insult at the almighty who created all races equal, in the beginning."[26] From these premises, Garvey concluded that "we have the same common right"[27] as "lords of the creation" to make our history and determine our social fate. This argument of common rights that derived from our place in creation was an important source of support for Garvey's position on racial equality.

The second important function of this spiritual philosophical anthropology was that it provided Garvey with a yardstick by which to measure our humanization. For Garvey, human self-realization, whether individual or racial, required an ever-deepening knowledge of one's self that included its spiritual foundations. Fully human individuals were rare in Garvey's view: "In the 1,500,000,000 human souls in the world, I hardly believe that we can find 5000 real men; that is to say, the individuals who know their possibilities and limitations."[28] Among African peoples, Garvey did not think he would find more than ten real or fully humanized individuals, that is, black men and women who really know themselves. Yet Garvey saw this self-knowledge as being necessary for our liberation: "If 400,000,000 negroes can only get to know themselves, to know that in them is a sovereign power, is an authority that is absolute, then in the next twenty four hours we would have a new race, we would have a nation, an empire."[29] In other words, for Garvey there is an important link between his spiritual humanism and his racial discourse.

Although conceived primarily in Christian terms, the self-knowledge of which Garvey is speaking parallels that of the *sunsum/Okra* relationship of traditional African thought and the ontological dynamics between ego and universal consciousness in Harris. Earlier we noted that Garvey left undeveloped the parallel he had established between the African and Christian discourses of spirit. This neglect was in all likelihood not an accident. It reflected an anti-African bias in Garvey's thought that established a rigid dualism between African and European religions. The two could not mix, fertilize, and creolize each other. Rather, like the early Blyden, Garvey was for the Christianization of Africans and the elimination of their religions. Consequently, the issue of self-knowledge could not be thematized in terms of these two religious registers even though they were attempting to represent and had feedback relations with the same domain of experience.

Creolizing tendencies were confined to the color symbolism of Garvey's spiritual humanism. Although a Christian, Garvey had a big problem with God's white representation in European Christianity. He argued that whiteness was not a permanent feature of God. Rather, it was a projection of Europeans onto God. For Garvey it was understandable that humans create God in their own image and give their color to Him. Consequently from the human standpoint, God should be as many colors as there are humans imagining Him. Thus in black communities, it would be both natural and legitimate for God to be imagined as being black. What is illegitimate and racist for Garvey was the insistence that God cannot be black even for black people. Thus in the tradition of Bishop McNeil Turner, Garvey insisted that Africans should think of God, Jesus, and other Christian figures as black while acknowledging this as a projection.[30] This attempt to legitimate a black symbolics for Christian spirituality represents an interesting but limited form of religious creolization. It occurs at the level of color but not at the thematic or discursive level. It is blocked by the binaries that separate European and African philosophical and religious thought in the Caribbean intellectual tradition, producing in Garvey's case the highly skewed patterns of creolization typical of Afro-Caribbean philosophy. Consequently, there is primarily a relationship of negation between Garvey's racial historicism and traditional African philosophy, in spite of Garvey's vigorous embracing of modern Africa.

This, in brief, is Garvey's racial historicism. It also has clearly outlined ethical (Christian) and poeticist tendencies[31] that I have not examined here. In spite of being more explicitly thematized than Blyden's, this is also an auxiliary discourse in a larger ideological project. Thus questions of epistemology are not addressed, although a number of tendencies can be identified. Consequently, like Blyden, Garvey's racial cycles and other claims about history are in need of firmer grounding. But in spite of this limited development, it is clear that we have here a philosophical formation that is an integral part of a project of world constitution of the reconstructive and transformative types.

THE RASTAFARIANS: BETWEEN RACIAL AND PROVIDENTIAL HISTORICISM

Unlike the written works of Blyden and Garvey, the philosophy of the Rastafarians has emerged for the most part through dialogues or "groundings" with each other. Hence it takes us back to the oral and popular sectors of the Caribbean intellectual tradition. Much of what we know about Rastafarian thought comes either from its music or from the ethnographic writings of scholars, raising in the context of the Caribbean the need for an ethnophilosophy.

Whatever position one takes on these issues, there can be no doubt about the incredible outburst of world-constituting activity in the 1920s among the sector of the Jamaican underclass that would become known to the world as the Rastafarians. Also, there can be no denying the impact of Rastafarian thought on racial discourses and racial consciousness in the region.

Philosophically, Rastafarian thought is uniquely positioned between the mythopoetic and historicist poles that have dominated the late- and postcolonial periods of Caribbean thought. In addition to fashioning a new mythopoetics of Afro-Caribbean origins and identity, it also attempted to address the historical experiences of Afro-Caribbeans. It is precisely its explicit treatment of Afro-Caribbean history that sets Rastafarianism apart from other Afro-Christian religions and brings it closer to the historicist tradition. Thus in analyzing its philosophy of history, we can best identify it as oscillating between the positions of racial and providential historicism.

Although quite distinct, Rastafarian thought emerged out of the tradition of Afro-Christian thought in Jamaica. This tradition began with the rise of Myalism in the mid-eighteenth century, and in the nineteenth century produced other Afro-Christian formations such as Zion, Revival Zion, and Pukumania. In all of these formations, the basic patterns of world constitution remained very African. The moderate African balance in the *sunsum/Okra* opposition was maintained, so that both the spiritual and material worlds were experienced as being equally real, although not of the same importance. The detailed construction of the spiritual world also remained very African. It consisted of a Creator God, a variety of good spirits and bad ones (or *duppies*), all very similar to what we described in chapter 1. Over time, the characters in this pantheon became progressively more Christian, as biblical figures such as the apostles or prophets were incorporated as spirits capable of possessing members of these groups. Religious life focused around the manifesting of the spirit through experiences of possession and the communications that followed. As a result, a highly historicized Christianity was incorporated into the primarily mythic framework of traditional African religions.

Rastafarianism is based on a very different type of Afro-Christian synthesis. In this case, it is the temporal structure and the historical framework of Christianity that encompasses and reorganizes into a new totalization of the African mythic tradition and the imploded historical experiences of Africans in the Western world. Within this Christian framework, direct access to the spiritual world was maintained through only a slight shift in the *sunsum/Okra* opposition in favor of the first half of this binary. Also, there was a monotheistic restructuring of the spiritual world that resulted in the negating of the nature deities. Jah, the creator God, reigned supreme much like Jehovah. However, the belief in evil spirits, or *duppies*, remained. One of the major consequences of the shift in the *sunsum/Okra* opposition and the rejection of the nature deities was a marked qualitative change in the nature of Rastafarian spirituality. Rather than centering their spiritual practices around experiences of possession, they grounded them in a meditative mysticism that did not reject the material world. The primary discursive manifestation of this mysticism is the highly original "I-language" and "I-identity" of the Rastafarians which I have discussed elsewhere.[32] Together these changes have made Rastafarian religious life quite different from that of Zion or Pukumania.

In spite of these shifts in a Christian direction, Rastafarianism remains quite distinct from Christian thought. First, the spiritual personae of Rastafarian thought are very different. God is Jah, who is also Jesus and also Haile Selassie, the "man" who became the emperor of Ethiopia in 1930. The color symbolism of God ceased being white and European, and became black and African. The Rastafarians went one up on Garvey. They didn't argue that God should be black, they just did it. Along with this shift in the color symbolism of divinity, Rastafarian thought racialized and Afro-Caribbeanized the Christian drama of the fall and redemption of human beings. Reconstructed in this way, the drama also told the story of the fall of Africans into slavery in the Western Hemisphere and of their coming redemption. The Christian drama now had an unprecedented sociopolitical dimension to it that has become one of the defining marks of Rastafarian thought. It also displays a much more open and egalitarian pattern of creolization than was the case with James, Blyden, or Garvey. Here African and European religious thought reinforce and negate each other in ways that should make Nettleford quite happy. These creole and sociopolitical dimensions of Rastafarian thought contain the historical elements that link it to the work of Blyden, Garvey, and other Pan-Africanists.

Like other major movements in Caribbean thought, the philosophical aspects of Rastafarianism are complex and multidimensional. The racial/providential historicism of the Rastafarians is indeed a complex philosophical formation with several dimensions to it. It has a strong existential dimension closely related to the mysticism mentioned earlier. It also has very explicit positions on ethics, ontology, philosophical anthropology, and the philosophy of language. Here my analysis is restricted to its historicism and the latter's place in the Pan-Africanist tradition.

As in the case of Garvey, who the Rastafarians continue to invoke, history is an arena of racial conflict resulting in forms of domination or "downpression" such as slavery and apartheid. They share Garvey's view of history as a process that takes the form of racial cycles that bring decline for some and hegemony for others. However, they do not see these cycles in the exclusively secular and Darwinian fashion that Garvey did. The present period is seen as the last decades of a two-thousand-year cycle of oppression in which the downpressors of the Rastafarians have been the imperial countries of the West, their local political supporters, the police, and the established Christian churches. Ironically, this constellation of oppressive forces has been given the biblical representation Babylon. Thus the actions of these "Babylonians" are not only politically oppressive but also morally evil. Consequently to be oppressed in Jamaica is not only to be in captivity but also to be living in sin. Hence both redemption and liberation are on the Rastafarian agenda.

This organic combination of liberation and redemption points to the unique positioning of the *sunsum/Okra* opposition that makes possible this inextricable linking of religion and politics in their thought. As already noted, the politico-racial order of Jamaican society was thematized by the Rastafarians in terms of the Christian drama of the fall. Consequently, theological statements are necessarily politico-racial, and politico-racial statements are necessarily theological. This makes sin not just an individual moral problem but also a politico-racial one for Jamaican society. As a social order that has practiced slavery and racial domination, moral recovery will require not just individual but also social redemption.

It is precisely this simultaneous politico-religious reading of the current cycle of racial oppression that separates Rastafarian historicism from Garvey's. For the Rastafarians, these cycles are both racially and providentially driven at the same time. Hence the oscillations between these two types of historicism. The key to these oscillations is Rastafarian ambivalence about both the meaning and cause of their suffering.

On the one hand, the Rastafarians attribute the cause of their suffering to the evil actions of their downpressors.[33] On the other, they attribute it to "the disobedient ways" of our African ancestors.[34] In the first case, suffering is seen as politico-racial in origin and has to be resisted as such. This view produced strong insurrectionary tendencies in the early phases of the movement that lasted until about 1960. During this period, the insurrectionary aspects of both Rastafarian theory and praxis were quite explicit and resulted in confrontations with Babylon. Here the overlap with Garvey's racial historicism was strongest. In the second case, the current cycle of Rastafarian suffering is seen as ancestral in origin and hence both punitive and expiatory in nature. This view is closer to Blyden's providential historicism and that of Crummell and Walker. Here repatriation or redemption would be accomplished by Jah in his own time, and not through Rastafarian self-assertion. In the post-1960 period, this became the dominant view, bringing with it pacifist tendencies and revolutionary symbols that are more spiritual than political.

With regard to the issues currently facing the Pan-Africanist tradition, four problems can be noted here. First, like Blyden, Rastafarian historicism leaves the social and developmental problems of Jamaican society largely unaddressed. Second, it ignores the fact that the vast majority of Jamaicans do not want to repatriate. Third, the social and developmental problems that it wants to abandon in Jamaica and the larger Caribbean are just as, if not more, severe on the African continent today. Fourth and finally, its providential historicism conflates divine and human agency in a way that we saw was problematic in the case of Blyden. Thus in spite of being a powerful subjective and legitimating force for black identities, we need to look beyond Rastafarinism as we examine the current crisis of Caribbean historicism.

WALTER RODNEY: RACE, CLASS, AND DEVELOPMENT

The labor uprisings of the late 1930s, followed by the formation of trade unions and mass political parties, dramatically changed the dynamics of racial struggles in the region. National independence via constitutional decolonization was finally on the political agenda, as well as political parties and trade unions for the masses of Indo- and Afro-Caribbeans. These organizations mobilized the latter groups more as workers in struggle against capital, and less as blacks in struggle with whites. Hence they marked an important move away from the racial mobilizations of the Garvey period.

Further, these prospects for nationhood and a politically organized working class, together with the opening of the University of West Indies in 1948, changed in an equally significant way the nature of Caribbean racial discourse. Both inside and out of the academy, the interactive dynamics between class and race figured more prominently in racial analyses, as well as the transformative capabilities that locally controlled states would bring. This greater prominence of postcolonial nation-states produced significant shifts in the emphases that punctuated Pan-Africanist thinking. What remained elusive possibilities for Blyden, Garvey, and the Rastafarians were now within the grasp of the new labor leaders such as Norman Manley, Grantley Adams, and V. C. Bird. Pan-African solidarity was no longer an issue of repatriation to Africa, but one of mutual support in the struggles for decolonization and national reconstruction.

This embedding of older racial struggles in the new dynamics of class and nation produced many scholarly attempts to rethink the issue of racial domination in the region. Among these were Gordon Lewis, M. G. Smith, R. T. Smith, Lloyd Braithwaite, Carl Stone, and Selwyn Ryan. Most of these scholars were liberal or socialist in outlook, rather than Pan-Africanist.

However, for the Pan-Africanist tradition, the most important was clearly Walter Rodney. Like James, Rodney was both a Pan-Africanist and a Marxist. He too in different works approached the social analysis of Caribbean society from predominantly racial or class perspectives, never separating the two, and was continuously redefining both of these perspectives. Thus, unlike Alex

Dupuy, I see a real continuity that is integral to Rodney's dialectical shifting of positions, rather than a major "epistemic break" in his thinking.[35]

As a Pan-Africanist, Rodney took Caribbean scholarship on Africa to new levels, particularly the scholarship on precolonial Africa. Thus, in his *A History of the Upper Guinea Coast*, Rodney is clearly addressing and attempting to correct many of the racist distortions about precolonial African societies that had solidified during the colonial period. Yet, within this Pan-Africanist text, we can find clear evidence of Rodney's Marxism. Central to the work is a class analysis of precolonial West African societies. Thus, in challenging Winterbottom's egalitarian view of society in Sierra Leone, Rodney writes, "Certainly, the principle of 'to each according to his need' did not operate when it could be said that 'he is the greatest among them who can afford to eat rice all year around.'"[36] This explicit reference to Marx makes it quite clear where this class analysis is coming from.

Even in his most explicitly Pan-Africanist work, *The Groundings with My Brothers*, we find this dialectical relationship with Marxism. It is a text in which the dynamics of class, political economy, and imperialism are raced. Race and processes of racialization within the context of Western imperialism become the points of view from which the postcolonial problems of the region are analyzed. The major flaw in Rodney's analysis is not so much its relations to class, but rather the failure of his racial categories to deal adequately with Indo-Caribbeans. Substantively, the process of racialization remains very much an African one and only formally includes the Indo-Caribbean experience. India does not figure in this text the way Africa does. Neither are the specifics of Indian racialization as visible as those of the African case. Thus, as thematized, the label "black" cannot adequately cover the experiences of both groups.

The role of class moves to the forefront in *How Europe Underdeveloped Africa* and *A History of the Guyanese Working People*. In the first of these two works, the shift is not so much from race to class, but rather from race to development. Here Rodney makes a connection with Marxist and dependency approaches to development. In this work, Rodney uses Marx's theory of historical materialism along with propositions from dependency theory to examine the problems of African development in a way that was new for Caribbean Pan-Africanism. In this treatment of development and underdevelopment, the changed nature of Rodney's historicism comes clearly into view. In *A History of the Upper Guinea Coast*, Rodney did not employ an explicit theory of sociohistorical development. Here he does. History emerges as a secular medium in which societies develop and underdevelop, driven by the motors of class/race conflict and technological change.

In spite of the dominance of this class-theoretic approach, Rodney consistently allows it to be de-centered by race as a factor in the oppression of

Africans. For Rodney, the ideological superstructure of European capitalism changed with its systematic exploitation of African slave labor. It increased the importance of white supremacist thought and the levels of institutionalized racism. This ideological production of racism generated new grounds for domination that were not identical with classism. Consequently, the "oppression African people on purely racial grounds accompanied, strengthened, and became indistinguishable from oppression for economic reason."[37] Rodney went on to suggest, "It can be further argued that by the nineteenth century white racism had become so institutionalized in the capitalist world (and notably in the U.S.A.) that it sometimes ranked above the maximization of profit as a motive for oppressing black people."[38] Like James, Rodney is here allowing his race-theoretic discourse to displace the class-theoretic one that he is laboring to construct. Thus, as in the earlier works, it is a dialectical relationship that emerges here, one that is growing in complexity and subtlety.

This argument for a continuously developing dialectical relationship between class and race as Rodney's primary contribution to the Pan-Africanist tradition is further supported by the interaction of class and race in A History of the Guyanese Working People. As in A History of the Upper Guinea Coast, this work begins with the land, its humanization, and the role of the working classes in that process of transformation. This was a struggle with both sea and river to reclaim land through empoldering. From this achievement, Rodney moved on to a detailed description of the development of the Guyanese working people, focusing on groups such as plantation workers, small farmers and miners. In tracing this development, Rodney looked at both the conflicts with capital that generated class solidarity, as well as those that created divisions between them. By far race is the most important of these internal contradictions discussed by Rodney.

In The Groundings with My Brothers, Rodney's racial discourse drew primarily on the experiences of the European/African encounter. Here it is expanded in three important ways. First, it is widened to include the distinct processes by which Europeans racialized Indo-Caribbeans. These entailed stereotyping, the devaluing of Indian culture, and its replacement by physical and attitudinal characteristics in European stereotypes of Indians. Thus Rodney discusses the "Sammy" stereotype and compares it to the "Quashie" stereotype that Europeans had of Africans. This made an approach to the race problem that drew only on Pan-African experiences untenable.

Second, there was now space in Rodney's discourse for the distinct ways in which Afro-Caribbeans and Indo-Caribbeans racialized the cultural differences between them as well as the economic competition. Stressing religion, language, and customs, Rodney writes: "The Creole-Indian immigrant antithesis at times took the form of an African racial confrontation. Differences in culture constituted obstacles in the way of working class unity across racial lines."[39] These processes of mutual stereotyping were further reinforced as conflicts over scarce economic resources were read in terms of these racialized images. However, Rodney insists, as he did in *The Groundings with My Brothers*, that the internalization of both "Sammy" and "Quashe" by Indo- and Afro-Caribbeans are potent forces in their processes of mutual stereotyping.

Third, Rodney argued that these tendencies toward racial divergence were being countered by processes of cultural creolization, which were creating important areas of overlap. Among these were common working environments, diets, funerary customs, and, of course, cricket. However, processes of racialization were clearly outpacing processes of creolization. This forced Rodney to observe that "there were in effect two semi-autonomous sets of working class struggles against the domination of capital—the one conducted by the descendants of ex-slaves and the other by indentured laborers and their fellow Indians."[40] Here again race emerges as a semiautonomous factor that can displace, but not break, its dialectical relationship with class. This was Rodney's contribution to the Pan-Africanist debates of the sixties and seventies. If, as Paul Buhle has suggested, James represented "the artist as revolutionary," then Rodney represented the historian as revolutionary. Both, along with Fanon, developed dialectical approaches that allowed them to embody very creatively both the Pan-Africanist and Marxist tendencies of Caribbean historicism.

PAUL GILROY AND THE POSTNATIONAL TURN

If decolonization and labor organizing set the stage for the convergence of racial liberation and nation building, then poor political performances in the postcolonial period prepared the grounds for their current separation. The dissatisfactions with political performances have been many and quite varied. Consequently, so are the articulated reasons for the break with nation-states. For purposes of this analysis, these articulated positions can be put into two broad categories: the politico-economic, and the cultural. Within the first, we need to distinguish between radical and neoliberal critiques. Both of these will be addressed more fully in the next chapter. Hence we will focus here on the cultural critiques.

The cultural critiques use as their criteria of evaluation not politico-economic performances, but rather the degree of reciprocity or dynamic convergence between the racial and cultural reproduction of state identity and the corresponding reproductions of individual and group identities. It is the emergence of postcolonial patterns of divergence between these sites of identity production that have led to the separating of racial from national discourses and the uncoupling of liberation and self-definition from the reconstructive projects of the postcolonial state. This withdrawal of identities from the ideo-logical totalizations that have legitimated postcolonial states have made them available for postnational deployments. The work of Gordon makes clear that one of these is existential in orientation. The work of Wynter and Glissant sug-gest that another of these has taken the form of theorizing race, racial identity, and racial liberation on the model of the open signifier.

However, the most provocative of these semiotically theorized postnational turns is to be found in the work of Paul Gilroy. His critique of the postcolonial state is a frontal one. Gilroy's primary concern is "whether nationalist perspec-tives are an adequate means to understand the forms of resistance and accom-modation intrinsic to modern black political culture."[41] His answer is a very definite no. Along with this rejection of the postcolonial state, there is also a separating of race and class that reverses the tendencies analyzed in Rodney. For Gilroy, racial discourses are now hegemonic and are largely on their own: "Their power, has, if anything, grown, and their ubiquity as a means to make political sense of the world is currently unparalleled by the languages of class and socialism by which they once appeared to have been surpassed."[42]

In Gilroy's view, national perspectives on race are inadequate for four basic reasons. First, they are founded on "premature totalizations of infinite strug-gles"[43] that are absolutist, essentialist, and exclusive. In short, they are guilty of the cardinal sins against poststructuralism. Second, they derive from Western Enlightenment notions of the nation-state, which have been "both a life line and a fetter"[44] for blacks. Third, nationalist perspectives encourage the pursuit of an authentic, stable, racial/cultural identity that is shared with others who live within the boundaries of the same nation-state. This produces an overinte-grated sense of cultural and ethnic particularity that Gilroy refers to as "ethnic absolutism." Fourth and finally, black political elites have exploited these nationalist conceptions of identity and culture to mask their misrule and grow-ing problems with the black poor.

Given these conditions, black identities can no longer be cultivated within the confines of these nationalist parameters. This cultivation must now take place in a new space—a postnational one. First, the geography of this new space for cultivation must be changed. Its center will no longer be located in African or Caribbean nations, or Afro-American communities. Rather it is to be found on the Atlantic Ocean and the ships carrying the slaves. The previous centers were cases of Glissant's atavistic and creole societies with their origin narratives and divinely legitimated identities. Hence they were problematic sites of essentialism and ethnic absolutism.

Second, in addition to this reterritorialization, racial discourses and racial identities had to be reinscribed. Race could no longer be thematized as an ide-ological construct that legitimated strategic projections of both the European self and European imperial projects. Instead, race was to be semio-linguistically modeled and posited as open or free-floating signifier, the new metaphor for freedom in poststructuralist thought. As a signifier, the dynamics of race would no longer be determined by sociohistorical factors such as projects of imperial expansion. Rather they would be determined by the semiotic play of the signifier.

Third, this reinscribing of race must be accompanied by a reinscribing of the black self. The latter can no longer be viewed in Pan-Africanist terms as a relatively permanent African structure that is organically linked to continental modes of self-production and cultural production along with their diasporic creolization. Rather the black self should be seen as "a constituted subjectivity, that emerges contingently from the endless play of racial signification."[45] From this black but de-Africanized position, Gilroy rejects as essentialist any notion of an African culture that would connect all blacks via a shared heritage of strategies for self-production and cultural production, such as I have argued for in this text. If indeed there is any common factor, then it is the experience of slavery itself and its imploding impact on African worldviews. Thus Gilroy has repeatedly referred to blacks as "descendants of slaves." Against this de-Africanized background, cultural factors such as religion and language become the accidental differences and "petty issues"[46] that stand in the way of real black unity.

This in brief is Gilroy's postnational reconstruction of Caribbean racial discourse. It represents a significant break with both classical Pan-Africanist positions and basic Marxist ones. Thus Gilroy's reinscribing of the black self represents a definite break with the labor-theoretic constructions of the self in the Marxist tradition. This is evident in Gilroy's assertion that "in the critical thought of blacks in the West, social self-creation through labor is not the center-piece of emancipatory hopes. For the descendants of slaves work signifies only servitude, misery and subordination."[47] In the place of the providential, racial, and class discourses of Caribbean historicism, Gilroy substitutes a racial semioticism. This unmistakable postnational turn in Gilroy is an important indicator of the crises of legitimacy and credibility confronting black postcolonial states. However, while registering very effectively this moment of crises, Gilroy's rejection of the Caribbean nation-state is premature, and it is not clear how its Atlantic recentering will solve the major problems it is currently confronting.

First, Gilroy's critique of nationalist and Pan-Africanist perspectives is severely weakened by its lack of references to specific writers. One is never sure who are the ethnic absolutists and national essentialists he criticizes. Given the variations in these positions, some of them need to be addressed specifically. Second, Gilroy does not make clear the specific implications of his claim that black nationalist discourses derive from the European Enlightenment tradition. Does this automatically invalidate them? Clearly not. As my analyses throughout this text have shown, this has been the norm for Caliban. Further, if it did, then it would invalidate Gilroy's use of both race and semiolinguistics. Third, the rejection of nationalist perspectives on grounds of premature totalization is a criticism to which his own work is subject. I will argue in the next two chapters that totalizing strategies are basic to the world-constituting activities of humans. This is clear in Gilroy's development of the concept of race. From these counterarguments, I conclude that Caribbean nation-states and Caribbean national discourses can make a vigorous comeback against Gilroy's critique.

However, any such comeback will require a broadly conceived and popularly legitimated project of reconstruction, one that addresses not only the cultural and ego-genetic foundations of racism but also the changing political economy of Caribbean racism. The need to liberate popular identities and racial discourses from the manipulations of postcolonial regimes with high-legitimacy deficits should certainly be on the political agenda and constitutes an important contribution from Gilroy. However, the separation of such liberated racial identities and discourses from Africa, from the political economy of Caribbean nations and Afro-American communities are major mistakes.

In Afro-America, the biggest challenges of the last two decades confronting racial liberation have come directly from the neoliberal reforms of the capitalist classes in the West. These politico-economic reforms have affected race relations in two important ways. First, they have reprivatized the regulation of race relations by minimizing state actions such as affirmative action. This model of privatized race relations was given its classic formulation by Hannah Arendt after federal troops were sent to Little Rock in support of integration policies.[48] Today, it has been updated by neosegregationists like Dinesh D'Souza.[49] What is new in current formulations is the metaphorical extension of the principle of the market to justify the removal of state regulations.

In place of affirmative actions, race relations are to be governed by market determinations of racial preferences, prejudices, and practices. The result has been a more Darwinian/Garveyite social context for racial struggle and competition that is increasing patterns of racial segregation and reinforcing old stereotypes. It is this free-for-all in race relations that has produced the current deteriorations in the state of black/white relations. These deteriorations cannot be separated from the decline in services in industries such as airlines, banks, and healthcare. Both have been negatively affected by the more intense competition encouraged by the neoliberal reforms. These racial dimensions of the neoliberal turn must be addressed. However, because of its inadequate conceptualization of class, they cannot be reached by Gilroy's racial semioticism.

As in Afro-America, any attempt to address current race relations in the Caribbean region must take these dynamics into account. Because of the continuing peripheral structure of our economies, we still import foreign capitalists, primarily from the West. Thus we import capitalists with these new attitudes and values. The stronger their positions as factions within local governing coalitions, the more they will influence or reinforce racist attitudes among local elites. In addition to these regressive tendencies in black/white relations, Caribbean societies still have much work to do on Indo- and Afro-Caribbean race relations. We need to build on and not take for granted the paths pioneered by Rodney.

Caribbean Marxism: After
the Neoliberal and Linguistic Turns

T hat Caribbean Marxism is in a
state of crisis is a well-recognized fact. The collapse of socialist experiments in
Grenada, Guyana, and Jamaica, as well as in the Soviet Union and Eastern
Europe have raised serious doubts about the viability of its praxis. These failures have given rise to several attempts at examination and criticism. For
example, there is Carl Stone's social democratic assessment, Folke Lindahl's
postmodern evaluation, Brian Meek's insurrectionary reflections, and David
Scott's poststructuralist critique.[1] Not surprisingly, the results of these analyses
are quite divergent. Stone's doubts about the future of Caribbean Marxism
derive from difficulties in its economic practice. Lindahl's rejection is based on
postmodernist evaluations of problematic discursive totalizations such as "the
people," or Clive Thomas's "the logic of the majority." Scott's critique is based
on a deconstructive reading of the concept of revolution, which shows that its
salience has evaporated in our time. In Meeks, concern is focused on the problem of structure and agency.

In this chapter, I undertake an analysis of Caribbean Marxism in the light of
two developments that have affected it adversely. These developments I've
called the *neoliberal* and *linguistic turns*. Like Stone, I will argue that the primary challenge confronting Caribbean Marxism is the "higher cost" of its
socialist practice in the globalized world created by the neoliberal turn. In

contrast to Lindahl, I will argue against the appropriateness of a postmodern lens for an assessment of Caribbean Marxism. Lindahl uses its critical power as a one-directional instrument that sees only the problematic totalizations of Marxism. Those of postmoderism (relativism, nihilism, grand narratives, binary opposites, particulars) and liberalism ("the people," the state, rights, the individual) are not subjected to the same doses of postmodern skepticism.

Although more carefully argued, my analysis of the linguistic turn will show that Scott's poststructuralist critique makes some of the same errors as Lindahl's. I will show that Scott's critique is of a type that can usefully be called *subtextual*. It is subtextual in the sense that it reads the fate of the concept of revolution in terms of the epistemic conditions that govern its textual elaboration. In my view, this is a reasonable suggestion. What is unreasonable is Scott's exclusion of all other factors that determine revolutions and the absolutizing of the epistemic factor. The *episteme* is elevated above the historical process in which Scott insists revolutions and other concepts must be immersed. From this monopoly position, epistemic readings then become criteria to which political theorizing must be subject. The fate of the latter is determined by the movement of *epistemes* without regard to explicitly political and sociological questions, which now become obsolete and illegitimate. At no time does Scott consider the possibility of a dialectical synthesis between these two levels of analysis. Rather, his position is one in which the epistemic displaces the political. Later, we will see that this is a persistent tendency in poststructuralist thought.

In contrast to this antagonistic relationship between the linguistic and political economy perspectives, I will argue for a more productive and dialectical relationship between the two. This will be a relationship in which *episteme* or sign de-centers labor as much as labor de-centers sign or *episteme*. My argument unfolds in four basic steps. First, I present a brief overview of Caribbean Marxism. Second, I examine the impact of the globalizing strategies of the neoliberal turn on both its theory and practice. Third, I critically assess the impact of four specific poststructuralist arguments: the dominance of the sign form, the "empty space" of discursive totalizations, specular doubling, and structural complicity. Fourth and finally, I offer some conclusions about the future of Caribbean Marxism.

CARIBBEAN MARXISM: AN OVERVIEW

The historic opposition between capitalism and socialism emerged in the early phases of European modernity. Particularly in its Marxist variant, socialism has always seen itself as an alternative to capitalism. Thus both the theory and praxis of Marxism has been closely associated with popular revolutions and upsurges against the contradictions and excesses of capitalism. The rise of Caribbean Marxism cannot be separated from the upsurges of Caribbean peoples against the racism and colonialism that Western capitalism imposed on them.

With the collapse of the Garvey movement in the late 1920s, the global struggles of African peoples against racism and colonialism took a decidedly laborist turn. It was in the course of this development that Caribbean Marxism was born, along with trade unions and mass political parties. At the intellectual level, the major statements of this early phase of Caribbean Marxism are to be found in the works of three Trinidadians—George Padmore, C. L. R. James, and Eric Williams. In these three, the basic lines of socialist praxis in the region were effectively demonstrated. In the early Padmore, an orthodox Leninist practice emerged, in James a popular insurrectionary practice, and in Williams a social democratic one.

This shift toward a class or labor-centric orientation did not eliminate the older Pan-Africanist tradition and its practice of racial mobilization. Rather the latter provided an important context in relation to which Caribbean Marxism would revise both classical and Leninist Marxism. This special role of race in Caribbean Marxism is clear in the work of the above three writers. The reworking is even stronger in Frantz Fanon, the leading Caribbean Marxist theorist of the next generation. Fanon's Marxism is a highly original mix that incorporated race theory, existentialism, and psychoanalysis.

With the regaining of political independence, there was a shift in emphasis from resisting foreign capitalism to pushing local economic development. This emphasis on development raised the issue of local capitalism. The consequences of this shift are most evident in the work of Arthur Lewis who moved from a proworker position in *Labor in the West Indies* to a procapitalist stance in his later works.

The failures and hardships produced by the procapitalist turn in the laborist tradition helped to set the stage for the next phase in the history of Caribbean Marxism. This phase was marked by the rise of the New World Group, which produced Caribbean dependency theory. Among others, this group included Lloyd Best, George Beckford, Norman Girvan, Clive Thomas, and James Millette. Caribbean dependency theory offered a radical critique of capitalism and advocated a social democratic practice that focused on changing the behavior of multinational corporations.

Also emerging out of the upsurges that accompanied the crises of the Lewisian development model were three other distinct approaches to Marxism. The first was the fairly orthodox Leninist approach of Trevor Monroe and his Workers' Party of Jamaica, which found echoes in the Peoples Progressive Party of Cheddi Jagan. The second was the insurrectionary

Marxism of groups like the Working Peoples Alliance (WPA) in Guyana, New Beginning in Trinidad, and the Antigua Caribbean Liberation Movement, which was led by Tim Hector. The leading theorists of the WPA were Walter Rodney and Clive Thomas. As we have seen, Rodney's Marxism was distinguished by its efforts to link the problems of class and race in a way that addressed Indo-Caribbean concerns. Rodney's Marxism had a strong influence on Clive Thomas, a figure in whom the New World and Rodney traditions meet.[2] Third and finally, we have the racially nuanced democratic socialism of Carl Stone. Stone's socialism centered around a basic-needs strategy that it shares with Thomas.[3]

The contemporary phase of Caribbean Marxism is distinguished by two important challenges: the first is the attempt to assimilate feminist critiques of the notions of wage labor that have been central to this tradition of thought. These critiques have suggested that in spite of its universal form and gender-neutral appearance, the concept has a male bias, which results in the systematic underrepresentation of the economic contributions of women. In this regard, the works of Paula Aymer, Rhoda Reddock, Patricia Mohammed, Joycelyn Massiah, and others come immediately to mind.[4] The second challenge is the attempt at a process of critical self-examination in the wake of the collapse of the major socialist experiments in the region except for the case of Cuba. Particularly difficult for Caribbean Marxism has been the tragic collapse in Grenada and the economic crisis that overtook Michael Manley's democratic socialism. These attempts at rethinking can be seen in the works of Clive Thomas, Norman Girvan, Trevor Monroe, Brian Meeks, and Hilbourne Watson.

This, in brief, is the field of Caribbean Marxism. It is a complex discursive field that allows for the taking up of quite varied positions. Thus a figure like the well-known journalist and activist Tim Hector clearly inhabits the Jamesian space of this field. Someone like Alex Dupuy occupies a space between Rodney and the New World Group. Much of my own work falls between the Jamesian and New World spaces.

What these varying positions share is the discourse of the commodity that opens Marx's *Capital* and, more specifically, its application to Caribbean labor power. The practice of class domination in capitalist societies is effected and legitimated through the commodification of labor. This domination is masked by the claim that, like all other commodities, labor power is bought by capital in a fair and equitable exchange. Consequently, there is no exploitation or unequal exchange. On the whole, Caribbean Marxism has rejected these claims and has sought to present counterdiscourses that make clear the unequal exchanges and practices of domination that surround the appropriation of Caribbean labor by both local and foreign capital.

From this common point, the varying positions inside the field of Caribbean Marxism diverge on a number of points, two of which are particularly important. The first is: Just how central are the dynamics of labor as a commodity (compared to other factors of production) for the growth of capital, on the one hand, and the poverty of workers, on the other? The second is to what extent do the contradictions arising from the representation and exploitation of labor as a commodity lead directly to a socialist alternative? On these points we find significant differences. Consequently, the impact of the neoliberal and post-structuralist turns will be different for the varying positions within Caribbean Marxism.

THE NEOLIBERAL TURN

As the persistence and nature of the socialist alternative have depended upon the anticapitalist contents of popular upsurges, the persistence of capitalism has depended upon special periods of hegemonic self-assertion and creative restructuring. These strategic and re-creative moves have often been in response to socialist challenges and to internal or systemic crises of capital accumulation.

The neoliberal turn is one of these periods of hegemonic restructuring. It is the set of policies with which Western capitalism has responded to the Third World's call for a New International Economic Order and to economic challenges from the Pacific rim countries. Together, these challenges had created a global environment in which Western multinational corporations were losing their hegemonic and competitive edges. Commodity cartels such as OPEC and IBA, the rise of Asian textile, automobile, and consumer electronics industries were sources of Western losses in hegemonic and competitive power. Steel, electronics, motorbikes, and textiles were just some of the major industries that collapsed. The neoliberal turn is the set of corporate-driven initiatives aimed at the reversing of this trend.

Toward this end, Western corporate elites have been able to mobilize both liberal and conservative parties behind their reforms, creating in effect a new model of the corporate state out of the earlier national security model. On the home front, these reforms have included lessening state regulation of capital, even of affirmative action guidelines; making capital more mobile; supporting it with supply-side incentives; weakening both unions and the enforcement of labor legislation; and reducing the support government gives to other classes and groups and the economic competition it gives to the private sector. On the international front, the initiatives have been oriented toward increasing Western access to Third-World resources and markets and rejecting the demands for a new economic order. Instead the neoliberal turn has pushed for liberalization of Third-World trading regimes, privatizing of state assets, export promotion, wage cuts, and reductions in both the size and role of government in the economy. The implementing of these policies in the form of structural adjustment packages (SAPs) was facilitated by the worsening debt crisis and rising levels of political instability in Third-World states, hence the emergence of the IMF and the World Bank as global financial policemen.

Within the economic spaces created by these policy shifts, Western corporations have been able to restructure themselves radically. Through mergers and acquisitions they have grown larger. Through massive layoffs, wage cuts, new technology, and the further globalizing of production, they have been able to cut dramatically labor costs. This reshuffling has resulted in two major sectoral changes in Western economies: the ballooning of the financial sector, and unprecedented expansions in both the retail and information-processing sectors.

Particularly important for Caribbean Marxism is the rise and restructuring of the retail sector. Both the rise and restructuring of this sector were the results of responses to Asian competition in apparel and durable consumer production. In the United States, retail chains such as Sears and J. C. Penney got larger in the 1970s as they gobbled up smaller independent retailers. In the 1980s, these enlarged chains became the objects of devastating competition from even larger discount chains such as Wal-mart, K-mart, and a growing number of specialty stores such as Montgomery Ward that catered to high-income shoppers.

Because of the size of the markets they control, these superchains have been better positioned to counter Asian competition in apparel and durable consumer goods than many older production companies. These giant chains have been able to contract out on unprecedented scales the production of these goods in Asia, the Caribbean, and Mexico to counter the labor cost advantages of their Asian competitors. Thus we have an important case of production being driven by the marketing and retail ends of these global commodity chains. It is the success of these "buyer driven"[5] strategies of the giant retail companies in meeting the Asian challenge that accounts for the rise of this sector.

The rapid expansion of the financial sector in the early eighties was due primarily to the growing inability of Western industrial production to profitably absorb surplus capital, hence the turn to investing profits in financial assets or privatized state enterprises. The phenomenal growth of speculative trading in foreign exchange, stocks, bonds, futures, loans to Third-World governments, and corporate mergers were indicative of the shift away from productive investment. The rise of the information-processing sector was a direct result of ongoing revolutions in communications and computer technologies, whose absorption by other sectors has spurred the growth of this sector.

The results of these changes in the organization of Western capitalism have been very mixed. They have restored dynamism to the U.S. economy, but they have also increased patterns of inequality in wealth and income. In Europe they have dampened economic dynamism, threatened the welfare state, and have also increased economic inequalities. To the Japanese economy, it has brought a long period of stagnation. More recently, it has brought both collapse and stagnation to the South Korean and a number of other Asian economies. To the Caribbean, Africa, and much of the Third World it has also brought stagnation, collapse, and dramatic rises in levels of poverty. Whether it is Kingston, Georgetown, or Accra we can see those who have been discarded by structural adjustment trying to sell just about anything on the streets of these cities. Neoliberal reforms have produced a ballooning of African and Caribbean retail sectors of a very different sort. Let us take a closer look.

CARIBBEAN MARXISM AND THE NEOLIBERAL TURN

Earlier I suggested that the theoretical core of Caribbean Marxism was its critical discourse on labor as a commodity. The three distinct forms of praxis associated with this body of thought have as their goals the ending of the class domination and surplus labor extraction that commodification masks particularly in the case of the working class. I also argued that the corporate restructuring of the neoliberal turn has made the production of a large number of commodities more global in nature. Thus any assessment of the impact of this turn on Caribbean Marxism must include its consequences for the latter's commodity discourse and its socialist practices. I shall argue that it confirms much of the theory while at the same time making the conditions for its practices more difficult.

Neoliberalism and Caribbean Labor Power
From the period of early colonization to the present, the peripheral function of the Caribbean has been that of a site for the reproduction of cheap, highly exploitable labor. On such sites the masks of commodification are often thin. The unequal exchanges, the extraction of surplus, the repression, and dehumanization that are generally concealed are here exposed in varying degrees to public viewing. This exposing of the violence of the commodity form is one way in which it has been affected by race. As Fanon noted, racial domination strives to other and exclude its subjugated masses and not to maximize surplus labor time. Its fulfillment is apartheid, not capital accumulation. Thus, with

the racist othering of black workers it has been possible to relax the masking that usually hides the violence that commodifies labor. Gender adds a similar dynamic to the process of commodification, the full significance of which we are now realizing.

In spite of its many restructurings, the production of Caribbean labor as a cheap commodity has remained the item of exchange by which Western capitalism has defined the peripheral role of the region. It is this highly exploitable labor power, rather than the specific commodities it produces, that continues to generate external interest and to determine the specific places we occupy in the ever-more global production networks of Western capitalism. Thus, whether it was the plantations of the mercantile and competitive phases, or the bauxite and tourist industries of the monopoly phase, our primary role in these production networks has been the supplying of labor. Girvan's analysis of the bauxite industry in Jamaica showed that the primary benefits to the Jamaican economy were payments to labor and taxes to the government.[6] Much the same could be said of the tourist industry.[7] Thus from a developmental view of Caribbean economies it is labor, and not bauxite or satisfied tourists, that we are really exporting.

This stark reality that for Western capitalism Caribbean economies are at bottom labor-exporting economies was indeed masked by the mode of commodification that came with the bauxite and tourist industries. The flurry of industrial activity together with the impact of trade unions created the impression that regional economies were industrializing and diversifying their output; that through significant percentages of value added they were exporting more than just labor; and that the peripheral function of the region had changed. However, with the neoliberal turn, this masking of the real peripheral role of Caribbean economies has been shattered by the competitive pressure that current modes of commodification must absorb.

Earlier, we saw that neoliberal restructuring produced important sectoral shifts and new forms of corporate organization in Western economies. The latter has emphasized flexibility, resulting in shifts toward subcontracting and away from earlier levels of emphasis on vertically integrated corporate structures. These subcontracting arrangements are designed to catch the cheaper labor of the semiperipheral and peripheral areas by shifting greater proportions of the production process to them. Hence the growth and greater visibility of global production networks in which semiperipheral and peripheral labor is being incorporated under the more competitive conditions created by the neoliberal turn.

In the Caribbean the changes in the mode of commodification can be clearly seen in the garment factories that increasingly "source" the U.S. apparel industry (and hence the new retail sector) through subcontracted production.

The dramatic rise of the Caribbean clothing industry since the early 1980s can be linked directly to the response of U.S. clothing manufacturers and retailers to the Asian challenge. The various bilateral agreements between the United States and the Caribbean such as 807 and Super 807 are clearly protectionist measures, which at the same time give U.S. capitalists access to Caribbean labor. By combining this labor with their inputs and technology, American businessmen have been able to retain their market shares by reexporting the finished products back to the United States. In this way, they have been able to counter the lower labor costs of their Asian competitors. Not surprisingly, the bulk of these investments have gone to Haiti and the Dominican Republic where labor is cheapest. Jamaica and Costa Rica come in third and fourth.

However, it is not just American clothing producers that are making use of Caribbean labor in this new competitive game. It is also the Asian producers. In all of these territories, substantial segments of this industry are Asian owned. By relocating to the Caribbean, Asian producers have been able to circumvent U.S. quota restrictions placed on their countries. This has been the Asian countermove to the U.S. response. Our involvement in this game is clearly the good location and the low cost of our labor.

As in the case of Girvan's analysis of the bauxite industry, a close examination of the clothing industry suggests that regional economies are unlikely to develop as a result of the growth of this industry. Because its competitive pressures require higher and more restrictive rates and conditions of labor exploitation, Caribbean economies are likely to derive far less from this industry.

In his study of the Jamaican clothing industry, Keith Nurse has shown that its potential as a leading sector is not very great as presently organized.[8] It shows few signs of generating significant backward and forward linkages. Further it generates little or no transfers of technology, low levels of value added, and only moderate amounts of foreign exchange. Nurse shows, in contrast to bauxite, the labor-intensive nature of the industry and hence the importance of low labor costs for profit margins. Thus even more than tourism or bauxite, the primary benefits from this industry will accrue through payments to labor. This is particularly the case as these firms operate in export-processing zones and are therefore exempt from major taxes. This outcome should reinforce the labor-exporting nature of Caribbean economies and their limited peripheral roles. Consequently, it would be a mistake to view this industry as a case of the export-oriented industrialization that is supposedly the key to Asian success.

Similar patterns of more exploitative commodification can also be seen in Caribbean agriculture, where traditional staples are being replaced by the production of off-season fruits and vegetables for the U.S. market. Laura Raynolds's study of these industries in the Dominican Republic shows the primary role of labor in these industries as well as the extent to which they have been using subcontracting practices.[9] It is still too early to say what the impact of the information-processing industries will be on the region. Studies of these such as the one in Barbados need to be done before we can assess their potential. However, from the cases of clothing and agriculture, we can conclude that Caribbean labor is being incorporated through a commodity framework that is more exploitative than the framework of the bauxite and tourist industries. This higher level of exploitation together with the impact of structural adjustment programs can only mean rising levels of immiseration in the region. Hence the growth of crime, informal activity, street vending in particular, and the overcrowding of the retail sector.

These outcomes of the neoliberal turn do not in any way undermine or invalidate the commodity discourse of Caribbean Marxism. On the contrary, they have increased the relevance of this discourse. More than before, Caribbean workers need a critical discourse that exposes the unequal exchanges concealed by the current commodification of their labor. As long as these masked, exploitative arrangements persist, the theory of Caribbean Marxism will be relevant.

Neoliberalism and Socialist Practices
If the impact of the neoliberal turn on Caribbean Marxist theory has been to increase its relevance, then the impact on its praxis has been to make it much more difficult. This is indeed a paradoxical outcome. However, it is one that derives from the introduction of the power factor into the implementing of this theory. Between structural adjustment and the semiperipheralization of formerly socialist countries, the neoliberal turn has been accompanied by dramatic increases in institutional power for the advanced capitalist societies. These increases have occurred both at home and abroad.

Although the difficulties created by these increases in capitalist power have affected all forms of socialist practice in the region, it should be clear that they affect some more than others. The negative effects have probably been greatest for the Leninists, then for the popular insurrectionists, and finally the social democrats. For the latter, the June 1997 elections in France which brought the socialists to power and the October 1998 elections in Germany have been important barometers for the future.

In spite of the differences in their praxis, there are some common elements around which there has been considerable consensus. First, the limited benefits from peripheral industries such as clothing point to the need for a more nationally oriented economic strategy, which would increase local control and root production more securely in local demand. Such a strategy has been given its most comprehensive and elegant formulation by Clive Thomas.[10] Caribbean

Marxists have argued that only such a strategy can put an end to the peripherally structured strategies of development that we have been repeating, and in which we never get beyond the exporting of labor. Thus is addition to the commodity discourse, the negative developmental impact of the neoliberal turn has brightly illumined the relevance of Marxist development strategies. This illumination has made it clear that dependence is a major problem, which neoliberal strategies are compounding by making the peripherally functioning sectors of the economy lead the growth process, hence the need for a development strategy in which the nonperipheral sectors lead the growth process. A second common element in the praxis of Caribbean Marxism has been the need for some measure of central planning that would result in more equitable distributions of the economic surplus. These concerns can be found throughout the tradition whether it is articulated by James, Thomas, Girvan, or Meeks.

Third and finally, Caribbean Marxists have been committed to ending the exploitation and commodification of Caribbean labor through structures of empowerment and self-organization such as self-managed enterprises or organizations that encourage popular participation.

Implementing all of the above will now be more difficult because of the politico-economic context that neoliberal reforms have created. Three things in particular stand out: (1) the new role assigned to the state; (2) the deepening and widening of the institutionalization of market competition; and (3) the increased technological minimum required for effective competition.

With the new American corporate state as the model, the pressure is increasing on countries whose political economies diverge too far from this norm. All of the above socialist strategies presuppose a strong interventionist state, and hence a political economy that is very different from the American model. The preference of the Left has been for a workers' or a worker-oriented state, rather than a corporate one. The strengths of these workers' states are different in the three traditions of practice. It is strongest in the Leninist tradition and weakest among the social democrats.

In Monroe's work, we can see the struggles of the Leninist tradition with the problems of authoritarianism.[11] In both the popular insurrectionist and social democratic traditions, these problems have been much less central. The works of James, Thomas, and Manley in particular make clear breaks with authoritarian models of socialist practice. Thus Lindhal's critique of Thomas really misses the mark, unless his point is that liberalism, and not participatory formations, represents the maximum measure of attainable democracy. Further, Lindhal never critically examines the authoritarian aspects and expressions of liberalism in a region and their possible roots in sources shared with authoritarian socialism. Thus the question of the management of power and the democratic organization of the state in the popular insurrectionary and democratic socialist traditions are poorly represented and not sufficiently distinguished from the authoritarian tradition. Of these three socialist state formations only the democratic socialist ones are likely to thrive during the life span of the neoliberal turn. Today, it is only the latter that has a chance of surviving without debilitating pressures from capitalist states. For the other two, the conditions are extremely adverse. So it is only those elements in the socialist agenda which social democrats affirm that can remain in place or get implemented.

Even more devastating for a socialist practice is the increase in the level to which economies all over the world are being marketized. This rise must impose greater limits on the scope and exclusivity of central planning as an organizing principle of socialist economies. Global markets have clearly become forces that socialist economies cannot ignore. Further, given the practical difficulties that Eastern Europe and the Soviet Union experienced with central planning, its limits and real capabilities must be reassessed. If Alec Nove is right, then the experiences of China, Eastern Europe, and the Soviet Union all suggest that there are overwhelming difficulties associated with the attempt to plan an entire economy, at least at our present levels of planning capability. Consequently, long before the socialist collapse and current levels of marketization, Nove vigorously argued for reforms that would have marketized substantial portions of these economies. He suggests a mutual dependence between plan and market such that the two cannot be absolutely separated.[12]

In the Caribbean, planning capabilities have been significantly less than they were in the Soviet Union and Eastern Europe. At the same time, levels of external dependence on the advanced capitalist countries were much higher. Given these two facts, it should come as no surprise that socialist experiments in Grenada, Jamaica, and Guyana never moved to fully or predominantly planned economies. On the contrary, the market remained the dominant organizing principle in these economies. In the present period, the power and global scope of the market is even greater than it was at the time of these experiments. Thus whatever the next major round of anticapitalist upsurges may bring to the region, it will be harder to pursue socialist strategies that exclude the market.

Along with restructuring the state and expanding global markets, the neoliberal turn has further increased the significance of technology as a factor of production. Like the market, technology imposes its own organizational imperatives on societies. These are often indifferent to or opposed to the redistributive and egalitarian goals of socialism. With the further globalizing of markets, appropriate technologies are determined less by national criteria and more by international ones. This external technological pressure can only make central planning more difficult. Insulating open economies like ours from such pressures will only get more difficult under present circumstances. In other words, local control over this factor of production is likely to lessen thus making planning and hence redistribution more difficult.

These three factors that have come with the neoliberal turn will force a serious rethinking of the praxis of Caribbean Marxism. In the area of politics, Leninist and popular insurrectionary approaches will encounter great resistance and little support. In development strategies, structural transformation has been limited to the possibilities of occupying higher value-added positions in production networks such as clothing and agriculture, than the labor-supplying positions we now fill. In central planning and redistribution, options are again severely restricted. Hence the need for rethinking the practicalities, technicalities, and the power dynamics of socialist practice in the region. In particular, new ways of mobilizing popular power and reorganizing the post-colonial state must be explored.

Language and Caribbean Marxism
In addition to these adverse changes in the objective situation of Caribbean Marxism, the linguistic turn in European philosophy has confronted this discourse with adverse changes in the subjective and ideological conditions of its practice. Here we cannot escape the question of how a shift in European philosophy has been able to affect Caribbean Marxism in this way. In truth, it is quite similar to the way in which the reorganization of the American retail sector has affected Caribbean labor. Both are explained by underlying patterns of dependence. In this case, it is philosophical, rather than economic. This philosophical dependence has been particularly strong in areas such as epistemology, ontology, and philosophies of the self. Thus the laborist/productivist notion of the self in Caribbean Marxism derives from the rationalism of the European Enlightenment period. The linguistic turn, particularly in its poststructuralist variant, has been deconstructing these Enlightenment conceptions of the self, hence the implications for the subjective foundations of Caribbean Marxism.

More specifically, the poststructuralist turn to linguistic explanations of human behavior have produced one set of arguments that challenge the commodity discourse of Caribbean Marxism, and three sets of arguments that challenge the viability of its socialist praxis. The argument against the commodity discourse is one that suggests that the consumption of commodities as signs has displaced in importance their production as commodities. The first of the arguments against a socialist praxis is that of the inauthentic or delusional nature of such discursively totalized projections. The second is that of specular doubling, while the third rests on the assumption of a structural (semio-linguistic) complicity between contested and contesting discourses. Because of the ways in which these arguments undermine the agency of subjects such as the Marxian revolutionary, their concerted effect has been to foster a subjective mood of postmodern malaise and an ideological outlook from which revolutionary transformation appears impossible.

However, I shall argue that in themselves none of these arguments are as prohibitive as poststructuralists often suggest. First, some of them are not really new and echo themes that have been stated less deterministically by Caribbean poeticists such as Wilson Harris and Sylvia Wynter. Indeed, had Caribbean Marxism drawn its conception of the self from this poeticist tradition, the linguistic turn would have affected us very differently. I will begin my response with a brief overview of the linguistic turn and then examine each of these arguments separately.

THE LINGUISTIC TURN

The linguistic turn refers to a major shift in the relationship between language and the disciplines of the humanities and social sciences. In these disciplines, language was for a long time seen largely as an instrument or medium of communication for the thinking ego. With the change in relations, language ceased being the neutral communicative medium that it was thought to be. Thus we can describe the linguistic turn as the gradual releasing of language from imprisonment in its communicative role as modern cultural systems become more internally differentiated. Freed from these communicative restrictions, language has emerged as a distinct domain of human self-formation, with distinctly linguistic explanations of human behavior that have fundamentally altered the relations between language and the established disciplines.

Both the structuralist and poststructuralist versions of the linguistic turn emphasize the unconscious enmeshment of human subjects in the semiotic aspects of the languages we speak. In other words, to speak a language is to be inscribed in the system of binary oppositions (male/female, right/wrong), their hierarchical ordering and functioning, that make the language possible. The names, categories, codings, and meanings that the system of binaries imposes on our social interactions give language the capacity to explain human behavior. In these explanations, it is the dynamic movements of signifiers, the textualities woven by their semiotic play, that is crucial. They are the explanatory competitors of the economic and political structures of Marxist discourses.

In the early phases of the linguistic turn, the tensions with Marxism were not particularly severe, as the works of Volosinov, Althusser, Bourdieu, and the early writing of Baudrillard suggest.[13] Those that did exist, centered around humanist notions of the subject that Marx inherited from the Enlightenment. For Marx, the central activity of the subject was his or her capacity to labor, that is, to transform subjective desires into objective realities. This creative/productivist view of the subject clearly concealed the constitutive powers of language that the linguistic turn has uncovered, hence the existence of mild tensions as in the case of Althusser.

However, with the passage of time, and particularly the collapse of the May 1968 student/worker insurrection in France, relations turned more opposi- tional. This collapse was the occasion for a major disengagement of French intellectuals from Marxism. Former Maoists turned "New Philosophers," such as Bernard-Henri Levy, Christian Jambet, and Guy Lardreau, all made their dramatic exits. In doing so, some turned to religion, others to themes in post- structuralist thought that were contained in the published works of Lacan, Foucault, and Derrida. More recently in *Spectres of Marx*, Derrida attempted to reassert some of the closer ties with Marxism largely in response to excesses of the neoliberal turn.

The Commodity versus the Sign

In the poststructuralist literature, the commodity discourse of Marxism is most directly challenged in the work of Jean Baudrillard, who counterposes the sign to the commodity. Baudrillard's argument for the hegemony of the sign form rests on the claim that the production and consumption of signs has taken pri- macy over material production in contemporary capitalism. Consumption is no longer the appropriating of a commodity for the satisfaction of a need. "It is not defined by the food we eat, the clothes we wear, the cars we drive, . . . but in the organization of all this as signifying substance."[14] To become "an object of con- sumption, the object must become a sign"[15] in a larger system of objects that have also become signs. Baudrillard then goes on to suggest that consumption is a "systematic act of the manipulating of signs."[16]

This imposition of the sign form transforms not only material commodities but also the subjective commodity of human labor power. It transforms the identity of the Marxian subject, which has been defined in terms of the com- modification of its capacity to labor. From the self-acting commodity, the sub- ject becomes the self-manipulating sign. Because this shift inscribes the subject in a consumptive discourse of the sign, Baudrillard speaks of a new humanism, the semiotic humanism of consumption.

In other poststructuralists, such as Michel Foucault, Jacques Derrida, and Roland Barthes, semio-linguistic analyses examine the self in relation to tex- tual and knowledge production, rather than consumption. Writing and knowl- edge production become crucial sites for reexamining the agency and creativity of Enlightenment conceptions of the subject such as Marx's. The result is a much more radical displacing of everyday, action-oriented models of the sub- ject than in the case of Baudrillard.

In these theorists, the author or subject is displaced as the real creator of texts and/or systems knowledge and is replaced by the unconscious combinatory activities of linguistic binaries, the founding analogies and metaphors of prere-flective *epistemes*. The subject does not make these *epistemes* that structure and make possible his or her textual or knowledge production. On the contrary, it is the subject that is made by the dynamic activity of these epistemic spaces. The subject inhabits these spaces and carries the signatures of their internal structures, which are seen as independent of human consciousness. From this subtextual perspective, the self appears radically de-centered and its agency severely compromised. It is similar to the quantum or subatomic perspective from which the solid objects of everyday life appear to be primarily empty space. David Scott's deconstructive analysis of the concept of revolution takes this approach. From the subdiscursive level of the *episteme*, very little of the everyday solidity of the concept remains. It is this quantum or subtextual view of the solid, unified self that results in its more radical displacement.

In general terms, poststructuralism's subtextual view of the self leads to major differences with the Marxian laborist/productivist model of the self. The latter is seen as a solid view of the self that ignores its own subtextual dimen-sions. This, in turn, leads to the rejection of a number of Marxian claims regarding the self: first, the claim that the self is the center of its own actions and experiences; second, that the self's primary activities are productive and transformative; third, that the creative elements in its primary activities are of its own making; and fourth, that the self becomes an authentic historical agent when through practical action it causes something new, such as socialism, to appear. These are all everyday, solid appearances that turn out to be primarily "empty spaces" when viewed from the subtextual perspective of poststruc-turalism. I will have more to say on this general perspective, but now we return to Baudrillard's critique.

Is Baudrilliard's claim regarding the hegemony of consumption correct for our region? I don't think it is. I am not even sure that it is correct for the advanced capitalist societies. There can be no denying the increase in impor-tance of consumption that Baudrilliard has attempted to theorize. However, I think he overstates his case and, in so doing, prematurely announces the death of production. The competitive and productivist nature of the economic battle between the United States and the Asian countries shows production and its global reorganization to be at the heart of neoliberal restructuring. Further, the attempts to revitalized the U.S. industrial base and not let a pure consumer society emerge as a result of foreign competition show the continuing impor-tance of production.

If the shift to consumption is questionable in the case of the advanced soci-eties, then it is even more so in the case of peripheral economies such as ours. Everything I've argued for in regard to the impact of the neoliberal turn on Caribbean economies works against Baudrilliard's claim. These arguments clearly suggest that production and a more exploitative commodification of labor will be increasingly important for the region. Thus Baudrillard's suggestion that we shift our conception of the subject from *homo faber* to *homo significans* is not one that is likely to advance our understanding of the new challenges confronting Caribbean labor.

In most other Third-World countries, such a shift is certainly not the reality. The heated debates in China over the commodification of Chinese labor power occasioned by the labor reforms of the 1980s demonstrate very clearly the dominant role of production in peripheral and semiperipheral economies.[17] As China continues to capitalize its economy, and redefine its relation to global capitalism, we can expect this role of production to grow as it will have the largest and cheapest supplies of labor on the global market.

These two cases suggest that the preponderance of consumption becomes a possible claim only when the global and polarized nature of capitalist production is overlooked. By focusing on the French case, Baudrillard is indeed able to make a plausible case for this claim. However, this plausibility declines sharply when the global and polarized (varyingly exploitative) nature of capitalist production is taken into account. This preponderance of production, even through increasingly located in the periphery, points to the dependence of consumption on production.

Further, this dependence helps to explain the rather forced nature of Baudrilliard's linguistic analogies. Commodities are more than signs and cannot be reduced to their semiotic dimensions. In Marx's commodity discourse, the semiotic elements are quite clear. Commodities are represented by their exchange value or their prices. The price is thus an important signifier in the representation, production, and exchange of commodities. Consequently, the behavior of the signifiers of commodities, exactly how and what they represent constitute an important semiotic dimension of the Marxian commodity discourse.

However, the order of this discourse is not determined by the set of general rules that govern the algebra of prices and other signifiers in this discourse. These formal semiotic processes are subject to an instrumental/productivist logic that systematically restrains and orders the constitutive and disseminative play of these signifiers. Thus the textuality of the Marxian commodity discourse cannot be reduced to the play or manipulation of signifiers. This textuality is necessarily shaped by feedback relations with productive activities in concrete factories, which impose instrumental, profit-oriented constraints on it. It is precisely this instrumental limiting of semiotic play that allows it to reflect critically the situation of workers. This nonlinguistic, productivist element embarrasses Baudrillard's linguistic/consumptionist reading. But in spite of such excesses, there can be no going back to the old conception of the relationship between language and the subject. The constitutive and behavior-determining powers of language must become an integral part of Caribbean Marxism.

DISCURSIVE TOTALITIES: THE SUBTEXTUAL VIEW

Unlike the critique of production, which affected the theory of Caribbean Marxism, our remaining three poststructuralist critiques regarding discursive totalities, specular doubling, and structural complicity all affect its practice. In particular, they focus on the capacity for practical action required for the realization of its socialist alternative. By practical as opposed to technical action, I am referring to the principled (ethical or political) actions of individuals that are oriented toward achieving a goal or bringing about a change.

Given poststructuralism's subtextual view of the self, it should come as no surprise that it takes a similar view of closely related discursive formations, such as universals, closed systems of thought, teleologies, and transformative totalizations such as historicism, humanism, or socialism. These formations have all been objects of deconstructive critiques and declared primarily "empty space" from this quantum perspective. Thus it is the apparent fullness and solidity of discursive totalities, rather than the superior power of the opposition, that misguide practical action and severely compromise its effectiveness.

Given the preference for difference, discursive totalities like all other constructions of sameness or identity are suspect for the poststructuralist. The unity and coherence that these totalizations offer are seen as forced and hence both oppressive and illusory. They are discursively produced or forged with the aid of metaphorical and analogical tricks that establish equalities and identities between things that are unequal and different. For example, are the identities between the workers of the world established by the Marxian notion of commodified labor real or illusory? Are there not real differences like race and gender that such a universal category suppresses? Thus discursive totalities can only be false totalities because they generate identities and equalities through the unacknowledged suppression of real differences. For the poststructuralist, all such universalistic or totalized constructions are discursively authoritarian; hence they should be deconstructed, and the suppressed differences given their play at the price of the totalized formation.

The fatal dependence of practical action on such problematic totalities is clearly demonstrated in the works of Lyotard, Lindahl, and Scott. As noted earlier, practical action needs not only strategic information but also a legitimating and transformative vision. For Lyotard practical action derives this vision from problematic totalizations such as the movement toward socialism, the dialectics of spirit, the emancipation of the rational, or the working subject.

Both Lindahl and Scott share Lyotard's view that these are all false totalizations, grand narratives that cannot deliver the alternatives they promise. They cannot because the images of equality, unity, and reconciliation that they offer are not genuine but misleading. As opposed to being real, they are the discursive effects produced by a masking of semiotic difference. For Lyotard and Lindahl, the mark of our postmodern period is precisely an incredulity toward such grand narratives. With this incredulity, the viability of practical action (particularly revolutionary action) collapses, giving way to a fin de siècle mood or to the reign of strategic and technocratic action.

As in the case of Baudrillard, I think Lyotard, Lindahl, and Scott overstate their cases against totalizing strategies. First, the problematic nature of discursive totalization is a well-recognized fact. This recognition is very clear in the work of Sartre, James, and Fanon, to mention a few.[18] Sartre analyzed the existential conditions that made totalizations problematic; James examined the social conditions; and Fanon brought both of them together dialectically.

Second, what these individuals recognized that our poststructuralist critics have overlooked is that unlike semiotic or interpretive action both strategic and political action function quite well and sometimes require problematic totalizations in which real difference have been suppressed. This oversight is particularly evident in the case of Scott who "normalizes" interpretation in this instance in the same manner for which he criticizes sociologists. In fact, the world of everyday life, its interactions, the everyday selves and linguistic analogies that poststructuralists project, all require such problematic totalizations. To resist neoliberal reforms or to struggle against capitalism does not require a subtextual, epistemic knowledge of all the difference and semiotic play suppressed by the strategic and practical stands taken in order to engage in these struggles. Some of this subtextual knowledge can be usefully integrated into these strategic positions but cannot replace them on the level of everyday interaction. The epistemic or semiotic microdynamics of interpretive action cannot be superimposed on the strategic and practical activities of political action at the everyday level of parties, states, and economies. Quantum physicists know that walls are primarily empty space, but they still use doors. Similarly, the empty subtextual appearance of capitalism or socialism does not mean that we can walk through the former and replace the latter with social criticism or liberalism.

Third and finally, to be consistent, our poststructuralist critics would have to abandon all forms of argumentation since even those they employ make use of analogical and metaphorical strategies for establishing instances of sameness or identity. The provisional eliminating of real differences is basic to human forms of argumentation. As we saw in the case of Baudrillard, the identity between commodities established by his concept of the sign rests on a rather forced analogy between language and consumption. In short, even poststructuralist critiques make use of totalizing strategies. The current resurgence in both James and Fanon studies in this high period of postructuralism points directly to the resilience of the dialectical solutions they gave to the problematic nature of discursive totalities. On this point, they anticipated the poststructuralist critique.

POLITICAL ACTION: IN THE GRIP OF SPECULAR DOUBLING

The phenomenon of specular doubling takes us from the subtextual world of semiotic play to the libidinal world of desire. This is, of course, the world of the Freudian unconscious that has been given a structuralist face-lift by Lacan. Critiques of political action that made use of specular doubling were prominent among "New Philosophers" such as Bernard-Henri Levy. The road traveled by Regis Debray from *Revolution in the Revolution* to *The Critique of Political Reason* certainly crossed the avenue of specular doubling. We also find them in poststructuralist figures such as Julia Kristeva and Helene Cixous.[19]

By "specular doubling" Lacan is referring to certain prelinguistic and narcissistic patterns of self-other identification that are really misidentifications. These misidentifications are in principle quite similar to the ones we encountered in the case of discursive totalities. Here the misidentification affects the self, rather than a discursive formation. By splitting or dividing the self, this false identification will leave it severely incapacitated. This incapacitation of the self will in turn condemn its practical actions to a tragic fate of Sysiphean repetition.

The errors in the misidentifications that ground specular doubling are precisely their inability to recognize and handle the differences that remain in spite of the identity posited between self and other. If a child identifies with his or her father, then an absolute identity requires the elimination of all differences that are not consistent with the image of the father, or vice versa. The nonrational or counterfactual elements in these misidentifications derive from the primary narcissism of the subject. This mode of self-identification through the internalizing of the other is both internally contradictory and self-alienating. It leaves the ego divided. It becomes a specular double as it is both itself and another. This *intrasubjective* impasse becomes the code for the specular doubling of *intersubjective* activity. Under the weight of this coding practical action is condemned to its tragic fate.

Particularly fatal for revolutionary or transformative action are the specular identifications that we make with others who will later be adversaries. Action against such an other will be ambivalent and internally contradictory as the ego must be divided in this instance. To resist such an other, the ego must also resist itself. To support this other is also to support itself. Thus deliberate attempts to defeat such adversaries are likely to end in failure or even worse, the reproducing of the adversary one is trying to overthrow. Specular doubling thus traps practical action in a tautological circle of abortive repetition, which condemns the revolutionary to reproducing the very order that he or she is trying to overthrow, hence Lacan's reference to "the revolutionary of today who does not recognize his ideals in the results of his acts."[20]

This portrait of political action is extremely problematic as it traps the political actor in the impasses of early stages of ego development. First, as in the case of the subtextual critique of discursive totalities there is a level-specific problem with this specular, subpersonal view of the political activist. Through a one-sided quantum shift in perspective the concrete historical actions of the activist are evaporated and made to disappear. The autonomy and integrity (limited as they are) of the ego's capacity for political action is eclipsed by a subpersonal view of its formative dynamics that is unable to adequately grasp the realities of the everyday level. Consequently, the problem is a level-specific one: To what extent are the apparent solidity and capabilities of the everyday ego determined by stadial ego-genetic problems such as specular doubling or an Oedipal complex?

These "hard" features of the ego cannot be wholly determined by such psychological conflicts as they are also shaped by cultural traditions, institutions, and other sociological factors. In other words, arguments of specular doubling make two problematic assumptions: (1) that the capacity for everyday political action is wholly or overwhelmingly determined by stadial conflicts in the process of ego formation, particularly the narcissistic ones that arise in Lacan's imaginary stage; and (2) that effective political action requires of activists that they are free of stadial conflicts and related divisions. These are, I think the conditions for spiritual action. For as Kierkegaard has reminded us, purity of heart is to will one thing. Such unity I am sure would improve the ethical quality of political action and hence must be recognized and encouraged as such. However it is not a precondition for successful battles against the injustices and exploitations that plague our world. What these struggles require is that we can say with Fanon: today I will take in hand my narcissism and my psycho-existential complexes.

Second, arguments that approach political action via its conditioning by ego formative processes are not new. They are standard in psychology and European existential philosophy. Further, throughout this text we've discussed many from the Afro-Caribbean philosophical tradition. Consequently, the real issue here is how are these psycho-existential dynamics to be brought into mutually critical and dialectical relationships with the social factors that also help to determine the reality of everyday egos and their interactions.

For Caribbean Marxists, the best response to this issue is still Fanon's. He deals directly with the problem of specular doubling in his examination of the pathological misidentifications made by Jean Veneuse/Rene Maran and Mayotte Capecia in *Black Skin, White Masks*. The latter case in particular has become a heated issue in recent feminist scholarship.[21] In both, the specular double of the ego is clearly the white colonizer. Hence their anticolonial activities take the form of whitening themselves through the specific seeking of white lovers, thus reproducing the colonial order. In spite of such tragic realities inherent in the colonial situation, Fanon was still able to declare his belief in love, political action, and revolutionary transformation. Such commitments are possible because the misidentifications that ground specular doubling are not all-determining. Fanon's dialectical weavings between this narcissistic/prelinguistic level and the everyday personal level of political action does the latter more justice than Lacan's or those of his appropriators.

Third and finally, the historical record of political action reveals more successes than the abortive and circular view of specular doubling would suggest. One can certainly think of cases that fit this cycle of repetition. In Antigua, the dramatic way in which Prime Minister George Walter, after such an aggressive struggle against Vere Bird, came to resemble the man he replaced is certainly grist for the Lacanian mill. It is quite conceivable that Mr. Walter misidentified with the neocolonialism that Mr. Bird had created in ways that were similar to the misidentifications of Veneuse and Capecia with the colonial order. However, in spite of this disturbing outcome, the movement led by Mr. Walter brought something new to the historical stage in Antigua. It deepened Antiguan democracy.[22] Similarly, in spite of their premature collapse the Afro-American Civil Rights movement did succeed in ending social apartheid, and the student movement succeeded in changing American attitudes toward gender and the environment. Finally, the original and influential heritage that Lacan himself has left behind shows quite clearly that the repetitive logic of specular doubling is not all-determining.

POLITICAL ACTION AND STRUCTURAL COMPLICITY

Perhaps the most recognizable political feature of poststructuralism is the way in which it has legitimated the relocating of oppositional action from the political to the cultural arena. In the world of Africana thought, the works of Cornel West, Henry Louis Gates Jr., Sylvia Wynter, Stuart Hall, David Scott, Paul Gilroy, V. Y. Mudimbe, and Homi Bhabha in different ways all register this shift away from party to cultural politics. According to West, the "distinctive features of the new cultural politics of difference are to trash the monolithic and homogeneous in the name of diversity, multiplicity and heterogeneity; to reject the abstract, general and universal in the light of the concrete, specific and particular; and to historicize, contextualize and pluralize by highlighting the contingent, provisional, variable, tentative, shifting and changing."[23] In short, it is a subtextual approach to politics that focuses more on the power relations that are inscribed in images, identities, discursive formations, and less on organized institutional structures.

Behind this emphasis on cultural politics are two important differences with Marxist practices. The first is a capillary conception of power, which sees it as extending beyond the state and the party and into the interstices of society via the languages spoken by its members. In the hierarchical structure of the latter's binary oppositions, is a political order that languages reproduce and transmit. This is the political order that is the primary focus of the new cultural politics of difference as opposed to the order of parties, elections, and corporate elites.

The turn away from the latter order is linked to a second argument. From the subtextual perspective, organized politics appears as semiotically structured where it is not "empty space." Its oppositional aspects in particular, such as government versus opposition, appear to be governed by a complicity that affects all semio-linguistic binaries. This semiotic complicity is such that binaries can suppress or oppose one another, recombine in different ways, but never absolutely separate. They are eternal pairs whose perpetual play is a necessary condition for semio-linguistic representation. On the level of everyday discourse and action, these semiotic conditions impose their fateful complicity on the dynamics between contesting and contested discourses. Thus oppositional political binaries such as socialism and capitalism are viewed as being caught in this structural stalemate, whose repetitive outcomes are similar to those of specular doubling.

Consequently the goal of the socialist or anticolonial revolutionary is a semiotically prohibited possibility because radical or absolute separations are barred. Given this binary impasse in which organized socialist politics is caught, the way out is to subvert the dominant signifier without aiming for a final overthrow. Within the complicities of this strategy, the political order of languages as manifested in identities, images, and discourses becomes the crucial site of political work.

This linguistic displacing of organized politics is particularly clear in the case of the French Left. In the work of Hélène Cixous, Julia Kristeva, Roland Barthes, and Jacques Derrida we see this transference of revolutionary activity to the realm of language. Cixous declares writing to be the place "that is not obliged to reproduce the system."[24] In the Caribbean, Scott's replacement of revolution with a writerly social criticism reflects this trend. On the whole, this turn to language and writing is reminiscent of the religious displacement of the organized politics of the Garvey movement by the more spiritual and discursive politics of the Rastafarians.

This shift to the linguistic realm is particularly clear in Roland Barthes. In his work, we can see the use of intermediary deconstructive strategies to circumvent the repetitive logic of structural complicity without a frontal attack on particular binaries. Rather than the political arena, the revolution will now occur in language. Barthes locates himself in the linguistic space between capitalism and authoritarian socialism. From this position, he rejects the unified languages of both for a third that would be outside of the complicity that has governed the relations between the opposing pair. That is, he will attempt to write the socialist revolution in a language in which it will be possible to think outside of the logics of both the commodity and the centralized political resource, as well as outside of the coercive strategies inherent in everyday linguistic discourses. A plural, disseminative textuality became the house and symbol of the revolution. This textual pluralism was seen as different from liberal pluralism because of its break with monolithic and centralized notions of power.[25]

With regard to these and other arguments based on structural complicity, I have three comments. First, as in the case of specular doubling, they are often overstated to the point of semio-linguistic determinism. The autonomy of the political disappears under the weight of its semiotic coding. Even political strategies are now semiotically determined. This overstating often rests in part on an isolated, analytic deploying of language, rather than a dialectical one that brings it into mutually de-centering relations with other determinants of political action. Of course such a centered and essentialized posture (neostructuralism) is precisely what poststructuralists have sought to deconstruct in other modes of thought.

Second, the turn to the micropolitical order of language, which we must welcome, cannot be seen as an alternative to organized party politics that focuses on the problems of state power. If it is viewed in this way it becomes a dishonest retreat. In spite of the snares of structural complicity the problem of state power must be addressed strategically and in organizational terms. If it is not, then micropolitics becomes either an alibi or is itself trapped in an equally fatal complicity with the macrostructures of state power.

Third, the real contribution of arguments of structural complicity to Marxist praxis will remain inaccessible if the above two issues are not resolved in a more satisfactory manner. As in the case of specular doubling, these arguments can be useful in dissecting some of the hidden constraints on political action that can cause it to fail. These would be good but level-specific contributions. However, when such arguments transform failures into absolute barriers, they become counterproductive. The activist is then forced to examine what exactly is behind such overreactions.

If the above assessments of neoliberalism and poststructuralism are correct, then the current situation of Caribbean Marxism is indeed a difficult one. It is sandwiched between the offenses that have been launched by these two movements, and hence is on the defensive. The first has adversely changed the material conditions of its practice, while the second has done the same on the subjective and ideological levels.

To reverse the shift in material conditions, Caribbean Marxism will require a new mandate from popular insurrectionary activity. This activity must be innovative and strong enough to change neoliberal and postmodern outlooks, as well as their economic and political agendas. These popular upsurges will have to bring new and strong anticapitalist images to the fore, as well as new symbols and discourses of equality, freedom, and cooperation. The future of socialism rests heavily on the specific contents that will emerge from the insurrectionary activities of the future. If the creative responses currently taking shape in the imagination of the Caribbean masses are no longer reflected in the socialist mirror, then indeed it will be time to move on. However, this new consciousness can only be known through some outward expression or manifestation. Without it, it is difficult to imagine the reinvigorating of Caribbean socialism.

Assuming the return of such popular infusions of power and legitimacy, there will of course be the new problems of higher levels of technology and market competition. The extent to which central planning can and should be undertaken in this new international environment has to be carefully reassessed. The credibility of a revitalized socialist economics will depend on this, particularly when groups will again seek state protection from the market. More than capitalism and socialism themselves, market and plan appear to be governed by a complementary complicity that is in need of closer examination. The involvement of one in the life of the other certainly echoes that of the eternal pairs of semiotics. We cannot overlook the excesses and inefficiencies of state action and state leadership that contributed to the neoliberal turn. This global loss of faith in state-led collective action must be recovered. Thus, in relation to the adverse conditions created by the neoliberal turn, socialist practice can only be restored through popular upsurges that are capable of empowering and legitimating a new socialist political economy in which market and plan complement one another.

With regard to the poststructuralist offensive, the ground to be covered is more subjective and ideological. An adequate response will require greater philosophical autonomy on the part of Caribbean Marxism, particularly in basic areas such as ontology, epistemology, and the philosophy of the self. Unless we can speak for ourselves and draw on our own experiences in these matters our response to the poststructuralist challenge will be inadequate. If my assessment of this challenge is correct then at least four important conclusions can be drawn.

First, it has introduced a subtextual, subpersonal, semio-linguistic perspective that yields very different views of basic concepts used by Marxism such as the self, history universals, and discursive totalizations. I've tried to show that, in spite of its epochal self-presentation, it's a partial perspective with level-specific contributions to make. Thus as long as this perspective is not deployed as an erasing of the "solidities" of the everyday world, there is much in it that can be dialectically incorporated into Marxism. Thus in considering the nature and status of important Marxian universals such as class, the proletariat, and commodified labor, the deconstructive insights of this subtextual perspective can most definitely be enriching.

Second, although they were often presented as decisive, the arguments based on the problematic nature of discursive totalities, specular doubling, and structural complicity have not really produced absolute barriers to successful revolutionary action. Hence we must reject the postmodern mood that has been created by the attempts to absolutize these arguments. Such attempts lead to what Lewis Gordon has called "political nihilism."[26] This we must avoid at all costs.

Third, there is an important lesson to be learned from the poststructuralist relocating of revolutionary activity to the domain of language. It may represent a temporary or strategic retreat that preserves the revolutionary impulse in what appears to be a dormant or inactive period. Preserved in this way it could again leave the safety of this linguistic haven and attempt to change the world.

Fourth and finally, the poststructuralist critique raised no barriers to new popular insurrectionary activity. Thus our analysis can only conclude with a call for Caribbean Marxism to revise and restructure itself in the creative ways that James and Fanon did. However, in this undertaking we must be guided by the writings that fill the pages of popular insurrectionary activity.

Caribbean Historicism: Toward Reconstruction

I declare myself for the broader and against the narrower view, . . .
for him who liberates the creative passion of the masses, against him
who channels and finally sterilizes it.

—AIME CESAIRE

I n the last two chapters, we exam-
ined some of the practical and technical problems confronting Caribbean historicism. We saw that these problems developed in relation to two basic trends:
first, the need for the region to insert itself more competitively in an increasing
marketized, technified, and still white-dominated world economy; and second,
corresponding declines in the performative capabilities of Caribbean states.
These two factors have created crisis situations for Caribbean historicism, in
both its racial and Marxist variants. Consequently any attempt at reconstructing this tradition must address these practical problems.

However, before dealing more comprehensively with solutions to these
issues of practice we must return to a number of theoretical and contextual

problems of Afro-Caribbean philosophy identified earlier. At the theoretical level, we indicated that Afro-Caribbean philosophy has been marked by a number of internal splits, dualities, and oppositional constructions that have blocked dialogue and hindered growth. At the contextual level, whether we were speaking of its African, Afro-Christian, poeticist, or historicist traditions, we saw that this has been an implicit body of philosophizing, in which philosophy has been the handmaiden of religious, ideological, political, and literary production. This has given Caribbean philosophy as a whole a rather low level of visibility and for related reasons an even lower level for its African heritage.

These problems of Afro-Caribbean philosophy paint a portrait of philosophical underdevelopment that shares significant features with the regions' political and economic underdevelopment. These similarities point to common roots in the colonial plantation societies of the regions. Like the contextual problems of politico-economic underdevelopment, those of Afro-Caribbean philosophy are rooted in specific sets of dynamic divergences and convergences between patterns of supply and demand established during the colonial period. In the case of Afro-Caribbean philosophy, these divergences were established between its supply of philosophical goods (ethics, ontology, and so on) and our three crucial sites of cultural production. The convergences that restored these disrupted equilibria were between the philosophical demands of these sites and Euro-Caribbean philosophy. Together, these divergences and convergences created many of the features of underdevelopment that have come to mark the philosophical tradition as a whole. In particular, they created the institutional bases for the overidentification with Europe and the underidentification with Africa.

Closely related to these patterns of misidentification were the long-term decline of African philosophy and the corresponding growth of European philosophy in the Caribbean intellectual tradition. The routinizing of these patterns of growth and decline gave rise to externally dependent modes of philosophizing. The more the position of European philosophy approached one of monopoly, the more these dependent practices increased, the more skewed were the patterns of creolizaiton, and the stronger the anti-African biases. Inserted in these dynamics, Afro-Caribbean philosophy responded by focusing its efforts on the production of a variety of reconstructive, strategic, and oppositional discourses.

As noted earlier, this tradition of thought experienced a major metamorphosis in the second half of the nineteenth century. Breaking with its Afro-Christian past, it emerged as a secular tradition that was divided along the lines of art and history. As a result, Afro-Caribbean philosophy became more divided, but also more assertive and ideological than its African and Afro-Christian predecessors, as it was drafted more directly into the effort to delegitimate colonial rule. The delegitimating strategies pursued, reinforced the earlier decline of the traditional African "sector," and the rise of the diverging poeticist and historicist ones. The latter, in spite of being caught in the above patterns of dependence, would attempt to overthrow the hegemony of the Euro-Caribbean (plantation) "sector" of this philosophical economy. Caribbean historicism shares these patterns and problems of philosophical underdevelopment with the tradition as a whole. Consequently, my attempts at reconstruction will address three sets of issues: (1) internal problems of unity and totalizing strategies; (2) contextual problems; and (3) problems of praxis.

PROBLEMS OF UNITY

My primary reconstructive goals in taking up problems of unity are those of raising Caribbean philosophy's general level of self-consciousness and its awareness of debates around discursive strategies that it has taken for granted. In other words, it is to make Caribbean philosophers (not just historicists) more aware of the unity of the creative space they inhabit, its rich subterranean connections, its latent possibilities for reconciliation between opposing positions, and the transformative power of these connections and reconciliations.

Earlier we noted that the regional constructing of worldviews was motivated by a consciousness of the colonization and racialization of African existences within the framework of Euro-Caribbean plantation societies. The imploding of worlds of meaning that resulted, gave rise to the distinct patterns of world constitution that have emerged in the region. We saw that these world-constituting activities moved in three directions: reconstructive activities that are oriented toward the past; synthetic or transversal activities whose horizon is the present; and transformative projects that are future oriented.

A basic discursive strategy shared by all three of these approaches is that of integrative totalizing. The resulting totalities are vision producing and vary widely in their scope. They are constructivist in orientation because they attempt to organize images, arguments, descriptions, rejections, and projections into coherent wholes. They have taken the form of a search for origins, or an attempt to create a myth of origins. If not, totalizing may take the cosmogonic form of an organic unity, which has the power to symbolically integrate human life into the rhythms of the cosmos. Or, we may get spirit as an ungraspable presence serving as a founding analogy or an order of meaning that is capable of resolving contradictions and oppositions that divide and split everyday thought. Finally, we have gotten totalizations that project alternatives to a present that is to be surpassed. These various types of totalities have been the bases for action whether cultural or political. However, as we have seen in several of the earlier chapters, the very strategy of totalizing has recently been called into question by poststructuralists, and before them by the logical positivists. Consequently, we will have to state in more positive terms than we've done so far the place of totalizing strategies in a reconstructed historicism.

Needless to say, these diverse responses to the colonizing and racializing of African existences have generated multiple splits and tensions between themselves that have obscured their deeper connections and common origins. These divisions are very different from the transversal asymmetries and oppositions produced by the peripheral dynamics of Caribbean cultural systems. They don't evoke horizontal images, but rather vertical ones. They are not primarily determined by racial or cultural differences as it is the vertical divisions between Afro-Caribbean philosophers that we will be examining. Rather I will argue that these fissures are rooted in the ego-genetic needs and patterns of ontic closure that shape the conditions and horizons within which historicists and others have been philosophizing. In making this argument, in addition to Harris, I will draw on the traditional African notions of *sunsum* and *Okra*, or ego and spiritual ground, as coperformers.

As a result, the solutions to these problems of unity will be seen as being more than just contextual or intellectual. They will also require real existential changes that can depolarize identity constituting oppositions that the ego found necessary to establish at earlier phases in its self-formation. In other words, some of these vertical divisions will only be eliminated by processes of personal growth as wider and more inclusive affirmations of ourselves replace earlier and narrower ones. This makes clear that these two problems are connected and that there may be something about the nature of totalizing practices and the way they are connected to self-formative processes that bear on our problems of unity.

THE DISTINCTIVENESS OF CARIBBEAN TOTALIZING STRATEGIES

The peculiar problems of unity confronting Caribbean philosophy come more clearly into view when we examine up close the particular nature of totalizing strategies in the region. We've already indicated the basic types that are often in use. Their uniqueness and specificity can be further amplified by a comparison with Western patterns of totalization. One of the major differences separating the Western from the Caribbean pattern is the dominant, but by no means exclusive, role of pure philosophical reason as a founding analogy in Western totalizing strategies. These have led to the great systems of Western philosophy. In the Caribbean this dominant role has been taken by art and history. Caliban's reason has been primarily a poeticized and historicized one. Thus James's rejection of philosophical rationalism is explicitly and directly tied to his historicism.[1] In short, the types of totalizing practices that until recently have been dominant in the West, are not the types we find in the Caribbean.

More specifically, we have not attempted the conscious construction of philosophical systems in which everything is assigned its meaning and validity according to the faculty of reflective reason. This is a type of world-constituting activity in which the norms and discursive order of philosophical reason serve as founding analogies. Further, this pattern of world constitution rested on ongoing scientific projects in which both natural and social environments were being transformed through feedback relations with scientific and other rational forms of knowledge production.

In the Caribbean, such scientifically mediated relations with surrounding environments have remained underdeveloped. We have already noted the failure to break the dynamic convergences that linked regional scientific needs to imperial scientific output and to replace them with local convergences. In this setting, it is difficult for pure reason to emerge as the dominant founding analogy, the heroic figure conquering all before it, defining the domains of spirit, religion, art, and science, and authorizing their epistemic claims. The image of Kant trying to establish metaphysics, religion, and spirituality within the bounds of the rational analogy is not the image that dominates world-constituting activities in the region. Neither is it the Husserlian conception of philosophy as the science of sciences with infinite ideals and infinite tasks. In the Caribbean, pure reason is not absent, but rather eclipsed by poetic and historical reason, which have been empowered by successful feedback relations with regional environments. The norms, discursive procedures, and practices of poetic and historical reason have provided the founding categories of Caribbean world-constituting activities. They have provided Caliban with his or her heroic, oppositional, and self-assertive identities in the face of Prospero's continuing metamorphoses from plantation owner to progressively more global developer.

Thus the bipolar structure of the creative space inhabited by Afro-Caribbean philosophers, its feedback relations or lack thereof with surrounding environments all make it quite different from the creative space inhabited by Western philosophers. In the latter space, art and history are clearly subordinate to reason as a founding analogy. This is a very useful perspective from which to view the tensions between poststructuralism and what the latter has called the logocentric tendencies of the main body of the Western philosophical tradition. In poststructuralism, we find a strong tendency to replace philosophical reason as founding analogy with the constitutive logics of art and language, hence its appeal to Caribbean poeticists. Similarly, the appeal of Marxism to Caribbean historicists rests on corresponding displacements of pure reason by the logics of historical constitution and historical action. In short, there are important differences in styles of philosophical totalization in these two regions. In our overidentification with the West, we have lost sight of some of these differences.

Closely related to these differences in styles of world constitution are the types of subjectivities and capacities for agency that they reflect and help to create. In spite of their differences, both the Caribbean and Western subjects are modern ones. Both have been exposed in different ways to the industrialization of economic activity and the rationalization of political and administrative practices that marked the beginning of the modern period.

However, the specific ways in which particular modern societies exited the symbolically integrated worlds of their traditional phases differ significantly. In the cases of India and Japan, the first way out of mythic orders was through the subjective universalism of Hindu and Buddhist thought. This universalism moved beyond mythic particulars and particular myths to mystic visions of universal spirit as a creative consciousness whose "activities" are beyond the grasp of all human discourses, mythic or otherwise. Thus the discursive manifestation of this subjective universalism was a negative theology and hence different from that of Husserl's phenomenology. The deconstructive practices of these theologies were more radical than those of poststructuralism as their approaches to the de-centering of the ego make clear. But what is important for us here is the discovery of a universal spirituality that demythologizes thought and pushes it out of the confines of traditional orders.

In the case of the West, this type of subjective universalism has played a much smaller role in the exit from premodernity. This exit has been driven overwhelmingly by forces of objective universalism. As noted earlier, Habermas has described the modernization process in the West as the colonization of the life world by systems of instrumental action. In other words, Christian and other traditional worldviews were systematically disrupted and displaced by the need to justify their truth claims in the light of scientific knowledge of objects. This rationalization manifested itself in the "reflective treatments of traditions that have lost their quasi-natural status," the universalization of norms, the generalization of values, and "the formation of abstract ego-identities."[2]

As members of peripheral capitalist societies, we have seen that the modernizing process in the Caribbean was quite different. It took the form of the colonization and racialization of one life world by another, with the impact of systems of instrumental action in the background. Modernization occurred within the context of African life worlds having to legitimate themselves and their truth claims in terms of European life worlds. Consequently, hybridization and racialization, rather than rationalization (whether of the subjective or objective type), were the dominant processes of cultural change that accompanied Caribbean modernization.

In spite of these differences in routes to modernity both rationalization and hybridization were rooted in processes of commodification, and were radically disruptive of the symbolic totalizations of traditional societies, sufficiently disruptive that self-redefinition required in both cases profound changes in the relation of the modern subject to itself and to its environments. Compared to the self in traditional societies, the modern self in both the Caribbean and the West is more assertive and interventionist. As we saw in the case of African existentialism, traditional totalizations usually present the ego in terms of its organic rootedness in the spiritual and psychic forces that shape its development rather than in terms of its own autonomy. In other words, although *sunsum* and *Okra* are coperformers in the making of the self, the *sunsum* understands itself more in terms of its determination by the *Okra* than by its own actions.

In the modern period, this duality in the ego's self-understanding gets reversed. The ego comes to see itself more through the lens of its own autonomy and self-assertiveness, and to lose sight of the organic ties to its spiritual ground. Here the tendencies to *Yuruguan* revolts are more evident. As Harris pointed out, the inverting of this binary necessitates the dismantling and delegitimating of the deities, which are mythological projections of the spiritual powers that shape the ego. As an autonomous subject, the modern ego finds it necessary to deny or minimize its spiritual determination. It is unable to see itself as both autonomous and spiritually determined. It has to be one or the other. This is an ego-genetic duality that traditional African thought long ago recognized as a major difficulty for the *sunsum*'s self-creative endeavors.

Given the modern reversal, it is clear that the traditional African formulations of this ego-constitutive binary are no longer adequate. It does not permit the de-godding and the varying degrees of polarization between *sunsum* and *Okra* that we find in the modern period, either in India, the Caribbean, or the West.

Even though the modes of self-assertion are different in the latter two regions, both share in different degrees the problems of subjects who have negated their spiritually determined modes of being and have separated themselves from the traditional totalizations they produced in the past. As Soyinka has pointed out, subjects in this state of separation are caught in dualities that they are not able to consciously resolve.[3] In other words, there is a unifying power in the unconscious totalizations of traditional thought that the modern separatist subject is unable to reproduce. In preparing the world for its autonomy, the modern ego has to de-god it. But in discarding these specific mythological representations of spirit, the modern subject often throws out the spiritual baby with the bathwater and is left without adequate powers of self-unification or discursive unification.

Habermas recognizes this problem in the self-constituting strategies of the Western subject confronting modernity: "It does possess, to be sure, an unexampled power to bring about the formation [Bildung] of subjective freedom and reflection and to undermine religion, which heretofore had appeared as an absolutely unifying force. But the principle of subjectivity is not powerful enough to regenerate the unifying power of religion in reason."[4] Consequently, both the thought and action of the modern Western subject remain caught in a number of dualities it is unable to resolve. The situation is much the same for the modern Caribbean subject. We have seen that Caribbean writers have not been able to reproduce the unifying power of spirit in either art or history, even though we have tried. Separated from the unifying powers of traditional totalizations, the knowledge and action of the modern subject are always partial, perceptual, and split by polarizations between these perspectives and positions, in spite of a striving for wholeness.

Even though Caribbean and Western subjects share these problems of dualities and fissures, their concrete manifestations have differed significantly. The primary reason for these divergencies is the different patterns of polarization that follow from the different founding analogies of the two regions. As Soyinka has pointed out, the rational analogy in the West has been the basis for the most radical rupture with traditional modes of life. Hence it has experienced the greatest need to reconstruct comprehensive totalizations of existence in terms of rationality. This has generated a lot of social and material knowledge, has released hidden potentials in partial positions, but has left the problems of dualities unresolved.

In the Caribbean, the poetic and historical analogies have produced less-polarized versions of self-determination/spiritual determination, *sunsum/Okra*, and other homologous binaries. The oppositions have been sharper in the historicist school than among the poeticists. As we have seen, there are direct connections in Harris's work with the traditional totalities of Africans and Amerindians. Gordon Rohlehr's excellent discussion of spiritual possession in some Caribbean writers supports this point.[5] Through the poeticist tradition, strong links to traditional totalizations have been maintained. In the historicist tradition, both Marxist and Pan-Africanist, these ties have been far weaker, due to the less intense focus on the self and the concern with future-oriented action. As we saw in the case of James, there is a strong tendency to read these oppositions in terms of the Western model. But together they have produced a different modern subject in the Caribbean, whose self-understanding, patterns of self-assertion, and sense of agency are quite different from those of the Western subject.

These are some of the distinctive conditions that set the totalizing practices of Caribbean philosophers apart. They are rooted in distinct founding analogies and are marked by distinct patterns of polarization and oppositional splits. As modern, creative subjects, they philosophize at distinct distances from the traditional totalizations of the past and hence have distinct problems of unity. From the perspective of traditional African existentialism, the autonomous projects of both the Caribbean and Western subjects need to be vetoed so that their self-understandings will include, rather than exclude, affirm and not negate their modes of being in which they are subject to creative determination by spirit.

TOTALIZATIONS AS PROBLEMATIC FORMATIONS

From the foregoing discussion of differences in totalizing strategies, it should be clear that these discursive formations are important to both Caribbean and Western philosophies. Yet both logical positivists and poststructuralists have declared wars on these processes of totalization. Karl Popper's attack is a logicist one. He begins by distinguishing two types of totalities: first, those that are the summation of "all the properties or aspects of a thing"[6]; and second, totalities as those aspects of a thing that "make it appear as an organized structure rather than a 'mere heap.'"[7] Popper then goes on to suggest that the scientific study of the second type is possible, while that of the first is a logical impossibility. He therefore directs his attacks on the first by making two points: (1) that science is always selective; and (2) that totalized studies are logically impossible because they will of necessity leave something out. Consequently, only particular studies that focus on limited areas are possible.

The poverty of Popper's logicism is evident in at least two ways. First, it is incapable of recognizing a greater variety of totalities. Second, as a critique of Marxian totalities, it fails to recognize the ones that are peculiar to it. From all that was said above, it should be clear that the symbolic totalities of traditional societies fall into neither of Popper's categories, and hence are largely unaffected by his criticism. Similarly, the totalizations of Caribbean Marxism are of a dialectical, rather than a mechanical, nature, because they tend to be both reconstructive and transformative in orientation. Thus it should come as no surprise that Caribbean and other totalizing practices have continued in spite of Popper's criticisms.

In the previous chapter, we examined the subtextual critiques that poststructuralists have directed at discursive totalities. There, the thrust of my response was to show that this rejection has forced poststructuralists into the contradictory position of having to use these constructs in spite of their rejection of them. The use of founding analogies, their centering and analytic hardening, the establishing of identities or equivalences between different objects are all totalizing strategies without which poststructuralism would be unimaginable.

The reading of texts via the linguistic analogy rests upon such constructive practices. Texts are not absolutely identical with language. In their specificity they are other than language and hence can be read on the basis of other analogies. Consequently, totalizing persists also in spite of poststructuralist criticisms.

This sturdy resilience aside, totalizations are indeed problematic formations. So, what exactly are the problems with them? Like logic, rhetoric, data gathering, and other discursive strategies, totalizations are imperfect and incomplete. Just as we have not thrown out the others because they are imperfect, we should not discard totalizations. They solve only in part, never completely, the problems of dualities that limit and fragment our knowing. Thus, in the case of dialectical totalizations, we often get the intersecting of two or more distinct analytically developed partial positions. This confronts dialectical totalizations with two major problems. First, between hardened analytic positions there are often antidialectics of reciprocal nonrecognition. As we saw in chapter 7, these antidialectics are existentially conditioned, and can be lessened but not completely eliminated by reconciliatory measures. Thus dialectical syntheses always take place in spite of residues of these antidialectics. Second, the analytical positions brought together are only a small fraction of the positions that can or should be interfaced. In spite of these limitations, dialectical syntheses help to lift us out of analytical positions that have hardened in the course of generating technical and practical knowledge. In doing so, they expand even though they may not perfect our vision.

Thus rather than excommunicating totalizations we need to take Wynter's advice and work hard at raising our consciousness about their imperfections, tendencies to error, and to closure. With this attitude toward our totalizing practices, we can now turn more directly to some of the errors and closures that have kept Caribbean histoicists from deeper ties with poeticists and the heritage of traditional African thought. In more positive terms, how can we bring to greater consciousness the hidden unities that we've glimpsed in the works of James, Fanon, Cesaire, Braithwaite, Short Shirt, and others.

CARIBBEAN HISTORICISM, LIMINALITY, AND ONTIC CLOSURE

As a modern discourse, Afro-Caribbean historicism shares the dualities, the incomplete totalizations, and other obstacles to unity and comprehensive vision that we've been discussing. It has assumed the self-constituting, assertive role of the modern subject, in particular, an activist one that is constantly attempting to realize historical projects. It has also established a good measure of ontic closure around this activist self-understanding, which has produced corresponding difficulties in knowing itself as spiritually constituted. Consequently, this activist stance embodies a highly polarized and one-sided resolution of this ego-constitutive duality, which has profoundly shaped the reach, outlook, and totalizing strategies of Afro-Caribbean historicism.

In spite of dialectical attempts to address some of its dualities, Afro-Caribbean historicism has remained trapped in others which have compromised its performance. The most important of these are the unbridged analytic gaps that separate it from the poeticist school, from traditional African thought, and from its spiritual ground. As a result, only in the rare cases of Fanon, James, and so on has it achieved the wider syntheses that are available to it. More often, it has settled for smaller affirmations of itself which negate the wider ones. Thus we've seen the narrow self-definitions around class that exclude race and vice versa. Here, I would like to address some of the new dimensions that a reconstructed historicism could acquire from a deeper dialectical engagement with the poeticist tradition.

In chapter 4, we examined some of the substantive differences between these two polar positions. However, we did not examine the specific contributions that a more dialectical engagement between the two would make to Caribbean historicism. I will take the position that such a synthesis would make two extremely important contributions. First, it would help to depolarize and raise our consciousness about the self-constituted/spiritually constituted binary that supports our activist self-understanding and many of our modern projects. This has the potential to expand and to change radically the concept of the subject in Afro-Caribbean historicism, and hence our philosophical anthropology. Second, a poeticist engagement would raise our consciousness about the operations of liminal dynamics and categories in historicist thinking. This has the potential to expand our awareness of epistemic formations, to open dialogues with excluded positions, and hence to change our epistemological outlook. Together, these contributions hold out the prospect of wider and more inclusive affirmations for historicists, which should have important implications for issues of unity and difference as well as for praxis.

With regard to the first of these contributions, depolarization must begin with the examination of poeticist arguments as to why the activist mode of self-objectification is not an optimal point for ontic closure. To start, this self is clearly a provisional choice that excludes other possibilities and is not a final one. From Harris and traditional African existentialism we know that in all such cases, a point of closure or revolt is often reached beyond which the ego experiences the resistance of excluded elements, because of the partiality of its position. Totalizing becomes progressively more forced, like a person trying to buckle a belt around an expanding waistline that insists on being recognized.

This metastability suggests that the historical rationality of Afro-Caribbean philosophy has its own problems with exclusion and liminal blindness that are comparable, though not identical, with those of Western rationality. As we saw

in the case of the latter, liminal blindness establishes an antidialectic of reciprocal nonrecognition between a self and its excluded opposites. In the case of
Caribbean historicism, this existentially conditioned antidialectic operates in
relation to the nonhistorical—particularly the spiritual and the poetic—hence
our inability to embrace these possibilities as our own. Instead our exchanges
with poeticists have been shaped by interests in ontological supremacy that
sustain one-sided modes of self-assertion. As in the case of Western rationality,
these existential foundations of the one-sidedness of Caribbean rationality can
only be constructively engaged by reconciliatory discourses of the Harrisian
and African types.

Thus from both poeticists and traditional Africans, we get a questioning of
the closed and one-sided sufficiency of historicism's activist self. It is seen as an
affirmation that rests on repressions and exclusion, the contents of which it
needs to integrate into wider affirmations. The exclusions are not just intellectual but also self-formative or ontic in nature. As a result, they make it difficult
for historicist subjects to recognize discourses and practices that are based on
experiences of the ego in other than historically constituted modes. Such discourses become alien territories into which we must not go. Here Harris's
notion of ontic closure joins Wynter's notion of liminal misrepresentation.
Both produce systematic interests in seeing incorrectly and in compounding
and defending these misrepresentations.

Thus the inability of historicists to really hear Harris, Wynter, Glissant, and
other poeticists has turned largely around the ontic and liminal effects of the
one-sided resolution of the metastability between our activist selves and their
binary opposites, particularly those of spirit and poetics. These writers have
been speaking to us from the excluded sides of these binaries, that is, from the
experiences of the Caribbean ego as a constituted entity that is enmeshed in a
variety of nonhistorical processes of formation. But we have not been able to
hear across the analytic divide created by those ego-constitutive dualities.
Consequently, before we can even get the message, we must be prepared to
work on these binaries and break the restraints they have placed on the existential transformation and intellectual growth of Afro-Caribbean historicists.

Assuming that we make some headway with these binaries, what are some of
the transformations in historicist thinking that we can expect? First a richer
and more original historicism, which is clearly another Harrisian message. He
has been telling us of the archetypal creativity and potential for renewal that
arises from including the other half of these binaries into our self-affirmation.
In Harris's view, to be open on these levels is to be open to the possibilities of
bringing something new into history. For him, the points at which ego and
spiritual ground interface are the front lines of world-constituting activities.
The latter begin at the spiritual level and then get recoded into everyday total-

izations and mythopoetic transformations of identities. Consequently, these points are primary sources of renewal and alternative imagining. This is the region where the waves never cease to wash the sandy shores, perpetually renewing hope through this ceaseless creativity. Here we find an ever-active creative intelligence, whose constant supply of new images should be the rock to which we return in times of crisis, such as the present, to revive our world-constituting practices.

James spoke repeatedly of the creativity of the masses, their ability to bring new solutions to human problems onto the historical stage. What did James have in mind while making these claims? This is one point at which his thought overlaps with and can be clarified by the thought of Harris. It was probably this openness to archetypal creativity that James had in mind even though he did not formulate it in the explicit way that Harris has done. This ocean of spontaneous creativity surrounding the ego was a reality that James as artist knew intuitively, but never formulated. Those of us who are not practiced in the ways of art, and are unable to intuitively engage these creative and transformative forces, produce Marxist and Pan-Africanist discourses that are much poorer in quality, originality, and vision.

Here, Fanon's existentialism emerges as a similar point of overlap with the poeticist tradition. Through his existentialism, Fanon fine-tuned his skills as a traveler on the creative waters surrounding the ego and against which the latter attempts to establish its self-sufficiency. Like Fanon, Caribbean historicists must be able to navigate these waters beyond particular ego projections and engage their creative powers to dissolve and reconcile binaries that clash violently in the ontically closed ego. This is the "authentic upheaval" of which Fanon spoke, that could emerge out of the zone of nonbeing. Thus Harris's archetypal life, James's notion of the creativity of the masses, and Fanon's authentic upheaval all point to a type of revolutionary creativity that is capable of bringing something new into history. However, it is linked to the ability of the ego to return to its spiritual ground and experience itself as being constituted. This is the change in our philosophical anthropology that would result from engagements with poeticists. This expanded philosophical anthropology should also help to facilitate deeper relations with that of traditional African philosophy.

However, the Jamesian legacy here is an ambivalent one. James often saw the masses as the only creative groups in Caribbean societies and understood their creativity primarily in secular terms. Yet he is, and did see himself as one of the region's creative genii, in spite of being middle class. The only solution to this dilemma is that James as artist was as open as the masses to the constituting creativity of this spiritual front line. James saw his creativity as complementing that of the masses. For the intelligentsia to continue this aspect of the

Jamesian legacy, we will have to fashion similar modes of openness. This is important as the burden of fashioning creative alternatives should not fall exclusively on the imaginations of the masses. We should all be responsible for these creative alternatives.

If we are to carry our share of these creative burdens, then historicists cannot remain locked in current modes of activist self-understanding. It is not enough for us to retain these affirmations. The crises of our times require that we go beyond them toward dialectical engagements with their repressed undersides and the discourses they support. Such engagements should release valuable creative resources and images from which new futures and wider affirmations of ourselves can be fashioned. In short, a more open and creative historicism could be the result of becoming more conscious of the deeper unity that connects us to what has appeared to be our poeticist opposite.

The second major contribution to Afro-Caribbean historicism from this deeper engagement with its poeticist twin would be much greater categorical awareness. Here, Wynter's poeticist/poststructuralist reading of historicist projects of transformation becomes absolutely crucial. Her analysis of the crises-ridden, dualistic nature of human cognition extends to colonized and colonizer, dominated and dominator, totalized and de-totalized formations. Consequently, many of the cognitive difficulties that plagued projects of domination reappear in emancipatory projects. Wynter's critique is profound, sobering, and hard-hitting. As we've seen, the thought of both historicists and their opponents have been trapped in the error-producing mythopoetics of founding schemas and their liminal categories. Thus, the level from which Wynter is operating is not that of a specific discursive claim or set of claims. Rather it is from the level at which specific historicist cogitos auto-institute founding and liminal categories and the manner in which they are socially deployed. This awareness should change our epistemological view of ourselves as knowledge producers.

Just as we have not been cultivating the creative resources of which Harris has spoken so eloquently, historicists have also not been cultivating a deeper awareness of the liminal patterns and dynamics of our thought. This too requires a significant extension of the self-reflective and epistemological practices in which we are currently engaged. We've been quite good at seeing these dynamics in the thought of others. But existing divisions among ourselves, the crisis in Grenada, the tensions between Marxists and Pan-Africanists, the late recognition of gender issues all point to the need to be more aware of how the liminal dynamics of our thinking have pushed us and are still pushing us to betray our best intentions.

Further, Wynter's liminal analysis has profound implications for our epistemological views of working-class and other insurrectionary forms of consciousness. From Harris, we learned that we cannot view the ontology of working-class consciousness as simply oscillating between periods of political activism and quietism around working and racial conditions. Rather in the latter periods it often returns to its spiritual ground to renew itself before becoming politically explicit again. Consequently, it must be viewed as a consciousness that is able to move between these two worlds partly because of its precarious insertion into the material world of global capitalism.

Similarly, if Wynter is right that the mythopoetics of founding and liminal categories affect both colonized and colonizer, then it must change our views of the knowledge constitutive structures of the revolutionary consciousness, whether in the colonized, blacks, workers, or women. In all of these cases, we will have to be sensitive to the liminal dynamics they contain and their potential when deployed for generating misrepresentations and for reproducing old and new forms of exclusion and domination. In other words these emancipatory projects do not emerge from unified epistemic subjects with easy access to the truth, but from subjects who are still caught in dualities and exclusionary practices.

This is another reason why the burden of mobilizing new symbolic alternatives cannot be left solely with the masses. They too are in need of critical commentary and engagement to avoid premature self-limitation and entrapment in oppositions. Wynter's liminal dynamics make it clear why returning to ground zero does not always result in an authentic upheaval. Some such returns are often overwhelmed by the tides to be navigated and degenerate into escapes. Others remain trapped in old dualities that result in new forms of domination. Wynter's analysis of the New Canaan community makes these possibilities clear. In our historicist tradition, we have cultivated the tendency to separate the revolutionary consciousness of workers and other oppressed groups from both the creative and liminal dynamics articulated by Harris and Wynter. A dialectical embracing of the poeticist half of our philosophical space should help to lessen this tendency.

In sum, it is my view that in reconstructing itself, Afro-Caribbean historicism can add archetypal and categorical dimensions to its self-understanding through an engagement with its poeticist half. There is a deeper unity that links these two that both must affirm if they are to remain open and creative. At this historical moment, we need to rethink more explicitly the problem of the self. As Fanon suggests, "It is through the effort to recapture the self and to scrutinize the self, it is through the lasting tension of their freedom that men will be able to create the ideal conditions of existence for a human world."[8] It is imperative that we end Fanon's exceptional status among historicists with regard to this issue. To follow his example more closely, we will have to move beyond established race- and labor-centered models of Caribbean subjectivity.

These models should now become dimensions of new and larger conceptions of the Caribbean self that embrace the archetypal and categorical dimensions so carefully thematized by Harris and Wynter. Crises such as the present one that require a radical rethinking of the self, or changes in its "subconscious alliances," will certainly be the sources for important periods in our phenomenological history of Africana subjectivity that was discussed in chapter 6. These crises require the inventing and using of those "silences" that Kincaid has demanded of us.[9]

Caribbean historicists can only emerge stronger from taking such a good look at ourselves in the poeticist mirror. We will no doubt experience a period of crisis, but we will get through it and be more aware of the larger unity that embraces us. How often has Nettleford said to us: to find a way out, we will have "to dig deeper within ourselves"? But we didn't really hear him. We didn't because we could not translate and concretize these poeticist claims into the language and practice of historicism. From this point on we must know how to do some poeticist digging.

CONTEXTUAL PROBLEMS

The second set of problems to be addressed in reconstructing Caribbean historicism are contextual in nature. These problems are not internal to the creative spaces of Afro-Caribbean philosophy, but have to do with the larger intellectual tradition in which this philosophy is situated. In particular, they are related to the peripheral dynamics of this larger tradition. In my introduction and in several other chapters, I've tried to formulate some of the consequences of these dynamics for Afro-Caribbean philosophy. We saw the implicit style they encourage, the anti-African and antiblack biases they produced, and the patterns of divergence and convergence that shaped the underdeveloped economy of Afro-Caribbean philosophy.

Given these problems of philosophical underdevelopment described at the start of this chapter, the first question on the road to reconstruction is one that goes beyond the historicist school and embraces the Afro-Caribbean tradition as a whole. This question raises the issue of whether or not we want to continue with our implicit mode of philosophizing. In other words, does the persistence of the imperial relationship necessitate the continuation of this style? Or, have the postcolonial changes in our relations to ourselves and to Western imperialism already taken us beyond this implicit mode of philosophizing? I will take the latter view and argue that given the problems facing the region and the major developments in Africana philosophy, Afro-Caribbean philosophy has little choice but to move in a more explicit and autonomous direction. This of course will not be an absolute autonomy, but rather a substantive change in the terms of the discursive compromise on which Afro-Caribbean philosophy conducts its intertextual relations.

From our samplings of some of the founding texts of Afro-Caribbean philosophy, it should be clear that the generation of James, Garvey, Fanon, Harris, and others did not succeed in freeing Afro-Caribbean philosophy from its enmeshment in peripheral dynamics and hence those of invisibility and underdevelopment. As noted several times throughout this work, they made valiant efforts and got us off to a very good start. In the case of Fanon, this failure emerged very clearly from our analysis of the ambiguities surrounding his attitudes toward African and European existentialism. In James, we saw it in his tendency to make the European philosophical tradition the lingua franca of all philosophy. Thus it is now up to us to complete the task of decolonizing Afro-Caribbean philosophy and freeing it of its old contextual problems.

To complete this project of philosophy's decolonization, there are at lease three important reforms that we must undertake. First, we will have to change significantly existing pattern of creolization. Second, we will have to increase the autonomy of philosophy in relation to other discursive practices. Third, we will have to change the current interdiscursive address of Afro-Caribbean philosophy. Basic to achieving of all three goals is the reestablishing of dynamic convergences between philosophical output and the philosophical demands of the major sites of cultural production. That is, we need a major transformation in the economy of Afro-Caribbean philosophy. Although many of the supporting arguments will apply to tradition as a whole, here they will be developed with special reference to the historicist school.

We've already noted in several contexts the unusually high levels of asymmetry that characterize the creole patterns of Afro-Caribbean philosophy. Compared to other fine arts such as dance and literature, the textual and normative dominance of European elements over African and Indian contributions stands out. This asymmetry emerges again when the comparison is with social sciences such as economics, sociology, and political science. In all three, there has been an indigenization, a reestablishing of convergences with local demands for economic, sociological, and political knowledge that has not occurred in the case of philosophy. Indeed, our philosophy's economy is closer to that of the natural sciences where these links have also not been reestablished. In both cases, these skewed patterns of creolization rest on peripheral patterns of divergence and convergence between cultural supply and demand. In other words, they rest on underdeveloped philosophical and scientific economies. Consequently, a conscious effort must be made to adjust downward the textual and normative dominance of European philosophies and to change the ways in which they interact and mix with African and Indian contributions.

In particular, a greater number of the texts of the latter need to be taken more seriously. We should be as familiar with the texts of Towa and Gyekye, and those of Sri Aurobindo and Sarvepalli Radhakrishman, as we are with Marx and Foucault. These texts should be allowed to mix on the basis of their contributions to Caribbean problems, and not on the terms of a European monopoly on philosophical knowledge. In short, as a creole formation we must be concerned with unequal distributions of authority and textual space between the three cultural traditions that have shaped Afro-Caribbean philosophy. On this point, the Rastafarian tradition provides an excellent model.

The distribution of authority and textual space in James's historicism can serve as a good illustration of these creole dynamics. As we have seen, James's historicism was both Marxist and Pan-Africanist. The dominant influence on James's philosophy was clearly European Marxism. The figures of Marx, Lenin, Trotsky, and Hegel all shaped the contours of James's thought, occupying large amounts of its textual space. The African spaces in James's historicism gave extensive play to Pan-Africanist figures such as Padmore, DuBois, Cesaire, and Nkrumah. In James, these traditions were open to each other and mutually influenced one another. By these particular criteria it has provided historicists with an excellent model of creolization.

However, there are two significant problems with the creole dynamics of James's historicism. First, as we saw in chapter 2, very little space and authority were allocated to traditional African philosophy. James's Africa was the Africa of Senghor, Nkrumah, and Nyerere, that is, modern, literate, and historically active. However, the contributions of traditional Africa to the vitality and distinctiveness of our other finer arts and to the poeticist school are well established. Thus it is highly unlikely that Afro-Caribbean historicism will achieve a vital creolization without it.

The second problem in James's creole dynamics is the role of authority in the exchanges between its European and non-European elements. In both the Marxist and Pan-Africanist wings of his historicism, James continued the practice of attributing near-monopoly authority to European philosophy in relation to all other traditions. The European was not just another tradition, but *the* tradition. Thus James saw the creolizing process as primarily one of creatively reformulating and adapting European philosophies such as Marxism, surrealism, liberalism, and so forth to the very real problems and questions of the Caribbean masses, hence the appeal of Cesaire, Nkrumah, and others. What we don't get are similar creative appropriations of solutions offered by African and Indian philosophies. On this point, there is a sharp difference with Harris who often makes these types of creative appropriations.

Thus as the formulation of an Afro-Caribbean Marxism, James's effort remains too asymmetrical in its distributions of intradiscursive authority. In it, we find an authorizing of European philosophy that excessively restricts the contributions of African and Indian philosophies. For Caribbean Marxism, this means that it has asymmetries to dismantle and more fluid and egalitarian patterns of creolization to establish. This is a problem that has plagued other attempts at formulating a black Marxism, whether it is DuBois's, Fanon's, James Boggs's, Rodney's, Cedric Robinson's, or Cornel West's.[10]

In Garvey's racial historicism, we can also discern creole dynamics that inhibit the free and egalitarian play of African philosophy. The latter was excluded from Garvey's creole mix and not allowed to compete and hybridize. This asymmetry was rooted in the authoritative status Garvey gave European civilizational, racial, Christian, and national discourses. These took the place of Marx and Lenin in James, and thus filled the European spaces of Garvey's historicism. However, the African spaces in Garvey's philosophy overlapped with James. They both drew on the same Pan-African tradition that had been created by Blyden, Robert Love, and others. With his strong emphasis on race, Garvey saw the creolizing process as one that involved the recoloring, reinterpreting, and adapting of the above European discourses to the problem of African liberation, both continental and diasporic. This is the open sector of Garvey's creolizing tendencies.

When examined more closely, we also discover a closed sector in which African philosophy was subject to microprocesses of surplus repression that helped to maintain the asymmetrical creole patterns of Afro-Caribbean historicism. Thus, in spite of his bold recoloring of European discourses, the latter retained much of their intellectual authority vis-à-vis African discourses. This we saw very clearly in the relations between European Christianity and traditional African religions. Between African and European philosophy the relationship was even more skewed as its greater invisibility suggests.

I am convinced that similar analyses of other historicists would produce similar results. As creole formations, they are all constructed upon the surpluses of discursive violence that have maintained the skewed patterns of creolization that have defined the field as a whole. If calypso and reggae are good examples of creole formations, then Caribbean historicism has a long way to go. These lingering patterns of surplus repression can only be removed by increasing the authority and textual space allocated to African and Indian philosophies. Their removal must be a part of the new discursive compromise of a reconstructed historicism. In the African case, our project of a phenomenological history of Africana subjectivity should be quite valuable, given its commitment to revalorizing the symbols of the African heritage.

The second major contextual reform of Afro-Caribbean historicism that we must undertake is that of establishing its discursive activities at a higher level of autonomy. We've already seen that the need for this shift derives from the contradictory tendencies that this discourse has inherited from its broader intellectual tradition. What would a more autonomous historicism look like and how would it operate? Fortunately, we already have some good glimpses of such a philosophy in the works of James and Fanon. The works of both of these authors are characterized by unusual levels of philosophical explicitness, which came close to breaking out of the confines of the implicit style.

More recently this trend toward greater explicitness has grown stronger in the works of philosophers like Lewis Gordon, Charles Mills, and Cleavis Headly. Indeed, it is safe to say that they have broken with the implicit style and have inaugurated a new phase in Afro-Caribbean philosophy. In their works, Afro-Caribbean philosophy ceases to be an auxiliary discourse and emerges as a major discourse with a more autonomous intellectual practice. Consequently, they have set a new standard of explicitness and autonomy that a reconstructed historicism must recognize.

Indeed Gordon's challenge to the historicist tradition is a multifaceted one. It raises not only the issue of the greater autonomy but also the problem of deeper ties with the poeticist tradition. Like Fanon's, Gordon's existentialism overlaps with many of the concerns of poeticists and Pan-Africanists. Its close relations to art, particularly music, make this very clear. Consequently there are not only problems of autonomy but also poeticist issues in Gordon's challenge to historicists. However, from the other side of the issue of unity, historicists hold out to Gordon the challenge of engaging more fully the political economy of social transformation.

In very different ways, Mills's challenge to contemporary Caribbean historicism also makes clear this issue of greater autonomy and explicitness. First, Mills's shift from a strong focus on the Marxist to the Pan-Africanist wing of this tradition, points to the dualities that we have been discussing and to the need to build on the dialectical bridges established by James and Rodney. Second, like the Ghanaian philosopher Anthony Appiah, Mills's analyses of racism pose an important logicist challenge to Caribbean historicism. The prominent role of logic in his work sets it apart from most historicist analyses. Consequently, these differences should force historicists to state more explicitly our position on this important discursive technique.

Recognizing these moves toward greater autonomy and explicitness would have at least two important implications for the tradition of historicism that we have inherited from James and Fanon. To participate in the new philosophical order, Afro-Caribbean historicism will have to thematize more explicitly its own concerns and criteria of knowledge production. For the most part, its concerns, its self-definition, and patterns of philosophical production have taken shape in response to problems that have been posed and formulated elsewhere. This auxiliary pattern will be difficult to maintain in the future. Rising to greater visibility will be the more formal aspects of Afro-Caribbean historicism as a discourse. These aspects of any philosophy usually emerge from feedback relations with its own attempts at self-understanding. Thus the very exercise in which I am here engaged is an example of the formal impact that new levels of autonomy and explicitness are having on the heritage of historicism.

Second, this more autonomous view of Afro-Caribbean philosophy will require changes in its historic interdiscursive subordination to ideological production. These changes confront historicists with two basic alternatives: an academic historicism that rejects politico-ideological embeddedness, or a more autonomous historicism that remains ideologically engaged while having stronger academic ties and more concerns of its own. I take the view that the persistence of imperialism and underdevelopment in the postcolonial period together with current trends in Africana philosophy are pushing us in the latter direction.

For some historicists, even this latter position may be a problem as they view philosophy as being necessarily embedded as it is in the implicit mode. In Tim Hector's view, philosophy is inseparable from political praxis. Historicism in particular has a relation to political transformation that is comparable to the relation between positivism and scientific production. In both cases philosophy has a supporting role to play in either an ideological or a scientific project. Consequently, Hector links the origins and development of Afro-Caribbean philosophy to major political events such as the Haitian revolution or the 1918 revolt of the West India Regiment while stationed in Italy. It is a portrait of Afro-Caribbean philosophy arising and continuing to exist as intertextually embedded in the politico-ideological alternatives that such insurrectionary movements projected. In other words, philosophy does not spring full-blown from the head of academics, but rather emerges out of the creative energy of popular upsurges.[11]

While there is much of great importance for historicism in this view, Hector's formulation restricts philosophy exclusively to its feedback relations with the reproductive needs of social orders. This exclusive formulation turns the anomalous seismic shift of the colonial period described in our introduction into a permanent feature of Afro-Caribbean philosophy. Prior to this period, and after it, philosophical creativity has been motivated by feedback relations with its own self-understanding, the ego-genetic needs of populations, and the information needs of economic production. With the receding of direct colonization, it has become possible once again to take up more of the diverse feedback relations of philosophy. In this period of growing autonomy, it is the relations with its own self-understanding that Afro-Caribbean historicism will have to thematize more explicitly.

Third and finally, to facilitate a more autonomous and regionally creolized historicism, we will have to change the current intertextual address of

Caribbean philosophy as a whole. As academics have played an important role in the growing autonomy of Caribbean philosophy, so also will the role assigned it in the division of academic labor be important for its new address. In searching for this new address our goal is not a hermetically isolated location, but rather one that will give philosophy more equitable and fluid relations with neighboring discourses. If indeed this is our goal, then Harris has made a very valuable suggestion regarding this new address for Caribbean philosophy.

In 1970, Harris pointed to the yawning communications gap between the traditions of creative and historical writing in the Caribbean. In particular, he pointed to a lack of exchange between historicists such as Garvey, James, and Eric Williams and creative writers such as Lamming, Walcott, and himself. After acknowledging his high regard for Elsa Goveia and James, Harris makes his bold assertion that "there does not exist a philosophy of history in the Caribbean correlative to the arts of the imagination."[12] Hence his accompanying suggestion that "some kind of new critical writing in depth needs to emerge to bridge the gap between history and art."[13] However Harris did not name or identify this new form of writing.

I would like to suggest that we make Caribbean philosophy this new critical writing. As a rational discourse that examines the human ego, its epistemic strategies, its objects of knowledge and transformation, philosophy is in an excellent position to mediate between these two traditions of writing. We have seen throughout this work that these issues are of great importance to writers in both of these traditions. Further, we saw the wide gap that still separates practicing artists and practicing historicists. It is unrealistic to expect artists to master dense economic or political text, and vice versa. Hence there really needs to be a bridge discourse here if indeed there is to be greater unity between the two. We certainly can expect philosophers to read both types of texts and provide the academic community with accounts that are accessible to both groups. Consequently, in its new abode it should be able to facilitate dialogues on topics such as differences in conceptions of the self, in approaches to objects of knowledge, and to praxis between these schools. These are the kinds of exchanges that are not taking place.

For Caribbean philosophy to fulfill this role, its various wings will have to make their particular adaptations. For historicists breaking the exclusive identification with the politico-ideological projects is the primary adjustment that we will have to make. To engage comfortably in this exchange historicists will have to recognize the value of feedback relations with ego-genetic needs, and those of philosophy's own self-understanding. We've seen that it has been primarily through the poeticists that convergences between regional cultural production and self-formative needs have been reestablished. Engaging in a deeper dialogue with this tradition should help Caribbean historicism to reestablish its linkages to self-formative needs and thus restructure its own economy. With such a transformed economy, it will be able to further creolize itself and thus become a more vital part of the creole identity-forming process.

PRAXIS

The major practical problems confronting Caribbean historicism were outlined in chapters 8 and 9. In its Pan-Africanist variant the project of strong Afro-Caribbean nations working in solidarity with Afro-Americans and Africans to ensure racial freedom, black equality, and black economic well-being has collapsed amidst the postcolonial and post–civil rights pressure on these political communities. In its Marxist variant, the socialist alternatives of workers' control and popular participation have also imploded under the weight of internal and external pressures. What is still very present is the peripheral status of the region that these historicist projects were to change. After suffering implosions of its own and being on the defensive, the peripheral condition is now in the ascendant position again. In other words, the above attempts at practical transformation have experienced voidings similar to these that destroyed the philosophies and worldviews of the region.

Elsewhere, I've examined in more institutional terms these repeated attempts at politico-economic and racial transformation under the rubric of the peripheral capitalist cycle.[14] These are cyclical tendencies in which peripheral states oscillate between periods of strong alliances with local working and lower middle classes. These cycles rest on the fact that peripheral states embody class/race compromises that legitimate the hegemony of white foreign capital. These compromises will of course vary with the model of development pursued, the specific nature of the peripheral state, the racial composition of the citizens and the current configuration of the political economy of the central capitalist countries. In the peripheral societies, these cycles usually begin with a strong alliance between dissident factors of the political elite and segments of local classes who are dissatisfied with their class/race positions vis-à-vis the state and the foreign capitalist class. With the support of these groups, this nonwhite elite faction often comes to power. But, once in power the structural dependence of the economy on international capital usually forces this elite into making compromises with foreign capitalist classes, which it had earlier opposed. These compromises often start a new period of increasing state responsiveness to the interests of foreign capital, and a decrease in its responsiveness to the interests of local classes. This alliance often continues to get stronger until shattered by new alliances between dissenting political factions and dissatisfied members of local classes.

The current neoliberal phase of central capitalism has brought to an unexpectedly dramatic end periods of state-local class alliances that had already been in major decline. With the reconfiguring of their political economies after the end of the cold war, the central capitalist countries have embarked upon a global drive to make peripheral states more responsive to their interests in capital accumulation. As a result, the Caribbean has entered a period of rapidly rising state responsiveness to the interests of white foreign capital. It was within the context of this new politico-economic order that external pressures combined with internal ones to implode the Pan-Africanist and socialist alternatives of the region.

Consequently, present-day Caribbean historicists find themselves very much in the paradigmatic position of the Caribbean philosopher. He or she has been thrown back to ground zero and is confronted with the task of retotalizing and revisioning the future of the region. The primary difference between the contemporary historicists and their earlier counterparts is that the pile of imploded worldviews has gotten higher. To the imploded bodies of African, Christian, Hindu, and other worldviews, we have the more recent additions of Pan-Africanism, dependency theory, and other regional variants of Marxism. The imploding of these worldviews parallels in so many ways the earlier ones, because they point to the persistence of the old peripheral dynamic of discursive competition.

This dynamic of discursive competition is clearest in the case of dependency theory. This was very much a homegrown discourse with strong convergences and feedback relations with regional economic demand. This has now been replaced by the externally imposed discourse of neoliberalism, recreating old divergences and patterns of external dependence. Nettleford's battle for discursive space continues unabated into the present.

Given the return to economic ground zero (the labor-exporting periphery), Caribbean historicists are currently confronted with a new set of reconstructive, transversal, and transformative tasks. The alternatives to our peripheral condition must be reimagined and retotalized around a revised praxis. First, because of the greater competitive pressures of our period, this new challenge must be undertaken with more of the creative resources of our discursive space. Anything in which we do not have a competitive advantage will surely be privatized and claimed by Western capital in the name of neoliberalism as a site for profitable investment. To paraphrase Marx, in this moment, Caribbean people are being forced "to face with sober senses the real conditions of their lives, and their relations with their fellow men."[15] This means that in the course of resolving the peripheral crises produced by this particular phase of central capitalism, more than ever, we will have to fall back on what is incontestably ours—our music, our food, land, beaches, territorial space, capacities for learning and for creative self-transformation.

In other words, with the eroding of humanitarian and market-compensating forces, the economic content of all new projections will have to be radically indigenized and made to rest on native qualities that resist foreign capture by the competitive logic of the market. Consequently, as Western capital continues its current drive of expansion and economic recolonization, we are being pushed back to the point of being able to engage only in those enterprises that specifically require native resources and our cultural distinctness. Until the current phase of demonizing state enterprises has passed, these "natal" activities will have to be the bases for nonperipheralized economic sectors. The option of state-led industries as basis for such a sector is precisely what the current neoliberal period has eliminated. Thus the specific entrepreneurial bases for a national economy will have to be rethought and new strategies pursued. Whatever these industries turn out to be, their organization and patterns of ownership must be such that they can be part of a larger process of increasing local economic control and the reestablishing of production more securely in local demand. These Thomasian convergencies must be a goal for any nationally oriented economic strategy.

Second, what we mean by the national economy will also be up for consideration in this revised praxis. As other countries around the world continue to organize themselves into larger blocs, we cannot continue to fragment if we are to move forward. More than ever, the current moment calls for a unified Caribbean state that would also be a part of even larger regional blocs. Again, the new conditions of economic competition are making these increases in territorial and market size imperative. The mobilizing of greater politico-economic power is vital for any substantive change in our relations with the world economy.

Third, any new attempt at transforming our peripheral status in the world economy must include new positions on the natural sciences and related technologies. Our inability to resist economic natalization is due largely to the level of our technological capabilities. The crises that have repeatedly overtaken our agricultural products such as sugar and bananas have been due in large part to inadequate technological innovations. Consequently a concerted effort must be made to establish convergences between scientific, engineering, and technological leaning, on the one hand, and the information needs of local economic production, on the other. This divergence has persisted far too long and needs to be addressed as a major priority. Without it, our peripheral status will only worsen.

Fourth and finally, we will have to rethink the nature of the Caribbean state. This rethinking is becoming all the more urgent as Caribbean private sectors have not really been able to launch regional economies, even though neoliberalism has declared this to be their time at the helm. Caribbean states have failed to deliver on a number of important points. We've already noted the problem of regional unification. Second, they have not met local demands for effective administration and political management. Levels of inefficiency in public sectors are much too high and will have to be reduced. Third, the state's developmental capabilities and policies have not been able to really move us out of our peripheral status. The current downgrading of these activities will only worsen this condition. Consequently, there has to be a rebuilding of the state's developmental capabilities beyond what they were before. This will be very difficult as the external pressure on the region is for a more corporate-oriented state that dishes out primarily corporate welfare. Fourth, for the most part Caribbean states have not delivered to the masses a political life that is high in quality and participation. Whether it has been in the party or the state machinery itself, the practice of politics has been driven by material incentives, narrow party loyalties, and the accumulation of power by "Maximum" leaders. Thus, it is not surprising that the politico-national communities of the region are in states of profound crisis.

We have clearly failed our first course in modern nation building. We have left largely unanswered the exam paper on the national question. But this is a required course. We cannot move forward without passing it. Unlike Gilroy, we cannot really afford to go postnational. So we are going to have to take it again. This time our aim must be for a larger and more unified political community, which offers its citizen better administration, better development prospects, and a higher quality of political life.

These fundamentals of a new praxis will require new archetypal power from a changed relationship to the creative spaces we inhabit, or from the legitimacy of a popular upsurge, or both. Historicists have no control over popular upsurges. They could come as Caribbean societies go through another peripheral capitalist cycle. However, we can look anew at our relations with the creative spaces that we inhabit, how they energize and limit our current affirmations of self, and how both of these have shaped our relations to both the local and external environments. Such a reexamination could release the new creative energies and legitimating images necessary for these types of innovative moves. In others words, the creativity and legitimacy for such a new project could emerge from the deeper unities of our divided creative space. I think this kind of empowering energy still exists within this historicist/poeticist space and that we are far from having exhausted its possibilities. In short, we can still count on it to bring something new into history. Its ceaseless creativity still has the power to renew our hopes and to legitimate our actions. We just need to increase our openness to its deeper unities and wider contours.

Conclusion

*For Europe, for ourselves and for humanity, comrades, We must turn
over a new leaf, We must work out new concepts,
and try to set afoot a new man.*

—FRANTZ FANON

The foregoing attempt to reconstruct Caribbean historicism should not be seen as an exhaustive effort to reorient Afro-Caribbean philosophy, or even the centerpiece of such attempts. I did indeed suggest reforms that extend beyond the confines of historicism and embrace the field as a whole. But these are clearly not enough for the comprehensive analyses that such a major reorienting of the field would require. My analyses of Caribbean historicism would have to be supplemented by an account of the place of scientific discourses, the responses of the poeticists, the voices of other historicists, the voices of women, and those of the rising generation of Caribbean philosophers. Together, we could indeed give Afro-Caribbean philosophy the new direction it needs.

In addition to these voices, the proposed reconstruction reflects and draws primarily on the experiences of the English- and French-speaking Caribbean, in particular their experiences with processes of racialization, creolization, and cultural colonization. Clearly absent are the experiences of the Spanish- and Dutch-speaking Caribbean with these same issues. This absence says nothing about their importance to the project of reorienting Afro-Caribbean philosophy, but a good deal about my own linguistic limitations and the patterns of cultural balkanization that persist in our region. Both the Spanish and Dutch traditions must be at the Afro-Caribbean philosophical table, so that we can all benefit from their distinct experiences. Last but by no means least, a program of reorientation would have to include a more detailed examination of our relations with Indo-Caribbean philosophy. Only when much more of these tasks have been completed can we really begin to talk about comprehensive reform and reorientation. In short, my analysis of Caribbean historicism is just a beginning.

Although just a beginning, the case of historicism brought to the foreground a number of important problems confronting the larger field of Afro-Caribbean philosophy. These are problems for which we can and do need to take collective responsibility. In other words, these problems are of significance not just for historicists but for poeticists and Afro-Christians as well. From my attempt to reformulate Caribbean historicism, three problems of significance for the field as a whole stand out. These are the underdeveloped nature of our philosophical economy, getting to know with greater care the creative spaces we inhabit, and the need to rethink the problem of the self.

Throughout the body of this text, I've tried to focus on the peculiar economy of our philosophy. I've attempted to thematize the patterns of convergence and divergence, demand and supply, dependence and external orientation that it shares with the plantation and other peripheral phases of our material economies. These features of underdevelopment are particularly evident in the areas of ontology, epistemology, philosophy of science, ethics, and philosophical anthropology. These have all been areas of voluminous importing, while local resources for such production have been left uncultivated. This is a philosophical economy that has both sustained and constrained Caliban's reason, whether historicist or poeticist, Spanish- or French-speaking. Changing the nature of this economy would lessen the current constraints upon us all and hence should be one of our collective goals.

Equally important to the analyses offered in this text was the need for new and more self-conscious relations with the creative spaces that we inhabit. In particular, their emergence and growth, their contours, binary structures, and overall unity. This means cultivating a greater awareness of the mythopoetic foundations upon which our philosophical practices rest. This increased consciousness of local creative landscapes will be vital for any attempt to creolize and reorient Afro-Caribbean philosophy.

However, these shifts in creative awareness will bring with them an important challenge that I did not make explicit: the challenge of knowing when creative spaces are blocked, exhausted, or about to undergo major changes. Directed at the present period, this challenge becomes: What is the current creative state of our poeticist/historicist space? We have been living and creating out of it for more than a century now. How is it holding up in the face of unprecedented scientific and technological growth? Have we absolutized its central images, and in so doing have we reduced its creative momentum and rhythms to a trickle? Or, is it still more than adequate for the transformation of our peripheral condition? These are some of the questions that will necessarily flow from our greater awareness of the mythopoetics of our creative spaces.

In the previous chapter, I made a case for reform and renewal on the basis of the energy that would be released by a unification of the two opposing halves of our creative habitat. I assumed that a more comprehensive grasping of this space, through "confessing" the partiality of its poeticist and historicist images, would be associated with enhanced capacities for renewal and creativity. But there is that enigmatic Hegelian saying: "When philosophy paints its grey in grey, then has a shape of life grown old."[1] This claim hangs menacingly over all that I've said in favor of new creative projects from within our current spaces.

If by "shape of life" Hegel was referring to the world-constituting potential of a particular creative space, then the possibility of my call for us to bring the underlying unity of our current creative habitat to greater self-consciousness could be a mark of its approaching demise. In other words, reading Hegel more positively, the world-constituting powers of a creative space have their springtime when we are only partially aware of its full dimensions and its nurturing activities. By the time we are able to perceive its contours and overall unity, it has entered its autumnal phase. If this is indeed the case, and my call is for us to paint our grey in grey, then we may be in for bigger changes than the reformist proposals that I've outlined. What these bigger changes would entail is beyond my current vision. But whether the changes confronting us are reformist or epochal, we will need to be more familiar with these aspects of our creative spaces.

Third and finally, a reformed Afro-Caribbean philosophy must assume as a collective responsibility a more important role in the task of rethinking the nature and dynamics of our self-formative process. The works of traditional African existentialism, Wynter and Harris in particular, pointed to the need for this reexamination. Further, the European philosophical anthropologies upon which we depended for discourses of self-analysis are currently in profound states of crisis. Thus, we are confronted with the challenges of inventing and creating our own. The challenges to this exercise in philosophical anthropology are twofold.

First, this rethinking must include the problem of reestablishing the linkages between the cultural demands of Afro-Caribbean ego genesis and our own production of philosophical discourses. The reestablishing of these ties will only take place in conjunction with the broader changes in our philosophical economy indicated earlier. If we are to retake control of the cultural aspects of our self-formation, then we must cultivate and produce the philosophical anthropologies, the ethical, ontological, epistemological, and other discourses that we continue to import from the West. The time for breaking these philosophical dependencies is now. The current conjuncture, by favoring cultural and identity politics, has made these issues visible in ways that they were not before. Hence the opportune nature of the present moment.

Second, our exercise in philosophical anthropology must take up Fanon's challenge "to try to set afoot a new man."[2] As a group, Afro-Caribbean philosophers must see themselves as included in the "comrades" to whom Fanon addressed this challenge. We should not let this responsibility fall so heavily on the shoulders of our artists as we have in the past. The need to "set afoot a new man" has only grown in the years since Fanon made his call. The global scope of the technocratic nightmare with which Western capitalism confronts projects of human self-realization, emerged very clearly from our analysis of the work of Habermas. From our own experiences of colonization and racialization, we know the depths of the dehumanization that have come out of the rise to power of Western capitalism. This was the dehumanization that led Fanon to remark: "When I search for Man in the technique and style of Europe, I see only a succession of negations of man, and an avalanche of murders."[3] These accounts of the darkness that has emerged from within the heart of the European Enlightenment make clear the nature of the crisis with which Prospero now confronts Caliban.

In the perennial struggles between ego and cosmic order, we have seen that the former is driven to attempt to conquer the forces of birth and death, health and illness, spiritual affirmation and spiritual negation that have reigned over the course of its life. Human discourses from myth to science and the practices of ritual and industry have been the means through which we have attempted to shift the balance of effective control in our favor. These are the struggles, along with those against various forms of sociohistorical domination, out of which different cultures have arrived at different conceptions of the nature, scope, and significance of human agency. As James has insisted, the collective projects we undertake profoundly shape the modes of self-objectification that give permanence and historicity to our identities. However, as we saw in chapter 2, James restricted these projects to the sociohistorical arena, which eliminated the anthropological significance of mythic/spiritual projects and made secondary that of scientific/natural projects. This we must correct. As these projects change, so do our modes of self-objectification. It is to the immanent tendencies and aims of these projects that some of the most profound questions of philosophical anthropology are addressed. Are the inherent tendencies of the ego toward cosmic revolt indicators of an ultimate destiny to rule over history, earth, and universe? Or, will mythic constraints continue to require some type of harmonic ego/cosmos balance as the ideal condition for human self-realization? What is the anthropological significance of our postcolonial projects and their accompanying modes of self-objectifications? If we are to take up Fanon's humanist challenge in the present period, then we cannot escape these difficult anthropological issues.

So far Afro-Caribbean attempts at revealing and defining the significance of human freedom and agency are recorded in our collective projects to increase the scope of our capabilities vis-à-vis spiritual, natural, and sociohistorical orders. These collective undertakings have ranged in self-assertiveness from the mythic ones of traditional Africa to the historicist and poeticist projects of our own times. For the most part this humanist tradition has given strong affirmation to the need for a mythically mediated compromise between the ego and the spiritual domain out of which it arises. However, this is not a fixed compromise. There is both elasticity and historicity in the ego's relationship with its spiritual domain, hence it has been the object of expansive and progressive redefinitions. But these redefinitions cannot continue to the point of complete severance at which the ego is completely on its own, determining itself, history, and the cosmic order of things. Such positions of mythic compromise have consistently occupied a central place in the projects through which we have imagined humanity. Consequently, these limits on our *Yuruguan* tendencies have emerged as important themes in our philosophical anthropology.

In relation to material nature, our scientific endeavors to shift the balance of agency and effective control have not been bold. The elasticity and historicity in this relationship remains underexplored. Indeed, they have been constrained by two sets of factors: (1) the analogical extending of the mythic compromise with inner nature to outer nature; and (2) the dependent practices of our colonial sciences. The first concealed the technical aspects of material nature, while the second revealed them only within the frameworks of oppressive and exploitative production regimes. These limitations have in turn affected our industrial practices and hence our ability to transform our peripheral economies. Consequently, the sense of agency that emerges from the natural and scientific aspects of our projects remains underdeveloped and does not provide us with good measures of human capability in this domain. In short, we need better answers to the anthropological significance of science.

Much better measures of human capability and agency emerge from our sociohistorical projects. In the struggles against slavery, colonialism, and racism, African peoples have given humanity some if its most revealing snap-shots of the anthropological significance of sociohistorical freedom and agency. They have revealed the dehumanizing consequences of the modes of self-objectification that came with the class/race structure of Western capital-ism and the heroic efforts that we have made to throw off these masks and reclaim our humanity. In short, our sociohistorical projects have given affirma-tive answers to the problems of full self-determination in relation to sociohis-torical orders of domination.

These responses to the problem of agency vis-à-vis spiritual, natural, and sociohistorical orders have provided the parameters within which we have engaged the problem of our humanity, its capabilities, and fate. If we are "to set afoot a new man," then this is the heritage that we will have to draw upon and reform. We cannot take up Fanon's challenge if our gaze is still externalized and focused on other traditions. This is the only humanist tradition that we can claim, from which we can invent something new and offer it to the world.

Although our estimates of our human proportions have been influenced by definite but changing mythic compromises, our colonial and postcolonial enmeshments in Prospero's projects of absolute control, have made it necessary that we consider this "infinite" conception of the proportions of humanity. In other words, we have been forced to ask: What is the anthropological signifi-cance of the Western project? What is the meaning of its complete rejection of the need for mythic compromises? Is it, as Foucault asks, that man's destiny includes "positing himself also as he who has killed God and whose existence includes the freedom and the decision of that murder"?[4] Is this *Yuruguan* hubris or is it the grandest vision of the human so far imagined? If we think that it is the former, then it is important that we disengage more radically from the momentum and rhythms of the Western project, while allowing the projects that have been taking shape in Caliban's reason to come to fruition. As we have seen, these projects have very different shapes from those of the West. In the main, they have been smaller in global proportions, restorative or revolutionary in nature, and nonimperial. They have attempted to reorder Prospero's history but not the course of human and planetary history.

In spite of these differences, Wynter's analysis of our historical projects showed that they too have had blind spots and liminal tendencies that have produced their own shares of dehumanization and historical wreckage. These common features Wynter attributed to the dualism and antinomies that are internal to human ego genesis, whether Caribbean or Western. We also saw similar claims in the works of traditional African existentialism and Harris. If these onto-epistemic explanations are correct, it means that we will have to break with the manner in which they were historicized and linked to Western capitalism by James and others. These onto-epistemic explanations suggest that our troublesome tendencies preceded capitalism and will also outlast it. The fact that we share them with the West means that we need to focus on our own and not just those of the West. After the tragic collapse in Grenada, and the strong tendencies toward parliamentary and nonparliamentary dictatorships throughout the region, we cannot afford to ignore the relationships between our ego-genetic process and our political practices. In other words, we must examine not only the othering practices of Prospero's reason but also those of Caliban's.

Further, these common features also point to scientific framing and empowering as extremely important differences separating the Western project from our own. The application of science and mathematics to the study of nature and society opened the possibilities of infinitizing the projects of European humanity. At the start of the modern period, Pascal caught very clearly this anthropological significance of mathematics and science. They revealed the environing universe to be a "twofold infinity," the infinitely large and the infinitely small.[5] Unlike Prospero, Pascal was terrified by this disclosure and the self-objectifications it made possible. Centuries later, Husserl echoed these views when he embraced these infinities as the "telos of European man." He notes that infinity was discovered "first of all in forms of idealized quantities, masses, numbers, figures, straight lines, poles, surfaces etc. Nature, space and time become capable of stretching ideally into infinity and also of being infinitely divided ideally."[6]

Is this infinity opened up by mathematics and science a bad, that is asymptotic, one? Is it an infinity that has created more space for human hubris and for the projecting of its constitutive binaries and antinomies? With the continuing production of new forms of poverty, new forms of liminal othering, spiritual and ecological crises of major proportions, it looks more and more as though the project of Western humanity is founded on the blind pursuit of a bad infinity. In the words of Adorno, it is "self-assertion gone wild."[7] In the shifting positions of language in relation to current discursive practices in the West, Foucault sees the reassembling of the mythic forces that will contain this pursuit and correct its hubris. Hence he speaks of the end or "the absolute dispersion of man" by the return of the gods.[8] The Western pursuit is blind because it has discarded its mythic mirrors that would keep visible reflections of the inflationary dynamics of its self-formative process. In the absence of these reflections, the Western ego is less able to see itself and hence to judge accurately its progress toward its infinite goal. In short, although scientifically empowered, the project contains no new solutions to the problems of othering and domination that have plagued the attempts of the "autonomous" ego to order history and nature.

The growing proportions of these crisis tendencies have increased the need for us to develop our own conceptions of humanity. The challenge confronting this particular endeavor is also twofold. First, it requires a project guided by interests in cosmic harmony even though the ego now has the sciences on its side. This would take us away from the excesses of the Western experience. Our project must avoid the polarization between the mythic and the scientific that has been so central to the Western case. Our particular path to modernity positions us for a good shot at such a project. Its resolutions of the self-determined/spiritually determined binary have been such that we can still register the mythic resistances and feelings of imbalance that are produced by the West's pursuit of infinity. Now more than ever, our world needs alternative projects in which the anthropological significance of science is construed differently.

Second, we will have to refine and enlarge the mythic mirrors in which our ego-genetic processes are currently reflected. That is, we will have to increase the powers of the discourses that we use to bring to consciousness the *Yuruguan* revolts, the binary projections and the liminal practices that are internal to our self-formative processes. The larger the scope of our projects the more we need these consciousness-raising and reconciliatory practices. This is the only way in which we can avoid the Western imbalances between ethical and technological growth so evident today. Technological growth in the West is creating whole new sets of ethical problems, from surrogate motherhood to euthanasia. If we are not able to renew and strengthen our own ethical traditions and sensibilities while engaged in scientific practices, then we will not be able to meet this particular challenge.

"To set afoot a new man" will require of us new mythic compromises and a deeper understanding of the ego's role in the establishing of these balances of power. We will have to be more conscious of our *Yuruguan* revolts, our liminal tendencies, and our states of ontic closure. These are key elements in mythic compromises that greatly affect ethical sensibilities and conditions for renewal. The ethical challenges ahead will require a different "languaging" of these ego-formative issues so that we can be more conscious of them and of the points where they share anthropological roots with the sciences. The task is not all that different from the one of finding the deeper unity that links our poeticist and historicist traditions. In similar ways, a different set of binaries have kept the mythic and scientific poles of the Western creative space apart. This is the unity that the West has been unable to achieve. With the emphasis again on language, Foucault describes it as "a unity that we ought to think but cannot as yet do so."[9] This opposition is weaker in our case and should make the discovering of this unity easier. In our case, the difficulties may be more on the mythic side. But, irrespective of sides, problems of human renewal in this technocratic era will only be resolved by the creative energies that will be released with the "confessing" of the partiality of scientific and mythic images and the discovery of their common anthropological roots. This is a unity that we must come to live. These moments of change in primal subjectivity cannot be put on hold, repressed, or kept separate from the activist struggles against Prospero in his current neoliberal mask. As we change (scienticize) our political economy, these are changes that must be made in the mythic economies of our primal subjectivity. Only with such wider affirmations of ourselves in which the two are kept together will we be able to fashion a more human project in response to the infinities of science.

In the fashioning of such a project of the human, a reformed Afro-Caribbean philosophy has a vital role to play. It can take as a primary responsibility the refereeing of the oppositional tendencies between myth and science. First, it can examine and define the cognitive interests of both. Second, it can critique and expose the tendencies toward ontic closure on both sides. Third, it can examine the roots of these tendencies. In short, philosophy's contribution to Fanon's challenge would be the encouraging of the kind of scientific thought that would not obscure the mythic and vice versa. In guarding against these tendencies, Afro-Caribbean philosophy will have to go beyond the recoveries of Husserl and Habermas. It will also have to reclaim the mythic and its unique capabilities for narrating the history of our primal subjectivity. In solving this riddle, we just might catch some good glimpses of the post-Caliban phases of our reason.

Notes

PREFACE

1. Merleau Ponty, *Signs* (Evanston: Northwestern University Press, 1964), 101.

INTRODUCTION

1. Kwame Gyekye, A *Essay on African Philosophical Thought* (Philadelphia: Temple University Press, 1995), 3–8.
2. William Shakespeare, *The Tempest* (London: Methuen and Co., 1954), 32–33.
3. George Lamming, *The Pleasures of Exile* (London: Allison and Busby, 1984), 13.
4. Charles Mills, *Blackness Visible* (Ithaca: Cornell University Press, 1998), 1–19.
5. Lewis Gordon, *Bad Faith and Antiblack Racism* (Atlantic Highlands, N.J.: Humanities Press, 1995), 104–116.
6. Gordon Lewis, *The Growth of the Modern West Indies* (New York: Monthly Review Press, 1968), 69.
7. Denis Benn, *The Growth and Development of Political Ideas in the Caribbean 1774–1983* (Kingston: ISER, 1987), 1–31.
8. Jurgen Habermas, *Legitimation Crisis* (Boston: Beacon Press, 1975), 47.
9. Rex Nettleford, *Inward Stretch, Outward Reach* (London: Macmillan Press, 1993), 80.
10. Clive Thomas, *Dependence and Transformation* (New York: Monthly Review Press, 1974), 59.
11. Ibid., 125.
12. For a more detailed treatment of these peripheral dynamics, see my "Towards a Theory of Peripheral Cultural Systems" (Working Paper #10, Center for Comparative Development, Brown University, 1986).
13. Wole Soyinka, *Myth, Literature and the African World* (Cambridge: Cambridge University Press, 1990), 37–8.
14. Edouard Glissant, *Poetics of Relation* (Ann Arbor: University of Michigan Press, 1997), 58.
15. Wilson Harris, *Tradition, the Writer and Society* (London: New Beacon Books, 1967), 31.

CHAPTER 1

1. Kwame Gyekye, *An Essay on African Philosophical Thought* (Philadelphia: Temple University Press, 1995); Alexis Kagame, *La Philosophie bantu-rwandaise de l'etre* (Academic Royale des Sciences Coloniales, Brunelles, 1956); Marcien Towa, *The Idea of a Negro-African Philosophy*, Trans. Tsenay Serequeberhan (forthcoming); Henry Oruka, *Sage Philosophy* (Leiden: E. J. Brill, 1990); Tsenay Serequeberhan, *The Hermeneutics of African Philosophy* (New York: Routledge, 1994).
2. Gyekye, *An Essay*, 64.
3. Robin Horton, *Patterns of Thought in Africa and the West* (Cambridge: Cambridge University Press, 1994), 197–258; Paulin Hountondji, *African Philosophy* (Bloomington: Indiana University Press), 7–70.

4. Towa, *The Idea* (forthcoming).
5. Ibid.
6. Emefie Ikenga Metuh, *African Religions in Western Conceptual Schemes* (Ibadan, Nigeria: Pastoral Institute, 1985), 43.
7. Ibid., 23.
8. Ibid., 4.
9. Robert Farris Thompson, *Flash of the Spirit* (New York: Vintage Books, 1984), 5.
10. Edouard Glissant, "Identity and Diversity" (paper presented at Brown University, Oct. 8, 1997).
11. Karl Popper, *Objective Knowledge* (Oxford: Oxford University Press, 1972), 106.
12. Mircea Eliade, *The Sacred and the Profane* (New York: Harcourt Brace & World, 1959), 21.
13. Alfred Schutz, *The Structures of the Life World, Vol. II* (Evanston, Ill.: Northwestern University Press, 1989), 105–6.
14. Plato, *Five Great Dialogues* (Roslyn, N.Y.: Walter J. Black, Inc., 1942), 403.
15. Placide Tempels, *Bantu Philosophy* (Paris: Presence Africaine, 1952), 35.
16. Alexis Kagame, "The Empirical Apperception of Time and the Conception of History in Bantu Thought," in *African Philosophy*, ed. Parker English and Kibujjo Kalumba (Upper Saddle River: Prentice Hall, 1996), 99.
17. Thompson, *Flash of the Spirit*, 5.
18. Gyekye, *An Essay*, 79.
19. Ibid., 98.
20. Ibid., 93.
21. Ibid., 70.
22. Metuh, *African Religions*, 25–26.
23. Wole Soyinka, *Myth Literature and the African World* (Cambridge: Cambridge University Press, 1990), 36.
24. Gyekye, *An Essay*, 70.
25. Basil Davidson, *The African Genius* (London: Little Brown & Co., 1996), 45–67.
26. Marcel Griaule, *Conversations with Ogotemmeli* (London: International African Insititue, 1970).
27. Soyinka, *Myth*, 28.
28. Sri Aurobindo, *The Life Divine* (Pondicherry, India: Sri Aurobindo Ashram, 1987), 131.
29. Gyekye, *An Essay*, 104.
30. William Wordsworth, "Ode: Intimations of Immortality," in *The Norton Anthology of English Literature*, vol. 2, ed. M. H. Abrams (New York: W. W. Norton & Co., 1968), 151.
31. Meyer Fortes, *Oedipus and Job in West African Religion* (Cambridge: Cambridge University Press, 1959), 14.
32. Melville Herskovits, *Dahomey*, vol. II (New York: J. J. Augustin, 1938), 201–30.
33. Rudolf Otto, *The Idea of the Holy* (Oxford: Oxford University Press, 1973), 88.
34. Tempels, *Bantu Philosophy*, 88.
35. Ibid., 82.
36. Ibid., 78.
37. Ibid., 79.
38. Ibid.
39. Fortes, *Oedipus and Job*, 22.
40. Gyekye, *An Essay*, 141.
41. Ibid., 132.
42. Ibid.
43. Ibid.
44. Ibid., 127.
45. Ibid., 141.
46. Tempels, *Bantu Philosophy*, 57.
47. Ibid., 58.
48. Gyekye, *An Essay*, 202.

49. Ibid., 83.
50. Soyinka, *Myth*, 49.
51. Ibid., 2.
52. Ibid., 36.
53. Leslie Demangles, *The Faces of the Gods* (Chapel Hill: Univeristy of North Carolina Press, 1992), 67.
54. Ibid., 68.
55. Diane Simmons, *Jamaica Kincaid* (Toronto: Twayne Publishers, 1994), 9.
56. Ibid., 9.
57. Ibid., 10.

CHAPTER 2

1. Winston James, "C. L. R. James: The Spell of 'European Civilization'" (paper presented at conference, C. L. R. James: His Intellectual Legacies, Wellesley College, April 19–21, 1991).
2. John Henrick Clarke, and Yosef ben-Jochannan, *New Dimensions in African History* (Trenton, N.J.: Africa World Press, 1991), 43–50.
3. For a good discussion of James's Pan-Africanism, see Paul Buhle, *C. L. R. James: The Artist as Revolutionary* (London: Verso, 1998), 130–161.
4. Norman Girvan, "The Development of Dependency Economics in the Caribbean and Latin America," *Social and Economic Studies* 22 (March 1973): 1–33; Selwyn Cudjoe, *Resistance and Caribbean Literature* (Athens, Ga.: Ohio University Press, 1980).
5. Paget Henry, "Towards a Theory of Peripheral Cultural Systems" (Providence, Working Paper #10, Center for Development, Brown University, 1986).
6. Homi Bhabha, "Signs Taken for Wonders," *Critical Inquiry* 12 (autumn 1985): 144–65.
7. Paget Henry, and Paul Buhle, "Caliban as Deconstructionist: C. L. R. James and Postcolonial Discourse," in *C. L. R. James's Caribbean*, ed. Henry and Buhle (Durham, N.C.: Duke University Press, 1992), 111–42.
8. "Discovering Literature in Trinidad: The 1930's," in *Spheres of Existence*, by C. L. R. James (Westport, Conn.: Lawrence Hill, 1980), 238.
9. "Black Power," ibid., 228.
10. Edward Blyden, *Christianity, Islam and the Negro Race* (London: Edinburgh University Press, 1967), 215.
11. Ibid., 368.
12. Rupert Lewis, *Marcus Garvey: Anti-Colonial Champion* (Trenton, N.J.: African World Press, 1988), 50.
13. Frantz Fanon, *Black Skin, White Masks* (New York: Grove Press, 1967), 110.
14. C. L. R. James, *The Life of Captain Cipriani* (Nelson, Engl.: Coulton, 1932).
15. "Dialectical Materialism and the Fate of Humanity," in *Spheres of Existence*, by C. L. R. James, 70–105.
16. "The Atlantic Slave Trade," in *The Future in the Present*, by C. L. R. James (London: Allison & Busby, 1977), 235–264.
17. C. L. R. James, *State Capitalism and World Revolution* (Chicago: Charles Kerr, 1986), 34–54.
18. "Presence of Blacks in the Caribbean and Its Impact on Culture," in *At the Rendezvous of Victory*, by C. L. R. James (London: Allison & Busby, 1984), 218.
19. Jurgen Habermas, *Knowledge and Human Interest* (Boston: Beacon Press, 1971), 306.
20. Wole Soyinka, *Myth, Literature and the African World* (Cambridge: Cambridge University Press, 1990), 140–60.
21. John Mbiti, *African Religions and Philosophy* (New York: Anchor Books, 1970), 23.
22. Cornel West, *Prophesy Deliverance!* (Philadelphia: Westminster Press, 1982), 17.
23. Soyinka, *Myth, Literature and the African World*, 153.
24. John Mbiti, *Introduction to African Religion* (London: Heinemann, 1975), 57.
25. Leonard Barret, "African Religion in the Americas," in *African Religions*, ed. Newell Booth (Lagos: Nok Publications, 1977), 185.

26. Mbiti, *African Religions and Philosophy*, 214.
27. Sri Aurobindo, *Letters on Yoga* (Pondicherry, India: Sri Aurobindo Ashram, 1988), 2:503.
28. Walter Ong, *Orality and Literacy* (New York: Methuen, 1985), 78–83.
29. C. L. R. James, *History of Pan-Africanist Revolt* (Washington, D.C.: Drum and Speare Press, 1969), 21–39.
30. Ibid., 40–780.
31. Anthony Appiah, *In My Father's House* (New York: Oxford University Press, 1992).
32. Kwame Nkrumah, *Consciencism* (New York: Monthly Review, 1965), 63.
33. Ibid., 68.
34. C. L. R. James, *At the Rendezvous of Victory*, 178.
35. Leopold Senghor, *Liberte I* (Paris: Seuil, 1964), English trans. Wendell Jeanpierre, Freedom I (Ph.D. dissertation, Brown University, 1974), 35–60.
36. Paul Hountondji, *African Philosophy: Myth and Reality* (Bloomington: Indiana University Press, 1983), 33.

CHAPTER 3

1. Frantz Fanon, *Black Skin, White Masks* (New York: Grove Press, 1967), 10.
2. Ibid., 10.
3. Pierre Bourdieu, and Jean Claude Passeron, *Reproduction in Education Society and Culture* (Beverly Hills: Sage, 1997).
4. Gordon Lewis, *Main Currents in Caribbean Thought* (Baltimore: Johns Hopkins University Press, 1987), 43–59.
5. Ibid., 94–170.
6. Ibid., 29–136.
7. C. L. R. James, *Modern Politics* (Port of Spain, Trinidad: PNM Publishing Company, 1960).
8. Lewis, *Main Currents in Caribbean Thought*, 109–116.
9. Sylvia Wynter, "Beyond the Categories of the Master Conception: The Counterdoctrine of the Jamesian Poiesis," in *C. L. R. James' Caribbean*, ed. P. Henry and P. Buhle (Durham: Duke University Press, 1992), 64–67.
10. Clive Thomas, *Dependence and Transformation* (New York: Monthly Review Press, 1974).
11. Fanon, *Black Skin, White Masks*, 10.
12. Ibid., 109.
13. Ibid., 140.
14. Ibid., 191.
15. Ibid., 110.
16. Ibid., 10.
17. Jean-Paul Sartre, *Being and Nothingness* (New York: Philosophical Library, 1956), 3–70.
18. Fanon, *Black Skin, White Masks*, 218.
19. Sören Kierkegaard, *The Concept of Anxiety* (Princeton: Princeton University Press, 1980), 155–162.
20. For a more detailed treatment of this discourse, see my "African and Afro-Caribbean existentialism," in *Existence in Black*, ed. Lewis Gordon (New York: Routledge, 1997), 13–36.
21. Meyer Fortes, *Oedipus and Job in West African Religion* (Cambridge: Cambridge University Press, 1956).
22. R. S. Rattray, *Ashanti* (London: Oxford University Press, 1923).
23. Fanon, *Black Skin, White Masks*, 184.
24. Ibid., 28.
25. Ibid., 130.
26. Ibid., 132.
27. Edouard Glissant, *Caribbean Discourse* (Charlottesville: Univeristy of Virginia Press, 1992), 17–26.
28. Ibid., 94.

CHAPTER 4

1. A. J. Seymour, "Introduction," in *Eternity to Season*, by Wilson Harris (London: New Beacon Books, 1978), 53–54.
2. C. L. R. James, "A New View of West Indian History," *Caribbean Quarterly* 35, no. 4 (Dec. 1989): 58.
3. Martin Heidegger, *Being and Time* (New York: Harper & Row, 1962), 164.
4. C. L. R. James, "A New View," 57.
5. Gregory Shaw, "The Novelist as Shaman: Art and Dialectic in the Work of Wilson Harris," in *The Literate Imagination*, ed. Michael Gilkes (London: Macmillan, 1989), 145.
6. Ibid., 146–47.
7. Ibid., 148.
8. Hena Maes-Jelinek, ed., *Explorations: A Selection of Talks and Articles* (Aarhus: Dangaroo Press, 1981), 98.
9. Ibid., 13.
10. Wilson Harris, "The Composition of Reality," *Callaloo* 18, no. 1 (winter, 1995): 20.
11. Wilson Harris, *Tradition The Writer and Society* (London: New Beacon Books, 1973), 8 and 21.
12. Alan Riach and Mark Williams, eds., *The Radical Imagination* (Liege, Belgium: Liege Language and Literature, 1992), 72.
13. Harris, *Tradition*, 7.
14. Harris, "The Composition," 16.
15. Riach and Williams, *The Radical Imagination*, 73.
16. Ibid., 69.
17. Harris, "The Composition," 17.
18. Harris, *The Guyana Quartet* (London: Faber and Faber, 1985), 112.
19. Ibid., 112.
20. Maes-Jelinek, *Explorations*, 125.
21. Harris, *Tradition*, 55.
22. Ibid., 51.
23. Ibid.
24. Wilson Harris, "The Fabric of the Imagination," *Third World Quarterly* 12, no. 1 (Jan. 1990): 182.
25. Ibid., 175.
26. Ibid.
27. Ibid.
28. Riach and Williams, *The Radical Imagination*, 72.
29. Harris, "The Fabric," 180.
30. Maes-Jelinek, *Explorations*, 45.
31. Harris, *Tradition*, 45.
32. Ibid., 74.
33. Ibid., 40.
34. Ibid., 44.
35. Ibid., 45.
36. Ibid., 44.

CHAPTER 5

1. Michael Dash, *The Other America* (Charlottesville: University of Virginia Press, 1998), 61–81.
2. David Scott, "Revolution/Theory/Modernity: Notes on the Cognitive-Political Crisis of our Time," *Social and Economic Studies* 44, nos. 2 and 3 (Sept. 1995): 1–23.
3. Jacques Derrida, "Structure, Sign and Play in the Human Sciences," in *Writing and Difference* (Chicago: University of Chicago Press, 1978).
4. Gayatri Chakravarty Spivak, *The Post-Colonial Critic* (New York: Routledge, 1990), 50–55.
5. Paget Henry, "Rex Nettleford, African and Afro-Caribbean Philosophy," *CLR James Journal* 5, no. I (1997): 44–97.

6. Derek Walcott, "The Sigh of History," *The New York Times*, Dec. 8, 1992, 25.
7. Ibid.
8. Sylvia Wynter, "1492: A New World View" (paper presented at the Smithsonian Institute, Oct. 31–Nov. 1, 1992), 27.
9. Derek Walcott, *Collected Poems 1948–84* (New York: Farrar, Strauss and Giroux, 1986), 364.
10. Sylvia Wynter, "After the New Class: James, *Les Dammes* and the Autonomy of Human cognition" (paper presented at Wellesly College, April 19–21, 1991), 1–2.
11. Gayatri Chakravorty Spivak, *The Post-Colonial Critic*, 17–34.
12. Walter Benjamin, *Illuminations* (New York: Schoken Books, 1976), 257–58.
13. Sylvia Wynter, *The Hills of Hebron* (New York: Simon and Schuster, 1962), 66–67.
14. Ibid., 260.
15. Jurgen Habermas, *Knowledge and Human Interests* (Boston: Beacon Press, 1971), 301–17.
16. Wynter, "1492: A NewWorld View," 21.
17. Ibid., 31–36.
18. Sylvia Wynter, "The Ceremony Must be Found: After Humanism," *Boundary 2*, no. 12 (spring 1984): 26–27.
19. Ibid., 22.
20. Wynter, "1492: A New World View," 72–74.
21. Ibid., 34–37.
22. Michel Foucault, *The Order of Things* (New York: Vintage Books, 1973).
23. Wynter, "1492: A New World View," 72–74.
24. Ibid., 52.
25. Ibid., 64.
26. Ibid., 59.
27. Sylvia Wynter, "Is Development a Purely Empirical Concept or Also Teleological?" in *The Prospects For Recovery and Sustainable Development in Africa*, ed. A. Y. Yansane (Westport, Conn.: Greenwood Press, 1996), 304–6.
28. Ibid., 309.
29. Wynter, "After the New Class," 16.
30. Wynter, "Is Development a Purely Empirical Concept?" 301.
31. Wynter, "After the New Class," 15.
32. Ibid., 98.
33. Ibid., 93.
34. Ibid., 92.
35. Frantz Fanon, *The Wretched of the Earth* (Baltimore: Penguin Books, 1973), 32.
36. Wynter, "After the New Class," 99.
37. Sylvia Wynter, "Beyond the Categories of the Master Conception: The Counterdoctrine of the Jamesian Poeisis," in *CLR James Caribbean*, ed. P. Henry and P. Buhle (Durham, N. C.: Duke University Press, 1992), 65.
38. Ibid., 65.
39. Wynter, "After the New Class," 120–22.
40. Wynter, "The Ceremony Must be Found," 39.

CHAPTER 6

1. Johnny Washington, *Alain Locke and Philosophy* (Westport, Conn.: Greenwood Press, 1986).
2. Cornell West, *Prophesy Deliverance!* (Philadelphia: Westminster Press, 1980), 24.
3. Ibid., 24.
4. Ibid.
5. Ibid., 15.
6. Ibid.
7. Ibid., 21.
8. Cornel West, "Philosophy, Politics and Power: An Afro-American Perspective," in *Philosophy Born of Struggle*, ed. Leonard Harris (Dubuque, Iowa: Kendal/Hunt, 1983), 52.

9. Cornel West, *The American Evasion of Philosophy* (Madison: University of Wisconsin Press, 1989), 139.
10. Ibid., 142.
11. Lucius Outlaw, "African, African American, African Philosophy," *The Philosophical Forum* XXIV, no. 1–3 (fall–spring, 1992–93): 71.
12. Ibid., 74.
13. Ibid.
14. Ibid., 73.
15. Ibid.
16. Ibid., 63.
17. Lewis Gordon, *Fanon and the Crisis of European Man* (New York: Routledge, 1995), 40.
18. Lewis Gordon, *Bad Faith and Antiblack Racism* (Atlantic Highlands, N.J.: Humanities Press, 1995), 94–103.
19. Gordon, *Fanon and the Crisis of European Man*, 24.
20. Rene Descartes, *Mediations on First Philosophy* (Indianapolis: Bobbs-Merrill, 1960); Immanuel Kant, *Critique of Pure Reason* (New York: St. Martins Press, 1965).
21. G. W. F. Hegel, *The Phenomenology of Mind* (New York: Harper Torchbooks, 1967).
22. Edmund Husserl, *Phenomenology and the Crisis of Philosophy* (New York: Harper Torchbooks, 1965).
23. Jean Paul Sartre, *Being and Nothingness* (New York: Philosophical Library, 1956); Martin Heidegger, *Being and Time* (New York: Harper & Row, 1962).
24. Jurgen Habermas, *Knowledge and Human Interest* (Boston: Beacon Press, 1971).
25. Frantz Fanon, *Black Skin, White Masks* (New York: Grove Press, 1967), 16.
26. Paget Henry, "African and Afro-Caribbean Existential Philosophies," in *Existence in Black*, ed. Lewis Gordon (New York: Routledge, 1997), 13–36.
27. Alfred Schutz, *The Phenomenology of the Social World* (Chicago: Northwestern University Press, 1967), 142–43.
28. Ibid., 28.
29. Anthony Appiah, "African American Philosophy?" *The Philosophical Forum* XXIV, no. 1–3 (fall–spring, 1992–93): 23.
30. Dale Bisnauth, *History of Religions in the Caribbean* (Kingston, Jamaica: Kingston Publishers, 1989).
31. C. Eric Lincoln, and Lawrence Mamiya, *The Black Church in the African American Experience* (Durham, N.C.: Duke University Press, 1990).
32. Jean-Baptiste Phillipe, *Free Mulatto* (Wellesley: Calaloux Publications, 1996); Mary Prince, *The History of Mary Prince* (Ann Arbor: University of Michigan Press, 1997); Michel Maxwell Phillip, *Emmanuel Appadocca* (Amherst: University of Massachusetts Press, 1997); Moira Ferguson, ed., *The Hart Sisters* (Lincoln: University of Nebraska Press, 1993).
33. David Walker, *David Walker's Appeal* (New York: Hill and Wang, 1995), 21.
34. Joseph Owens, *Dread* (Kingston, Jamaica: Sangster, 1976), 192–93.
35. W. E. B. DuBois *(The Souls of Black Folk* (New York: Vintage Books, 1990), 10.
36. Alain Locke, "The Legacy of the Ancestral Arts," in *The New Negro*, ed. Alain Locke (New York: Athenaeum, 1968), 254–68.
37. See chapters 2 and 3 of this text.
38. Deotis Roberts "Religion-Ethical Reflections Upon the Experimental Components of a Philosophy of Black Liberation," in *African American Religious Studies*, ed. Gayraud Wilmore (Durham, N.C.: Duke University Press, 1989), 249–69.

CHAPTER 7

1. Edmund Husserl, *Phenomenology and the Crisis of Philosophy* (New York: Harper & Row, 1965), 149.
2. Jurgen Habermas, *The Theory of Communicative Action*, vol. II (Boston: Beacon Press, 1987), 322.

3. Jurgen Habermas, *Legitimation Crisis* (Boston: Beacon Press, 1975), 79.
4. Ibid., 70.
5. Edmund Husserl, *Ideas: General Introduction to Pure Phenomenology* (New York: Collier, 1962), 8.
6. Edmund Husserl, *Phenomenology and the Crisis of Philosophy*, 122–23.
7. Edmund Husserl, *The Cartesian Meditations* (The Hague: Nijhoff, 1960), 150–55.
8. Husserl, *Phenomenology and the Crisis of Philosophy*, 192.
9. Jurgen Habermas, *Towards a Rational Society* (Boston: Beacon Press, 1970), 1–12.
10. Theodor Adorno, *Against Epistemology* (Cambridge: MIT Press, 1983), 3–8.
11. Jurgen Habermas, *Knowledge and Human Interests* (Boston: Beacon Press, 1971), 306.
12. Ibid., 307.
13. Jurgen Habermas, *Theory and Praxis* (Boston: Beacon Press, 1974), 142–62.
14. Habermas, *Knowledge and Human Interests*, 316–17.
15. Herbert Marcuse, *One Dimensional Man* (Boston: Beacon Press, 1964).
16. Habermas, *Knowledge and Human Interests*, 44.
17. Ibid., 42.
18. Peters Dews, ed., *Habermas: Autonomy and Solidarity* (London: Verso, 1986), 91.
19. Introduction to Jurgen Habermas, *The Theory of Communicative Action*, vol. I, ix.
20. Ibid., xL.
21. Ibid., 302.
22. Atu Sekyi-Otu, *Fanon's Dialectic of Experience* (Cambridge: Harvard University Press, 1996), 62–67.
23. Frantz Fanon, *Black Skin, White Masks* (New York: Grove Press, 1967), 216–22.
24. Husserl, *Phenomenology and the Crisis of Philosophy*, 158.
25. Ibid., 158.
26. Ibid., 156.
27. Ibid., 171.
28. Ibid., 170.
29. Ibid.
30. Habermas, *The Theory of Communicative Action*, vol. I, 44.
31. Ibid., 46.
32. Ibid.
33. Ibid.
34. Ibid.
35. Jean-Paul Sartre, *Search For a Method* (New York: Vintage Books, 1968), 3–34.
36. Habermas, *Theory and Praxis*, 268–70.
37. Paul Feyerabend, *Against Method* (London: Verso, 1979), 17–46.
38. Habermas, *The Theory of Communicative Action*, vol. I, 21.
39. Ibid., 68.
40. Ibid.
41. Otu, *Fanon's Dialectic of Experience*, 79.
42. Jean-Paul Sartre, *Being and Nothingness* (New York: Philosophical Library, 1956), 361.
43. Ibid., 73–79.
44. Ibid., 244.
45. Sören Kierkegaard, *Fear and Trembling and the Sickness Unto Death* (Princeton: Princeton University Press, 1970), 148.
46. Sartre, *Being and Nothingness*, 68.
47. Habermas, *Legitimation Crisis*, 48.
48. Wilson Harris, *Carnival* in *The Carnival Trilogy* (London: Faber and Faber, 1993), 44.

CHAPTER 8

1. Douglas Massey, and Nancy Denton, *American Apartheid* (Cambridge: Harvard University Press, 1993).

2. Hollis Lynch, ed., *Black Spokesman: Selected Published Writings of E. W. Blyden* (London: Grank Cass & Co., 1971), 42.
3. Edward Blyden, *Christianity Islam and the Negro Race* (London: Edinburgh University Press, 1967), 368.
4. Hollis Lynch, ed., *Black Spokesman*, 26.
5. Ibid., 26.
6. Ibid.
7. Ibid., 27.
8. Ibid.
9. Ibid.
10. Ibid., 29.
11. Ibid., 30.
12. Amy Jacques-Garvey, ed., *The Philosophy and Opinions of Marcus Garvey*, vol. 2 (New York: Athenaeum, 1970), 15.
13. Ibid., I: I.
14. Ibid., I.
15. Ibid., 24.
16. Ibid., 2: 34.
17. Ibid., I: 24.
18. Ibid., 37.
19. Ibid., 23.
20. Ibid., 80.
21. Ibid., 21.
22. Ibid., 18.
23. Ibid.
24. Randall Burkett, *Black Redemption* (Philadelphia: Temple University Press, 1978), 6.
25. Ibid., 38.
26. Amy Jacques-Garvey, ed., *Philosophy and Opinions*, vol. I: 32.
27. Ibid., I: 90.
28. Burkett, *Black Redemption*, 30.
29. Jacques-Garvey, *Philosophy and Opinions*, I: 39.
30. Ibid., 44.
31. Tony Martin, *Literary Garveyism* (Dover, Mass.: The Majority Press, 1983).
32. Paget Henry, "Rastafarianism and the Reality of Dread," in *Existence in Black*, ed. Lewis Gordon (New York: Routledge, 1997), 157–64.
33. Joseph Owens, *Dread* (Kingston, Jamaica: Sangsters, 1976), 69.
34. Ibid., 193.
35. Alex Dupuy, "The Evolution of Walter Rodney's Thought on Race and Class in the Post-colonial Caribbean" (presented at Caribbean Studies Association Meetings, Antigua, May 26–30, 1998).
36. Walter Rodney, *A History of the Upper Guinea Coast* (Oxford, Eng.: Clarendon Press, 1970), 36.
37. Walter Rodney, *How Europe Underdeveloped Africa* (Washington, D.C.: Howard University Press, 1974), 89.
38. Ibid., 89.
39. Walter Rodney, *A History of the Guyanese Working People* (Baltimore: Johns Hopkins University Press, 1981), 179.
40. Ibid., 179.
41. Paul Gilroy, *The Black Atlantic* (Cambridge: Harvard University Press, 1994), 29.
42. Ibid., 2.
43. Ibid., 30.
44. Ibid.
45. Ibid., 36.
46. Ibid., 28.

47. Ibid., 40.
48. Hannah Arendt, "Reflections on Little Rock," *Dissent* 6, no. 1 (winter 1995): 45–56.
49. Dinesh D'Souza, *The End of Racism* (New York: Free Press, 1995).

CHAPTER 9

1. Carl Stone, "Whither Caribbean Socialism? Grenada, Jamaica and Guyana in Perspective," in *A Revolution Aborted*, ed. Jorge Heine (Pittsburgh: University of Pittsburgh Press, 1990), 291–308; Folke Lindahl, "Caribbean Diversity and Ideological Conformism. The Crisis of Marxism in the English Speaking Caribbean," *Social and Economic Studies* 43, no. 3 (Sept. 1994); Brian Meeks, *Re-reading the Black Jacobins: James, the Dialectic and Revolutionary Conjuncture, Social and Economic Studies* 43, no. 3 (Sept. 1994); David Scott, "Revolution/ Theory/Modernity: Notes on the Cognitive-Political Crisis of Our Time," *Social and Economic Studies* 44, no. 2 and 3 (Sept. 1995): 1–23.
2. Clive Thomas, *The Poor and the Powerless* (New York: Monthly Review Press, 1988).
3. Carl Stone, "Whether Caribbean Socialism?" 293.
4. Paula Aymer, *Uprooted Women* (Westport, Conn.: Greenwood Press, 1997); Rhoda Reddock, *Women Labor and Politics in Trinidad and Tobago* (Kingston, Jamaica: Ian Randle Publishers, 1994); Patricia Mohammed, "Midnight's Children and the Legacy of Nationalism," *Small Axe* no. 2 (1997): 19–38.
5. Gary Gereffi, "The Organization of Buyer Driven Global Commodity Chains: How U.S. Retailers Shape Overseas Production Networks," in *Commodity Chains and Global Capitalism*, ed. Gary Gereffi and Nigel Korzeniewiz (Westport, Conn.: Praeger, 1994), 96–100.
6. Norman Girvan, *Foreign Capital and Economic Underdevelopment in Jamaica* (Kingston, Jamaica: ISER, 1971), 39–74.
7. Paget Henry, *Peripheral Capitalism and Underdevelopment in Antigua* (New Brunswick, N.J.: Transaction Books, 1985), 121–36.
8. Keith Nurse, "The Developmental Efficacy of the Export-oriented Clothing Industry: The Jamaican Case," *Social and Economic Studies* 44, no. 2 and 3 (1995): 195–227.
9. Laura Raynolds, "Institutionalizing Flexibility: A Comparative Analysis of Forest and Post-Forest Models of Third World Agro-Export Production," in Gereffi and Korzeniewiz, eds., *Commodity Chains*, 143–61.
10. Clive Thomas, *Dependence and Transformation* (New York: Monthly Review Press, 1974).
11. Trevor Monroe, *Jamaican Politics: A Marxist Perspective in Transition* (Kingston, Jamaica: Heinemann, 1990), 1–20.
12. Alec Nove, *The Economics of Feasible Socialism* (London: George Allen and Unwin, 1983), 68–81.
13. V. N. Volosinov, *Marxism and the Philosophy of Language* (Cambridge: Harvard University Press, 1973); Louis Althusser, *For Marx* (London: Verso, 1979); Pierre Bourdieu and Jean-Claude Passeron, *Reproduction* (London: Sage Publications, 1977); Jean Baudrillard, *For a Critique of the Political Economy of the Sign* (St. Louis, Mass.: Telos Press, 1981).
14. Mark Poster, ed., *Jean Baudrillard: Selected Writings* (Stanford, Calif.: Stanford University Press, 1988), 21.
15. Ibid., 22.
16. Ibid.
17. Jung-Hee Lee, "Government and Urban Labor Reforms in post-Mao China (1978–95)" (unpublished Ph.D. dissertation, Department of Sociology, Brown University, 1997).
18. Jean-Paul Sartre, *Search for a Method* (New York: Vintage Books, 1968), 85–181; C. L. R. James, *Notes on Dialectics* (London: Allison and Busby, 1980), 34; Frantz Fanon, *Black Skin, White Masks* (New York: Grove Press, 1967), 12–13.
19. Julia Kristeva, *Revolution in Poetic Language* (New York: Columbia University Press, 1984); Helene Cixous and Catherine Clements, *The Newly Born Woman* (Minneapolis: University of Minnesota Press, 1986).

20. Jacques Lacan, "Some Reflections on the Ego," *International Journal of Psycho-Analysis* XXXIV (1953): 12.
21. T. Denean Sharpley-Whiting, *Frantz Fanon: Conflicts and Feminism* (New York: Rowman and Littlefield Publishers, 1998).
22. Henry, *Peripheral Capitalism*, 121–27.
23. Cornel West, *Keeping Faith* (New York: Routledge, 1993), 3.
24. Cixous, *The Newly Born Woman*, 42.
25. Roland Barthes, *The Pleasure of the Text* (New York: Hill and Wang, 1978).
26. Lewis Gordon, *Her Majesty's Other Children* (Lanham, Md.: Rowman and Littlefield, 1997), 92.

CHAPTER 10
1. C. L. R. James, *Modern Politics* (Port of Spain, Trinidad: PNM Publishing Co., 1960), 19–25.
2. Jurgen Habermas, *The Philosophical Discourse of Modernity* (Cambridge: MIT Press, 1990), 2.
3. Wole Soyinka, *Myth, Literature and the African World* (Cambridge: Cambridge University Press, 1990), 33–36.
4. Jurgen Habermas, *The Philosophical Discourse*, 20.
5. Gordon Rohlehr, *The Shape of that Hurt* (Port of Spain, Trinidad: Longman Trinidad, 1992), 66–96.
6. Karl Popper, *The Poverty of Historicism* (New York: Harper Torch Books, 1964), 76.
7. Ibid., 76.
8. Frantz Fanon, *Black Skin, White Masks* (New York: Grove Press, 1967), 231.
9. Jamaica Kincaid, *A Small Place* (New York: Farrar Strauss Giroux, 1988), 53.
10. W. E. B. DuBois, *Black Reconstruction in America* (New York: Harcourt, Brace, 1935); James Boggs, *The American Revolution* (New York: Monthly Review Press, 1963); Cornel West, *Prophesy Deliverance* (Philadelphia: Westminster Press, 1980); Cedric Robinson, *Black Marxism* (London: Zed Books, 1983).
11. Tim Hector, "The Making of Caribbean Philosophy," *OUTLET* 26, no. 43 (May 29, 1998).
12. Wilson Harris, *History, Myth and Fable* (Wellesley, Mass.: Calaloux Publications, 1995), 41.
13. Ibid., 41.
14. Paget Henry, *Peripheral Capitalism and Underdevelopment in Antigua* (New Brunswick, N.J.: Transaction Books, 1985), 161–64.
15. Karl Marx, and Frederick Engels, *The Communist Manifesto*, in *The Marx-Engels Reader*, ed. R. Tucker (New York: Norton, 1978), 476.

CONCLUSION
1. Georg Hegel, *Philosophy of Right* (London: Oxford University Press, 1967), 13.
2. Frantz Fanon, *The Wretched of the Earth* (New York: Grove Press, 1968), 316.
3. Ibid., 312.
4. Michael Foucault, *The Order of Things* (New York: Vintage Books, 1973), 385.
5. Blaise Pascal, *Pensées* (New York: Harper and Row, 1962), 149.
6. Edmund Husserl, *Phenomenology and the Crisis of Philosophy* (New York: Harper and Row, 1965), 183.
7. Jurgen Habermas, *Philosophical-Political Profiles* (Cambridge: MIT Press, 1983), 100.
8. Foucault, *The Order of Things*, 385.
9. Ibid., 386.

Index

Earth god(s), 39
Edwards, Bryan, 4, 72, 75
egalitarianism, 65, 265–66
Ego, the, 29–37, 61, 149, 188–89; collapse of, 78–87, 240, 253, 258, 268–69; modern, 192; subexistence of, 32, 41–43, traditional African, 150–57; transcendental, 137, 169–71, 279. *See also* the self
egogenesis, 10–11, 33–46, 118, 153, 279–80, 281–82
egoism, 62–67
Egypt, 22, 62, 77
Electra, 165
Eliade, Mircea, 24, 284 ch. 1, n12
empiricism, 42–44, 161
England, 199
episteme(s), 125–42, 185, 221, 222
epistemic violence, 119
epistemology, *passim*, but esp. 12, 41–43, 51, 60, 126, 146, 151, 173, 203, 233, 260–61; C.L.R. James's, 61; Robin Horton on, 183–84
Equiano, Olaudah, 44
equiprimordiality, 140–41
Erzulie (Yoruba deity), 159, 165
ethics, 37–41, 78–89, 146–47, 238, 280–81; analogical, 38
ethnophilosophy, 64, 66–67, 153–54, 163, 209
eugenics, 75; Nazi, 136
Eurocentrism, 2–4, 47–50, 75–89, 200
Europe, *passim*, but esp.: Eastern, 221, 232; denied tribalism in, 77–78; hegemony of, 2–4, 73–89, 145. *See also* Eurocentrism
European philosophy, 163
everyday, the, 25–37, 60, 118, 151, 171, 239, 243, 246, 258–59; as inauthentic, 91–104
evil, 38–39
existence, *passim*; African attitude toward, 37; socio-, 142
existential deviation, 3, 93–94, 152, 156. *See also* nonbeing
existential phenomenology, 148–56, 187–94
existentialism, 23, 90–104; African, 31–37, 62–63, 78–89, 98, 179, 188–94, 256; European, 81. *See also* Fanon; Lewis Gordon; Wilson Harris; Jean-Paul Sartre
experience, 154, 163, 263–64

family, 33
Fanon, Frantz, 3, 6, 17, 46–7, 68–89, 93–4, 113,118–120, 124, 136–8, 148, 151, 156, 160–162, 168, 179, 188, 198, 202, 207, 223, 227, 239–242, 246, 256–7, 259, 261, 263, 265–6, 273, 276–8, 285 ch. 2, n13, 286 ch. 3, n1, 2, 11–16, 18, 23–26; 288 ch. 5, n35, 289 ch. 6, n17, 19, 25; historicism

of, 81; limitations of, 83–89; Marxism of, 223; overall philosophy of, 89; on invisibility, 51; ontology, 52, 69–89; the self, 78–87
fate, 34, 84–85
Faust, 12, 73
Ferguson, Moria, 289 ch. 6, n32
Fichte, Johann, 173
Firmin, Joseph-Anténor 73, 79
Fodeba, Keita, 78
folktales, 22, 88
force, 25–26, 38
formal logic, 2
Fortes, Meyer, 34, 36–37, 39, 85, 284 ch. 1, n31 and 39; 286 ch. 3, n21
Foucault, Michel, 125, 235, 264, 278–79, 288 ch. 5, n22
foundationalism, 2; textual, 67
France, 230
Frederick Sperling Award, 13
freedom, 47, 55–56, 122, 160; of the will, 40
Freud, Sigmund, 33, 81, 173; the unconscious, 240
Frobenius, Leo, 86

Garvey, Marcus, 6, 47, 58, 51, 69, 73, 77, 79, 83, 120, 169–62, 198–99, 203, 204–9, 211–13, 219, 223. 263, 265–66; on economic mobilization, 204–5; equality, 208; God, 209; history, 205–6; nation states, 207–8; philosophical power, 207; racial conflict, 206–7; self-knowledge, 208; philosophical anthropology of, 207–8;
Gates, Jr., Henry Louis, 242
Gates, Thomas, 4
Gauls, the, 77
gender, 228
geography, 129–31
Germany, 230
Ghana, 61, 227 . *See also* Akan; Ashante
Gilroy, Paul, 120, 198–99, 216–20, 272, 242, 271; against nationalism, 217; on race, 217–18, 272; poststructuralism of, 218
Girvan, Norman, 83, 223, 224, 228–29, 231, 285 ch. 2, n4
Glissant, Edouard, 6, 15, 23, 27, 73, 87–88, 118, 121–22, 162, 217, 258, 283 intro. n14; 284 ch. 1, n10; 286 ch. 3, n27 and 28
Gnostics, 37
God, 22–46, 56–7, 74, 129, 278; as Black, 209–13; Akan conception of, 26; Dogon, 32, Igbo, 23, 26; Rastafarian, 209–13; Tellensi, 27; Yoruba, 26; "de-god," 253
Gordon, Lewis R., ix, 8, 51, 145, 147–52, 156, 162, 168, 179, 188, 199, 207, 217, 246, 266, 283 intro. n5; 286 ch. 3, n20; 289 ch.